Storytelling
Organizations

Storytelling Organizations

David M Boje

Los Angeles • London • New Delhi • Singapore

First published 2008

Apart from any fair dealing for the purposes of research or
private study, or criticism or review, as permitted under the
Copyright, Designs and Patents Act, 1988, this publication
may be reproduced, stored or transmitted in any form, or by
any means, only with the prior permission in writing of the
publishers, or in the case of reprographic reproduction, in
accordance with the terms of licences issued by the
Copyright Licensing Agency. Enquiries concerning
reproduction outside those terms should be sent to the
publishers.

SAGE Publications Ltd
1 Oliver's Yard
55 City Road
London EC1Y 1SP

SAGE Publications Inc.
2455 Teller Road
Thousand Oaks, California 91320

SAGE Publications India Pvt Ltd
B 1/I 1 Mohan Cooperative Industrial Area
Mathura Road
New Delhi 110 044

SAGE Publications Asia-Pacific Pte Ltd
33 Pekin Street #02-01
Far East Square
Singapore 048763

Library of Congress Control Number: 2007928857

British Library Cataloguing in Publication data

A catalogue record for this book is available from the British
Library

ISBN 978-1-4129-2976-9
ISBN 978-1-4129-2977-6 (pbk)

Typeset by C&M Digital (P) Ltd, Chennai, India
Printed in India at Replika Press Pvt. Ltd

CONTENTS

ACKNOWLEDGEMENTS AND DEDICATION

I am grateful to Kiren Shoman for taking this book to the SAGE board, and making me do the revisions. I think it's a better story.

I want to thank every one of my doctoral students, and everyone at *Standing Conference for Management and Organization Inquiry* (sc'MOI, pronounced c'est moi, as in the French way). This list is too long, but many of you are mentioned by name in the book.

I want to thank the STORI group, Ken Baskin, Carolyn Gardner, Terence Gargiulo, Theodore Taptiklis, Jo Tyler, and my wife Grace Ann Rosile. Your experiments in the Socratic Circle and doing the eight ways of sensemaking experiment was an inspiration throughout.

I am thankful for ghosts of Mikhail Bakhtin, Walter Benjamin, Lou Pondy, and Gertrude Stein, for our dialogic conversation in this book.

Thank you SAGE for allowing the use of Story in the title, and letting story out of narrative's prison. When I wrote *Narrative Methods for Organizational and Communication Research* (2001), I was told to use narrative, not story.

I dedicate the book to Grace Ann Rosile, who has horsesense and has restoried me.

David M. Boje

PART I
THE COMPLEXITY OF STORYTELLING ORGANIZATIONS

What is a Storytelling Organization? It is defined as, a 'collective storytelling system in which the performance of stories is a key part of members' sensemaking and a means to allow them to supplement individual memories with institutional memory' (Boje, 1991: 106).

What is new in this book? It's a theory of the differences between narrative and story that constitute self-organizing forces of Storytelling Organizations. Specifically, in *Storytelling Organizations*, narrative-control and story-diffusion are the force and counter-force of self-organizing. Each Storytelling Organization achieves a unique balance between narrative order and story disorder.

The central thesis of this book is that narrative, over the course of modernity, has become a (centripetal) centering force of control and order. The counter-force is that story (when not totally subservient to narrative order) can constitute a (centrifugal) decentering force of diversity and disorder. Narrative has been influenced by modernity to aspire to abstraction and generality, while story, here and there, has retained more grounded interplay with the life world, and its generativity. Several contributions become possible in Part I of this book.

The first contribution is to develop a theory of sensemaking types. In the book's introduction, I expand Weick's theory of narrative as retrospective sensemaking for control. I do this by theorizing an interplay of several kinds of narrative story sensemaking: retrospective, here-and-now, and prospective.

Organization scholars have devoted most attention to *retrospective narrative sensemaking*, that is, noticing Aristotelian narratives with a beginning, middle, and end (BME) plot structure that is quite linear and whole. Less noticed is retrospective sensemaking of narrative fragments, the kinds of disrupted, interrupted, and socially distributed communication that occurs in complex organizations. In the *here-and-now*, in the moment of Being, there are several modes of story sensemaking: Tamara (means simultaneous stories played out in different rooms, as actors network to make sense of the patterns); horsesense (my wife Grace Ann Rosile's term for intuitively noticing our embodied relationships, not only with horses, but in human-bodied relationships); and, emotive–ethical (being compelled by complicity in story to act or intervene – what Mikhail Bakhtin calls our ethical-answerability that has no alibi when we are the only ones who can act now to make a difference).

Relatively ignored in organization studies are more *prospective* ways of sensemaking. The antenarrative (the bet that a before-story can become a narrative) is transformational because it's a traveler, picking up and jettisoning context as it moves, inviting a different sensemaking of the future. *Antenarrative* is defined as 'nonlinear, incoherent, collective, unplotted, and pre-narrative speculation, a bet, a proper narrative can be constituted' (Boje, 2001a: 1). Retrospective narrative, here-and-now storying, and prospective antenarratives are not the only relationships of narrative and story sensemaking. There are ways of narrative and story sensemaking that are not fixated on a temporal axis, and instead are more vertical, more about transcendental, and reflexivity.

Reflexivity is, for me, more about the dialectical, such as George Herbert Mead's I–we, or Paul Ricoeur's dialectic of identity of sameness with identity of difference, Kant's containment of metaphysics to what is a priori to sense-making (time and space reasoning), or Hegel's thesis, antithesis, and synthesis. But these kinds of dialectic reflexivities are different from a number of dialogisms. Bakhtin is the pioneer in theorizing that whereas narrative is a mono-logic bid for order, story can be more dialogical. My contribution is to apply several types of dialogisms to Storytelling Organizations. I use the term 'polypi' to mean the interplay dynamics between polyphonic dialogism (many voices), stylistic dialogism (many styles), chronotopic dialogism (many time–space conceptions), and architectonic dialogism (discourses of cognitive interanimating with ethical and aesthetic discourses). It is this dialogical story sensemaking (along the more transcendental as opposed to dialectical) that allows us to open up an exploration of complexity, collective memory, strategy, and organization change.

A contribution developed in Chapter 1 is the paradigm shift from systems think-ing to complexity thinking about Storytelling Organizations. Systems thinking has been a monological narrative about organizations, as if there were a linear ordering of levels of reality, a tower of systems that is an all-encompassing deep structure of our world. The first challenge to the field is to go beyond mere open system think-ing. Storytelling shapes systemicity at the level of image, symbol, and transcenden-tal aspects of dialogism. The move to complexity thinking can be informed by looking at the variety of narrative and story sensemaking. My contribution to com-plexity thinking is harnessed under a new word, '*systemicity*.'[1] Systemicity is defined as the dynamic unfinished, unfinalized, and unmerged, and the interactiv-ity of complexity properties with storytelling and narrative processes. The second challenge I make is to break the hierarchic ordering of the properties, to see them in any combination, as holographic.

In Chapter 2, (how story *dialogism* differs from narrative), the contribution is to posit story dialogism as quite different from narrative monologism. Dialogism is a word Bakhtin never used, and is defined as different voices, styles, and ideas expressing a plurality of logics in different ways, but not always in the same place

---

1 Bakhtin (1981: 152) uses the term 'systematicalness' to denote unmerged parts, and unfinalized wholeness of systems. I prefer a new word, 'systemicity.'

and time.[2] Dialogism is defined as different voices (polyphony), styles (stylistics), space–time conceptions (chronotopes), interanimating discourses (architectonics), and dynamic interplay of these varied dialogisms (which I call the polypi). Story is more 'dialogized' than narrative, with fully embodied voices, logics, or viewpoints (Bakhtin, 1981: 273). There is something called a 'dialogized story' (Bakhtin, 1981: 25) that is not only the polyphonic (many-voiced) story, but one dialogized with multi-stylistic expression, diverse chronotopicities, and the architectonics of interanimating societal discourses, including cognitive, aesthetics, and ethics. It is a rare and endangered species. Out of the polypi of dialogisms, wells up emergence.

In Chapter 3, the contribution is to develop types of collective memory that interplay in Storytelling Organizations. Exploring collective memory is a project I began with the office supply company ethnography (Boje, 1991) and at Disney (Boje, 1995) where I noticed more than one collective memory, interacting in complexity. *Collective Memory* is like a tapestry of group's and some errant individuals' collective memories, interpenetrated by strands or threads of thoughts interwoven across many groups. The chapter explores the relation between collective memory and emergent stories. *Emergent story* can be defined as absolute novelty, spontaneity, and improvisation, without past or future. Emergent stories are conceived in the here-and-now co-presence of social communicative intercourse of narrative-memory prisons ready to capture and translate emergence. Managerial collective memory posits a center point. Punctual collective memory develops silos, while feigning multiplicity, which it seems to suppress. Multilineal collective memory breaks with horizontal and vertical points to break from the unitary memory. Polyphonic collective memory has multiplicity of memories (or anti-memories) that deny the kinds of center points of memory endemic to managerial memory. Narrative and story research in organizations has been particularly negligent of non-oral ways collective memories are renarrated or restoried. For too long it was assumed only one BME rendition exists (i.e. managerialist). If there are several collective memories vying for recognition or control, then you can see that this makes an organization holographic, punctuated by currents of sensemaking-storytelling, and out of all the dialogic plurality wells up emergence.

The ideas in Part I inform what follows: Part II deals with the application of these key concepts (self-organizing opposition of narrative and story forces, interplay of narrative-story varieties of sensemaking, dialogisms of emergence, and interacting collective memories) to the field of strategy; Part III applies concepts of Part I to how story consulting is, and could be, done; and Part IV examines frontier issues of living story method, and the book closes with a Socratic Story Symposium.

---

2 Bakhtin used dialogicality. I use *dialogism* and *dialogic* interchangeably to mean *dialogicality*. Holquist's (1990) reading of 'dialogism' describes Bakhtin anti-Hegelian dislike for Absolute Spirit dialectic. Bakhtin preferred neo-Kantianism more 'speculative epistemology' (Holquist, 1990: 17), a move from Newtonian to Einsteinian worldview (i.e. relativity of time/space).

INTRODUCTION

torytelling *Organizations* is about how people and organizations make sense of the world via narrative and story. Narratives shape our past events into experience using coherence to achieve believability. Stories are more about dispersion of events in the present or anticipated to be achievable in the future. These narrative-coherence and story-dispersion processes interact so that meaning changes among people, as their events, identities, and strategies get re-sorted in each meeting, publication, and drama. This book will identify eight types of sensemaking patterns of narrative coherence in relation to story dispersion that are the dynamics of Storytelling Organizations.

For 15 years I have written about what I call the 'Storytelling Organization.' Every workplace, school, government office or local religious group is a Storytelling Organization. Every organization, from a simple office supply company or your local choral group, your local McDonald's, Wal-Mart, to the more glamorous organizations such as Disney or Nike, and the more scandalous such as Enron or Arthur Anderson is a Storytelling Organization.[1] Yet, very little is known about how Storytelling Organizations differ, or how they work, how they respond to their environment, how to change them, and how to survive in them. Even less is known about the insider's view of the Storytelling Organization, its theatre of everyday life. Where you work, you become known by your story, become promoted and fired for your story. It is not always the story you want told, and there are ways to change, and restory that story.

Obviously the glamorous entertainment companies such as Nike, Disney, and even McDonald's and Wal-Mart are Storytelling Organizations. But, think about it, so are the less glamorous, less boisterous, ones like your hardware store, your building contractor, your realty company. They all live and die by the narratives and stories they tell.

This book is not an argument about there being only one way, narrating or storying, or a choice between narrative and story. It is not that there is only one form

---

1 We have done research on each of these Storytelling Organizations (Goldco Office Supply: Boje, 1991; Disney: Boje, 1995; Nike: Boje, 1999a; Choral group: Boje et al. 1999; McDonald's: Boje and Cai, 2004; Boje and Rhodes, 2005a, b; Wal-Mart: Boje, 2007c; Enron: Boje et al. 2004, 2006).

of narrative coherence and story dispersion. Nor, being only *retrospective, in-the-now*, more *prospective*, or the neglected *transcendental* and *reflexivity*. It is that retrospective, now, prospective, transcendental, and reflexivity are in interplay creating dynamic forces of change and transformation of an organization with its environment. To treat what is different, as the same, blinds us to dynamics, with important implications for how these multiple ways of sensemaking dance together. It is this dance among sensemaking differences that gives us new understanding of complexity, strategy, organization change, and methodology.

The structure of the book is as follows: the introduction will map, for the reader, eight ways of sensemaking (two are narrative-coherence; six are story-dispersion processes). Part I of the book looks at the complexity and collective memory implications of storying and narrating. The key point is the transition businesses and public organizations are making from Second World War system thinking (in one logic) to complexity thinking (that is a dance of diverse logics and languages of sensemaking). Part II is five chapters applying implications of the dance of narrative coherence and story dispersion to strategy schools. Each chapter contributes a new frontier for traditional strategy schools to explore. Part III is a couple of chapters on how narrative and story are being used in organization development and change programs. The final part of the book gives attention to method implications of how to study the interplay of narrative and story, as well as storying and narrating processes. Key is the concern for a 'living story' method in relation to 'dead narrative' text ways of study. In the final chapter, I have a bit of fun, and give tribute to dead narrative and story scholars who have influenced ideas expressed in this book. They are people I always wanted to meet and have a conversation with (Bakhtin, Benjamin, Dostoevsky, Heidegger, Ricoeur, and Stein).

MAP OF SENSEMAKING TYPES

At this point, putting together the eight ways of sensemaking into a map, will simplify their presentation, and give you, the reader, a way to visualize important interrelationships. Figure I.A maps important dynamics among eight ways of narrative and story sensemaking.

More research has been done on the past ways (BME and Terse fragments) of sensemaking, than on future ways (antenarratives), or the now ways (Tamara, Horsesense, and Emotive–Ethical). Even less is done with reflexivities (Dialectics), and hardly anything with the transcendentals (Dialogisms).

Reflexivity refers to the (often subconscious) processes by which we know ourselves, and story our identity, in ethical appraisal. Like Roshomon, we retrospectively recall past events in a way that supports our concept of who we are. Thus if I see myself as kind, I may narrate my act of firing an employee as helping them to move on to a job better suited to them, a better 'fit' where they will be happier and more successful. If I see myself as efficient and business-like, I may see the firing as nothing personal, just a matter of performance numbers. In the now,

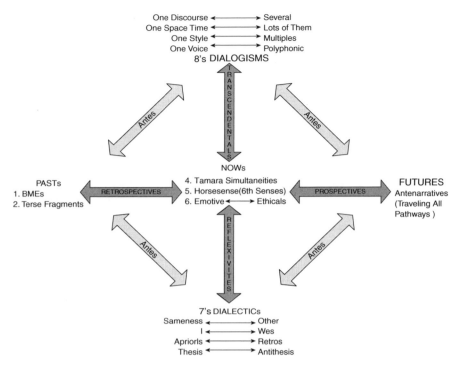

FIGURE I.A *Dynamics of narrative and story sensemaking*

Note: Arrows indicate key relationships among retrospective, prospective, now, reflexivity, and transcendental ways of sensemaking. Narrative forms include BME (Beginning, Middle, and End) linear narrative and Terse (Narrative) fragments, and the Antenarratives. The Now's, Dialectics, and Dialogisms are what I refer to throughout as story. Antes (short for antenarratives) besides leaning to the future, are also integral in moving in-between other ways of sensemaking.

I might reflexively notice that I am uncomfortable in the presence of the person I just fired. I might attribute this discomfort to the person's unpleasant personal qualities. Or, I might story the situation such that I am nobly carrying out an unpleasant but necessary job for the good of my organization. I might extend this sense of ethical self into the future, and incorporate change, by telling myself that I am too soft-hearted to do this type of unpleasant task in the future. In such a telling, I plan to delegate it to an assistant. Or, I may decide such firings are immoral, and that I cannot participate in this ever again. I begin to look for another job where I can be (prospectively) the kind of person I want to be or see myself as already being. Upward reflexivity includes the spiritual aspects of sorting out my life path. Downward reflexivity is about the many netherworlds, be they Dante's inferno, or worlds alive with ancestors and animal guides (as in native traditions). The middle world, the here-and-now, is the path I am on, the choice point between several paths open to me.

The key point about reflexive storying is that stories are about who I am, who I ought to be (be they spiritual aspects of self or higher self, or religious doctrine), and my relation to many other people, sometimes to people and animals in other worlds (higher or lower than this one, in many native traditions). The remaining ways of sensemaking take us in directions other than retrospective narrative-wholes or narrative-fragments. We will explore each aspect of Figure 1A, but first I want to give some explanation of why I treat story as something other than narrative. Many readers, no doubt, use narrative and story interchangeably.

How Narrative and Story Differ

Treating narrative and story as the same serves to erase any understanding of their interplay, the ways their dance creates transformative dynamics that work to change organizations. Narrative ways (1, 2, 3) and story ways (4 to 8) of sense-making are oriented differently among our multiple pasts, multiple nows, and multiple futures, as well as, what is the breakthrough science, the study of dynamics of reflexivities (dialectics), and the transcendentals (dialogisms). The key differences are that narrative is a whole telling, with the linear sequence of a beginning, middle, and end (BME); is usually a backward-looking (retrospective) gaze from present, back through the past, sorting characters, dialog, themes, etc. into one plot, and changes little over time.

The act of narrating, in the information age, gives full explication of a backward-looking (retrospective) chronology that leaves little to the imagination, in hindsight reassemblage, in order to achieve coherence. Often the past is reimagined from the vantage point of the present. Yet, there is the future-oriented (vision) narrative, and, to stay with temporality, the storying taking place in the now.

The most important of the story dynamics come into play because there are so many pasts, nows and futures. In my antenarrative concept (Boje, 2001a), I asserted telling can be about the future (prospective sensemaking).

Story, in contrast to narrative (that is centering or about control) is more apt to be dispersive (unraveling coherence, asserting differences). Narrative cohesion seeks a grip on the emergent present, which story is re-dispersing. The dynamics of the nows (simultaneous storytelling across many places or in many rooms at once) is what I researched in Tamara (using Disney as an example, in Boje, 1995). The emergent present keeps changing, but since we cannot be in every room at once, we interact with others taking different pathways to make sense of it all. The act of storying usually leaves the explication to the listener's imagination, in acts of co-construction, in an emergent assemblage sensemaking, across several (dialectic or dialogical) contexts. Participants oriented differently to pasts, nows, futures, dialectics, or dialogisms will have wildly different audience expectations about what a story ought to include and exclude. Walter Benjamin (1936) and Gertrude Stein (1935), in particular, argue that in the narrative-telling age, storytelling has been deskilled, and in particular we have lost skills in how to notice and listen to stories in the now. Fully explicated BME narrative is somewhat easier to identify in doing research. One can aspire to be a detective, reassembling tersely told narrative fragments. This ease of discovery has put narrative, with its drive for whole, coherence, full explication, in the upper hand. The contribution of this book is to emphasize that narrative and story are not the same, and are in interplay in ways not yet researched. There are instances, for example, where people assume a narrative whole to exist, but in story, the dispersion is so varied, layered, and in contest, no overall narrative whole may ever have existed.

Storytelling Organization is an 'and' relation between processes of narrating and storying, and between narrative and story forms. To simplify the writing, I prefer the term 'storying' to 'storytelling,' since 'telling' is orality, and an important dynamic is the relation of oral to text, and these to the visual ways of narrating and storying. Oral, text, and visual mediums are juxtaposed in ways that help us understand new aspects, and differences among Storytelling Organizations. Noticing the interplay of narrative and story's oral, text, and visual mediums will afford a more rigorous inquiry than has occurred to date in organization and communication research. In sum, the specific contribution this book intends is an inquiry into the interrelationships of narrating and storying processes with narrative and story forms, across the juxtaposed mediums of orality, textuality, and visuality. I believe this nexus to be at the heart of understanding new ways of sensemaking, that have important insights to be gleaned about complexity, strategy, organization change, and methodology. These topics are discussed in the book, with chapters composed of everyday and well known organizations.

Let us start with a new rendition of sensemaking.

EIGHT WAYS OF NARRATIVE AND STORY SENSEMAKING

Karl Weick (1995) presented a narrative sensemaking in a chapter on organization control. Indeed one facet of narrative sensemaking is the retrospective gaze from present into the past that assembles a beginning, middle, and end, demanding narrative coherence in a way which controls sensemaking by deselecting that which does not fit with the chosen beginning, middle, and end. In the past decade Weick has lamented limiting sensemaking to only retrospection, and to only the five-empiric perception senses (touch, smell, taste, sight, and hearing).[2] He specifically wants to look at emotion as a sixth sense. We can heed Weick's call, and look at how multiple ways of sensemaking interplay, in relationships among ways of narrating and storying, and in the forms, narrative and story. I propose eight types, knowing full well, there are others, to be discovered.

---

2 See Weick et al. (2005)

1   BME Retrospective Narrative

BME stands for Beginning, Middle, and End, and for their retrospective assemblage into a rather linear narrative coherence. It is a form that Aristotle (350BCE) immortalized in the *Poetics* of six elements: plot, character, dialogue, theme, rhythm, and spectacle. Aristotle dictated that these be in a particular order, with plot the most important, and spectacle the very least. Nowadays, however, one can see that that order is reversed, and spectacle rules supreme, and plot is hard to find. Spectacle includes the spin, the costuming, the razzle-dazzle substitutes for good old-fashioned BME plot development, in politics and in organizations. BME retrospective narrative, and all its poetic elements, is important to business. Rhythm, for example, helps us understand the processes of complexity. Dialogues among stakeholders constitute a frontier issue for strategy. Changing organizations so that spectacle has the substance of characters with integrity and authenticity, and so that the plot espoused is what gets enacted, has ethical import. Kenneth Burke (1945: 231) made two simple changes to Aristotle's six poetic elements. He combined dialogue and rhythm into one (agency), and renamed Aristotle's elements, resulting in Burke's famous Pentad model.

Aristotle's Six → Burke's Pentad

Plot → Act

Character → Agent

Theme → Purpose

Dialogue + Rhythm → Agency

Spectacle → Scene

Burke (1937, 1972) regreted not having included 'Frame' as a Pentad element. By the way, Aristotle also wrote about frame. To the end Burke remained fixated on Aristotle, on the ratio aspects of Pentad, and BME. Given that there are now many plots, many characters, many dialogues, many themes, many different rhythms, and multiple spectacles in a complex enterprise, there is a major research methods challenge: how to trace all these interactions.

Czarniawska (2004) takes a petrification approach, arguing that in strong culture organizations, founding BME narratives are immutable, with later tellings just adding concentric rings to the narrative, like a tree trunk, year-by-year. It is assumed that founding narrative emerges fully formed, as in the mind of Zeus. Or that strong corporate cultures have 'many strategic narratives [that] seem to follow a simplified variation of … the epic Hero's Journey' (Barry and Elmes, 1997: 440, bracketed addition, mine). But, results of my founding narrative research, such as at Wal-Mart, suggest there is no originary Beginning narrative telling. For example, in 1972, when Wal-Mart began filing annual reports, all one finds is 'Our eighteen Wal-Mart stores that already existed as of February 1, 1970' (p. 4) and 'Wal-Mart Stores Inc. began through an exchange of common stock Feb 1 1970' (p. 8).[3] In 1973, there is mention of a 'twenty-eight year history' (p. 2). In 1974, there is more, 'We're all proud of our record to date, and we're confident this is just the **beginning of our Wal-Mart story**' (p. 3, bold mine), and there is this more complete BME rendition:

> ... President and Chairman, Sam M. Walton, who opened his first Ben Franklin variety store in Newport, Arkansas in 1945. One year later, Mr. Walton was joined by his brother, J. L. 'Bud' Walton, now Senior Vice President.
>
> In 1947, Bud Walton opened a Ben Franklin store in Versailles, Missouri. The two brothers went on to assemble a group of fifteen Ben Franklin stores and subsequently developed the concept of larger discount department stores. The Company's first Wal-Mart Discount City store opened in Rogers, Arkansas in 1962.
>
> In October 1970, Wal-Mart Stores, Inc. became a publicly held corporation and became traded in the over-the-counter market. August 25, 1972, the Company's stock was listed and began trading on the New York Stock Exchange.... **Wal-Mart's success story** has always been one of people who are completely dedicated to the performance of their jobs to the total good of the Company' (p. 4, bold, mine)

This raises the question, 'do originary founding narratives exist, or are they retrospective concoctions, retrofitted, after the fact, after many years?' The brothers were opening stores in the 1940s, but not putting together a coherent narrative (in the reports) until 1974. I also found, that, in subsequent Annual Shareholder Reports (through to 2007), the BME journey is never petrified exactly the same way, from one year to the next. The important implication is that a lack of petrification may be the key strategic force of BME hero's journey narrating. The reason is, strategic journey narrative faces a dilemma: how to appear to be the same over time, and to appear to be different, reflecting shifts in innovation and the environment. The balancing of sameness and difference in narrating identity is the subject of Ricoeur's (1992) work. We can see sameness and difference played out during Sam Walton's leadership, when founding narrative was skillfully told in nuanced ways. But after Sam's death, two of his successors, David Glass, and Lee Scott Jr., rarely refer to the petrified narrative, trotting it out when there was a scandal, to claim they were operating within the founder's vision. Or Sam Walton's son (John), or his wife (Helen), are introduced into the report, to answer charges being brought against the executives that they are not following in Sam's footsteps (1997 Wal-Mart Annual Report):

> *John Walton*: 'I've grown up with the company' says the son of founder Sam Walton ... before Sam Walton died, John told him that 'what he had done went far beyond Wal-Mart to make American business better' (p. 7)

---

3 See Wal-Mart.com for annual reports for years 1972 to 2007

Helen Walton: Wal-Mart's First Lady … 'As our Company has grown questions have come up about where Wal-Mart is going and if Sam would approve,' Helen said. 'I believe he would. I feel good about our leadership, especially in this last year.' (p. 10)

By 2001, Wal-Mart's Annual Report is including long lists of lawsuits it is facing, and by 2003 this list includes the Dukes vs. Wal-Mart class action lawsuit brought on behalf of 1.6 million past and present female employees, which becomes the largest punitive suit in corporate history (expected award could be as high as $11 billion, US). By 2004, CEO Scott is saying, 'We must always do the right things in the right way, but we can also **be more aggressive about telling our story**. It is after all, a great story, from the jobs we provide to the consumers we help, to the Communities we serve' (p. 3, bold, mine).

There are at least four implications of a focus on the changeable aspects of founding narratives (rather than their more stable or 'petrified' qualities). One implication is that BME retrospective sensemaking can be highly adaptive, and its lack of petrification-stuckness, is a strategic advantage. A second implication, is that Storytelling Organizations, such as Wal-Mart, struggle to adapt their reputation asset (BME journey narrative rendition to founding story), to *balance* what Ricoeur (1992) calls their sameness-identity, with a difference-identity, that is, claims that they are changing radically from their past ways. Third, whereas Sam Walton was acknowledged as a talented storyteller, it is not clear that his successors are. This is another reason, in annual reports, to hark back to Sam's stories rather than successors to offer new ones. Finally, there is a dance between telling BME full-blown narratives, and telling more fragmented narratives.

It is the narrative fragments we explore next, which, in organizations, are more common than BME narratives.

2   Fragmented Retrospective Narratives

In 1991 I published an article in *Administrative Science Quarterly*, about narrative and story that now seems so obvious, I hesitate to restate it. In transcribing eight months of participant observations of the talk among customers, vendors, salespeople, secretaries, managers, and executives in Goldco Office Supply (as in the above Wal-Mart study), there was rarely a BME retrospective whole narrative to be found. In business, it seems that BME is quite a rare form. Instead, there were mostly fragmented retrospections, so coded, and so well understood by participants, that a word, a nod, a photo, could each imply some whole narrative moments. So coded, that to an uninitiated observer, the narrative exchange went completely unnoticed. I called this 'terse telling' of fragments.

But these fragments are *not* like the archaeologist's bits of pottery, for which there was once a 'real' pot as an originary artifice, at some specific time and place in the past. Rather, these narrative fragments are like pieces of a jigsaw puzzle, whose box cover has been lost. To our dismay, we discover that someone has mixed several puzzles together, and further, these puzzles may have some portions of their pictures in common, and other sections just missing. And we do not know how many puzzle makers were there to start with, or if they're ever was one or more whole, or originary puzzles. As Gabriel (2000: 20) cautions, the originary telling may be imagined, but actually never existed.

Narrative fragments are distributed across many different characters, meetings, texts, and visual displays. It was when I began to piece fragments together, to juxtapose different renditions, in varied mediums (oral, text, photo), that I detected (like a detective) what was being communicated, that participants all seem to understand, but that I had been trained (based on BME schooling), to ignore: that there was no whole narrative, never had been, but everyone assumed someone had heard it somewhere. It was this study of a medium-size, rather common-place office supply company (Goldco), operating in a few states (a region) that afforded my first understanding of the Storytelling Organization, defined as a, 'collective storytelling system in which the performance of stories is a key part of members' sensemaking and a means to allow them to supplement individual memories with institutional memory' (Boje, 1991: 106).

Goldco (tersely told) fragment of Founding Narrative

Doug: I look at Goldco as a toy that somebody decided to put in the company because it was fun and it also brought in/

Sam: Well, I'll tell you how that came about

Doug: I thought you would [*lots of laughter from the group*]

Sam: Sam Coche worked for Sea Breeze or something like that, oh you know the story/

Doug: No go ahead tell it, really it's important.

Sam: He got out there and he came over and they formed Goldco and Goldco does not mean Gold Company or anything else they took the first four initials from Billy Gold, which is G O L D and from Cochec., and that's how they got Goldco.

Doug: And it was a good living for a couple of people. It was a nice toy for Billy, he made a few bucks on the thing. He had some fun for it but then the motivation at that time was a whole lot different than it is today. We don't have the luxury of screwing around with something like that/ [*lots of cross talk at this point*].

[*Returns to turn-by-turn talk*].

So what? Most of the narrative is left untold ('you know the story'), and is not told in BME fashion, is interrupted, starts in the middle, is revised by the group, unfolds in animated conversation. Second, there are many frameworks in play: the old school ways of a salesperson's culture are challenged by the conglomerate that brought Doug in to get the numbers in order so it can be bundled with other regional office supply firms, and sold as a potential national office supply enterprise. And what was ethical in the old time sales culture is now unethical in the more bureaucratic frame that Doug (and the conglomerate) expect (i.e. 'I look at Goldco as a toy,' is a powerful pronouncement by any CEO; once a 'good living,' 'he had some fun with it;' but 'we don't have the luxury of screwing around.') Especially since this is a meeting to decide which division to scrap, to make the year end numbers come out the way the conglomerate expects. In short, the telling is terse, it takes heaps of context understanding to notice when it is that which is between-the-lines, unspoken, yet conveyed, really matters.

In this book I make some changes, based upon subsequent research, to the concept. While my *Administrative Science Quarterly* article (Boje, 1991) introduced the concept of 'Storytelling Organization,' this book significantly adds to that concept. I go beyond retrospective sensemaking. This book introduces in-the-moment, as well as prospective and reflexive ways of sensemaking. Now I see *Storytelling Organizations* as an interplay of retrospective-narrative control (e.g. Doug's 'it was a nice toy,' or Wal-Mart's, 'Sam would agree with what our executives are doing') with prospective and reflexive (inward, soul-searching, or ethical) sensemaking. Some attempts that are backward-looking, seemingly whole, and tersely told fragments of narrative, along with more forward-looking (prospective), and some emergent (now-looking) glances, mingled with attempts are reflexive ('is this what we ought to be and do'). In short, whether in wholes or fragments, retrospective narrative sensemaking studies seem fixated on sorting the past according to the logic popular in the present. What seems so obvious now is that fragments are more abundant than the whole BMEs, some fragments purport to derive from BMEs that never existed, and many (perhaps most) fragments are not always retrospective. They look forward (prospectively) to invent the future.

3 Antenarratives

Antenarrative, along the 'arrows of time', is more attuned to prospective (future-oriented) ways of sensemaking. I invented the term *antenarrative* in my last SAGE book (2001a), *Narrative Methods for Organizational and Communication Research*. I wanted to contribute an alternative to the narrative-retrospective ways (BME and Fragments), which the fields of organization narrative and folklore seemed to ignore. Antenarratives are prospective (forward-looking) bets (antes) that an ante-story (before-story) can transform organization relationships. Forward-looking antenarratives are the most abundant in business, yet the most overlooked in research and consulting practice. These fragile antenarratives, like the butterfly, are sometimes able to change the future, to set changes and transformations in motion that have impact on the big picture. More accurately, antenarratives seem to bring about a future that would not otherwise be. The key attribute of antenarratives is they are travelers; moving from context to context, shifting in content and refraction as they jump-start the future. What is most interesting about them is how they morph their content as they travel. As in the Wal-Mart report examples they are rarely told, shown, or written the same way twice. They are travelers that pick up context (perspective, logic, situation) and transport it to another context. They are also discarding (forgetting, or choosing to ignore items previously acquired in other contexts).

For example, the following demonstrates some dynamics of antenarrative. In the 2007 Wal-Mart Annual Report there is a quote from the late Sam Walton (died in 1992): 'The best part is if we work together, we'll lower the cost of living for everyone, not just in America, but we'll give the world an opportunity to see what it's like to save and have a better life' (p. 3).

While Wal-Mart executives are making antenarrative retrofits of what Sam said, *What's Up Wal-Mart* and *Wal-Mart Watch* (both founded in 2005 by unions) are antenarrating a different story. They suggest that Sam must be turning over in his grave at the number of lawsuits for violations of labor standards (forced overtime, not paying for overtime), discrimination (among women, races, disabled), etc.[4] For example Wal-Mart Watch lists seven Sam Walton quotes concerning moral responsibility principles that Wal-Mart's current executives are not living up to:

1 **Protect Human Dignity** 'If you want people in the stores to take care of the customers, you have to make sure you are taking care of the people in the stores' – Sam Walton

2 **Ensure Quality and Affordable Health Care Coverage** 'You can't create a team spirit when the situation is so one-side, when management gets so much and workers get so little of the pie' – Sam Walton

3 **Use Market Power to Improve Supplier Conditions and Wages** 'We still want to drive a hard bargain, but now we need to guard against abusing our power' – Sam Walton

4 **Enable and Embrace Self-Sufficiency** 'Maybe the most important way in which we at Wal-Mart believe in giving something back is through our commitment to using the power of this enormous enterprise as a force for change' – Sam Walton

5 **Buy Local First** 'For Wal-Mart to maintain its position in the hearts of our customers, we have to study more ways we can give something back to our communities' – Sam Walton

---

4 The United Food and Commercial Workers Union (UFCWU) started WakeUp WalMart.com. The Service Employees International Union (SEIU) started up Wal-MartWatch.com in 2005.

6 **Keep it Clean** 'I'd like to believe that as Wal-Mart continues to thrive and grow it can come to live up to what someone once called us: the Lighthouse of the Ozarks' – Sam Walton

7 **Prove Worthy of the Public Trust** 'As long as we're managing our company well, as long as we take care of our people and our customers, keep our eyes on those fundamentals, we are going to be successful. Of course, it takes an observing, discerning person to judge those fundamentals for himself' – Sam Walton

Successor CEOs Glass and Scott have asserted repeatedly that their philosophy, core values, and business ethics are just the same as Sam Walton's, but the unions are claiming just the opposite. Each is recasting elements of context into a forward-looking interpretation of Sam's way. Research into antenarratives has only just begun. For a recent study, see work on Sears UK (Collins and Rainwater, 2005), or work about Enron (Boje et al., 2004), or more on Wal-Mart (Boje, 2007c).

Antenarratives, therefore, morph as they move about. As such, these most fragile of travelers are prospectors, and they can be the most powerful transformative sensemaking of all, particularly, in complex organizations, picking up and dispersing meaning from one context to the next.

4   Tamara

Tamara is now a seemingly obvious insight into how Disney's Storytelling Organization operates, one I first developed in 1993 (with Dennehy), and more rigorously in 1995 (in *Academy of Management Journal*). The problem Disney faced is the same for every complex organization, how to make sense of storytelling in many rooms, around the world, when you can physically only be in one place at a time. In the 'Now' (Figure 1), there are people in any given organization, narrating and storying, but situated in different rooms. Not being God, it is impossible for someone to be in all the rooms at once. In this simultaneous situation, people must choose which rooms to be in each day, stitching together a path of sensemaking. This phenomenon is so ubiquitous (to all organizations) it seems obvious. Yet it has not been researched, and the field of story consulting does not address it at all. The implication that needs to be explored is how do distributed, simultaneous storying and narrating processes work? This fourth type of story-sensemaking allows different and even apparently contradictory stories to be simultaneously enacted across different rooms (or sites) of an organization. However, the meaning derived by people in any given room, depends upon their path (what rooms they have been in). These insights come from a play called *Tamara* (by John Kriznac). Characters unfold their stories in the many rooms of a huge mansion, before a walking, sometimes running, audience that splinters into fragments, chasing characters from room to room, in acts of situated sensemaking. At each moment (in-the-now), audience members must choose which actors to chase into which room (yet cannot be in more than one room at a time). This sets up a myriad of complexity dynamics that follow from the rather straightforward insights that storytelling is simultaneous, you have to ask others about stories performed in rooms you did not attend, and pathways influence what sense people take away from any given room.

For example, how do people find out what stories were performed in the rooms they are not in? How are the many choices of a sequence of rooms to be in during just one day, by each person, affecting the differentiated sense made to a story enacted in a current room? In strategy, the fact that people in different rooms are making strategy all-at-the-same-time, and are trying to sort their simultaneous action out, is why strategy-in-planning is different from strategy-in-implementation. In organization development, Tamara has important, yet unexplored implications. For example, since narrating and storying is simultaneous, yet distributed across different rooms where people meet to converse, as well as hallways, and cars (etc.), people are making sense of what they are missing in other rooms. If this is the case, then training executives in two-minute story pitches, or collecting archetype stories in focus groups, are rather shallow, flat-earth ways to try to change or lead a rather more complex, dynamic, moving Tamara-Storytelling Organization! Finally, for research methods, the implications of Tamara are in tracing the dynamics that are simultaneously distributed over time, to get at processes of emergence, pattern formation, and the ways sensemaking pathways (of room choices, and in which order) affect sensemaking. If a researcher is stuck in one room, not privy to what is happening in all the other rooms, then traditional methods (interviews, focus groups, etc.) are too low a variety way of doing the inquiry. A more dynamic story-tracing method, for example, would need to involve a team of researchers, experiencing the on-going, shifting frames of action. Across the disciplines of complexity, strategy, change, and research methods, one way to proceed is to look at the interplay of forces to gain more narrative control (forces for coherence may employ BME-coherence or enforce control by consistency), while the forces of story diffusion recognize the process of making room choices, choosing among multiple stories being dispersed, or among polyphony of voices or logics.

We have not begun the task of sorting out differences in patterns of sensemaking (how eight ways interplay differently) in simple versus more complex Tamara-Storytelling Organizations. Goldco Office Supply, as a regional firm, with a fairly flat structure, was rooted more in orality (of salespeople's way of telling). Goldco is less complex than Disney (with its workers being cast members), McDonald's (where a clown has a leader role), Nike (where 'spinning' a story is routine), Enron (where spin came undone), or Wal-Mart (whose founding story in annual reports is not told the same way twice).[5]

---

5 See Boje and Rhodes, 2005 a,b for more on Ronald as a leader, even a board member at McDonald's; Boje (1995) for Disney studies; Boje (1991) for office supply. See Enron studies already cited above. Wal-Mart study of morphing founding stories, not behaving in petrified manner predicted by traditional theory, was presented to Critical Management Studies conference (Manchester, July 2007).

5   Emotive–Ethical

Emotional intelligence is now all the rage. Yet, in his early writing, in the 1920s, Bakhtin's (1990) notebooks were all about the relation of emotion to something all but forgotten: ethics. In the now, in the moment-of-Being, when one makes that choice of which door to enter (and all the doors not to enter), there is a once-occurent ethical choice, that is also an emotional prompting (beyond just cognitive sensemaking calculus). We feel that there are times and places that if we do not act, no one else will. It is in those once-occurent (now) moments, we have an emotive–ethical obligation to act, to intervene, to no longer be a bystander, to move from being spectator (bystander) to being the actor. This is what Bakhtin calls our *in-the-moment* answerability.

Answerability is our answer (in action) to a compelling story, told by the 'Other' that tugs our emotional passion, our outrage, and invites our capacity to act, to help, to do something for someone. For example, when Greenwald's 2005 documentary film, '*Wal-Mart: The High Cost of Low Prices*' was released, Wal-Mart commissioned a more expensively produced counter-film, Galloway's '*Why Wal-Mart Works and Why That Makes Some People Crazy.*' The film wars are over the issue of Wal-Mart's answerability, its ethics record, and both films make emotive–ethical appeals in their way of telling. Justification for emotive–ethical sensemaking can also be found in basic neuroscience studies. Work by Josh Green (and colleagues, 2001) at Princeton, using fMRI (functional magnetic resonance imaging) found that presenting subjects with a Runaway Trolley Car story, elicited emotional responses to an ethical dilemma. Would a bystander, the only person next to a track switch, let a runaway trolley hit and surely kill a family of five, or throw the switch, so only one man would die. While such a moral dilemma engages the cognitive, it also stimulates the emotion area of the brain. There are circumstances in an organization that engage our emotion, and we make an ethical judgment, in-the-moment. These results in cognitive neuroscience suggest that there may be a middle-path between the age old argument, of cognition versus emotion. For me, I want to explore how emotive–ethical is a rediscovered mode of sensemaking. In short, what I am calling 'emotive–ethical' sensemaking is storying *in-the-now*, that addresses the important question of how an answerable decision to act (or to be the bystander) to change what happens to Others, gets done and undone in complex organizations. What is becoming clear in cognitive neuroscience has yet to be researched in organization studies. Yet, it is happening, every day, many times a day, in any complex Storytelling Organization, in any Tamara, when one chooses one door to enter a room of conversation, and chooses to speak out, or does not enter, or not engage, while the tug of emotive–ethical prompts that key moment of reflexivity: '*I am the only one who can act, and if I don't act, no one will act. I am therefore complicit with what will happen next to the Other.*'

6   Horsesense

Grace Ann Rosile (1999) gave her presentation on horsesense at Jeffrey Ford's exclusive gathering of the most esteemed narrative and story scholars, at Ohio

State University. Karl Weick encouraged Grace Ann to write up her talk and send this new way of sensemaking into publication at *Journal of Management Inquiry*. Grace Ann wrote it up, many times, but did not submit it for publication.[6] Horsesense is the most difficult of the eight ways of sensemaking to define. I can only define horsesense by telling you a personal experience story. It was June 2007. I had just returned from a plane trip, and had pulled the luggage too often and a side muscle was paining me. I approached Grace Ann, in her home office. Her back was to me. She said, 'Nahdion says he can cure your muscle pain.' Without another word, and retaining all my science skepticism, I marched from our house to the barn, opened Nahdion's stall door, did not look at him, and turned my back to him, clamping both hands, arms extended, to the high-bar of the stall. Nahdion, a 27-year-old Arabian stallion, noisily circled behind me, breathing hard, and snorting. He approached deliberately, putting his entire forehead against just the spot where I ached. He then gave me the best and most professional deep tissue massage I ever had. At times Nahdion was so vigorous, he lifted me off the ground. I held on to that bar, kept my eyes closed, and let it happen. When Nahdion was done, I thanked him, hugged him, and left. The pain was all gone. And it did not return on the next trip. What kind of sensemaking is going on between Grace Ann, Nahdion, and me? Surely cat and dog-lovers, and all horse-lovers, will have similar stories of inter-species sensemaking. Yet, horsesense is more than this. Horsesense is not just about communicating between people and horses. It is also about body-to-body energy connections, not by noise, smell, sight, taste, or touch, but some other kind of energy sensemaking. In biology, we know dolphins, whales, and some birds have a magnetic compass, can register pressure changes, and can sense radiation. Surely, we scientists are not so myopic as to deny energetic body sensemaking? There is, for example, Patricia Reily's *Seasense*, the sense sailors have of their relation to waves, currents, winds, and tides.[7] There is 'printers' sense,' the aesthetic sense compositors have for energetic graphic design, and the kind of 'energeia' sense (being-what-something-is even as it is changing) that Aristotle wrote about. Jerome Bruner (1986: 48) suggests a traffic sense and channel sense: 'My traffic sense is a different model from the one that guides my sailing into a harbor full of shoals, when, as the saying goes, I depend upon my channel sense.' Several implications of horsesense follow.

---

6 For more on Grace Ann Rosile's horsesense, see http:horsesenseatwork.com
7 'And there we were'…An exploration of the role of sea stories in the United States Navy and Coast Guard' by Patricia Reily, University of San Francisco, School of Education, Organization and Leadership Program. Pat Reily coined the term 'seasense' at a STORI workshop in Las Vegas, Nevada (April 2007). Printer's eye is a sense I was exploring while working at UCLA in the early 1980s. STORI is Storytelling Organization Institute, http://storyemergence.org

The first implication is, in horsesense, identity is unchanging, its energetics some-how discernable. In seasense terms, waves, currents, tides, and winds are in flux, but their energy is discernable, to those experienced and gifted enough to make sense of their configurations. A second implication is people, animals, and some indige-nous people believe stones and even this planet (Gaia) are energetic beings. American Indians believe that stones are alive; directions have energy, as do the ele-ments (water, earth, air, and fire). In India (and elsewhere) it is thought that there are seven charka (Sanskrit – Çakra) energy points in the human body: root, spleen, solar plexus, heart, throat, brow, and crown. I have a breathing coach named Toni Delgado, and she has been teaching me to balance charka energy points, to release and replace energeia.[8] I do not know how it works, but the beneficial results are self-evident. What has this to do with business? Perhaps Sam Walton, as he walked through a store, began bagging products at the register, asking associates what items were moving, etc., was doing a form of horsesense, a way of story noticing, that was about tapping into the flow of action, putting his body in that flow, and keying into the energies around him. They say some people have business-sense, can read the market, like a seaman reads the waves. Or, they can sustain the energy of a change effort, can read the mood of the organization. In sum, Tamara, emotive– ethical, and horsesense are storying *in-the-now*, in the once-occurent choices made in the present moment. From here we move in Figure 1, to map the reflexivity modes of sensemaking.

7 Dialectics

In the language of business, there are multiple identities, the officially narrated identity, and all the other ways of storying identity, not forceful enough to be the dominant sensemaking currency. Here, we will look at four types: sameness versus otherness (Ricoeur's dialectic of identities); I versus We's (Mead's con-cept of internalized we's from parents, society, etc. battling with our I-ness); the a prioris of cognition that come before retrospective sensemaking (Kant's idea of intuitive sense of time and space before the five empiric senses); and of course thesis versus anti-thesis (Hegel's idea includes synthesis and spiritual, no spiritual for Marx, and no synthesis for Adorno).

We have already looked at Wal-Mart's problems in having an identity of same-ness (unchanging petrified BME narrative) that is dialectic to an identity of dif-ference (innovation, nuanced telling in answer to contemporary situations); this dialectic of sameness and differences of narrated identity is seminal in the work of Ricoeur (1992). Narrative control makes one way of coherence, the only (approved), talked about way of sensemaking in an organization. Yet the officially

---

8 Toni Delgado's breath meditation energetic charka methodology is available at http: anextstep.org

narrated identity (of sameness), is always susceptible to some new (different) way of making sense of an organization, that can turn into some new complexity, envisioning some new strategic plot, or devise some way to transform a privileged way into a restoried way to make sense in a Storytelling Organization. Dialectics is at the heart of any business, and its transformations of one story, restoried into another, one identity becoming reimagined. There is always one way of sensemaking, at the apex of the managerialist hierarchy, a way of thinking that is the one accepted logical way to organize, while those in the middle, at the bottom, or customers and venders looking in, believe their own logics would work a whole lot better, and even resolve problems so obvious. Stakeholders cannot fathom why those standing atop the pyramid cannot see them in the very same way. There are several dialectic ways of sensemaking. First is to explore the relation of an official narrative of control (often a managerialist BME) or retrospective fragments in need of a detective, and all the other ways of story sensemaking (antenarrative, tamara, emotive–ethical, horsesense, etc.) that too often are left in the margins of a business (ignored customers, vendors, employees without voice, etc.). This is a common, and easily recognized dialectic, yet quite difficult to change.

Second, is what George Herbert Mead (1934) coined as the 'I–we' dialectic. It is the 'I' of narrative identity, and the many ways of storying the 'we's (our parents, siblings, teachers, and various identity groups – (occupation, politics, gender, race, ethnicity, geography, students, etc.). We internalize many we's through socialization in the family, education, military, career, media, etc. We have been socialized to think in we-ways, and are said to struggle to define our I-ness. I–we is a form of reflexivity, when we pause to reflect upon how many we's control our I-ness. To the extent that I–we's include the spiritual, some may wish to stress more transcendentals (see Figure 1).

A third dialectic comes from the work of Immanuel Kant. He wanted to tame metaphysics of spirituality, and limit transcendental to a way of sensemaking that is quite different from BME and fragmented retrospective narrative. For this reason, I located it in Figure 1 among the kinds of dialectic reflexivities. For Kant, the five empiric ways of sensemaking perception did not deal adequately with intuition, and did not address what was a priori to retrospection. In particular, Kant argued that ways of temporality and spatiality were a priori and transcendental retrospective sensemaking. In business terms, some departments will take a longer term view looking at transformations rather than other departments staffed by people concerned with short term (some almost immediate) transactions with short-term time horizons (accounting, sales, public relations). And spatially, there is an obvious dialectics between those with a focus on local affairs, more regional ones, and those treating the global situation as their landscape. For example, a McDonald's chain in India will alter the menu radically to deal with local foodways, change the employee dress code in a Muslim nation, and offer much more aesthetic styles of décor in France. The key point in these dialectics are that there is always other stories than just the official one, there are many we's that affect (psychosocial) I-ness, the synthesis is not always happening, spirituality is struggling to redefine transcendental, there are multiple time horizons, and local is trying to co-opt global (and vice versa).

The remaining kind of dialectic is what Hegel expressed about the teleology of spirit, which Kant and Marx soundly rejected (and readers following a more spiritual sensemaking path, may wish I located this among the dialogisms in Figure 1). For Hegel, the arrow of time, is of a path guided by the Spirit, but for Marx and then Adorno, it is not about transcendental appeals.

Marx, for example, thought a non-spiritual teleology, a determining political economy (instead of Spirit) would bring the working class (antithesis) to oppose the pesky capitalist (thesis), and yield a new synthesis: a democratic form of organizing, with workers and capitalists deciding together how to invest and organize the enterprise. But the dialectic ran a more Soviet course, and the revolution of the workers' liberation from oppression, did not occur.

Many critical theorists (e.g. Adorno, Horkheimer) decided to forget synthesis, and focus on the relation of thesis to antithesis. A non-theological (i.e. non-deterministic) dialectic has everything to do with complexity, strategy, and change processes.

These dialectics interplay with the modes of sensemaking discussed.

8   Dialogisms

This strange word comes from Mikhail Bakhtin. There are four dialogisms. Most research has been done on one voice (usually management's speaking for shareholders) and the many voices of polyphony. We are just beginning to look at the dialogism of styles, at the multiple styles of speaking, writing, and art that are involved in narrative and story ways of sensemaking. The third dialogism (its technical name is chronotope) gets at the interplay of lots of space–time ways of storying any situation. It can be storied as an adventure, as a trip into the future, as a descent into some netherworld. For Bakhtin (inspired by Einstein physics), there are space–time relations that are relativities. The most accessible example is the relativities of space–time in being global (pushing the future onto local) and being local (tending to tradition to keep the local coming into the global future). A fourth dialogism extends Kant's work on the cognitive discourse of how systems are constructed in language. Bakhtin takes this dialogism (called architectonics) into the interanimation of cognitive, aesthetic, and ethical discourses.

In business, for example, there is an effort to be ethical. For Bakhtin, as our discussion of emotive–ethics stressed, ethics is not always just cognitive, or a retrospective glance at precedent. Bakhtin stresses how our emotion gives us ethical awareness, something in the now, needing our attention.

Bakhtin also, even during his days of Soviet oppression, wrote often about the spiritual and religious. Unlike Kant, Bakhtin wrote of netherworlds, gave attention to transcendentals, beyond Kant's attempt to tame the metaphysical. This has implications for organizations.

For example, there is a burgeoning, very popular movement to reunite the spiritual (and/or religious) with leadership, strategy, and other organization practices. If we look at system and complexity, one of the key debates is over, what to do with Boulding's (1956) 'transcendental' level of complexity? Strategy is wrestling with how to become more spiritually and ecologically attuned (Landrum and Gardner, 2005). And in the field of organization change, there is more writing about spirituality than ever before. While I was editor of JOCM (*Journal of Organizational Change Management*), there were 68 articles, written by colleagues, on the relation of spirituality and business. There were so many spirituality and religion submissions that I finally helped co-found the *Management, Spirituality, and Religion Journal*, to handle the demand.

In business language, a dialogism is when people with different logics meet in the same time and place, and engage in something transcendental, on their differences, allowing for the possibility of something generative to happen, out of their explorations.

In the broader scope, dialogism, as we have seen, is difference in how different stakeholders hold a firm accountable for the stories they tell. It is definitely not about consensus, nor is any one logic going to sway people to their point-of-view. In the best case scenario, some new way of viewing how all the logics interrelate can emerge. It is more about learning to listen at a deep level of reflexivity, than it is about arguing to make one's story, the story the group adopts.

Dialogism is not the same as having a dialogue. A dialogue, in business (and the university), is about persuading, or facilitating consensus. The dialogue in Wal-Mart annual reports, would have everyone believe that all the stakeholders have happy faces, are part of the Wal-Mart success story, and have no complaints. People, in corporate settings, often learn the hard way to only express the logic the boss most wants to hear! In a business dialog, we are rarely free to express what we think, feel, believe, or intuit. Nor do we engage (very often, or more than once) in emotive–ethical acts, and be that one person who speaks back to power, asking power to be answerable to what is happening to the Other. And if one does, there are always more than one emotive–ethical counter-storying going on.

Dialogism in business can be about bringing stakeholders together, to express themselves, but more often narrative control (by a boss or some dominant coalition) is so powerful, so threatening, so terrorizing, that people are mostly silent, saying and posing whatever power wants to hear and see.

Dialogism is not the same as dialectic. Bakhtin, the inventor of dialogism, was exiled, got deafly ill, lost his leg, and had his dissertation rejected by Moscow, for daring to pose something different than the dialectic. So when I say dialogism is neither dialogue (as practised in business), nor the dialectics (above), this is quite definitive. Especially since Sorbanes-Oxley, companies are responding to challenges stakeholders (and even exposé journalists and activists) are making. A contemporary annual report is a mix of styles: numeric accounts, photos of happy stakeholders, letters by CEO, interviews with managers, and (favorable) comments by employees, customers, vendors, and community members. In short, there is a dialogism of very different styles of text (charts, strategy stories), the attempt to mimic orality (interviews or letters by the CEO), and some visual artistry. Reports are looking more like magazines. It is a level of collective writing by artists, accountants, executives, consultants, and division heads that has yet to be studied (Cai, 2006).

Another example is the décor and architectural storying. For example, at Disney the executive suite is held aloft by the Seven Dwarfs (giant size). In the Dean's suite of my Business College, are paintings of all the white-haired male deans before this one, and on another wall statements about the importance of diversity. What is key to analyze is the juxtaposition of styles, the orality, text, and visual storying and narrating going on all around us, that is not being noticed. Story awareness (noticing stories, noticing what is getting story attention and story action) can yield some Nova experiences (Nova – Chevy car sold in Mexico, where the meaning is 'no go'). McDonald's seems to be ahead of the curve in awareness of stylistics, and has coined the term, 'McStylistics' (the ten choices of décor and architecture that franchisees can select from, but only in France).

The third dialogism (chronotopes) builds on what we said earlier about ways of narrating time and space. Putting this in business language, there are several adventure chronotopes in how people story a business history, or story its strategy: an adventure of conquest (our strengths and opportunities overcoming each weakness and threat), or application of a chivalric code (McDonald's clean, efficient, friendly service), an encounter with accident or novelty (Enron's off-the-balance-sheet transactions come undone), or the heroic CEO's biography of exploits (such as Bill Gates, or Phil Knight). There are also folkloric ways of narrating, such as the idyllic appeals to family, knowing one's shire versus the more global ways of doing business. McDonald's Corporation exhibits ten chronotopes, as we will review when we look at their strategy.

The fourth type of dialogism (architectonic of one discourse becoming several interacting discourses), in business terms, is all about the concern over how to think like a business. Does that mean just the purely cognitive ways of storying business, or does it include, as well, the aesthetic (such as the styles of a restaurant design or the graphic design of a report), and does it include the ethical? In complexity terms, how is the business being constructed in the stories and narratives? Is the emphasis on the cognitive (bottom line, nuts and bolts), or is there a more artistic appeal, and a whole section of meetings and reports devoted to stories of ethical practices?

In an era of collapsing business ethics (Enron, WorldCom, Arthur Anderson's collapse, etc.), there is a growing concern for being ethically answerable to each stakeholder of a business (and that list is getting longer each year). Business ethics was once just about the answer to the question what is the business of business? In the 1990s the narrative changes to testimonies about having a 'code of ethics' and then lately to monitoring that code of any violations. Not all, but many, ethical codes are hypocritical: say one thing, do another. The business ethics on the horizon, by my reading, is all about engaging in acts of reflexivity, on how to make the expressed stories realized in day-to-day organizational behaviors. This dialogism is concerned with how to align cognitive, aesthetic, and ethical sensemaking narrating and storying, in ways that satisfy multiple, diverse logics of very different stakeholders. Everything from the annual report, to photos in the lobby, to the theatrics of expression in meetings, is telling customers, employees, and communities, what kind of business is active there.

There is ever increasing stress in the business of answering the charges of one's critics. Each annual shareholder report is an answer not just to investors, but to exposé journalists, activists, unions, regulators, and community members. Each line of a narrative or story is an answer to something (either from an old battle, or some new one brewing). In short, these four dialogisms are happening already in and around every complex Storytelling Organization. People are coping with them, but without a language to make sense of them.

I have one final dialogism (named polypi, a hydra named in Hans Christian Anderson's 'Little Mermaid') that is the interplay of the first four dialogisms. There are important, groundbreaking implications of these interacting dialogisms, and their interplay with the other seven ways of sensemaking, for complexity, strategy, change, and methodology (the parts of this book).

Complexity   The eight ways of sensemaking constitute dynamics of complexity that business and public organizations are enduring, that is beyond open system thinking. System thinking worked well for post-Second World War industry, but there are now orders of complexity that exceed the vantage point of first cybernetic (control of deviations), and second cybernetics (amplification of variety). The two cybernetics are the yin and yang of open system thinking, and are critical to understand. But in Part I of this book, I want to try to move beyond system, to another level of complexity, one that Ken Baskin and I call the 'Third Cybernetics' (Boje and Baskin, 2005). Third cybernetics is about the interplay of the eight sensemaking modes, and develops Boulding (1956) and my mentor Lou Pondy's (1976) dream of going beyond open system, to multi-brained, multi-languaged, and multi-story, as well as multi-narrated organizations, engaged in acts of co-construction, and the kinds of co-generativity that the study of dialogisms opens up.

Strategy   Part II of this book is five chapters, laying out possible frontier issues for schools of strategy. Each chapter takes up a particular kind of dialogism. The cutting edge in strategy is how to enact successful, collaborative, multi-logic, and multi-voice strategies (polyphonic). A second area is how to align visual, textual, and oral ways of showing, writing, and telling a strategy to a variety of different stakeholders (stylistics). A third chapter deals with the interplay of ways of conceiving the strategy adventure in terms of different time and landscape horizons (chronotopes). A fourth chapter is concerned with perhaps the most important topic of strategy making, how to align espoused and enacted strategy so instead of spin, it is about ethical action that is answerable to a variety of stakeholder positions (architectonics). Finally, how can these four dialogisms interact in ways that are productive, so the hydra has some legs (polypi).

Change   Two chapters in Part III are devoted to change and organizational development approaches involving narrative and story. The first of these is about single organization change efforts, where the BME retrospective narrative is often the tool of intervention. I assert that other sensemaking modes can be even more effective, and achieve better results for more complex organizations. The claims of the two-minute BME narrative that is expected to transform an organization are greatly exaggerated. The other chapter is about large system or change in networks of organization that is done using narrative and story. The focus is on comparing dominant methods, and showing how they use narrative and story in different ways.

Method   The last part of the book is about methodology. One chapter is about living story method. My colleague Jo Tyler and I believe that stories live, that they can have a life of their own. I offer an autoethnography, a storying, in different ways of a family tragedy: the death of my Aunt Dorothy. Was it a suicide, or was it murder? A network of organizations produced narratives (some whole, mostly just fragments). But my extended family wanted a different kind of storying to occur. And it has kept the family divided for over 30 years. Doing living story research, changes the ground. And this one is no exception. I am now in contact with people I had not spoken to for far too long. The final chapter is a sort of Plato's dialogue, but meant to be more of a dialogism, a meeting of people I wanted to have a story circle with, and to see what might be generated.

1

FROM SYSTEMS TO COMPLEXITY THINKING[1]

omplexity is a turn away from linearization, from hierarchic levels, to something holographic. Complexity is not lines! It's spirals in the dialogical interplay of narrative-order with story-disorder that produces the self-organization of Storytelling Organizations. This chapter is about the paradigm shift from systems thinking that is linearization to complexity thinking that is spiralization, as depicted in Figure 1.1.

What does complexity have to do with Storytelling Organization? Everything! There are those of us that profess that narrative and story have important differences. Narrative and story are typically treated as synonyms: different words that mean the same thing. Derrida raises two questions. First, what if narrative and story are homonyms: words that *seem* the same but refer to *different* things? Second, what if story and narrative form the border for each other to comprehend each other:

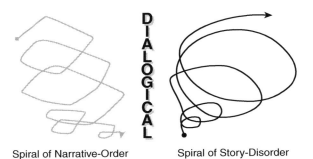

Spiral of Narrative-Order   Spiral of Story-Disorder

DIALOGICAL

FIGURE 1.1   *Holographic complexity spirals of narrative order and story-disorder*

1 I would like to thank members of my PhD seminars, especially Al Arkoubi Khadija, Yue Cai, David Tobey and Joe Gladstone for their written comments.

> Each 'story' (and each occurrence of the word 'story,' (of itself)) each story is at once larger and smaller than itself, includes itself without including (or comprehending) itself, identifies itself with itself even as it remains utterly different from its homonym. (Derrida, 1991: 267)

Derrida puts narrative into a relationship to stories larger and smaller than themselves:

> ... The question-of-narrative covers with a certain modesty a demand for narrative, a violent putting-to-the-question an instrument of torture working to wring the narrative out of one as if it were a terrible secret in ways that can go from the most archaic police methods to refinements for making (and even letting) one talk that are unsupposed in neutrality and politeness, that are most respectfully medical, psychiatric, and even psychoanalytic. (1991: 261)

The violence is methods that force a narrative linearization out of the interrogation of story, to put an origin, one middle, and one end into a BME linearization. Retrospective sensemaking is the demand to return to the scene to 'tell us exactly what happened' (1991: 260), 'to force a narrative out of the narrator' (p. 263), or to assemble 'narrative fragment' (p. 263) after narrative fragment into some originary detective puzzle in a 'linearity' of writing narratives.

The story (*récit*) is the homonym to narrative, not the synonym. The problem this interplay of narrative–story poses for systems thinking is that various hierarchic ordering models of systems complexity are flat grand narratives of linearization that wash out the stories of multiplicity and difference.

Bakhtin, in the 1920s anticipates Derrida's theory of *difference*, as well as the strange interplay of narrative-control and the more dialogic manner of story. Bakhtin's (1968, 1973, 1981, 1986, 1990, 1993) work on dialogical story gets us to the complexity of convergent-order (centripetal narrative) in opposition to divergent-disorder (centrifugal story) in their language moves.

PARADIGM SHIFT FROM SYSTEM THINKING TO COMPLEXITY THINKING

We begin this chapter by comparing the hierarchic linear levels of systems models of Kenneth Boulding (1956), Louis Pondy (1979), Michael Polanyi (1966), and Robert Pirsig (1974) as shown in Table 1.1. Not only is each a linearity ordering of systems stacked upon systems into a hierarchy of realities, these are each transcendental narrative subtext that is often ignored by previous reviewers.

The dialogism of order with disorder in acts of self-organization was also written about by Edgar Morin (1977, 1996). It is an escape from hierarchic order linear models of systems thinking, into complexity thinking. Boulding, Pondy, Pirsig, and Polanyi, as we shall see, also did not anticipate Morin's complexity ways of looking outside the rule of order into the disorder, self-organization of emergence

TABLE 1.1 *Comparison of systems-hierarchic-levels models with non-levels-holographic-complexity*

Boulding, 1956	Pondy, 1979	Pirsig 1974	Polanyi's 1966 tacit knowing and emergence	Bakhtin/Boje 2007c non-hierarchic, Non-levels, Holographic
N/A	? As yet unspecified level	N/A	N/A	? As yet unspecified Holographic Multi-dimensionality (4th cybernetics)
9 Transcendental	N/A	Transcendent nature of motorcycle technology (p. 285)	Transcendental values (e.g. Plato's Meno and past lives recall, p. 56)	Polypi-Dialogism of dialogisms (3rd cybernetics)
8 'Role' Social Organizations	Multi-cephalous System	Motorcycle as social construction	Mutual Social Control	Architectonic strategy (3rd cybernetics)
7 Symbolism (Human)	Symbol Processing System	Motorcycle as idea systems (mythos shaped by logos, p. 343–4)	Composition (e.g. literary criticism)	Chronotopic strategy (3rd cybernetics)
6 Image (Animal)	Internal Image System	N/A	Style (stylistics)	Stylistic Strategy (3rd cybernetics)
N/A	N/A	Rhetoric as reduced rational system of Aristotelian order (p. 353)	Voice (phonetics), Words (lexicography), Sentences (grammar) (i.e. 3 levels)	Polyphonic Strategy (3rd cybernetics)
5A Plant	Blueprint Growth System	N/A	Organic/Biotic	Organic
4 Cell (Open)	Open System	N/A	Chemical	Open (2nd cybernetics)
3 Thermostat (Control)	Control System	Motorcycle as control systems	Engineering/ Physics	Control (1st cybernetics)
2 Clockworks	Clockworks	Motorcycle as mechanical	Mechanistic	Mechanistic
1 Frameworks	Frameworks	Motorcycle as framework of concepts and functions	Frameworks (p. 17)	Frameworks as semantic vocabularies

in the everyday practical social communication activity of organizations that is not system parts merged into wholeness, because the parts do not merge, and the whole never seems to be finalized except in narrative imagination.

Systemicity is my replacement word for the outdated static linear-hierarchic conceptions of whole '*system*.[2] Systemicity is defined as the dynamic unfinished, unfinalized, and unmerged, and the interactivity of complexity properties (such as dialogic, recursion, and holographic yielding emergence and self-organization) constituted by narrative–story processes, in the dance of sensemaking (see Introduction). I invoke the word 'systemicity' in order to attack the 'illusion' that 'whole system' exists, because given the paradigm shift to complexity, and the focus on emergence (and self-organization), organizations are continually being reorganized, and never seem to finish long enough to have merged parts or some kind of fixity of wholeness. Morin (1977, 1993) for example, asserts that 'the whole is greater than the sum of the parts' and has become an illusion, or to put it more bluntly mantra so taken-for-granted, that wholes are being sighted everywhere, and way too often. This I think is Harold Garfinkel's (1967) main message, that people get upset when you start to question that some wholeness exists to sort out the meaning of a conversation (Shotter, 1993) or its complexity (Morin, ibid.). This shift to complexity paradigm, alters my earlier definition: I redefine Storytelling Organization as, 'collective storytelling system[icity] in which the performance of stories is a key part of members' sensemaking and a means to allow them to supplement individual memories with institutional memory' (Boje, 1991: 106, bracketed is my 2007 definition amendment). In sum, my concept, systemicity, builds upon system thinking of Bakhtin, but takes it along the paradigm shift into complexity thinking (i.e. Morin) and into deeper aspects of reflexivity (e.g. Garfinkel, Shotter, and the eternal return-recursivity of Nietzsche's 1967 *Will to Power*).[3]

There may be a challenge made that Bakhtin has nothing to say about system or systemicity-complexity. Yet, I have found a good deal of Bakhtin's writing is not only relevant to systemicity of complexity theory, but is pioneering. For example, in Bakhtin (1981, *Dialogic Imagination*) four essays from his notebooks, begun in 1929–1930, supplemented with conclusions in 1973, but unpublished till after his death in 1975, is a section relating closed system theory to oral and textual stylistics:

---

2 Bakhtin (1981: 152) uses the term 'systematicalness' to denote unmerged parts, and unfinalized non-wholeness. I prefer my own term, 'systemicity.'

3 There is a piece of work that needs to be done, to look at the differences in what is reflexivity, and how Stein's (1935) recursive writing is a way to get at it, how that differs from Garfinkel's (1967) ethnomethodology, and work by Nietzsche (1967) on eternal return, and how this differs from Argyris and Schön's (1974) espoused-theory and theory-in-use. I used to have engineer-managers at Hughes Aircraft (when it existed) fill in the left column with what they said, and the right side with what they were thinking, but did not say. The differences were amazing. While Garfinkel (1967: 25–26. 38–39) does a left-right column it is I think more about a kind of reflexivity that bridges with Morin's (1996) theory of dialogical complexity.

[System theory has theorized] stylistics as if it were a hermetic and self-sufficient whole, one whose elements constitute a closed system presuming nothing beyond themselves, no other utterances. (1981: 273, bracket addition mine)

Bakhtin is therefore aware of closed systems thinking (before the term was popularized after the Second World War) and aware of the 'wholeness-illusion' quite early on. However, in his dialogisms, and within the chronotopes, in particular, properties, as with Boulding and Pondy, are set in accumulating hierarchic arrangement.[4]

In Table 1.1, the first column recovers some of the original labels of system thinking properties that Pondy morphed in the second column. Pondy dropped Boulding's transcendental word (9) altogether, reworded 'social organization' (8) into multi-cephalous, reworded image (6) into 'internal image' (the difference is image orchestration is image for others), substituted 'blueprint growth' for Boulding's 'plant' (5), and 'control' for 'thermostat' (3). The third column suggests at what hierarchic system thinking levels, Bakhtin's dialogisms are relatable. The last column in Table 1.1 combines Boulding's original concepts, retains Pondy's idea of yet undiscovered levels. In sum, Pondy (i.e., unspecified holographic multi-dimensionalist changed the label and meaning of five of Boulding's nine concepts as summarized in Table 1.1 (numbers 9, 8, 5A, 4, and 3).

For example, Boulding's (1956: 205) highest systems level is called 'transcendental' but he worries that he will be accused of erecting 'Babel to the clouds.' Boulding reasoned that from the lowest to the highest order of systems complexity could be modeled in nine levels. From lowest to highest these are: frameworks, clockworks, thermostat, cell, plant, animal-image, human-symbolism, role in social organizations, and transcendental. Boulding views general systems thinking as trapped in various 'mysteries,' where 'up to now, whatever the future may hold, only God can make a tree' and even 'living systems' medicine hovers 'between magic and science' (1956: 206). But this is not the only transcendental aspect. The entire stack of nine systems levels, one atop the other, is a transcendental line, a Babel Tower of systems levels, a linear tower 'systems of systems' (p. 202). The very last line of his essay says it all: 'The skeleton must come out of the cupboard before its dry bones can live' (p. 208). His Babel Tower of Linearization of Hierarchic Order self-deconstructs pages

---

4 This may be an artifact of the way of writing, since for example in *Dialogic Imagination*, Bakhtin sets out the chronotopes in a kind of order by virtue of the chronology of their use in the novel. But in the stylistics and architectonics, those dialogisms are styles and discourse (respectively) without presumed hierarchy (leaving order in counterplay with disorder, as in heteroglossia.) Heteroglossia is the interplay of two spirals, one is counteracting (centripetal) and the other is amplifying disorder (centrifugal). That move by Bakhtin is what makes dialogism of language something to explore in terms of complexity theory of organization.

earlier: 'There may always be important theoretical concepts and constructs lying outside the systematic framework' (p. 202). Exactly!

Lou Pondy, my mentor in the University of Illinois PhD program was seduced by Boulding's linearization of a hierarchy of systems, and became, like me, trapped in its linear logic. Pondy ignored Boulding's transcendental model, and redefined several other levels, but stayed trapped in the Babel Tower. Pondy sees from this tower that there is some kind of difference between 'objective reality' and 'phenomenological' representation or 'socially constructed reality' (1979: 33) and that there is 'language-using, sense-making' by administrators skilled in 'creating and using metaphors... but also poetry' (p. 36). Pondy, however, does not see the limits of Boulding's general linearization, systems stacked upon systems into a Tower.

I think a story told outside the lines of narrative, of Lou Pondy's rejection letter, can introduce the paradigm shift underway from systems thinking to complexity thinking, from linearity to spirals. I was in Lou Pondy's office the day he opened his rejection letter from the editor of *Administrative Science Quarterly* (*ASQ*). It was 1976. He read parts aloud. I tried not to listen but I had to listen. He gave me the letter to read the rest. I tried not to read but I had to read. The editor wrote that while 'interesting' the article was too rooted in the 'cute school of organization.' Each word 'cute,' 'interesting,' and every 'etcetera' and every 'space' between-the-lines, meant so very much more.

There are *reflexivities-to-fill-in-gaps-in-between-these-lines*: Lou was the Associate Editor of *ASQ Journal*. Lou had published there before. Most of the board of editors had come to the University of Illinois, where Lou is department head of organizational behavior, and went to conferences on symbolism and radical organization theory. There was *prospective-antenarrating-going-on*: Lou and I were revising a paper (Pondy and Boje, 1980) called 'Bringing Mind Back In', a positioning of social definitionism (our terms for social constructivism) in relation to other paradigms of sociology (social factist), and psychology (social behaviorist). My work on 'Bringing Mind Back In' would lead me, step-by-step, to choose qualitative studies over quantitative studies, to publish both kinds in the venerated *ASQ* (Boje and Whetten, 1981; Dewar et al., 1980; Boje, 1991).

More filling-in-the-blanks, more acts of spiraling reflexivity: 'What was cute about it?' Lou, a former physics major, had adapted noted economist, Kenneth Boulding's (1956) hierarchy-complexity model that says there are nine levels of systems complexity. And in the now, I have an emotive–ethical question: who or what is answerable, because Lou, with tears welling in his eyes, rages, and painfully could not believe his masterpiece had been dismissed, not even sent out for formal review (and that is something I do now for journals I edit). 'Going beyond open systems thinking... is not cute!' Lou says, as I am turning Lou's voice down, giving him some space, and turning up some voices in my head, deeply listening to inside my head and to the drama of Lou in his office (Steiner, 1935 talks about how we tell and listen at the same time). I tuned in, in spirals of reflexivity, to what we were doing in Lou's organization design class, to my marriage, to the reason I was in Lou's office, and then it dawned on me (see Garfinkel, 1967; Shotter, 1993).

Pondy saw immediately that Boulding's level 4 (cell) was open systems thinking (the interplay of variety-order-control and variety-disorder-amplification), and that the upper levels (especially 6 to 9), were all about the use of language in everyday practical social interactions. Pondy and Boulding saw that Ludwig von Bertalanffy's (1956) *General System Theory* had overlooked non-physic-biological ways in various complexity language-properties such as image, symbolism, social organization (networks of discourse), and transcendental (that as I said Lou dismissed). Unfortunately, Pondy, like Boulding, chose an overly simplistic language model, the *information processing* (sender-message-receiver-feedback loop) model of Shannon and Weaver (1949), and then the Chomsky grammar model. There is no reflexivity there, nor is there transcendental. Both models assume one-logic (mono-logic) thinking about systems. They do not account for ways fragments of experience are recounted socially throughout organizations. Systems thinking ignores how the ways of sensemaking we looked at in the last chapter (Introduction) interact in self-organizing complexity without being hierarchically ordered. Pondy and I had become bystanders, systems theorists who stood outside as omniscient narrators, looking in.

Cooper (1989) castigated Pondy for continuing to use information processing models that were overly simplistic. Cooper explored a Derridian communication model which has the trace, the intertextual, and ways to deconstruct one text, showing its outcropping in many other texts (a kind of reflexivity). Cooper missed Pondy's (1978) attempt to move out of information processing language models, for example adopting Chomsky's language-grammar model in a paper titled 'Leadership *is* a language game.' In this paper was not only the ordering effect of Chomsky grammar, but the disorder of the language games of Wittgenstein. I go beyond it because 'systems thinking' ignores not just language, but also story and narrative.

I prospected (several antenarratives); I was going to get letters like this. I had to learn to deal with rejection, since I would likely get my fair share, or more. It is now 30 years later. I am getting acceptance and rejection letters, teaching a systems/complexity theory class, exploring and changing Lou's model for making language part of systems thinking to get deeper into reflexivity in what I call 'the zone of complexity' that is deep within, and the transcendental (the really spiritual, more cosmic sphere). I have worked out a storyteller's way to fulfill my mentor's dream, to go beyond, to transcend open systems thinking, to even bring in transcendence that Boulding talked of as the highest level, whereas Lou had tossed it out of his narrative. I go beyond it because 'systems thinking' does ignore, not just language, but story, and narrative.

At the time, in the late 1970s, Pondy had us read Robert Pirsig's (1974) *Zen and the Art of Motorcycle Maintenance*. We thought we were escaping hierarchy, noticing something different was going on. Pirsig argues that there is an 'a priori' motorcycle: 'The sense data confirm it but the sense data aren't it' (p. 128). But this Kantian move by Pirsig, this a priori transcendental has its own fixed hierarchy:

'What we think of as reality is a continuous synthesis of elements from a fixed hierarchy of a priori concepts and the ever changing data of the senses' (Pirsig, 1974: 26). As a Harley (after market) builder and rider, I can appreciate that the a priori motorcycle is continually changing; the vibrations alone throw out bolts, loosen wires, send cracks through the paint and metal. I think what Boulding, Pondy, and Pirsig have missed is that the hierarchies of systems are as Pirsig (1974: 121) puts it 'hierarchies of thought.' Pirsig's narrative of systems of hierarchic order, his linearization tries to escape the Babel Tower with some lateral thinking:

> Lateral knowledge is knowledge that's from a wholly unexpected direction, from a direction that's not even understood as a direction until the knowledge forces itself upon one. (Pirsig, 1974: 114–15)

Pirsig is almost aware of the Babel Tower, that these tower levels and shapes are 'all out of someone's mind' (p. 95). It's the stories that are prospective and lateral ways to find one's way out of someone's mental hierarchies of logic. But Pirsig is not consistent: at points a motorcycle is ideas and concepts, 'systematic patterns of thought' and on the same page 'a motorcycle is a system. A *real* system' (p. 94).

Michael Polanyi (1966) has yet to be compared by scholars of organization to Boulding or Pondy, or to Pirsig. Polanyi reviews systems in neuroscience, Gestalt psychology, physics, chemistry, engineering, and linguistics. At first, it looks as though tacit knowing is just a matter of a process of subception (1966: 15), something rooted in cognitive neuroscience, and in a footnote it can be easily confused with sense-making: 'Our tacit knowing of a process will make sense of it in terms of an experience we are attending' (footnote, p. 15). But most reviewers skip the more transcendental metaphysics in Polanyi, tidying up not only tacit knowing but also emergence. Like Boulding, Pondy, and Pirsig, Polanyi is all about linearization, and making a 'tacit framework' for our 'moral acts and judgments' (Polanyi, 1966: 17). For Polanyi the engineer's understanding and comprehension of a machine is deeper than that of the physicist, and since the biologist tends to sentient matters, their understanding is at a higher level than the chemist-physicist-engineer, and since language is so important, those who comprehend language are at a much higher level, and since the universe is ordered, there is some moral sensemaking at the top of his Babel Tower.

Like Boulding and Pirsig, Polanyi sees much mystery in tacit knowing, in thought forms indispensable to explicit knowledge, such that any project that would eliminate tacitness would be 'fundamentally misleading and a possible source of devastating fallacies' (p. 20). But, let's inquire further. What is his transcendental onto-theocracy? It is rooted in Plato's theory of anamnesis (*Meno*), as Polanyi (1966/1983: 22) puts it 'all discovery is a remembering of past lives.' Instead of knowledge just acquired through the senses, in acts of sensemaking, tacit knowing is a recollection of memory of past lives, what Polanyi calls a 'tacit foreknowledge of yet undiscovered things' (p. 23), or 'foreknowledge which guides scientists to discovery' (p. 33) is defined as the 'tacit act of comprehending'

(p. 33). It's as if tacit knowing is taken right out of Plato's (1957: 27–28) *Theory of Knowledge*: 'all learning is the recovery of latent knowledge always possessed by the immortal soul.'

What of emergence? For Polanyi (1966: 35), the 'universe [is] filled with strata of realities' and as with Boulding, Pondy, and Pirsig, with 'higher and lower strata' all 'forming a hierarchy.' As with the others, at each level there is a principle of control that we can see in some great hierarchy of comprehension (p. 36). And not only chemistry, physics, engineering, and biology, but speech acts get ordered into his Babel Tower: 'hierarchy constituting speechmaking' (p. 40) where 'successive working principles control the boundary left indeterminate on the next lower level' and 'each lower level imposes restrictions on the one above it' (p. 41). For example in speech acts, without the hierarchy of control, 'words are drowned in a flow of random sounds, sentences in a series of random words, and so on' (p. 41). We finally arrive at emergence as a totalization of levels, as an elevator in the Babel Tower: 'but the hierarchic structure of the higher forms of life necessitates the assumption of further processes of emergence' (pp. 44–55).

> Thus the logical structure of the hierarchy implies that a higher level can come into existence only through a process not manifest in the lower level, a process which thus qualifies as an emergence. (Polanyi, 1966: 45)
>
> ... Tacit knowing [is] ... seen to be the relation between two levels of reality, the higher one controlling the marginal conditions left indeterminate by principles governing the lower one... Such levels were then stacked on top of each other to form a hierarchy, and this stacking opened up a panorama of stratified living beings. (Polanyi, 1966/83: 55)

The rhetoric is seductive. Hold on! We almost fell into the same hierarchic-ordering trap that caught Boulding and Pondy! Table 1.1 is way too ordered hierarchically. The 'whole' 'levels' theory is the trap of hierarchic ordering of systems thinking.

For example, Figure 1.1 explores how Boulding's complexities would fit with Bakhtin's dialogisms in a hierarchic-linearization model, the Babel Tower turned into Inverted Pyramid. Boulding theorized nine hierarchic levels of accumulating complexity properties and delineated five master metaphors holding back systems thinking (frame, machine, thermostat, cell and plant). Bakhtin's oeuvre theorized four hierarchically ordered dialogisms, each more complex than the next: polyphonic, stylistic, chronotopic, and architectonic. I fell deep into the hierarchy trap in Figure 1.2, by making Boulding/Pondy/Pirsig/Polanyi and Bakhtin's hierarchic-levels models *seem* combinable, and stackable-strata. The trap is of course the linearization assumption, that effects of properties at each higher level are cumulative, not successive. You do not just stop having mechanistic systems when you become open. For example, Level 4 (open) is theorized to exhibit properties 1, 2, 3, and 4. Unlike duality models (e.g. open–closed, mechanistic–organic), properties after level 1 do not displace the lesser complexities. Similarly, with Bakhtin, you do not just stop polyphony when you enter chronotopicity. In Figure 1.2, I

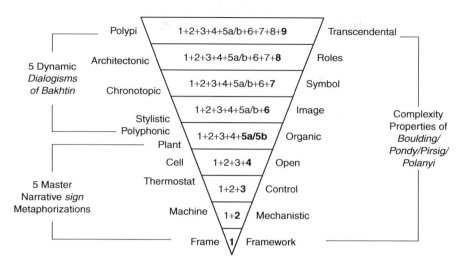

FIGURE 1.2   *Combined hierarchic-complexity models of Boulding and Bakhtin*[5]

split Boulding's level 5 into 5A and 5B to accommodate Bakhtin's polyphonic dialogism. However, there are major flaws in doing hierarchy modeling.

The problem is how to theorize dialogisms in relation to complexity properties, without falling into the trap of hierarchic systems thinking. There is some kind of Heisenberg observer-effect, a linguistic erection of linearization, a Babel Tower with systems stacked atop one another that seems to me to be highly arbitrary. Each level, be it framework or clockworks is someone's lexicon, someone's grab bag of words to comprehend it.

Back to the past! Something went wrong that day! Boulding, Pondy, Pirsig, Polanyi, and I got hopelessly trapped for decades in *system's thinking*, in the logic of order that drives out disorder to erect the Babel Tower. I was a prisoner of the systems thinking tower, its doctrine from 1976 (the event of Lou's rejection) to 2006 (when I began to move away from systems thinking). I ran from the Babel Tower and began to think of complexity spirals, somehow interlocking with all the rejections I had faced, was facing, and would likely face.

In the next section, we examine how to escape the hierarchic-order trap of systems theory.

OUT OF THE SYSTEM THINKING TRAP

I feel like I have discovered the location of the Holy Grail. Just this week (September 2007), in doing some rewriting of this chapter, I came across the work

---

5 My thanks to Yue Cai (2006) for redrawing my original model, and granting permission to use her more stylized graphic here.

of Edgar Morin (buried in a teaching material box, in a folder I have been mean-ing to read for the past eight years). Low and behold, Morin and Bakhtin are both using the word *dialogic*, but defining it differently.

Edgar Morin (1992) came up with a dialogic principle to facilitate the paradigm shift from system to complexity thinking. He defined it as the '"dialogical" relationship... between order, disorder and organization' that is 'antagonistic, concurrent and complementary' (Morin, 1996: 11).

Mikhail Bakhtin defines several types of dialogisms: polyphonic, stylistic, chronotopic, and architectonic. These are developed more fully in the next chapter. I will only point out that both Morin and Bakhtin made language their primary focus.

Besides the dialogic of order/disorder/organization, Morin (1996: 14) in two sentences specifies a way out of hierarchic order, to let the properties of what I call systemicity interact without the presumption of hierarchy:

> The 'hologrammatic' principle highlights the apparent paradox of certain systems where not only is the part present in the whole, but the whole is present in the part: the totality of the genetic heritage is present in each individual cell. In the same way, the individual is part of society but soci-ety is present in every individual, through his or her language, culture and standards.

The flaw of hierarchic systems thinking can be overcome by looking at holo-graphic combinations of complexity. If we apply Morin's dialogic and holographic properties together, we can see that complexity properties, and dialogisms, may or may not be hierarchic to one another.

Morin, like Bakhtin treats language as the motor of complexity. For Bakhtin, it is the heteroglossia of language, the opposition of centripetal (centering spiral of order) and centrifugal (decentering spiral of disorder) forces of language (see Figure 1.1, above). For Morin the speech acts are dialogic in social activities of order/disorder/organization.

In sum, Edgar Morin (1977, 1992, 1996) proposes three properties of com-plexity: dialogical, hologrammatic, and recursivity.

1 **Dialogical** Dialogical is the interplay of order, disorder, and organization that is antagonistic, concurrent, and complementary (Morin, 1996: 11). Like Pondy and Boulding, Morin wants to go beyond open system thinking, and its prede-cessor, von Bertalanffy's General Systems Theory 'Moreover, General System Theory, which is founded solely on the notion of the open system, is wholly insuf-ficient when applied to living or social systems' (Morin, 1992: 382). The dia-logical property of complexity comes from the work of Henri Atlan, and not (as far as I know) from Bakhtin. As Morin (1996: 13) explains: 'At the birth of the universe there was an order/disorder/organization dialogic triggered off by calorific turbulence (discord) in which, under certain conditions (random encoun-ters) organizing principles made possible the creation of nuclei atoms, galaxies

and stars.' It is the dialogic (order/disorder/organization) that auto-produces self-organization in the physical, biological, and human worlds. We can apply dialogism to Storytelling Organizations, where past-looking narrative histories, founding narratives and future-looking strategy stories are retrospectively prospectively sensemaking (see Introduction).

2 **Hologrammatic** As in laser photography, the whole is present in the part (i.e. the photo embeds multiple perspectives). The Hologrammatic Principle is where the *dynamics of the whole are present in the part*, as in laser photography. Holography allows complexity properties to be non-hierarchic. Holography is implicated in processes of complexity beyond mere open system thinking and is what I call *'systemicity' thinking*. I want to suggest that eight sensemaking registries are holographic, rather than hierarchic to one another. In holography various lenses combine to consummate dimensions without presuming hierarchic ordering. Eight ways of storytelling sensemaking constitute an octagonic holographic holography. Each sensemaking registry has its tragic flaw (see Introduction for these). Each of the sensemaking ways can become a way to control social interaction.

3 **Recursion** Recursivity is a 'dynamic and generative feedback loop' between whole and parts where 'order and disorder, observer and observed' (Morin, 1992: 371) are situated. The Recursion principle moves beyond open system theory's opposition of feedback-regulatory loop and feedback-amplification loop by situating a self-organization (generative) loop. An example of recursion is narrating and storytelling shapes systemicity, and systemicity shapes narrative–story.

Systems theory, trapped in cybernetics, narrated a view of organization that privileged order over disorder, thereby obscuring emergence, self-organization, and especially the language games of narrative–story that constitutes phenomenal complexity in dialogic/holographic/recursion. Complexity theory paradigm allows for reflexivity-transcendence, as well as retrospective-prospective sensemaking.

It's time to move from hierarchic systems thinking to holographic complexity thinking. To get at the holographic nature of story emergence in systemicity complexity we need to define emergence more carefully.

What is Story Emergence in Complexity?

Jeffrey Goldstein (1999) reviews how G. H. Lewes first used *emergence* over a century ago. In the 1920s the word combined with evolution, 'emergent evolutionism' (Goldstein, 1999: 53), and did not define the process of emergence. With the advent of complexity theory, emergence took on many new meanings (Langton, 1990; Lewin, 1993; Waldrop, 1993; Kauffman, 1996; Holland, 1998; Goldstein, 1999; Stacey, 2006, to name a few). Ralph Stacey (1996: 287) defines it this way:

> Emergence is the production of global patterns of behavior by agents in a complex system interacting according to their own local rules of behavior, without intending the global patterns of behavior that come about. In

emergence, global patterns cannot be predicted from the local rules of behavior that produce them. To put it another way, global patterns cannot be reduced to individual behavior.

I think it's important to point out an alternative definition to the way Polanyi, and Stacey are defining emergence. For Foucault (1977b: 148–9) emergence is the 'moment of arising ... always produced through a particular stage of forces ... or against adverse circumstances.'

It will also help to define qualities of emergent stories. I theorize at least five: *authenticity, contagion, institutional support, entertainment value*, and *cultural force*. Most emergent stories lack the quality of authenticity, where they are believable beyond those present. Most also lack the quality of contagion, where gossip jumps to outsiders to become rumor (Lang and Lang, 1961). Most emergent stories lack the quality institutional support to where they become legend. A few have entertainment value.

In and between *Storytelling Organizations*, at least eight ways of sensemaking intertwine to constitute a systemicity that is more complex than just an 'information-processing network' approach so prevalent in system thinking (Boje, 1991: 107).

My reference to emergent story (dispersion) in relation to control narrative (centering) is in its more dialogical manner than a mere information processing model. Storytelling complexity does not obey hierarchic order. What Boulding proposed and Pondy embraced, is a narrative teleology. The wrong step was to miss the fact that people in everyday life narrate in ways that are out of control. They mix a level 1 framework with say a level 9 transcendental, while skipping the intermediate levels (e.g. 2). Out of intense simplicities, intense complexity can emerge. And vice versa, as Winston Churchill once said, 'out of intense complexities intense simplicities emerge.'[6] There is this unity of consciousness in hierarchic-systemicity theories, a narrative control reduction of the Polypi dialogic manner of storytelling complexity and simplicity.

My contribution is to integrate Boulding and Pondy with Bakhtin, but without hierarchic thinking, to launch what we call the 'Third Cybernetics Revolution' (Boje and Baskin, 2005). First cybernetic is control by deviation-counteraction feedback loops; second cybernetic adds to first cybernetic, the open systems complexity property of deviation-amplification (requisite variety making to organize environmental complexity). To get beyond open systems is to invoke the third cybernetic revolution of jettisoning dualities, hierarchies, and especially levels. This brings us to holography.

In this next table (Table 1.2), I give the integration of Boulding, Pondy, and Bakhtin some storytelling sensemaking flesh, in an integration of storytelling sensemaking registries and systemicity complexity thinking.

---

6 This is an often cited remark. See Churchill Quotes web, http://www3.thinkexist.com/quotation/out_of_intense_complexities_intense_simplicities/15826.html

TABLE 1.2   *Sensemaking registries of systemicity storytelling complexity*

Antenarratives	That emergent story has not escaped narrative prison is missing from Boulding/Pondy. Narrative police are still trying to arrest emergent story and antenarratives, as always. Small antenarratives (bet and before fragments that aspire to narrative coherence) can transform a calcified image narrative.
BME Retrospection	Retrospective sensemaking with BME (beginning, middle and end) progressive sequencing is missing from Boulding/Pondy.
Emotive–Ethical	Emotion sensemaking can convey an ethical urgency, a sense of what Bakhtin calls answerability of the teller to tell a story of oppression or the listener to act to bring about social change. Answerability is also part of architectonics, but not conceived as emotive reflexivity.
Fragmentation Retrospection	No whole stories, just fragments told in ongoing discourse are missing from Boulding/Pondy.
Horsesense	Horsesense is Rosile's term for describing how one body registers the sensemaking of another's body. Embodied sensemaking is not part of Boulding/Pondy's modeling of complexity properties.
I–We, Sameness–Other, Transcendental, and Hegelian Dialectics	Dialectics is missing from Boulding/Pondy.[7] In Mead there is self-reflexive awareness. In Ricoeur is the Sameness–Other dialectic of narrative identities. In Kant transcendental reason and aesthetics are reflexivities a priori to retrospection of BME or fragmentation sensemaking. For Hegel, antithesis and thesis oppose each other. Horkheimer and Adorno dispute if some kind of synthesis results.
Polypi	Dialogisms of polyphonic, stylistic, chronotopic, and architectonic that invite reflexivity commingle with what Boulding calls image, symbol, social network. Boulding misses the polyphonic. • Polyphonic is fully embodied voices, not in hierarchy. They fully engage and debate one another, including author's voice. • Stylistic is juxtaposition of visual, oral, and textual ways. In managerialism there is telling through *image orchestration* to make it appear debate or dialogism is happening. • Chronotopic is interplay of pluralized ways of conceiving space–time in the symbolism, reflexive, retrospective history, and prospective teleology of storytelling organizations. • Architectonic dialogism is the interanimation of cognitive, ethical, and aesthetic discourses in social and societal discourses that prescribe and co-produce roles.
Tamara	Boulding/Pondy ignore the context of sensemaking. Sensemaking ways are contextualized in the physicality of space–time, in the impossibility of people being everywhere at once to hear all the simultaneous storytelling going on. The reflexivity on what went on in rooms you are not in is never-ending.
? Sensemaking registries not yet discovered	Pondy (1976: 2a) holds with 'systems of unspecified complexity.' that is, what other sensemaking registries might be in interplay with storytelling complexity and systemicity.

---

7 In his last paper, which I had published in a special tribute issue of *Journal of Organizational Change Management* to Lou Pondy, he reflects upon how the Boulding model is too much about harmony and ignores social conflict (Pondy, 1989).

Next, I develop the holography theory which I will apply to an early study I did of storytelling systemicity.

HOLOGRAPHY THEORY AND COMPLEXITY THINKING

Instead of hierarchy, I seek a more holographic understanding, where all complexity properties may be refracted in any of the other ones. *Holographic inquiry is defined as interrelationships of storytelling-sensemaking and complexity-properties in any order, with from 1 to 13 or more dimensions (facets) reflecting one another.* It is concerned with the interactivity of hierarchic as well as dialogic systemicity complexity with storytelling. 'Gon' is the root-word of each of the dimensions, and means 'angle.' I mean it more in the 'agonic' sense as *does not have a bent or angle or an 'end.'* Agonic is therefore opposite of 'gon' and means not an angle, but all the 'agons' from digon to tridecagon, and beyond. For example, the 'E' in BME is an 'End' that can drive people to an imposition of values (ends). In short, the connotation of the 'gons' is double meaning with 'agons' (without an end-value). What is holographic, is that pick up any one 'agon' and you see the refractions of the other dimension lenses. To date, the interactivity of various complexity properties has not been theorized or studied empirically. My adjusted interactive holographic model is presented in Figure 1.3. I purposely put them out of clockwise hierarchic ordering.

This holographic model exhibits the interactivity of properties of systemicity–complexity, including emotive–ethic, fragmentation, antenarrative, and Tamara that were left out of the Boulding/Pondy system thinking model (see Introduction and Table 1.2 above).

TABLE 1.3   Holographic complexity chart

Monogon – 1 dimension

Digon – 2 dimensions

Trigon – 3 dimensions

Tetragon – 4 dimensions

Pentagon – 5 dimensions

Hexagon – 6 dimensions

Septagon – 7 dimensions

Octagon – 8 dimensions

Nonagon – 9 dimensions

Decagon – 10 dimensions

Hendecagon – 11 dimensions

Dodecagon – 12 dimensions

Tridecagon – 13 dimensions

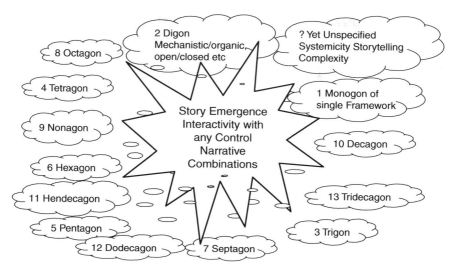

FIGURE 1.3   Holographic systemicity complexities

We know nothing of the combined interactive effects of different combinations of holographic dimensions and about their reflexivity in Storytelling Organizations. Yet, it is these combined effects at triadic, quadratic, and more complex groupings that produce what I am calling *reflexivity-transcendental sensemaking* that is beyond retrospective-prospective-sensemaking.[8] With each combination beyond dyadic, from triadic to tridecagon (should we be able to imagine such complexity), the interactions produce dialogic relations among control narratives, systemicity complexity, and emergent stories. Without a theory of holographic complexity, we cannot sufficiently appreciate the dynamics of at least the eight (octagonic) sensemaking ways. We remain trapped in monogon, digon (dualities), or at best trigon (hierarchic) system thinking.

To summarize, my thesis is that in contemporary times, Storytelling Organization complexity exhibits highly interactive properties of storytelling systemicity complexity in holography that is not always about hierarchy. Most narrative research is stuck at BME linear sensemaking and hierarchy thinking. Theories of systemicity complexity are stuck at Boulding/Pondy's first four hierarchic levels, and are blind to storytelling emergence because the information processing model of communication is not sufficiently robust and holographic, and does not deal with interactivity of non-hierarchic relationships with hierarchic ones. Holographic storytelling can run from one dimension (monogon) to multiple

---

8 Refer back to the Introduction, to Figure 1, and the temporality is retrospective-prospective, but there is the other zone of complexity in sensemaking that is all about reflexivity-transcendental.

complexity property interrelationships, from two dimensions (digon) to many more complexity dimensionality up through tridecagon (13 dimensions and beyond). Storytelling is *holographic* in the sense that it can interrelate more than one complexity property.

Next I elaborate on how holographic systemicity-complexity properties are relevant to various organizations that I have studied.

STORYTELLING ORGANIZATION SYSTEMICITY

One of my earliest empirical investigations of the Storytelling Organization theory was the Gold Office Supply study (Boje, 1991). I transcribed over 100 hours of tape and video recordings of talk, week-by-week, over an eight-month period. This was accompanied by participant observer field notes and by document analysis. I retheorize the study from ordinal, hierarchic to dialogic associations of storytelling complexity properties. I did not find BME retrospective narrative sensemaking as prominent as the literature then (and since) suggested. What I did observe at Gold was the inextricably intertwined relation of highly fragmented (tersely told) narrative sensemaking and the ever changing and rearranging dynamic complexity of 'systemicity.' That is, to interpret the transcript required months of participant observation, hundreds of hours of transcription, and investigation of what words, phrases, and stuff left out meant to them, and to me.

My position that a dialogical story is not just the lines of the narrative retelling, but the silences between the lines, and what the hearer is filling in in-between-the-lines is a source of controversy in narrative studies. In Gold Office Supply, I found that a phrase as short as 'you know the story' (lines 1163–4) or even a nod, could indicate I was to fill in the blanks.

How do other narrative scholars interpret Gold? Yiannis Gabriel (2000: 20) argues that my terse telling does not meet his BME stricture of what is a *proper* story, that I sacrifice what makes a story a story in order to explore systemicity. Barbara Czarniawska (1997, 1998) once thought only BME defined *proper* story, but her 2004 book picks up on the fragmented, high interruption, code-nature of telling I studied. For me, storytelling is to systemicity what precedent cases are to the courts. In a courtroom, various stakeholders perform sensemaking narratives and stories to cope with the equivocal situation of inquiry into the many sides of tellings told by defense and prosecution witnesses. Accounts of eyewitnesses often do not agree, and may also disagree with forensic accounts.

Storytelling and antenarrative trajectories pass through the event horizons of space–time stitching together, weaving together many agons.

Next, I work out holographic theory using examples from Gold Office Supply study.

Monogonic thinking

Systemicity-complexity is an improvement system writing, which presumes 'monogon.' Monogon is defined as monologic, monovocality, and mono-languagedness of one-dimensional system theory. With monogon (one) dimension thinking, there is this reductionism:

> Every correct judgment corresponds to a particular unified systematic-monological context, rather than being attached to a personality. (Bakhtin, 1973: 65)

The implication is that our personalities live and work, in a 'plurality of consciousnesses' that is multi-dialogic (Bakhtin, 1973: 65). Yet, from monogon to tridecagon, and beyond, it's always about some kind of control of one sensemaking against many others. For Bakhtin (1973: 12) 'narrative genres are always enclosed in a solid and unshakable monological framework.' Coherence narrative posits mono-system-wholeness, mergedness, and finalizedness. The single observer posits unitary mono event horizon wholeness with one complexity property. Heisenberg's *Uncertainty Principle* applies here. Even the monogonic observer is an intrusion to systemicity, altering the event horizon.

In the Gold study, there are several monogonic frames, the conglomerate, the sales culture, and the mechanistic enterprise. Each tries, like some kind of black hole, to absorb everything into itself. Mechanistic narrative, for example, imprisons Gold in linear storytelling of a BME plot of coherence, and a resolute belief in whole-system, with merged part-relations predetermined by the conglomerate, by Doug's mechanistic and control training, or by reversion to Billy Gold's feudal sales culture.

A story can be more than backward-looking BME or fragmentation retrospection. It can convey a forward-looking prediction of future organizational behavior. What is interesting is that most of the telling is left unstated in the terse telling. Besides trailing people around in most every situation taping their talk in their work situation, my colleague and I conducted a vendors' focus group. It becomes obvious to those in the next room, that vendors are also aware that Gold is 'a ship without a rudder right now and I think it concerns their salespeople as well' (362–4). What is being tersely told is expounded upon by Doug and his upper echelon after the event. There is terror. What if the sales people are about to jump ship for some other office supply company? It has happened before to Gold, and the really devastating prediction is once again they will take the most valuable customers with them.

CEO Turnover Story by Vendors

Dan: Yeah, my boss will call from	337
We're based out of the Northwest and	338
he'll say 'Well Dan who is running the	339

ship at Gold now?' He can see a	340
lot of the proposals that we've	341
presented and were accepted six months	342
ago still in effect because there's	343
been turnover[***]	344
You know is the next administration	356
going to come in and make changes to	357
that? One point that Jeff made	358
earlier that I want to touch on is our	359
concerns are shared with their	360
salespeople. They definitely know	361
sometimes that they're kind of a ship	362
without a rudder right now and I think	363
it concerns their salespeople as well	364

Relationships with vendors and contract customers, as the animated discussion following each focus group reveals, constitutes an important interorganizational systemicity for Gold, but reading the dynamics requires lots of fieldwork to understand context of textuality, orality, and visuality that is in interplay in the moment of Being.

Gold's history is propaganda generated by the powerful conglomerate, and each CEO agent, to control the sales force, vendors, and customers. Such narrative frameworks of monogonic, simplistic, monologic, complexity have been unchallenged since Aristotle's (350 BCE) *Poetics*. Yet, even Aristotle complicated the frameworks. Narratology remains blind to Aristotle's extra-narrative framework categories, 'epic-story' and 'history.' Epics are longer, more complex than narratives, with more characters, and shifting dramatic personae, yet it is still an imitation. History 'has to deal not with one action, but with one period or all that happened in that to one or more persons, however disconnected the several events may have been' (Aristotle, 350 BCE: 1459a, #21: 256). As in simple narrative, and epic stories, the whole of the *living story* is not performed, only a portion, a simple or complex plot of a few characters and incidents, a narrative telling to give the desired cathartic effect (pity, fear, authenticity, believability).

Digon holography

Digon inquiry explores dualities, such as closed–open, mechanistic–organic, male–female, emotive–rational, etc. For example, in Gold Office Supply, at the digonic two-dimensionality, one monogon polarity is hierarchic to some other one.

Storytelling organizations, such as Gold, can be analyzed according to the distribution and frequency of various framework types that are in digonic relations.

In recent work, we have mapped the relationship between fragmented narrative tellings and the more epic stories of Enron Corporation (Boje and Rosile, 2003a). In Gold, the sales culture framework is being opposed by the conglomerate's demands for a more professionally bureaucratic framework.

> **The story was not found to be a highly agreed-upon text, told from beginning to end, as it has been studied in most prior story research.** Rather, the stories were dynamic, varied by context, and were sometimes terse, requiring the hearer to fill in silently major chunks of story line, context, and implication. Stories were frequently challenged, reinterpreted, and revised by the hearers as they unfolded in conversation. (Boje, 1991: 106, boldness mine)

Founding story tersely told In over hundred hours of taped talk, this was the most complete rendition of a BME organization story. Refer to the Introduction for the example of how tersely told is the Goldco founding story. More frequently, bits and pieces of narrative fragments were shared and the listeners were left to fill in the blanks, based on their knowledge of stories behind the tersely told fragments. Much of the story being told is not actually uttered. There is no whole story, and even in this rendition, Doug is tilting the telling to make his point – 'nice toy' 'fun,' and 'we don't have the luxury of screwing around.' Listeners around this meeting of Doug, several managers, and myself, are expected to know the details, to read what is in-between-the-lines. Doug is steering Sam's telling, fitting it to other instances when Gold had picked up a division or entered new territory, on a whim. This storytelling is intertextual to many other storytellings people are expected to know. The story left implicit (in-between-the-lines, in what is oral or written), is embedded in a systemicity of eight, and like more, sensemaking currencies. For example, a conglomerate owns Gold, and is about to sell Gold with a Midwest and an eastern office supply company. They need the numbers to look right for investors.

What was ethical in the sales culture is now unethical in a bureaucratic frame. It's the story of Weber's bureaucracy in context with feudalistic nepotism, and charismatic sales frame. The fact that ethics is at issue in frameworks speaks to the need to develop a more holographic model of complexity. The problem for the dyadic holographic of any two frameworks, such as the salesperson and bureaucratic culture, is that they easily become a duality, rather than a conjunctive relationship.

Over the eras, epic story has gotten shorter, since the attention spans of audiences no longer span a month or weeks or days to tell an epic. Epic story is 'made up of a plurality of actions' including simultaneous episodes of diverse kinds, but is not as nuanced as history (Aristotle, 350BCE: 1462b, # 7: 265). Now epic can be told in 90 minutes or split into a series of narrative-episodes, told one by one. The whole concept of simultaneous telling in an outdoor festival, as in Aristotle's day, is now unthinkable.

Mechanistic–organic duality has a long history in *digon* system thinking. For example, Thomas Hobbes (1958: 180–1, caps in original) wrote Leviathan in 1651 as mechanistic system that dominated over the organic: 'And first of systems, which resemble the similar parts or muscles of a body natural. By SYSTEMS, I understand any numbers of men joined in one interest or one business.' The Leviathan was the Commonwealth or State, which Hobbes (1958: 23) describes as 'an artificial man, though of greater stature and strength than the natural... in which the sovereignty is an artificial soul, as giving life and motion to the whole body' with nerves and motion, and 'having an artificial reason.'

Narratives are stereotyped, and are not only typed and counted, their machine-like movements are tracked across space–time. This is a technical (clockwork) sensation of time being narrated, within the limits of linear plot-lines. Humans imitate the machine, repeating highly scripted behavior, to behave as Leviathan cogs with artificial souls. Leaders mimic clockwork-machine masters, and everyone else is a clock-slave. Machine temporality is only one possibility, but others such as biological or historic time, can only be inter-polated into machine temporality, into linear plot-sequence.

Trigon

Trigon interrelationships of three complexity properties can be enacted with or without hierarchy. For example, one of Gold's trigons is frameworks, chronotopes, and architectonic combinations.

Boulding (1956) specifies 'social organization' complexity, as an awareness of roles – there is not compliance, the square peg does not fit neatly in a round 'hole' iden-tity construction. Architectonic interanimation of cognitive, ethical, and aesthetic dis-courses, of which story is domain (with metaphor and trope) is manifest, as the organization adapts to societal discourse, and actively shapes it. Metaphorization is mimicry. Boulding does not say that complexity properties of mimicking framework, mechanistic, control, open, organic, etc. have vacated discourse.

Contesting frameworks (sales, conglomerate, etc.) interact with various Bakhtinian chronotopes (romantic, chivalric, biographical adventure, etc.), as well as with architectonics (ethical-answerability, cognitive frames, and aesthetic dis-courses) constructing trigon complexities. We can relate a number of chronotopes that expand narrative types, to interaction with frameworks and architectonics.

Architectonics was first only a cognitive project by Kant (1781/1900: 466): 'By the term *Architectonic* I mean the art of constructing a system... Reason cannot permit our knowledge to remain in an unconnected and rhapsodistic state, but requires that the sum of our cognitions should constitute a system.' Bakhtin (1990) preferred the term 'consummation' to construction, and was careful to not assume a monophonic, monologic, or mono-languaged system (rather he pre-ferred to look at the unmergedness, the unfinalizability of system, or what I defined above as *systemicity*. Bakhtin added ethical and aesthetic discourse to Kant's cognitive architectonic. Ethics here is not ethics of conceptions of beauty, but the very notion of answerability. Ethics is interanimated by cognitive and aesthetic discourse (of which story is a domain). Bakhtin (1981, 1990) posits what I will call an A-B-C-D model of storytelling, and its more architectonic dialogism:

A – Who are the authors consummating the systemicity?
B – Who are the beholders of the systemicity?
C – Who are the characters in the scripted systemicity?
D – Who are the directors of the storytelling systemicity being consummated?

Romantic narrative, for example, is an adventure-time chronotope that begins with a 'flare-up' (Bakhtin, 1981: 81) happening to some hero or heroine, and by the end of the plot, they make a successful overcoming of initial obstacles, where relationships are tested, but not broken. One obstacle for Doug is the old salesperson's culture of nepotism. Greek romance is the earliest of the chronotopes, one that dominated narrative writing for centuries, and is still a way in which organization tales are told. Doug in the Gold study is such an adventure hero. He becomes the 'savior' figure, able to protect Gold from the conglomerate monster. In the Greek romance adventure chronotope there is no biographical maturation, no transformation of the basic character. Billy Gold remains as he always was, and Doug does not change.

Tetragon

At the quadratic level, four complexities become storied in either hierarchic or dialogic ways. For Boulding and Pondy, framework (frame) precedes control (clockwork), and is followed in higher order complexity by mechanistic (thermodynamic), and open (cell). Each of these is obvious in the textual examples I presented from Gold. For Bakhtin, four dialogisms (polyphony, stylistic, chronotopic, and architectonic) are hierarchic. Voice, styles of writing and orality, chronotopes of space–time that compete, and architectonics of Doug trying to install a moral ethical discourse where the aesthetics of sales culture and the cognitive framing by the conglomerate run differently, are examples I have drawn out of the study. It is possible that neither hierarchic model is borne out in organizations, or in all cases. It is possible that the theory is holding back our observations of complexity relationships that do not follow hierarchic patterns. Or, it is likely that there is some combination of hierarchic with some complexity properties in certain situations, and these interact with some that are not behaving hierarchically. Several chronotopes such as the ones about adventure may be hierarchically ordered complexities, but perhaps the others are not. For example the idyllic (number 9) may interact with romantic, everyday, and chivalric adventure.

Pentagon

Storytelling that holographically stitches together five event surfaces seems a performance too intricate to contemplate. Yet Euclid described pentagons in 300

BCE. In the US the five main armed forces are installed in the Pentagon building constructed in 1943, shaped as concentric pentagons, with corridors stretching 17.5 miles. Here I am more concerned with conceptual pentagons. Boulding's signs of frame, machine, thermostat, cell, and plan are hierarchically conceived conceptual pentagons. In Gold Office Supply, the storytelling is not anomalous, with tellings plucked out of their natural setting. They occur in the complexity of space–time, which can have at least five dimensions.

Rather the storytelling is multi-dimensional, sometimes with the intertextuality of a pentagon. The founding stories of Goldco specialties and Printing divisions, and Reno Branch denote patterns that are no longer acceptable by shifting frameworks. These stand in relationship to other complexities. For example, a pentagon holographic story network in Gold would be that (1) founding stories are refracted in shifting frameworks, (2) that reverberates in the word being on the street about selling Gold, (3) exciting storytelling among salespeople vendors and customers about future scenarios such that (4) deal contracts may shift yet again, and (5) provoking a restorying of what is and is not ethical behavior at Gold. In short, frameworks, polyphonic social networks, open, and architectonic complexities are interactively dynamic.

Hexagon

Kenneth Burke's (1945) infamous pentad (act, scene, agent, agency, and purpose) could become a hexagon. Burke (1972: 23) says that 'many times on later occasions' he 'regretted' not adding a sixth element, called 'frame' (Burke, 1937). Aristotle's (350 BCE) narrative elements are hexadic and hierarchically ordered: plot, character, theme, dialog, rhythm, and spectacle. Aristotle also wrote about frame but did not include it in his one list of six. Burke got his pentad by collapsing Aristotle's dialog and rhythm into 'agency.' In Burkean narrative theory, the translation of Aristotle hedadic is as follows: plot is act, character is agent, theme is purpose, dialog and rhythm are agency, and spectacle is scene (see Boje, 2002). Burke, unlike Aristotle, developed ratio relationships among dyadic pairs, such as the famous scene–act ratio. We could easily analyze Gold and find the pentagon in play.

Septagon

If we retheorize Aristotle's narrative elements without hierarchy and include his focus on frames, which is something Burke wanted for his own work, then we have a septet or septagon. Further we can pluralize the elements, so that there are many plots (and counterplots), characterizations, themes, rhythms, dialogs, spectacles, and frameworks that are interactively dynamic complexity properties of the Storytelling Organization. We can do this in the Gold Office Supply study. Doug and the conglomerate have a plot being resisted by counterplots preferred by salespeople, customers, and vendors. There are characterizations of the divisions as 'toys' and 'play things' and of founder Billy Gold, and an executive named 'Fox' that speak to ethical character flaws. There are themes I call ante-narratives that are emergent, such as customers and vendors, and sales crew 'in the know' about the pending sale of Gold. The rhythms of the CEO and upper management turnover is wreaking havoc with cycles the customers and vendors would prefer, and what can emerge is the exit of the top sales people, taking their accounts with them to a competitor with a more attractive cycle. The dialogs in the hallways, in boardrooms, and focus groups are interanimating and highly intertextual. The spectacle of moral crisis is in play and it affects the other elements. I used the septagon in the Enron spectacle study of some 5,000 Enron narratives, as well as antenarrative clustering traversing and morphing in space–time (Boje and Rosile, 2002, 2003a; Boje et al., 2004).

Octagon

I did the dance of eight sensemaking registries in Gold (in previous section) and need not recount them again. What I did not do was to show the eight factorial ways in which these ways of sensemaking constitute the dance of simplicity and complexity. Each of the eight sensemaking frameworks of narrative control is exacting about the selection of incidents and characters. BME puts them in linear relation, the others in non-linear. Polypi dialogisms, for example, are still narrative control, at the level of dialogism interactivity, when one dialogism dominates the others.

In the next example, from a customer focus group, all eight sensemaking ways are in play. Several antenarratives are clustering: 'turnover in senior management' (line 343), 'change in philosophy' (lines 346–7), agreements are worked out and new management changes the agreements (958–61). These antenarratives are 'bets' and 'pre-stories' that some BME narrative will emerge, such as 'we have to reinvent the wheel' (961–2) every time a new CEO is installed at Gold because they are not honoring old deals. Frank is a customer, from a large corporation, a purchasing agent, who expresses emotive–ethical concerns. 'I don't care how they resolve their internal politics' (350–1), 'I need the product' (352), but with the turnover each 'president has [their] own stamp of how he is going to operate and things change' (347–9). The video of Frank shows very emotive behavior, and the audio reveals an inflection of tonality that vibrates in ways that the words of the transcript below do not capture. The audiotape of intonations and pauses, and videotape of body language reveals a *horsesense-making* going on that is occurring beyond the words. Several I–we dialectics are evident in the transcript. The 'I' of the purchasing agent is opposed by the turnover in CEOs, as well as new vice presidents, and sales managers. The rapid turnover has resulted in systemicity problems of stability and access in Gold's relations to customers. Doug, the CEO who hired a marketing professor and me as consultants, is the latest in a succession of five CEOs brought in just two years.

A Customer Story

Frank: And I'm seeing symptoms of the	342
turnover in senior management they	343
have had senior management that they	344
have had in the past 14–15 months	345
where they have had a change in	346
philosophy. A certain president has	347
own stamp of how he is going to operate	348
and things change. My major concern is	349
the end result. I don't care how they	350
resolve their internal politics	351
I need the product	352
[***] They do listen but with half an	954
ear maybe because of the change in	955
management.	956
Certain management we have had	957
discussions and we have come to agreements	958
and the systems have been worked	959
out. New management comes in a new	960
president of the company and we have to	961
reinvent the wheel and we go back and I	962
mean it's in writing it's documented	963
these agreements are documented and then	964
go to the next person	965

The polypi of dialogisms is part of what I learned (but did not, at that time, have language to express) in eight months of participant observation. There is a polyphony of frameworks in play, from the old school ways a salesperson's culture worked, to the new expectations of a conglomerate that wants to bundle the regional Gold company with two others to make a national office supply company, to be put up for sale (this becomes evident in other exchanges in this focus group). I am working on stylistics, helping the CEO restylize the annual report to reflect a better image to the conglomerate, to give the bottom line numbers and ratios a story that the conglomerate will buy into. Doug, the latest CEO, is changing the ways of sensemaking, adding a way of making sense that is from his prior job, where the kinds of unprofessional behavior he observes in his sales force, in not keeping deals that were made, does not keep recurring. Doug is shaking up the ways of making sense, and does so with some very emotive–ethical as well as answerability ethics dramatics.

For example, one story that was repeated in many office conversations concerns how, upon Doug's arrival as the latest CEO, there were assigned parking spots. Doug, in almost his first meeting with the executives, uprooted a 'reserved for the CEO' (one was also reserved for each of several VPs) parking sign and threw his on the executive meeting table, demanding to know 'who put up this sign? This is not the kind of leadership I will have around here.' He is holding the VPs at the meeting accountable. There was also a guy who supposedly worked in the warehouse that spent much of his day washing and detailing executive's cars. The offending executive, for this and other good reasons, was fired by week's end. Not only this but there is a general moral crisis he perceives, where prizes the vendors think are going to sales people for selling more than others, are going to managers, and to executives' family members instead of to sales people. Doug is shaking up the fabric of operating philosophy in its architectonics, in the new cognitive, new aesthetic, and especially new ethical ways of sensemaking. Storytelling about the shakeup at Gold helps customers and vendors make sense of a shift in operating philosophy that is apparent the customers have noticed. This telling is quite terse (347–9, 957–66). There are narrative fragments of retrospective sensemaking (342–51, 954–65). Yet, there is also reflexivity, not just BME or fragmentation-retrospection, about how the senior management listens with half an ear (954–5) and how customers and management come to agreement and work out systemic-agreements, but new management comes in to reinvent the wheel, voiding past agreements (954–62). Finally, there is a Tamara here I did not specify in the published article. The focus group in the recording room is being conducted at the behest of Doug, his VPs and senior managers, who are behind a one-way mirror in another room. After the customers head out for more gourmet food in another room, the upper echelon of Gold begin to discuss with their consultants what is going on, what are the implications of what they just saw and heard. By the way, the customers did remark, 'that looks like a one-way mirror' and 'It'll be Doug and his VPs behind it, watching us.' They are not strangers to Tamara, to how there is simultaneous storytelling in different rooms, how people chase storylines from room to room.

In organizations, storytelling is the preferred sensemaking currencies of human relationships among internal and external stakeholders. I have asserted eight are in interplay. The institutional memory of the Storytelling Organization is embedded in the distributed Tamara-systemicity of talk, written records, and in the living memory of how people do what they do across many times and places. People are more than just limited information processors. People are symbolic, reinterpret history, bring multiple discourses (ethical, cognitive, aesthetic) to bear in the moment of performing stories, especially collectively told ones. Sensemaking storytelling is highly embedded in *talk*, in *visual* image and body language, and in the *textuality* (i.e. writing) done by Gold.

The storytelling at Gold was oftentimes reflexive upon ongoing moral crises. In the Goldco founding story (above), Doug the CEO is eliciting a telling from Sam in the context of a discussion about which division and which offices in other cities and states might have to be sold off. Doug is managing the transitions of this office-supply firm from a company of nepotism and questionable ethics, steering it away from further moral failure. Keep in mind that the framework of a sales culture may have practices that are ethical, but to more bureaucratic (play by rules) framework, those same practices are considered unethical.

Some practices are unethical in any framework. Doug told me he had come in after midnight to meet the night warehouse crew. In walking past his office, he noticed a light on in his secretary's outer office. Thinking that she had forgotten to turn out the lights, he entered. He saw a pair of men's trousers, tie and jacket, and a woman's dress, high heels, and panties, all strewn about the floor. He heard groans of apparent ecstasy and pleasure coming from his own office. He opened the door and there was the vice president of marketing atop the sales manager, and oblivious to his presence, on top of Doug's expensive leather couch. He grunted, 'I just bought that couch!' and withdrew, closing the door behind him.

The next day, Doug asked me, 'Dave, what should I do? Fire one, fire them both, what?' I said firing the executive seemed appropriate, since this was the latest of many incidents of sex in the workplace, not to mention some drunken excesses at various affairs with employees, clients, and vendors. Doug replied, 'this morning I accepted his resignation, and wrote him a letter of resignation.' 'Why not fire him?,' I asked. He explained that if he fired him, the word would get on the street in ways that would drag down the image of the company. 'What about the sales manager? Do I fire her or let her go?' 'Have you talked to her? Maybe it was forced or coerced. He is her boss, after all,' I added. Doug did talk to her and established that it was apparently consensual sex mixed with quite a bit of alcohol. Doug and his remaining executives kept her on. To release her at the same time as the VP of marketing would create way too much chaos among salespeople, customers, and vendors. There is a grey area here. Upholding the moral shift from salesperson's to more bureaucratic framework, also meant the practicality of ethics: to not offend the conglomerate who want a squeaky clean image for Gold.

There was the matter of the Laker's tickets, Hawaii trips, TVs, stereos, and other prizes given by vendors to reward salespeople that were moving their products. Doug told me something I was hearing from VPs, managers, salespeople, vendors, and customers in confidence: the prizes were being taken by VPs, some managers, and their families, and very few actually went to the sales people.

I dug out in subsequent field interviews with them, that this had been a problem in the link line of successive CEOs. CEO Ed Fox engaged in very questionable behavior and was replaced by yet another and another CEO, until our current CEO Doug took the job. Doug put an end to the unethical practice. Each new CEO sent in by the conglomerate was supposed to change the salesperson culture into something more professional, and sellable to investors.

There were nepotism practices of Billy, which were understandable, but not for the next four CEOs. For example, those-in-the-know would tell me that Raymond, a former CEO, was once a hero figure for adding several branch offices (tersely told in lines 727–31). The full meaning is inaccessible unless one explores

Gold extensively to unpack extended meaning in intertextual referents of context, other stories, and history.

Although many researchers might challenge if this next excerpt is a story at all, the teller, Sam, does identify the telling as a story by interjecting, 'I guess you heard this all already' (732) and 'I guess you heard the whole story before' (736–7). Even the words 'you know' (739–40) invite the hearer to fill in the blanks. My point is that story and narrative fragments are in-between systemicity and context. This is an example of a storyteller briefly referencing a fuller storyline, which I observed throughout the stories shared by executives, managers, salespeople, vendors, and customers. I am Dave in this one.

Reno Branch Story of Nepotism

Sam: I think five years ago there was no	727
Executive Committee. He just ran	728
the place the way he wanted as if you	729
wasn't here. Raymond was [conglomerate's]	730
man and he did what he pleased.	731
I guess you heard this all already	732
Dave: I heard about the high growth (nodding)	733
Sam: Yes we picked up San Diego	734
Dave: Reno?	735
Sam: Ed Fox picked up Reno and I guess	736
you heard the whole story before.	737
That's why we picked up Reno because	738
Ed Fox had that with his father. You	739
know.	740

These stories and other stories made the rounds and reinforced Doug's image as the reformer–savior who would not put up with special privileges for executives that had been perfectly OK in the old framework. This Doug-as-savior theme resurfaces in stories from vendors and customers. The ripping-out-the-parking-sign, the required resignation of the VP, the end to nepotism site growth were all enforcements of ethics since Doug became CEO. A year from now this might be tersely referred to as the parking-sign story, the couch story, Reno story, and may all be part of institutional symbols and terse telling.

Beyond Octagon

From nonagon to tridecagon, the relationship of storytelling to complexity properties must await empiric (ethnographic) investigation. Even hendecagon (11 dimensions) yields some 40 million combinations. Tamara-land is my name for many storytelling episodes going on simultaneously across a landscape of stages of one or many storytelling organizations (Boje, 1995). Anecdote, or story, on one stage or fixated on one screen, with stationary audience, has succeeded what was once epic story, of the fragmented wandering audiences that even Aristotle with his BME preferences wrote about.

LIVING STORY SYSTEMICITY

In sum there is no whole story. One never gets the whole story. There are only narrative fragments in systemicity. Whole story is just BME narrative fiction. Nihilism is forever announcing the end of coherence, in the restorytelling of our living story, as we and others reframe in acts of exclusion, embellishment and terse-telling. Any claim to whole story violates the nihilistic principle of infinity of interpretations (Vattimo, 1988). Whole story is *poetic* illusion. We keep hoping that someday the whole story will come out, but it never does. Instead I am proposing a theory of living story, one intertwined with systemicity complexities.

Living stories are transitory antenarratives changing in the moment, becoming reinterpreted, restoried, told differently in each situational context, just plain unstable, as versions proliferate and emerge. Living story is all that happens to all the persons, simultaneously, in all the space–time horizons where storying is going on. Living story is simultaneous, and includes the little people, not just the victors with the swords writing hi-story. People in living stories cannot know the whole story because stories have contextual meaning. Story-sensemaking is betwixt and between persons and context.

Living stories are intertextual, betwixt and between texts, posing answerability to Others' counterstories we know in part, and our acts of *discovery*. Aristotle seemed aware of discovery, 'as the very word implies, a change from ignorance to knowledge' by reading signs, disclosures, re-membering, reasoning, composite discovery, or discovery from the incidents themselves (Aristotle, 350 BCE: 1452a, #30: 237). We cannot split ourselves to be simultaneous in the Tamara-land of the landscape of the chronotopic diversity of space–time the tellings are happening in. Living story is the dance of lust for coherence of whole with differences, contingencies, multifinality, unmergedness, unfinalizedness, and plurivo-cality of systemicity.

Collective Memory is our next chapter. It is also collective forgetting, collective rehistoricizing, and collective striving for coherence.

2

HOW STORY DIALOGISM YIELDS EMERGENCE

This chapter is about emerging dialogic story. Emergence is defined as an absolute novelty, spontaneity, and improvisation, without past/future. Dialogism is defined as different voices, styles, and ideas expressing a plurality of logics in different ways, but not always in the same place and time.[1] Story emergence is getting lost. The reason is that dialogism is not being understood. Bakhtin taught me there are 'dialogic stories' which means they are social, imprinted with many voices and logics that are 'dialogic' to one another, and entirely unfinished, unfinalized, not whole like narrativists say they are. Pondy taught me that stories are socially defined. Latour taught me that every aspect of our life has a narrative expectation of our role and what will be the sequence of events. Emerging story can break us out of that prison. From Stein I learned that between the lines of story is the stuff we fill in, are expected to fill in, but we do so in our own way. From Benjamin I learned that over the last decades, our organizations have lost important competencies to be able to interpret living stories, redefine narrative expectation, understand many voices, and read between the lines of story.

A five-act play, but first the playbill.

Playbill: What is Emergent Story?

Emergent story can be defined as absolute novelty, spontaneity, and improvisation, without past/future. Emergent stories are conceived in the here-and-now co-presence of social communicative intercourse of narrative-memory prisons ready to capture and translate emergence. For Foucault (1977b: 148–9) emergence is the 'moment of arising ... always produced through a particular stage of forces ... or against adverse circumstances.' It will also help to define qualities of emergent stories. I theorize at least four: *Authenticity, contagion, institutional support, entertainment value*, and *cultural force*. Most emergent stories lack the *quality of authenticity*,

---

1 Bakhtin used dialogicality. I use *dialogism* and *dialogic* interchangeably to mean *dialogicality*. Holquist's (1990) reading is 'dialogism' and describes Bakhtin anti-Hegelian dislike for Absolute Spirit dialectic. Bakhtin preferred neo-Kantianism more 'speculative epistemology' (Holquist, 1990: 17), a move from Newtonian to Einsteinian worldview (i.e. relativity of time/space).

where they are believable beyond those present. Most emergent stories lack the *quality of contagion*, where gossip jumps to outsiders to become rumor (Lang and Lang, 1961). Most emergent stories lack the *quality institutional support*, to where they become legend. A few have entertainment value.

BRINGING EMERGING STORY BACK IN!

Act 1: Enter Pondy!

I was in graduate school when Lou Pondy asked me in 1977 to co-author a paper, 'Bringing mind back in' (Pondy and Boje, 1980). Treating story as object is what Pondy and I call 'in-place metering device' science. Ours was a clever narrative of paradigm wars between organization sociology, organization behavior, and organizational phenomenology. We gave them sexier labels. Sociology we derided as *social factist*. Social behavior, in particular leadership, we derided as *social behaviorism*. Sensemaking and phenomenology we called *social definition*, in deference to Silverman and Weick's emerging viewpoints.

- **Social Factism** sociology caged 'mind' of the storyteller into factist frameworks, where survey was easy to apply, and ethnographic roots could be forgotten.
- **Social Behaviorism** imprisoned 'mind' by removing it from free interplay between stimulus and response, making it a black box that facilitated lab and survey studies, instead of behavioral observation in situations of 'real' life.
- **Social Definitionism** was a new candidate for paradigm of the year. Philosophically it's rooted in Husserl and Shutz's social phenomenology. We could sense it was migrating into organization studies. Weick's enactment sensemaking we saw as a way to 'Bring mind back in' to the two paradigms that had excommunicated them.

We just wanted parity. Our efforts to do more anthropological and phenomenological story study were opposed by leader-behaviorists, and sociologists doing lab and survey method. People in our department like Jerry Salancik, Greg Oldham, Michael Mock, Jean Bartuneck, Manuel London, David Whetton, and others were suspicious. We needed the *Social Definitionism Manifesto* to compete with the superpowers Social Factism and Social Behaviorism.

Of course you know the story. Fill in the blanks. The 'Bringing mind back in' paper was popular in its day, circulating in the underground, for those who did not buy into the two-by-two cage narrative of Burrell and Morgan (1979). The four-cell prison became widely popular on Broadway, while our three-cell narrative played in the underground, Off-Broadway. Now, social phenomenology, symbolic interactionism, discourse, and intertextual analysis of poststructuralism are no longer fledgling disciplines. Not containable in Social Definitionism of the Burrell and Morgan cells. Our cells and theirs are narrative constructions, to contain the 'mind' of living emergent story behind the seven bars.

Act II: Enter Latour!

I was awakened by Bruno Latour's 1993 performance at the plenary session of EGOS conference in Paris. He sat on the stage in a chair, violating the narrative expectations of the several hundred academics in the audience. One expectation is to stand behind the podium and narrate. Latour did more of a nightclub comedy act. There were further violations of narrative expectations of every academic discipline of organization study. I remember him saying that each social situation has its story. Now I know it also has its narrative control. More accurately, it's an implicit narrative script. We know intuitively by socialization how to improvise to fulfill our narrative roles in some emergent storytelling. It's not all that spontaneous. Latour explained the hermeneutics of pre-story (what I came to call antenarrative), with story emplotment, and the understanding it takes to interpret, retrospectively, narrative plot.

Latour said, in passing, it was his first presentation in Paris. Suddenly, Latour's performance was interrupted, never to resume. How ironic it was. An international conference invited him to speak, when no Paris University had ever done so. French professors leapt out of their seats, and began shouting and pointing, arguing in that way only the French know how to do. Some shouted agreement. Others were affronted. Such a discounting of a distinguished French academic in Paris was impossible, unthinkable. The moderator had to breakup the ruckus. I wrote about the incident in *Management Learning Journal* (Boje, 1994). I believe Latour was breaking out of a French academic narrative prison, breaking the bars to bring emergent story back in.

Act III: Enter Bakhtin!

I began keeping notebooks, conversing with Mikhail Bakhtin, several years ago. What Bakhtin (1973, 1981) calls *dialogized heteroglossia* is, for me, the 'mind' and 'life' of story that continues to be ignored in organization studies in general (with few exceptions), and in particular in system, strategy, leadership theory, as well as in narrative inquiry, and in general by organization empirical studies, as well as the practice of story consulting, which is more accurate to call 'narrative consulting' since story dialogicality or variety making is banished. Dialog is not the same as dialogism. In practice no dialogism is beyond what passes as 'dialog' consulting.

Act IV: Enter Stein!

It is just recently I read Gertrude Stein. Ever notice that when we escape narrative security, the ways of emergent story are very different, and quite telling? Stein (1935) first noticed this in leaving developmental narrative linearity and sequencing behind. She stayed in the moment of telling, before narrative retrospective or reflexivity sensemaking takes over. I began to recall my challenge from Pondy, the episodes in our department, the performance of Latour, and how I imagined Bakhtin and Stein performed.

Act V: Enter Benjamin!

Reading Walter Benjamin's (1936) classic piece, *The Storyteller* happened only this year. This amazing essay argues that ways of storytelling are dying, being replaced by information processing, BME ways of writing novels, and it's all due to changes in the regime of capitalism. Storytelling for Benjamin is a craft, one that grew up in the pre-capitalist world of people sitting around telling and listening to stories while they did their sewing, weaving, or seafaring crafts. When late modern capitalism imposed workers' silence and division of labor as ways to enhance performativity of production, the arena for workers practising the ancient arts and secrets of storytelling was destroyed. It is a wildly fantastic hypothesis. It roots orality skills in the ways of craftspeople telling stories, the ways journey-persons traveled from town to town carrying tales, the ways those who did not travel had deeply reflexive ways of listening and memories to recount a retrospective tale in great detail, all while not dropping a stitch. Like Ivan Illich (1993) and Walter Ong (1982), Walter Benjamin thought that orality storytelling was being corrupted by ways of textuality, ways that written narrative imposes a BME prison onto oral telling. In oral telling lie the secrets of polypi.

SECRETS OF POLYPI DIALOGISM

Polypi Dialogism comes from work I did on Wilda stories (Boje, 2005e, 2005f) an inquiry into the intertextuality of Bakhtin's four dialogisms (polyphonic, stylistic, chronotopic, and architectonic). As Bakhtin (1981: 156) tells it, 'regardless of whether they corroborate one another, mutually supplement one another, or, on the contrary contradict one another or have any other sort of dialogical relationship.' In the polypi manner of story, the dialogic plurality can degenerate into mere polyphony or stylistic plasticity, or polemic speech, or what Bakhtin (1981: 181) terms 'abstract allegoricalness' or 'dialogical disassociation' (1981: 186). As such, polypi is heteroglossic, the struggle of centripetal (story control) with centrifugal (counter-story amplification).

This produces the highest order of dialogism that Boulding imagined, which he called 'transcendental', a move that Pondy dared not make. Polypi resists the move of modernity to excommunicate what Boulding (1956) calls transcendental (relation of unknowable to knowable) from all social and physical science, as well as from all societal discourse. What else is the Enlightenment project, if not an excommunication of transcendental?

Oral storytelling, once upon a time, was not the same as written narrative retrospective or reflexive 'systematic-monological *Weitaschauung*' (Bakhtin, 1973: 64). The more centripetal 'centralizing tendencies in the life of language have ignored this dialogized heteroglossia' in the social sciences (Bakhtin, 1981: 273). For Bakhtin, 'the image of the idea' becomes dialogic to the preceding ways of sign-representation narratives (frame, machine, cell, plant, etc.), those '*foreign* ideas' (Bakhtin, 1973: 71) organizations are so fond of in system thinking. Image is not the same as sign, so popular in simple BME narratives. Dialogism is not the Hegelian, Marxian, or Mead dialectic of evolution and revolution teleology.

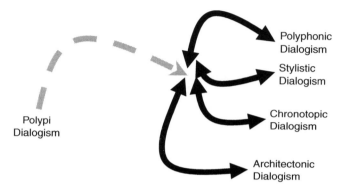

FIGURE 2.1   *Model of polypi systemicity complexity of dialogisms*

Polypi is my term for the dialogism of dialogisms. The word *Polypi* comes from Hans Christian Andersen's (1974) adult fairytale *The Little Mermaid* and is literally a colony of hydra, and for me a metaphor for understanding the interanimation of the four dialogisms (polyphonic, stylistic, chronotopic, and architectonic). Polypi, at the time of Andersen's writing, was thought to be both vegetative and animal. Polypi is a manner of story with 'jolly relativity' (Bakhtin, 1981: 102).

My purpose is to 'Bring story back in' to organization studies, all has been taken over by BME narrative prisons. Each narrative prison cell is an unique manner of emergent story control and discipline. I explore the polypi theory of dialogisms, polyphonic, stylistic, chronotopic, and architectonic, as the interplay of emergent story and narrative control. My contribution is to theorize five types of dialogism interplaying in the Storytelling Organization: polyphonic, stylistic, chronotopic, architectonic, and the polypi (dialogism of these dialogisms at more complex systemicity complexity than each individually). *Polypi dialogism* is defined as the dialogism of dialogisms of systemicity complexity (Boje, 2005 b, e, f). I develop each of the dialogisms in relation to the Storytelling Organization.

Polypi is a manner of story at an order of complexity above the separate dialogisms. In polypi there is dialogic interplay between official master narratives (sign-representation monologisms) and the more dialogic intercourse among respective dialogisms. Polypi, then, is a plurality of dialogisms, in struggle with modernity. The polypi manner of the story forces a Socratic interrogation of modernity. Its problematic questions of unknowable, unfinalizedness, unmergedness, indeterminacy of systemicity combine with the most problematic question of all the transcendental. At any moment the plurality of dialogic story can degenerate, be reduced to mere plasticity of individual dialogism or just narrative monophonic.

In Hans Christian Andersen's (1974) adult tale of *The Little Mermaid*, the transcendental question is raised, as the crude underworld of the sea comes into an encounter with the human world – the purgatory of sea-foam and the world of here-after. In my Wilda storytelling, I pick up on what I see as a further problematic, how late (post) modern capitalism tells stories of its own spirituality and religiosity. Wilda is my grandmother's name, and my sister and I believe she too was an enchantress, who lived in the wildness. In Andersen's tale, the enchantress is protected by the polypi (hydra colony), where she lives and works, selling her mystic potions for a dear price.

'Dialogism' is a term never used by Bakhtin (Holquist, 1990: 15). Bakhtin (1981) preferred the term 'dialogicality.' Here I use dialogism. Dialogism predates Derrida's (1978) *play of difference and differance* and *de-centered discourse*. Writing in the late 1930s Bakhtin (1981: 284) said, 'Discourse, lives as it were, on the boundary between its own control and another alien context.' Dialogism overcomes binary opposition of signifier/signified, text/context, self/other, etc., in order to look at Einsteinian relativity. In terms of emerging story, the implication is that each story is socially in motion, relative to sensemaking between bodies (physical, political, social, bodies of ideas, etc.), and to another way of telling (Holquist, 1990: 20–1). Each dialogism is a systemicity complexity property that is 'unfinalizedness [in] its open-endedness and indeterminacy' (Bakhtin, 1973: 43).

Bakhtin (1981: 139) says 'capitalism brings together people and ideas just as the 'pander' Socrates had once done on the market square of Athens.' To me, Wilda brings capitalism onto the market square, where an interrogation can take place. I intend an interrogation of the relation of multiple spiritualities and religiosities to the storytelling of capitalists and their enterprises; how the transcendental is brought into business. Globalization, for example, is quite the evangelical project.

Polypi is a manner of story that addresses the struggle of story control and more critical counter-story of transcendental business of business. The official utopia is opposed by counter-stories of transcendental fakery. The plurality of dialogisms becomes a struggle of the phantasmagoric interrogation on the public square (now just a market place), with the legitimating of business in transcendental storytelling. And 'life seen in a dream makes normal life seem strange' (Bakhtin, 1981: 122).

For example, McDonald's has a rich fantasy life, with grotesque characters (burger-headed sheriff, mayor, and child-burglar), and a clown, who in recent years, has an executive office, a seat on the board of directors, and is spokes-clown for the 'Go Active' nutrition and fitness global strategy. But also, this clown is a transcendental figure, contemporalized as a savior, as a Christ-like super-figure. And what is 'McDonaldland' if not the netherworld, capitalism descending into the underworld, then born again into the human world, with special powers. Polypi is a manner of story that invokes the holography of systemicity, with a special role for transcendental. As we shall explore in subsequent chapters, the polypi of dialogisms can be orchestrated quite strategically by storytelling organizations. Yet, our theory and empirical work lags behind what is common practice to so many storytelling organizations.

The polypi manner of story exceeds single dialogic context, subtext and intertext, to invoke transcendental dialogic angles. The polypi manner of story does not replace or nullify monogonic monologic narrative. Dialogized story is interactive with the linear manner of BME narrative. As we address more complexity the circle of discourse widens, and modernity comes into conflict with its banishment of transcendental discourse. Enlightenment seeks once again to exorcise transcendental from secular ways of telling capitalism. Wilda, the enchantress of the polypi, is a business women, willing to exact a dear price of suffering for a shot at immortality. The fantasy life of corporate storytelling organizations, here and there, does embrace the transcendental, and on the public square, now the market place, once again there is an interrogation about ultimate questions. Yet, in a moment, the polypi can self- deconstruct, into separate dialogisms, no longer an encounter of unknowable with knowable, this world, the underworld, and what's next. Polypi is emergent story complexity antecedent and interactive to transcendental and retrospective sensemaking.

Heteroglossia is defined as opposing language forces of centripetal (centralizing deviation-counteraction) and centrifugal (decentering variety-amplification). 'Polyphonic manner of the story' is only one of the dialogisms implicated in story's relation to narrative control (Bakhtin, 1981: 60). Emergent story is thoroughly 'dialogized,' 'heteroglossia' until narrative control sets in (Bakhtin, 1981: 14, 273).

Dialogism is not the same as dialog!

Dialogism is beyond the trope of people in the same (or virtual) room doing problem-solving dialog. Dialogism is beyond dialog of a focus group or the interview. Nor is dialogism some form of Habermasian rational consensus dialog. Dialog is multi-voiced elucidation, but each voice is not polyphonically fully-fledged, nor is there a polylogic collision of embodied viewpoints and logics. One form of dialogism, Socratic Dialog, died with Socrates. Managerialism positivity dialog is diametrically opposed to debate. Managerialist dialog is diametrically opposed to debate, dialectic, and all dialogisms.

Dialogism is not the same as dialectic!

Dialogism is not Hegelian or Kantian transcendental dialectic nor Mead's (1934) 'I–we dialectic' of I-self with internalized 'Others' (the We's).

One form of dialogism is polyphonic debate!

The contribution of polypi theory is to show emergent story is interactive with narrative control in dynamic complexity of five dialogisms. When emergent story is not multi-dialogic, it's being merely narrative. When multiple dialogisms are in play, the term 'emergent story' takes on its deepest complexity systemicity meaning. It interacts with control narratives, even in their least complex (frame, sign, monologic) variety. Dynamics of emergent story and narrative control sensemaking and variety making interplays in systemicity complexity. It highlights what is dialogic in systemicity complexity, leadership, change, and organization sociology, critical theory, poststructuralism, and postmodern disciplines.

Storytelling emergence is still under control of narrative expectations. Bakhtin's (1968, 1973, 1981, 1986, 1990) dialogisms, do not set story emergence free of narrative. This means a revolution in system theory.

Next, I want to point out how polypi of dialogisms fare in cybernetic-systemicity, leadership, and strategy.

THIRD CYBERNETIC REVOLUTION

Whole-system thinking is BME narrative until you get beyond the first and second cybernetic revolutions, and get into complexity properties that Boulding (1956) envisioned, and that Pondy (1976), and now in 2006, colleagues and I re-vision as the third Cybernetic Revolution (Boje, 2004b, forthcoming c; Boje and Al Arkoubi, 2005; Boje and Baskin, 2005). System narrative is monogonic, mono-voiced, mono-logical, and linear in its retrospective narrative sensemaking. It ignores more reflexivity ways of sensemaking we have discussed in the Introduction and Chapter 1. The ways of retro and reflexive narrative are dialogic to one another and with story emergence.

Third Cybernetics Revolution is defined as the substitution of polypi dialogism theory for the Shannon and Weaver (1949) information processing theory (sender-receiver-feedback loop) model that has been in vogue since von Bertalanffy's (1956) general system theory.

The first cybernetic revolution was mechanistic, cybernetics of deviation-counter-action; in Bakhtin's term it is centripetal forces of language, including retro-narrative.

The second cybernetic revolution was the open system (cell) narrative of deviation-amplification, known as Law of Requisite Variety, including variety making. It takes more variety in organization to process the variety in the environment. This is a simple sign theory of narrative that ignores image, or symbol, or intertextuality multi-story dialogical storytelling variety making of human social organization.

The third Cybernetic Revolution is underway, making whole system monologic singularity a dialogical whirlwind. There are no whole systems, only unfinished ones. In the Third Cybernetic Theory, the first dialogism is polyphony, the second is multi-stylistic, the third is multi-chronotopic, the fourth is architectonic, and the fifth is at the highest imagined order of complexity, the polypi dialogism of dialogisms. Yet, there is no need to order them hierarchically and fall into the death trap of system thinking. Narrative is too much about coherence. Incoherence plays with coherence, non-linearity animates linearity, multi-stylistic stimulates mono-stylistic telling, and the unknowable transcendence is interplay with the fantasy of whole system. Third Cybernetic is 'Bringing emergent story back in.' The first and second cybernetics are sign-based information processing models that in cumulative complexity theory interact with one another and emergent story. Emergent story dynamics plays with images, symbols, history in social organization, and transcendent reflexivity in free form, but is never free of narrative expectations.

BRINGING EMERGENT STORY BACK INTO LEADERSHIP!

Leadership is imprisoned in not only social behaviorism, but also a narrative prison that is blind to the role of the dialogic manner of story. Narratives in leadership are coherent, with heroic leader as beginning, middle, and end of all organization. The leader does oral narration, too busy to write (Mintzberg, 1973). Leaders take one stage, doing one monologue. Story theory says there are distributed stages in many rooms I have called *Tamara-land* theatrics (Boje, 1995). Leadership theory is fixated on narrative-wholeness, rather than the unmergedness, unfinalizedness interplay of the dialogic manner of story.

Transaction and transformation narrate leader behaviors, as part of a general framework typology (system thinking) along with traits, and situation. Framework is the first order master narrative that imprisons the leadership paradigm. It is a framework that has not changed remarkably since I was in graduate school in 1974–8. Frameworks lend themselves to survey/lab method. Recall, here-and-now, Latour's theatric performance at the Paris conference. His ways of storying broke narratively scripted expectations.

Leadership is dialogically imagined in Storytelling Organization Theory. Leadership is highly theatrical, involving orality, writing, and visual-gesture effects. Leadership is no longer ordinary modern theatre, with one room for all spectators, with actions of leaders acting on an elevated stage. Now leadership theatre has multiple stages in many rooms distributed globally, and a fragmenting of wandering audience choosing emergent storylines to investigate, while running from room to room, and stage-to-stage, unable to take in the 'whole' mystery of the fragmented narrated lines. Dramaturgically, leader is part co-author, beholder, character, and co-director in this *Postmodern Storytelling Organization* (Bakhtin, 1990).

BRINGING EMERGENT STORY BACK INTO STRATEGY

Strategy is the polypi of dialogisms. We will define each dialogism, and illustrate with strategy examples.

Polyphonic Dialogism

Polyphonic dialogism is defined as fully embodied plurality of multi-voicedness and unmerged consciousnesses, viewpoints or ideologies where none takes primary importance, not able to impose monovocal or monologic synthesis or consensus integration. Polyphonic dialogism theory assumes 'multivoicedness of an epoch' and is rendered in narrative history. Epic history is just a few voices in a '*systematic monological philosophical* finalizedness' (Bakhtin, 1973: 25–6, italics original). The monologic and monovocal consciousness is still dominant.

Yet, as theorized in Third Cybernetic, there is a heteroglossic collision of centripetal (centering deviation-counteraction first cybernetic) complexity properties with centrifugal (decentering deviation-amplification second cybernetic) ones. It's what Bakhtin (1973: 12) calls 'polyphonic dialogicality,' a 'complex unity of an Einstein universe.' The materials of emergent story and narrative control have deep socioeconomic roots in capitalism, in the writing of capitalism. Dostoevsky anti-causality, and anti-evolution is a 'deliberate and fully formed polyphony' (Bakhtin, 1973: 28), beyond the system thinking of von Bertalanffy/Boulding/Pondy.

> Every act of creation is bound by the laws of the material on which it operates as well as by its own laws. (Bakhtin, 1973: 53)
>
> The plurality of independent and unmerged voices and consciousness and the genuine polyphony of full-valued voices… plurality of equal consciousness and their world'. (Bakhtin, 1973: 4)
>
> His self-conscious lives on its unfinalizedness, its open-endedness, and indeterminancy. (Bakhtin, 1973: 43)
>
> The unmergedness in polyphonic dialogic complexity is of 'unmerged consciousness(es)'. (Bakhtin, 1973: 6)
>
> It is precisely on polyphony that the combination of several individual wills occurs and the bonds of an individual will are fundamentally exceeded'. (Bakhtin, 1973: 17)

In Dostoevsky's novels, Bakhtin (1973, 1981) implies in polyphony an equality of author's voice with any hero's voice, each equally valued in the dialogism. Keep in mind this is not saying that there is no power and domination. It's not an idealized equality of voices; there is hegemony here, as well as equality. 'Polyphonic manner of the story' (Bakhtin, 1973: 60) is beyond the four master narratives (framework, control, mechanistic, open) but not quite beyond organic narrative hegemony. 'The story is told … oriented in a new way to this new world' (Bakhtin, 1973: 5). There is in Dostoevsky novels a 'destruction of the organic unity of materials' but that narrative metaphorization is still in force (Bakhtin, 1973: 11). Story is no longer presented 'within one field of vision, but within several complete fields of visions of equal value… joined in a higher unity of a second order, the unity of the polyphonic' (Bakhtin, 1973: 12). Bakhtin's material conditions of narrative and story presages Derrida's (1978) preference for writing over orality; the difference is that Bakhtin treats the modes of telling (oral and writing) as dialogically implicated.

Polyphonic strategic dialogism implies the interplay of multiple logics, or polylogicality. It's not a monologic, as in SWOT (strengths, weaknesses, opportunities, threats). Strategic consensus (S1) is no longer a polyphony of fragmented narrative

(S2). The breakthrough in strategy narrative (Barry and Elmes, 1997) calls for polyphony of perspectives that remain in plurality. Some are more dominant than others. There is unmergedness and unfinalizedness of systemicity.

Strategy in multi-layered polypi dialogism is not restricted from relating to any other sensemaking registries. Polyphonic does achieve self-reflexivity beyond mere image-management.

The narrative cannon (or prison) of strategy still requires unity of coherence. Even beyond open system, at the organic 'narrative fabric' (Barry and Elmes, 1997: 11), there is also an antenarrative, in emergent story fabric, where the lucidity of narrative coherence is interwoven with antenarrative (pre-story and bet) incoherence. There's a strategic bet that antenarrative can be fossilized into narrative. Or become a polyphonic manner of story, a whirlwind force that is centrifugal, and therefore transformative to the organization. 'Narrative genre[s] are always enclosed in a solid unsinkable monological framework' (Bakhtin, 1973: 13). So too is emergent story enclosed, imprisoned. Antenarrative is replete with fits and starts, and an erratic form that is not yet narrative cohesion or story polyphony (Boje, 2001a). Antenarrative is a wandering unfinalizedness that violates the cannon of narrative-modernity ways of telling story.

Strategy is within a 'whirlwind movement of events' and distributed telling (Bakhtin, 1973: 11). In organic-imagined systemic complexity, narrative strategy unity of vision, mission, etc. is violated by antenarrative and polyphonic manner of heterogeneity of holographic interacting complexity properties. Polyphonic manner of story combines voices of systemicity complexity way beyond mere strategic homophony. Monophonic strategy narrative is too tightly causally sequenced. 'There is no causality in the Dostoevskian novel' and polemicized 'against the theory of environmental causality' (Bakhtin, 1973: 24).

Monogonic strategy is a reduction of the more polyphonic manner of emergent story and fragmented narrative into reductionist whole narrative, reducing multiple properties of complexity to the one.

The generativity of polyphony strategy is in collision with many complexity properties. Boulding (1956) and Pondy (1979) are trapped in the 'blueprint-growth' acorn-becomes-oak-tree metaphorization. They do not intuit or theorize polyphonic dialogisms. In polyphonic strategy it is debate, not dialogs of positivity (or consensus). Polyphony strategy explores the collision of systemicity consciousnesses.

Stylistic Dialogicality

Stylistic Dialogicality is defined as a plurality of multi-stylistic story and narrative modes of expression (orality, textuality and visuality of architectural and gesture expressivity). Multi-stylistics juxtapose and layer in an intertextual complexity manner that may or may not be polyphonic.

> A dialogically agitated and tension-filled environment of alien words, value judgments and accents [that] weaves in and out of complex interrelationships,

merge with some, recoils from others, intersects with yet a third group and all this may crucially shape discourse, and leave a trace in all its semantic layers, may complicate its expression and influence its entire stylistic profile. (Bakhtin, 1981: 276)

Stylistic modalities of Storytelling Organization construct dynamic image complexity. Image storytelling can be more than simple sign BME narrative vision, value, and mission adventure strategy. Stylistic dialogism does not succeed or displace polyphonic dialogism. Stylistic dialogism is dialogic among the polypi of dialogisms.

Holographic strategy is multi-voiced, multi-languaged, and polyphonically and now multi-stylistically dialogic. Holography moves the field of strategy beyond oral telling or analysis of text. Some styles are visual tellings without words. Stylistic strategy is all about image management in a variety of stylistic modes that are dialogic. There is a widening of the circle in a multiplicity of expressive modalities.

Strategic branding is the sign narrative control of image. Sign representation of environment in narrative is still part of interweave. Branding narrative unity is opposed by antenarrative and story polyphonic. Branding is an example of a reduction of stylistic dialogicality into a singular expressivity and faciality.

Strategy has the problem of contemproalization. What is styled must become restyled to retain contemporary enthusiasm in acts of re-contemporalization of established images. A 'finalized monological whole' stylistic is uni-modal. An anathema to ongoing renewing of a plurality of stylistics. The stylistic modes of story and narrative are accomplished in an assemblage of stylistic modes that are in 'constant renewal' (Bakhtin, 1973: 87).

Strategy balances centering and decentering forces of narrative and story. Heteroglossic forces of entering-centripetal and decentering-centrifugal historically shape and reshape stylistics. At each historical moment, stylistics 'brush up against thousands of living dialogic threads, woven by socio-ideological consciousness' (Bakhtin, 1981: 276). Emergence is never spontaneous.

Strategy theory locks away stylistic dialogism in a dungeon of monologic context, where 'multi-languagedness, has remained outside its field of vision' (Bakhtin, 1981: 274). The orientation of strategy theory is towards unity, a singular field of vision. It is the multi-stylistic verbal, written, and artistic genres that carry the decentralizing tendencies of heteroglossic dialogicity. Yet, in strategy practice, the stylistics are now exploding in variety (Cai, 2006).

There are five stylistic modes (Bakhtin 1981: 262): artistic, *skaz*, everyday writing, scientific writing, and official writing that I will illustrate in McDonald's strategic stylistics.

Artistic style   Includes the architecture that tells its own story, as well as artistic décor of French McDonald's restaurant choices called 'McStyle.' McDonald's even has a 'McStyle' website where customers and owners sort through some nine décor and architectural themes, selecting their preference. Any given city across the US, Europe, Asia, or Australia, may exhibit a variety of artistic styles in photos, sculpture, décor or architecture. Each style took shape in an historical moment (classical Americana Speedy drive-in of 1950s, nouveau modern drive-through of 2000s, etc.). These restaurant styles intersect with seasonal themes. There is something about French social aesthetics that demands such differentiated styles. The chronotope of Clown-Rogue-Fool (Ronald, Hamburglar, and Grimace) is expressed stylistically differently in Europe (except Netherlands) where a younger version of each occurs, as compared to the older characters in the US.

Skaz   taking a fragment of someone else's everyday speech, and re-narrating with another narrator's intention (e.g. a corporate one) through it (examples: 'I'm lovin' it,' or Nike's 'Just Do It!'). Skaz 'lives, as it were, on the boundary between its own context and another, alien context' (Bakhtin, 1981: 284). McDonald's is filled with alien, accented, a Tower of Babel of extra-artistic skaz, with 'Mc' words, such as McJob, McWork, McMeal, McFamily, McFun, etc. It's the McDonaldization of language. McJob, for example, for the corporation once meant the hiring of the physically or mentally challenged, who would work for less. McJob has become an alien word meaning from the point of view of the corporation. It was described as 'a low-pay, low-prestige, low-dignity, low bene-fit, no-future job in the service sector. Frequently considered a satisfying career choice by people who have never held one' (Coupland, 1991: 5). The term was redefined to mean dull, repetitive, low-pay, dead-end work, and became an entry into first the Meridian-Collegiate Dictionary, then the Oxford Dictionary, and many others. The corporation struggles to dominate the meaning put to 'Mc' words by culture jammers, living wage, animal rights, environmental, slow food, vegetarian, anti-sprawl, and other activist groups. In an open letter to Merriam-Webster's, former CEO Cantalupo said that 'more than 1,000 of the men and women who own and operate McDonald's restaurants today got their start by serving customers behind the counter'.[2]

Everyday writing   (For example, a letter, a diary, annual report, and so forth). There are storied bits from CEO letters to shareholders with references to dead CEO Ray Kroc in McDonald's websites and annual reports, and many references to Ronald, a simulacra virtual leader strategically constructed (Boje and Rhodes, 2005a, b). Kroc and Ronald speak to the shareholders, and employees, through the everyday writing by executives, and quotes of their folksy speech.

Scientific, non-artistic writing   (For example, a scientific statement, a chart of numbers from an account, an ethnographic description, or a philosophical treatise). For example, look on the tray-liners at McDonald's and the brochures available – they have scientific narrating of how nutritious, and fitness-conscious parents are who give their children fast food.

---

2 BBC News Online 2003 http://news.bbc.co.uk/2/hi/americas/3255883.stm

Official writing   (For example, Ronald McDonald, Grimace, Hamburglar, but also Bob Greene, Ray Kroc, or a new CEO). An official sign about do or don't do this or that on the wall is part of the telling. As is a pamphlet quoting what McDonald's official position is on this or that issue.

In sum, stylistic dialogicality is strategic interactivity of multiple modes of expression (oral, written, theatric, architectural, and so forth).

I situate stylistic strategy dialogism as a property of 'image' management. In organization's more managerialist attempts to control story, there is a strategic, centered (or centripetal), orchestration of multiple stylistic modes of expression. In more 'bottom up' governance, the stylistic multiplicity that consummates the firm's image is more a living story than a managerialist orchestration of public faciality or image.

Now consider the global challenge of orchestrating stylistic multiplicity, caging any pluralistic story and counter-story, into managerialist central administration of story to craft the image of the corporation around the world. The stylistic modes of McDonald's corporate, interact with more local traditions. The architecture itself, for example, varies from locality to locality, keeping the familiar 'M' emblazoned everywhere, accenting with 'Mc' skaz. In France for example, McStyle web page lists some 13 thematic choices of restaurant architecture and décor.[3] In a country with over 400 official cheeses, consumers are unwilling to limit their stylistic choice to the plastic styles of American McDonald's. We will explore the range of stylistic differences in the next part of the book, with a chapter on stylistic dialogic strategy. Here, I want to continue to list the types of dialogisms.

Chronotopic Dialogism Strategy

Chronotope is defined as the relativity of time and space. For Boulding it is complexity where symbols differentiate from signs and images. Chronotopicity is literary fusion of space and time. It's admix is temporalities and spatialities. The chronotopic manner of story is exhibited when idea images of past, present, and future mix with a diversity of spatial images narrated to become its own dialogism. Chronotope is 'vertex of dialogically intersecting consciousness' that also interacts with 'polyphonic' and other dialogisms (Bakhtin, 1973: 73–4).

There are ten ways Bakhtin (1973, 1981) conceptualized 'chronotope' defined as the relativity of time/space in the novel. The theory is the chronotopes are embodied in ways of writing, visualizing, and telling stories and narratives. I have sorted the types into my own categories (adventure, folkloric, and castle room). Chivalric is actually number five in Bakhtin's (1981) historical presentation of the first nine. The tenth (Bakhtin, 1973) is disputed, a mystery I choose to tackle.

---

3 Go to McDonald's France website, click 'Entrez', then 'Tout Sur McDo' menu, for 'McStyle' page; http://www.mcdonalds.fr/

Storytelling Organizations have inherited ten chronotopes. In contemporary organizations, the ten are dialogic to one another. Like Boulding, Bakhtin's properties are cumulative rather than independent or successive. In other words, the third chronotope would have properties of the proceeding ones.

The dialogic nature of chronotopes is a cutting edge research topic in strategy. In subsequent chapters I will assert that most strategy writing is about adventure chronotopes, leaving the folkloric (especially orality) ones untheorized. Meanwhile, as I will illustrate briefly, in practice, the folkloric ones are quite strategically realized. Complex strategy may exhibit combinations of ten chronotopic properties. For Bakhtin, they are hierarchically ordered. For me, they are not.

TABLE 2.1   *Ten chronotopes in dialogicality*

Adventure Chronotopes

1	Greek Romantic
2	Everyday
3	Chivalric
4	Biographic

Folkloric Chronotopes

5	Reversal of Historical Realism
6	Clown-Rogue-Fool
7	Rabelaisian Purge
8	Basis for Rabelisian
9	Idyllic
10	Castle Room

Greek Romantic Adventure   Abstract, formal system of space and adventure time; link to time and space in more mechanistic than organic ways. Time sped up to overcome spatial distance and conquer alien worlds. Adventure time in systemicity is a large space with diverse countries, but without ties to place or history. The strategic systemicity of McDonald's is well known. Its campaign to invade the world is well known. The telling of Ray Kroc's founding is a romantic adventure narrative of the franchise expansion. He succeeded the McDonald brothers, who invented the system of fast food Taylorism. Heroes in Greek Romantic adventures have Aristotlian 'energia.' Their dramatic persona does not change, traits are merely discovered; energia is consistent with Kroc's autobiography.

Everyday Adventure   Chronotopes are cumulative. This one mixes romantic adventure with everyday adventure. The hero's life is sheathed in context of the metamorphosis of human identity. The course of the hero's life corresponds to travel and wandering the world. McDonald's operates in global space of diverse countries, avoiding local historical ties when possible, adapting the menu when it must. This chronotope is about strategic emergence and adaptation of the grander narratives of McDonald's. There is a type of metamorphosis in the mythological cycle of crisis, so a person becomes other than what she or he was by chance and accident. McDonald's heroes wander the world, such as Charlie Bell, Jim Cantalupo's successor (after his fast-food heart attack). Suddenly CEO Charlie Bell fell ill, was replaced, and passed away. Both CEOs had health issues that are allegedly related to fast food diet. McDonald's everyday adventure story has been overcome by has a lot of suddenlys when you include the McLibel trial of Helen Steel and Dave Morris, the celebrated trial of José Bové in France, McFat children trials, and sudden McDeaths of CEOs Jim Cantalupo and Charlie Bell.[4] Since Cantalupo's heroic turn around of the company's failing stocks and sliding same store sales record, and the sudden entry of 'McJob' into many dictionaries, strategic narrative of McDonald's has had to adapt to everyday emergence.

Chivalric Adventure   Hyperbolization of time with other-worldly verticality (descent). This one mixes with previous chronotopes, in the testing of heroes' fidelity to love or faith in chivalric code. Sometimes its fairy tale motifs linked to identity and enchantment. This is the epitome of McDonaldland. A more mundane example is the chivalric creed of Quality, Service, Cleanliness, and Value code at McDonald's. Portraying one's corporation as chivalric (or ethical in its code) is a narrative strategy. Corporations like McDonald's have war rooms to track their narrated lines, to spin more favorable press, and hire many story consultants to run focus groups, author and direct story behaviors of the corporations.

(Auto) Biographical   The interrelation of hi-story biographical with lo-story untellables. Formally, biographical time in metamorphosis seeking true knowledge of the self. There are many conversion narratives of biographical time that dissolves into abstract time of ideal era. It's laying one's life bare, illuminating it on the public square in a theatre of self-glorification, a masked identity completely on the surface, an exteriority (energia and bios). Early biographies in ancient times had energia personalities, not the kind of personality that transforms in reply to growth experiences. Energia is Aristotle's more ideal time–space. The struggle is with the public square, where the non-hero, the invisible servant or slave may come forward and deconstruct the lionizing story told by (auto) biographers. McDonald's official (auto) biographies are plagued by counter-story biographers, who tell the other side of the story. See Kroc (1977) and Westman (1980) for official story biographies. There is

---

4 McLibel http://www.mcspotlight.org/case/

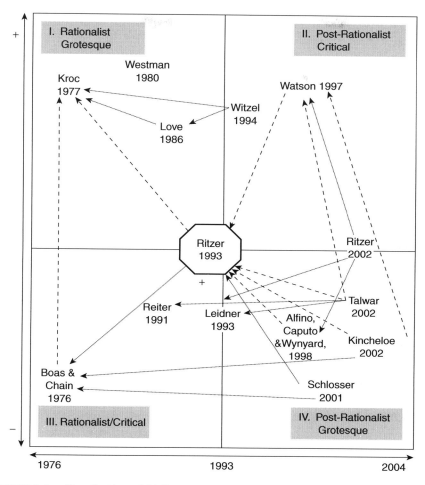

FIGURE 2.2   *Novelization of McDonald's (auto)biographies*

counter-story writing that began with Boas and Chain (1976), was repli-
cated by Schlosser (2001), and Ritzer's (2002) McDonaldization thesis
countered by Watson (1997), etc. Graphic that follows is part of Boje et al.
(2005a) work.

The more folkloric chronotopes are absent in traditional strategy writing, but
is very much a part of everyday practice. There's a website I maintain for illus-
trations and study guides on McDonald's dialogic strategy.[5]

Reversal of Historical Realism   Reversal of here-and-now time–space into a futuristic ephemeral temporality. An inversion to folkloric fullness of here-and-now reality, and material world (folkloric realism) becomes transformed by mythic thought into either epic past or ephemeral future (given more concreteness by the appropriation); the here-and-now of systems becomes exceeded by the historical inversion. Examples include the six McDonaldland videos produced by Klasky-Cuspo studios (makers of Rugrats, The Wild Thornberrys, and The Simpsons).[6] McDonaldland was strategy enacted by Ray Kroc to imitate his war buddy, Walt Disney's success with Disneyland; there is now an online version of McDonaldland.[7]

Clown-Rogue-Fool   Out of depths of folklore pre-class structure, three medieval masks emerged. Obviously at McDonald's this is Ronald McDonald, the clown, Hamburglar the rogue, and Grimace the fool. It's ironic that the world's number one fast food corporation has perfected Bakhtinian Clown-Rogue-Fool chronotope, and all its grotesque humor (Boje and Cai, 2005; Boje and Rhodes, 2005a, b).

Rabelaisian Purge   The purge begins with the suddenlys of a *Supersize Me* documentary or a McLibel or a José Bové trial. It continues when those servants and slaves begin to express counter-stories to the official corporate vernacular. And in this chrontope, the Rabelaisian Purge – grotesque humor that is used by the activists to poke fun at the McDonald's icons, and at their spiritualization, such as McSupper, and the McJob skaz controversy, already mentioned.[8]

Folkloric Basis for Rabelaisian   This is grotesque humor. Time is collective and part of productive growth, measured by labor events; generative time is pregnant time and concrete here-and-now, a time sunk deeply in the earth, profoundly spatial and concrete, implanted in earth and ripening in it (metamorphosis). For example, the slow food movement is focused on slow time to eat, on using organic foods, on avoiding the fast and furious. It's the antidote to McDonaldization by home cook festivalism, visiting the non-chain, local restaurants, where people take their time. McDonald's strategic move is to invoke grotesque humor of hybrid characters, such as Hamburglar, part burger-head and part boy. Their humor resets the culture jamming into a more romantic adventure chronotope. Animal

---

6 See http://www.klaskycsupo.com/data/questions.html

7 See McDonaldland in Wikipedia Encyclopedia http://en.wikipedia.org/wiki/McDonaldland

8 See McSupper image at http://peaceaware.com/McD or at http://xray.bmc.uu.se/cgi-bin/gerard/image_page.pl?image=dombo/pics/last_mcsupper.jpg

slaugher is countered with McFry Kids, and the McNuggets, as well as Birdie. Each is part animal or human and part fast food.

Idyllic   Idyllic is organic localism that fragments modernity's quest for global. Idyllic folkloric time is agricultural, craft and labor time. It's family organically grafted to time events and spatiality (place), living organically in familiar territory, in unity of place; rhythm of life linked to nature and cyclic repetition that is separated from progress myth; not a stage of development; a rebirth. Growing your own food, taking time to be rooted in a community, its non-fast food places. It would be a form of labor where workers own their tools, apply their trades, learn in apprenticeship. The previous chronotope is extended in the idyllic. McDonald's apes the idyllic by invoking a family trope in its McDonaldland stories, complete with McNugget aunts and uncles, McFry kids, a sort of gay marriage of Ronald the Father, and Grimace the Mother; parenting of sister and brother, Hamburglar and Birdie.

Castle Room   Bakhtin refers to time–space of trope of being in a Gothic 'Castle' or 'Salon' that affects the sense of temporality and spatiality in the story-ing going on there. 'Meeting' at McDonald's is its own type of chronotope.[9] This is 'a real-life chronotope of meeting constantly present in organizations of social and governmental life' (Bakhtin, 1981: 99). In such Gothic, as compared to more modern and postmodern meeting spots, there is a change in the discourse, in the atmosphere, in temporality and spatiality. A medieval castle, in novels, carries a premodern temporal resonance, of feudal oppression and irrationality (Bakhtin, 1981: 246 for castle; see pp. 97–8 for meeting as device).[10] In Lincoln there is a castle converted to a prison in the eighteenth century, where prisoners attended church, seated in an arrangement where they could see and be seen by the speaker at the podium, but could not see other prisoners. One could argue that various kinds of meeting places in modern corporations have an historic way of orienting our discourse, such as the Mahogany board room, a Playplace at McDonald's where plasticity of play is different from play in the forest, or meeting in a McDonald's without a Playplace is different from one with.

Architectonic Dialogism

Architectonic dialogism is defined as the interanimation of three societal dis-courses: cognitive, aesthetic, and ethic. Cognitive architectonic was invented by

---

9   The Everyday chronotope of meeting in travel adventure, is different from the tenth chronotope of meeting in salon or gothic castle that is more knitted into expectations about domination, plastic setting, etc. that loom over the kinds of conversation in tenth, as opposed to meeting in travel; the two chronotopes are dialogic to each other.

10 See www.literaturecompass.com/images/store/LICO/chapters/784.pdf and http://clcwebjournal.lib.purdue.edu/clcweb00-2/keunen00.html

Immanuel Kant (1781/1900: 466): 'By the term Architectonic I mean the art of constructing a system... Reason cannot permit our knowledge to remain in an unconnected and rhapsodistic state, but requires that the sum of our cognitions should constitute a system.' Bakhtin preferred the term 'consummation' to construction, and was careful to not assume a monophonic, monologic, or mono-languaged system (rather he preferred to look at the unmergedness, the unfinalizability of system, or what I defined above as systemicity). Bakhtin (in 1990) added ethical and aesthetic discourse to Kant's cognitive architectonic. Ethics here is not ethics of conceptions of beauty, but the very notion of answerability. Aesthetics is about how and for whom a given systemicity is consummated. There are no strategy studies or theories of architectonic strategy (exception, Boje et al., 2005).

I relate architectonic dialogism to what Boulding (1956) calls the 'social organization' and what Pondy (1979) terms 'multi-cephalous' (meaning multi-brained). As I reviewed in the last chapter, I prefer 'social organization'. It is complexity property at the societal level of discourse, as the storytelling organization is shaped by its role in a network of storytelling organizations.

Collective memory that is fragmented retro sensemaking supplants individual memory (Bakhtin, 1973: 24):

> They remember from their past only those things which have not ceased to be current for them and which continue to be expressed in the present, an unexpected sin or crime, an unforgiven insult.

Collective memory occurs in textuality, orality, and visuality. It's the topic of Chapter 3.

3
TYPES OF COLLECTIVE MEMORY IN STORYTELLING ORGANIZATIONS

Collective memory has not been adequately theorized, much less researched in story and narrative studies. Collective memory varies according to groups embedded in organizations and their environment. It is dynamic, under continual revision, selective forgetting, and extension to accommodate emergence. The chapter begins with an autoethnography example of emergent story types vying for collective memory change. This emergent story begins in improvisation, quickly takes other forms of emergence as secret gossip-emergence jumps official channels to become rumor, and takes the rare turn of an emergence that is reforged into the narrative form of legend and myth. It is this dynamic quality of emergence, its morphing into narrative form at differing paces in various groups spread across time and space that makes for dynamics of collective memory in storytelling organizations.

Collective memory that is fragmented retro sensemaking supplants individual memory (Bakhtin, 1973: 24):

> They remember from their past only those things which have not ceased to be current for them and which continue to be expressed in the present, an unexpected sin or crime, an unforgiven insult.

Emergence has less to do with the duration of the social process, than with its significance in dynamics of collective memory. At our symposium on deconstruction, in the 1995 Eastern Academy of Management Meetings held at Cornell University, something unusual happened. The night before, and leading up to this event, gossip about something 'unusual is about to happen' was confined to an inner circle of presenters and close friends. Rumor circulated until everyone at the Eastern Academy except Grace Ann knew something was about to happen. The room was packed. People were standing along the walls, and stuffed into the doorway. We presenters wore t-shirts with fragments of the word, '*de-con-struc-tion*' on them.' Deborah Summers wore '*de*' on her shirt. I of course was the '*con*.' Grace Ann was '*stru*.' Bob Dennehy wore '*tion*.'

Grace Ann remarked without appreciation of the irony, 'you all came here to learn about deconstruction?' In the middle of Grace Ann's '*stru*' presentation, Judi Neal pulled out her guitar, and began to play the wedding song. I invited Grace Ann to dance. When I proposed someone asked, 'is this real or deconstruction?'

Laughter erupted for the longest time. Some elements were pre-arranged such as the ring I hid in my pocket, the request for champagne, and the invitations to old friends. But, how to propose, that was strictly improvisational. Grace Ann paused, and was dead silent. She confided later, she did not know whether to joke or say 'yes.' She said 'yes.' Roaring applause filled the room. Gil Boyer, the session chair, passed around a tray of champagne. When the glasses were distributed, and the toast was made, he used the tray to take up a collection, netting $40.

We went from our session to the luncheon as the gossip of our engagement took another turn. People seated at the luncheon tables, most not at the session, began without prompt clinking glasses with forks and spoons. We kissed. The President of the Eastern Academy resumed his interrupted speech, remarking 'for the first time in the history of this Academy, two professors got engaged. Next year please come back. We will host your wedding reception!' More thunderous applause.

Email turned the emergent story into more rumor of the event. People not at the Eastern Academy sent us congratulatory messages. Grace Ann got a call from Professor Bill Torbert, who said, 'Congratulations! Your engagement has now passed from story to myth. People not even at the conference are telling other people, who told me, and I wasn't there either.' Events of such extraordinary proportion, so out of the ordinary, emblazon themselves on collective memory. But, what pray tell is emergence of story and what is collective memory? Let's begin by defining emergence and its various types, and turn then to collective memory. Table 3.1 summarizes the basic Storytelling Organization Model of collective memory and story emergence dynamics.

EMERGENT STORY PATTERNS AND COMPLEXITY

This is not one emerging story, but several types. My opening story of proposing to Grace Ann is not one emergent story, but many types of emergence, and many kinds of sensemaking, with a kind of collective deliberation. It is improvisation (E7), rebellion (E5), innovation (E6), that becomes gossip (E1) and Rumor (E2), before settling into retrospective BME (S5), and it's a kind of dialog interplay of antenarratives (S1) as well as Tamara (S2). *In short, sensemaking registries are holographic lenses, but embedded in collective deliberating, and contexts where emergent story patterns interplay.* What precisely is holographic complexity? Bakhtin (1981: 277, 1993: 60) does not use the word 'holographic,' but his trope imagines words as rays of light radiating uniqueness, 'passing through time' penetrated with 'the light of value' (1981: 60), in dialogic interplay of ray-light-words that are unrepeatable plays of colors, with 'facets' giving a sort of 'spectral dispersion' of the 'ray-word,' passing through alien ray-words on their way to social spaces in 'facets of the image' that 'sparkle' (1993: 277).

Most emergent stories lack what Malinowski (1954: 102) calls the 'cultural force' to enter the 'retrospective narrative pattern of moral values, sociological order, and magical belief' to become myth.

TABLE 3.1   *Storytelling organization collective memory dynamics*

Storytelling Sensemaking Complexity Thinking (Holographic)	*Collective Memory Types*	*Collective Deliberation Processes (4 ways interact)*	*Emergent Story Patterns*
S1 Antenarratives	CM1 Manageria (Horizontal and vertical lines to retrospective center point)	D1 Dialog – often Managerialist	E1 Gossip
S2 Tamara			E2 Rumor
S3 Horsesense		D2 Debate among fragments	E3 Fad
S4 Emotive–Ethical			E4 Propaganda
S5 BME Retro whole (myth, legend)	CM2 Punctual (Didactic silos, horizontal and diagonal, some feigning of multiplicity)	D3 Dialectic (I–We; sameness/difference identities)	E5 Rebellion
S6 Retro fragments Improvisation (some folktales)		D4 Dialogism- Polypi	E6 Innovation
			E7 Improvisation
S7 I–We Dialectic Reflexivity Unity (villain, hero, rogue, clown fool, martyr archetypes)	CM3 Multilineal (Transhistorical, break with horizontal or vertical points)		E8 Quasi Object
S8 Polypi Dialogic Transcendental	CM4 Polyphonic (Acts of anti-memory, mutations make points indiscernible)		

The columns of Table 3.1 are not meant to be independent. For example, Tamara can be context for system thinking, where various ways of deliberation occur in different rooms, and where emergent stories whirl in-between rooms. Antenarratives can carry emergent gossip, etc. The point is collective memory is comprised of all four areas.

The patterns, hierarchic or not, interplay in various modalities of collective deliberation (D1 to D4), sensemaking (S1 to S8), emergence (E1 to E8) and Collective Memory (CM1 to CM4, sorted out in the next section). This is what I mean by Storytelling Organization Collective Memory Dynamics. All eight sensemakings ways (S1 to S8) and emergent ways (E1 to E8) are co-present, and affect collective memory, in the embedded context of holographic systemicity complexity.

EMERGENT TYPES OF STORY[1]

E1 Gossip is defined as a type of emergent story, divulging personal information by 'those in the know' about others. Secrets are usually confined within a social group, or organization.

---

1 First five types of emergence come from Lang and Lang (1961).

E2 Rumor is defined as a type of emergent story that jumps the official or agreed channels of communication. Rumors come in subtypes: pipedreams (hopes), bogeys (fears), wedge-drivers (distrust among subgroups), and projective (illusory correlations). Rumors change as they are told and retold in serial repetition. Characterizations, more than basic facts, morph and sharpen slants in grapevine transmissions of speculation.

E3 Fad is defined as a type of emergent story, part of fashion and what stylistic image is in vogue. The ephemeral fad quickly fades away.

E4 Propaganda is defined as a type of emergent story, one that is premeditated, and planted to spread, and transform hero into fool, villain into victim, rogue into idol, victim into martyr, or any combinations of idol, clown, rogue, fool, hero, villain, or victim. Each transformation of character is a rallying point for opposition, dehumanization, and more hostile impulses. One dethrones another. Vilification by one group meets lionization of hero by another. Martyr is victim that willingly becomes scapegoat. Trumped up emergence lacks the quality of contagion. E4 propaganda is a kind of emergence that lacks authenticity and contagion, but may have institutional support. Enron is now the legend of villains and the myth of Enron-economics. Most folktales lack the *quality of entertainment value*, the coherence and embellishment, to keep dispersing. Enron folktales and jokes keep dispersing.

E5 Rebellion is defined as a type of emergent story characterization. Deviants from collective status quo stir up controversy, sometimes rebellion. Rebellion opposes dominant power by organizing the fringe of out-groups. Rebels become symbols of cleavage, and widespread unrest among subgroups. Rebels define and blur intergroup boundaries, define in-group and out-group. Social authorities tend to marginalize, co-opt rebels.

E6 Innovation is defined in managerial circles as a type of emergent story. It is what Schumpeter calls *creative destruction*. It's initially unorganized. What it's good for is unclear. New technologies, social organization, self-awareness, discourse, and sentiments are all innovation emergences. It's more about emergent idea and paradigm shifts than physical products.

E7 Improv is defined as a type of emergent story. Spontaneous theatrics works best (Boal, 1979, 1992, 1995; Stacey, 2006). Conjuring emergence in managerial consulting often lacks quality of authenticity for contagion, but has institutional support.

E8 Quasi object is defined as a type of collective emergent story. It's the focus of collective action. A quasi-object, says Steve Brown (1999) is an object that passes through a social group. For example, Enron's emergent stories were deception, the financial re-engineering of off-the-balance-sheet partnerships that circulated as 'quasi objects.' The 'L' in *LJM partnership* stands for Lea, as in Lea, Andrew Stuart Fastow's wife (also heiress to a Houston real estate fortune). 'J' and 'M' are the initials of their two children (Maier, 2002). Fastow has admitted that he pocketed $45 million from the off-balance-sheet partnerships he created, with names like LJM, Raptor and Chewco. Recent work on quasi-objects by Bruno Latour Michel Serres, and Pierre Lévy has significantly changed actor network theory.

Serres (1983, 1987) and Latour (1987, 1988a,b, 1996) show how quasi-objects mediate and transform personal and collective identity in network relations (Serres and Latour, 1995). The major concern in Lévy's writings (1995a, 1995b, 1997, 1998) is with the relations of community and personal 'cyberspace' virtual identity. Gossip and rumors of Enron's decline and the fictitiousness of LJM and other quasi objects, did not save people and institutions from financial ruin.

The result is holographic collective dynamics of systemicity complexity and deliberations that disrupt control (BME and fragmented) narratives already embedded in collective memory of Storytelling Organizations.[2]

EMERGENCE IN RELATION TO LEGEND, MYTH, AND FOLKTALE

Three kinds of retrospective sensemaking narrative forms need introducing – legend, myth and folktale. Emergence gets imprisoned sooner or later, if they survive for any duration, in one of them. Most fall under the retrospective BME sensemaking genre.

Legend is defined as a type of retro control narrative where an historic event testifies to the greatness of people and/or organization lineage. It rarely is crystallized or solidified during legend's lifetime. It can become retrospective BME, leaving its cyclic renditions behind. Its most common form is the founding story.

Myth is defined as a type of retrospective control narrative about heroic beings, arranged in coherent, also most offing in linear BME or cyclic, sequence. Present day life is justified by precedent that supplies a retrospective pattern of moral values, sociological order, and magical belief (adapted from Malinowski, 1954: 102). Myth stabilizes a character (rogue, clown, fool, villain, victim, hero, etc.) into idol. Idols personify the collective imagination at each instant. Unchallenged gossip, rumor or propaganda socially reify or crystallize into myth. While myth was supposed to be purged by the Enlightenment (the progress of rationality in science and technology), it seems to have more accurately been the dialectic of Enlightenment promising to vanquish myth, then reverting to myths of progress or emancipation at every turn (Bauer, 1999).

Folktale is defined as a narrative, which dissociates heroic, or spiritual value link to leadership, and is retold for entertainment value. It's more about the esteem of the performer than veracity or exactitude of content.

In modern times, linear BME rules over other ways of telling myth, legend, and folklore. Other orderings can happen, such as the ever popular hero's

---

2 I resist appropriating butterfly effect, bifurcation, power law, and other complexity properties worked out in mathematics and computer simulations. There is a difference between local/global complexity properties (Stacey, 1996; Mihata, 1997) and the phenomena of emergence. My approach is closer to what Hugo Letiche (2000) calls 'phenomenal complexity.'

journey myth, more a cycle than linear: getting the call, denying the call, heeding the call, meeting up with helpers, being bested by villains or monsters, then vanquishing them all, returning to village with the boon, then resuming the cycle all over again (as in Star Wars, Star Trek, Lord of the Rings, or the Matrix).

Most emergent stories do not survive long enough to become myth, legend, or folktale. Most are forgotten. Survivors become quickly translated into retro-BME-narrative expectation. Such as, should not the hero look for helpers after taking the call to adventure?

Emergence has less to do with the duration of the social process, than with its collective significance in collective memory. Emergence of the improv was in the moment, in the instant. Emergence of the gossip began spontaneously the evening before and continued to emerge the next day. In the opening example, rumors emerged from the session rapidly through the luncheon. From these emergences, the control narratives of legend, myth, and folktale took shape. More emergences of rumors took flight in the Internet, during and after the conference. Emergent stories, control narratives, and complexity systemicity interplay in collective memory dynamics.

My contribution here is to make the role of narrative sensemaking control, and story emergence explicitly in relation to ways of deliberation. The benefit is researchable phases to emergence: excitation, deliberation, and storytelling appropriation into collective memory.

Excitation phase   Once the excitement phase of story emergent spontaneity subsides, or before short-term memory becomes long-term, narrative control and coherence of style institutionalizes what does not disappear. This is where rules of textuality dominate ways of orality and visuality.

Deliberation phase   This kicks in rather quickly in combinations of D1 to D4 to set expectations on storytelling to have proper narrative ways. D1 in managerialism is dialogs of positivity, without D1 debate. D3 is dialectic processes. D4 is dialogism of organizational and societal discourse. Modes of deliberation (D1 to D4) nihilate story emergence, one-by-one or in combination. This is what I mean by Collective Memory imprisoning story emergence. Story emergence is impossible without considering the apprehension of a Past, as For-itself (Bauer, 1999: 169). As Sartre (1943/1956: 138) put it, 'Consequently it is impossible at any particular moment when we consider a For-itself, to apprehend it as not-yet-having a Past.'

COLLECTIVE MEMORY

Maurice Halbwachs' (1950/1980) *Collective Memory* is fascinating reading.[3] Maurice was a student of Bergson the phenomenologist and Durkheim the

3 I am grateful to David Tobey for recommending it to me.

sociologist. Maurice has some disagreements with his mentors, which are summarized in a fascinating introduction by Mary Douglas (always great).

Collective memory is defined to be like a tapestry of group's and some errant individuals' collective memories, interpenetrated by strands or threads of thoughts interwoven across the groups. The point is there are a multiplicity of them and several types.

Halbwachs is convinced that individual memory is intertwined with group memory. He does not anthropomorphize. He is asserting that when we have a remembrance we do so, 99 per cent of the time, with the thoughts, ideas, and feelings of various groups, of which we are a part.

> In particular, the individual memory, in order to corroborate and make precise even to cover the gaps in its remembrances, relies upon, relocates itself within, momentarily merges with, the collective memory. The collective memory, for its part, encompasses the individual memories while remaining distinct from them. (1950/1980: 51)

There are two kinds of stories (narratives) that intrigue Halbwachs. The first is a story that I can evoke as an easily accessible story. The second is harder for one to access. The first type is easier to recall because we can base it on the memory others in my group have of some past event. The second type of story is only available to oneself and only that person can know of it. Ironically, the story (type two) that is the most personal possession, is the most difficult to constitute.

The Storytelling Organization is a tapestry of multiple interacting, interpenetrating collective memories of members of various groups. Halbwachs in the first part of his book stays close to a typical retrospective sensemaking view of collective memory, how several groups a person is a part of, can socialize a person to collective memories. He then veers into a more space and time approach, one where groups of individuals imprint collective memory onto their spatiality and their ways of partitioning temporal sequences of activity. As he moves in the later direction, he moves further from Bergson, closer to Durkheim and Kant.

Storytellers possess a social competency of storytelling that Walter Benjamin (1936) believes to be dying. My own view is that storytellers lack the social bonds they once enjoyed in tribal or working artisan communities to tell and not only listen but decipher stories without today's need for elucidation and coherence.

Of particular interest to me is the antenarrative, the emergence of pre-story that is a bet of transformation of not only collective memory, but also reflexivity on what might be future possibilities. Those antenarratives of novelty–discovery give the socially competent storyteller (if there be any more of them) leverage to restory collective memory of times and places, inviting listeners to fill in content and scope of interpretation of past and future, all of it between the lines. It also occurs by demarcating the partitions of time differently than before as well as after emergence, to reap the advantages of novelty. That novelty can also be a great fear of catastrophe that will befall the collective, just as it did in the past, and proposes to do again, unless a drastic reorientation of currents of thoughts, feelings and ongoing behavior takes place.

Halbwachs' theory of collective memory has not been applied to narrative or story studies for several reasons. First, as a student of Bergson and Durkheim, his theory is a bridge between Bergson's sensemaking of individuals and Durkheim's social solidarity of social construction by groups. It therefore falls in between the scope of phenomenologist and social psychologist. Second, the theory has not been applied to narrative because Halbwachs is a Neo-Kantian. He seeks to place collective memory on the myriad of conceptions of time and space, instead of fixing them to some universality. It is therefore difficult for narrative theorists to assimilate time and space ways of storytelling that are not universal in their form with the requisite BME across individuals, and across groups or organizations. Third, Halbwachs is perhaps most difficult for narrative theorists to wrap their hands around because he has an unstated theory of complexity and emergence. Novelty, as I have suggested, emerges in various manifestations and is assimilated, or not, into revisions of collective memory of individuals, and the several groups of which they are a part. But, only partially, since we are not complete members of all aspects of groups in all spaces of action, nor rarely over their entire duration.

The stories of past events, according to narrative theory are fairly stable in collective memory, and so-called stronger cultures have more petrified stories to stabilize the culture. However Halbwachs' theory is more akin to Bakhtin, where stories and collective memory are more dialogic, answering questions of concern to several groups in a storytelling organization and its environment. Traces of antenarratives of novel emergence begin to suggest answers that require a restorying of collective memory, its retrospections of past as well as its future projections of storied strategy, and its a priori senses of temporality and spatiality (this later bit very Kantian).

Such restorying of past and future is not just a matter of consultants convening storytellers in a room and asking them to pass a talking stick (or microphone) until collective memory has been storied to meet novel challenges emerging in their environment. One has to ask more Bergsonian, Durkheimian, and Kantian questions about collective memory. To the Bergsonian, where are the more self-enclosed collective memories? For the Durkheimian, where are the pockets of organic solidarity? For the Kantian, what are the a priori conceptions of space and time?

Halbwachs' major contribution is in calling attention to the multiplicity of collective memories in a given storytelling organization. These are sustained and negotiated by groups of unequal power in organizations and society. Halbwachs favored theory metaphors are the tapestry, the relay race, and the sea current.

In the sea currents metaphor, collective memory is currents of thoughts, feelings, and images that crisscross the groups. In the relay race, a story is like a baton that in a relay race one group would handoff to the next, but here Halbwachs deviates from narrative theory. He asks how can such a story (baton) possibly be considered to be the same story, when it is so radically changed, context shifts, and shades of meaning substituted, one for another? The first two theory-metaphors for understanding collective memory, are probably more palatable to narrative theorists and folklorists determined that story remain constant, whole, and its BME intact through its trajectory across groups.

All three metaphors give us an image of collective memory as highly variegated across groups defined by age, gender, occupation, ethnicity, race, hierarchic level, education, socioeconomic class, etc. One metaphor that Halbwachs detests is assuming collective memory is like a book, where the pages are stories, and one only has to recall the story, as one would recall a page from a book. Such metaphor theory of collective memory is common among knowledge management, and too many textualists. Textualists, in particular, fixate on collective memory being a text, and stories being texts, recalled like some kind of hypertext in a computer memory. The problem with the book or computer metaphor, is collective memory is not an imprinting that is invariant, or hidden for all times in one's subconscious library of permanent texts or computer chips, all stored away neatly in the brain.

The implications for storytelling organizations of Halbwachs' (1950/1980: 124) theories of collective memory is akin to Derrida's difference, Bakhtin's heteroglossia, or my own Tamara (storytellers being chased room to room by fragmenting audience):

> The fact that people are not immersed, within a given time and space, in the same collective currents already permits one element of individual differentiation.

That is, in a given interval of lived group duration, each sensemaker is occupied with a dureé of represented time, meaning there is within and between groups a wide variation of differences of temporal partitioning and spatial imprinting.

Whereas Henri Bergson as well as William James 'picture the individual consciousness as isolated and sealed off within itself, Halbwachs (p. 125) stresses a more open system, with contact of groups with their environment, and that means with 'continuous currents, so many waves pushing after one another' one has to try very hard to be isolated.

In terms of complexity theory, Halbwachs contributes the idea that collective memories are in flux, that flow of thoughts, feelings, and images cuts across 'numerous branchings off, as it were' (p. 125).

Finally, he reminds us, as does Kant, that there is more than retrospective sensemaking going on: 'of course, thought is still active in [collective] memory, shifting and moving about' (p. 125).

Time and Collective Memory

Conceptions of time vary within and between organizations, and are intertwined with collective memory. Societies mark their calendars by 12 months, and 12 hours, because of the spiritual meaning of that number, and mark AD and BC as well. A military has a 24-hour clock, and the key before and after, is date of enlistment, tours of duty, etc. A university marks time by dates of enrollment, exams, class times, and graduations for students, and dates of tenure and promotion for faculty. But a legislature funding state university marks time by when its members run for election, the convening of sessions, the dates of votes on bills, etc. A sweatshop is run on quota and as any Marxist knows, its all about stretching time, stretching the working day by haggling on meal time, break time, and making people stay until their quota is accomplished. These ways of marking the demarcation and duration of time become embedded in the collective memory of storytelling organizations, and can vary by groups within them.

Space and Collective Memory

Besides orality and textuality, the way we organize our décor, arrange our furnishings, even the design of space in a building tells a story, and imprints collective memory. There is an arrangement and choice of books in any faculty's office that tells as much of a story of their exposure and reverence for streams of thought as do the photo and paintings and knick knacks they cherish. There is a spatially 'physical coherence of place and person' (p. 129). Bill Wolfe, when visiting my office at UCLA, said he could tell I did not fit in, I was not part of the institution. He was right of course, but I could not, at the time, discern how he figured it out.

The story is imprinted on space, in the surroundings. It's this story that tells of a way of life. This imprinting of space gives a group a sense of its continuity (p. 130). Years of routine uses of buildings constitute a spatial framework that tells a collective story. Does the building change radically from one year to the next, with a shuffling of office occupants? Maybe it hardly changes at all. Maybe there are renovations, allocations of more space to certain groups, the downsizing of space for other groups. It's these changes in space utilization that demarcate a before and after, either expansion or downsizing, or remaining just the same.

The story is also adapting to the space. The space is also adapting to the story, the strategic story of which groups get what resources. The story, however, can get to be so fragmented, so full of emergence of innovative projects, assigned monotonous ones, or accidental ones, it is difficult to read any coherent story.

The external milieus can invade organizational spaces, and often do, 'ermeating every element of its consciousness, moderating and governing its evolution' (p. 130). At Loyola Marymount the new business building had to have windows in the door, to get the insurance for faculty harassment of children, and you could not cover them over with posters. Any administrator is supposed to stroll the hall looking for faculty touching any student, by spying in the little window. The designs the building are often for surveillance of its faculty by administrators.

Spatial images tell us heaps about the equality or the hierarchy: the corner office, the number of secretary cubicles in an outer office, the size of an office, whether it has a window. Often new faculty and staff are assigned to smallest offices, or to cubicles, and must wait for a location near a window. I waited four years, in an office without a window.

Thereby every place of the group can be translated into spatial terms, and its residence is but the juncture of all these terms. (Halbwachs, 1950/1980: 130)

What stories spaces tell!

The dean's office where I work has huge paintings of the line of successive deans, all white males. Visualization of space is the group's imprint onto collective memory. Storytellers, by their architecture and décor, bring awareness to demarcations of the past, and point out the implications of duration on spatial appropriations or downsizings to a group's line of continuity. The current dean has lots of cushioned chairs and fancy tables in a carpeted lobby of the college, inviting students to sit and chat, or to study.

Story is also imprinted by economic spatial memory of habituated transactions, how space is allocated to what kinds of transactions, for how long. An economic boon, or downturn, can imprint its remembrance on spatial occupation, on vacant spaces, or overcrowded spaces. Collective memory records transactions in spatial terms, just as it does in textual terms and oral manner of economic memory.

The loss of space can lead to protest, resistance by members to allocations. In our hallways, at my university, there are wastebaskets, piles of papers, discarded books, the occasional broken or otherwise unwanted piece of office furniture. You have to walk a gauntlet of trash. What's the story? The university gave its VPs pay upgrades, and was rather miffed the working slobs formed a union, so they 'sanded' (the in word for downsizing) the janitors, and now faculty take out their own trash and put it in the office, so far fewer janitors, can toss it in a cart.

We have just had a disagreement over economic collective memory, the one by the administration and the one by our department not agreeing. Our production of credit hours was up each year, but to the administration, by their way of calculation, it was down year after year, so they 'sanded' two open positions. Turns out the university MIS software can only award credit hours for team-taught courses to one department, and it wasn't ours getting the boost. The formula used by the President and upper administrators was flawed. We offered corrections that were ignored. Now we have to create a new story of performativity (input to output ratio) that will be in line with the administration's need to develop this year's niche that is in line with the priorities of the State legislature, which change from session to session. Our need to restory, to develop a new story is paramount. And it's happening more rapidly than ever before. Of course, this is from the view of the collective memory of my department, and is at odds with collective memory of the administration, where the flawed formula was just a guideline, and positions had to be sanded or reallocated to growing departments, so that's that.

Medium of Collective Memory

Collective memory is created out of orality (speeches, conversation, and chatter), textuality (files, reports, web pages, and accounting), and visuality (photos, décor, architecture, and gestures). Derrida argues that writing is not a supplement to orality. He does not support the privileging of orality over textuality. He concludes, 'Writing has no effect on memory' (Derrida, 1991: 136). I disagree. The way a formula of allocation is written has a major impact on the allocation of budget, faculty lines, office, and classroom space. Especially in formal organizations orality is subordinated to textuality, to writing everything into files, to collecting work knowledge for downsizing ends, to getting sign-offs for anything textual.

Ethics is at stake in what passes for collective memory. Knowledge re-engineering and knowledge managing raises ethical and moral dilemmas. Why? Because stories have rights that are tied to localized collective memory. Can one entrust their story, collective memory, to be reduced, fragmented, indexed, for retrieval, put to who knows what use? Re-engineers, for example, plumb the depths of collective oral memory to acquire property called 'tacit knowledge,' to mine it and capture it, so it can be transferred to organizationally owned computer databases. At issue is the state of individual and group story rights, over what is passed from ear to ear, and becomes appropriation in the knowledge writing. 'Story rights' has a tradition of answerability ethics, faithfully reciting history by permission of the community, being steward. Writing, especially computer writing repeats without knowing orality or visuality creation, without sensitivity to story rights.

Storytelling in orality is living discourse. Textuality, even intertextuality, is a crypt, not an exercise of living memory, just mechanical memory in the book, computer, or worldwide web. With the rise of information by machine, storytelling competencies, skills in faithfully recounting, story rights competencies, have died off (Stein, 1935; Benjamin, 1936; Ong, 1982; Illich, 1993). Writing allows the 'surveillance of knowledge' [work] and 'forgetfulness in the soul' (Derrida, 1991: 132). The internet is limitless memory, but living memory of oral storytellers is finite. Ironically, the internet, while limitless, dulls living memory, our ability to recall without the machine.

Researchers have yet to study collective memory in relation to textuality, orality, and visuality, much less the types of collective memory that follows.

TYPES OF COLLECTIVE MEMORY

While Halbwachs is certainly to be celebrated and credited for conceiving a theory of collective memory that is more than mere sensory representation, he did not elucidate types of collective memory. For that we turn to work by Gillies Deleuze and Felix Guattari and some critical theory.

- CM1 Managerial (Horizontal and vertical lines to retrospective center point)
- CM2 Punctual (Didactic silos, horizontal and diagonal, some feigning of multiplicity)
- CM3 Multilineal (Transhistorical, break with horizontal or vertical points)
- CM4 Polyphonic (Acts of anti-memory, mutations make points indiscernible)

CM1 Managerial Collective Memory

This is the erection of horizontal and vertical narrative lines of retrospection to one or more center points. CM1 is a 'General Linear Reality (GLR) model of the processes of social reality; where 'social world consists of fixed entities' (Abbott, 1988: 170). The example demonstrates, I hope, that collective memory does not proceed by linear development. In the opening rendition of the engagement to Grace Ann, it is clear that the emergent story keeps morphing in a very short time horizon. Collective memory does its processing non-linearly, then as an after-thought it is rendered linear. Eventually all the antenarrative sway and swag becomes reduced to something that never was.

BME narrative models, for example, do not attend to story location in space and time (its context) or to its historical passage points (its sequence or trajectory). BME sensemaking theories of story assume stories tap memory with 'stable' common cultural meaning. BME historical narratives assume wholeness, with fixed attributes of finalized meaning. But this is indeed a plundering, a rejection of emergence and genealogy. Managerialist story always embraces the chimeras of origin and ending.

Tamara sensemaking, by contrast, assumes story location in space–time context, and sequence of story trajectory, as well as how the sequence of stories each person experiences affects the meaning ascribed in the present. Genealogy is defined as traces of the emergences, accidents, deviations, and reversals and false appraisals (Foucault, 1977b: 146; Bauer, 1999; Nietzsche, 1956). The BME story model, by contrast, goes against event-based stories, such as antenarratives, in which the attributes and social meaning changes with trajectory (lines of flight). In short, CM1 posits collective memory as a GLR model in which BME retrospection narratives win the day.

Managerialist storytelling organizations try to possess collective memory by the linear-positional, hierarchically anchoring of narratives to one or more center points. Collective memory becomes a matter of re-representation and re-production of a present in fictionalized retrospection.

Deleuze and Guattari (1987: 15) argue that 'accounting and bureaucracy proceed by tracing: they begin to burgeon nonetheless, throwing out rhizome stems, as in a Kafka novel.' Centralized, organized memories can become a rhizome (defined as stem roots that penetrate a lawn or envelope a tree trunk, rupturing in discontinuity and multiplicity). Short-term memory is mostly rhizomatic, full of forgetting, emerging in the instant while 'long-term memory is arborescent and centralized (imprint, engram, tracing, or photograph)' inscribing long-term concepts like race, society or civilization (ibid, p. 16). Arborescent refers to a tree-hierarchy of trunk, branches, and sub-branches (Henri Fayol's image of organic organization). In tree-organization, the 'individual has only one active neighbor, his or her hierarchical superior… the channels of transmission are preestablished' (ibid, 16). Managerialist collective memory is a centered logic of processing, in the 'phallus-tree' (ibid, 17). It is perspective discrimination in manager-standard accounts.

Applying Derrida, collective memory goes through spacing and temporalization we might call *différance*. Différance is for Derrida (1991: 71) a double meaning: *spacing* (discernability, distinction, separation, and diastema) and a *temporalization* (detour, relay and reserve). Collective memory becomes the image orchestration (see stylistic strategy chapter) in acts Derrida terms effacement and selective recall (Derrida, 1991: 14–15). In managerialist collective memory the storytelling goes through spacing and temporalization points that constitute lines of retrospective sense-imposing (story control, not just sensemaking). This can create discord of differences between official and other stories of events (Boje, 1995).

Tracing the breach that occurs in filtering the experience of others into the managerialist experience traces circuits of power (Clegg, 1989). Managerialist collective memory, despite all the financial and accounting systems, the annual reporting to investors, can be quite imaginative re-presentations of history, a fictitious image, for example of environment commitment record that is plain greenwashing. On every storytelling interaction of managerialist collective memory, managerialist logos wins, all others lose. It is easy to concoct an ideality or idolatry of former CEOs. Despite the re-presentation of sensory empiric perception, the differences re-produce a drift into fiction. Under the guise of image management, a past is created that never was.

All eight registries of sensemaking can take place in managerialist reconstruction of collective memory. Of these the favorite is retrospective BME. The difference between official BME collective memory and fragmentation sensemaking is on only the différance of the detour, or setting out a relay or reserve schema. In I–we dialectic, the I and We are both managerialist logos. Any antenarratives are run point-to-point, and are quickly captured and converted to BME rehistorization. For Weickians, to retrospect is to travel back by simple BME sensemaking. BME is easy prey for managerialism.

Managerialist collective memory is what Derrida (1991: 42) might call an 'undermining of an ontology' that accomplishes its feat by the trace of BME. Managerialist BME authoritarian consciousness strives toward reduction trace, subordinating and usurping memory to one logic.

Managerialist collective memory is a restricted economy of sense-imposing, a différance that can make profit out of memory displacement. It suppresses horizontal and diagonal communicative interaction, captures memory into center point. Managerialists live in their own world of collective memory. Dissipating the mirage requires moving to some other collective memory. If we can get beyond managerialist story and memory control, then what John Berger says could come true: 'never again will a single story be told as though it's the only one' (quoted in Roy, 1997). There is a second version of managerialist collective memory: punctual.

CM2 Punctual Collective Memory

Managerialist collective memory can become punctual. Punctual means having a point in space, and its second meaning, acting or arriving promptly at an appointed time. Deleuze and Guattari (1987: 294) define it this way:

Memory has a punctual organization because every present refers simultaneously to the horizontal line of the *flow* of time (kinematics), which goes from an old present to the actual present, and the vertical line of the *order* of time (stratigraphy), which goes from the present to the past, or to the representation of the old present.

CM2 has vertical didactic silos to one or more centers, as well as horizontal and diagonal communicative interactions. By itself, for example, Norwest Bank (without the shroud of Wells Fargo, after 1998; see next type) operates silos from its center point at corporate headquarters, to the thousands of branches, with firewalls at the local and corporate level in-between checking/saving, home mortgage, business banking, investment banking, etc. There can be some feigning of multiplicity.

Transversal (diagonal) antenarratives coexist with BME sensemaking narratives. However, BME narratives ignore story change, whereas antenarratives are all about amalgamation with context, picking up and shedding meaning, during transversal. The basic problem antenarrative poses to managerialist collective memory and to BME narratives in general, is one of appearance/ disappearance of attributes of meaning, as story traverses context.

Restorying (White and Epston, 1996) is movement from dominant memory to some newly constructed memory. Of course, a punctual collective memory can be restoried into another official option in acts of subjugation, superimposition, and selective attention (forgetting). Restorying retraces the relationship between dominant story and marginalized counterstories and what Foucault (1977b: 160) calls 'counter-memory.' Counter-memory is parodic masquerade, dissociation of identity, and sacrifice of the subject of knowledge for a will to knowledge (ibid, 160–4).

In CM2, antenarrative is not just vertical-to-vertical or horizontal-to-horizontal along pre-established channels. Players are liberated in diagonal lines of flight. This introduces dynamics of collective memory, not as present in managerialism gigantic hierarchic-centered-tree-memory. There is rather a multiplicity of interactive lines of becoming. These forms of antenarratives do not have beginning or end, and instead emerge in lines of emergence, becoming middles (but not some average of middles). The middles are in absolute movement taking lines of flight that are not point-to-point, and are 'perpendicular' (Deleuze and Guattari, 1987: 293). Punctual collective memory becomes opposed to single-center-point collective memory. Antenarrative lines free themselves from points.

'Memories always have a reterritorialization function' (ibid, 294). This is as true for managerialist as other types of collective memory. BME and diagonal antenarratives may coexist on respective lines of reterritorialization. A given form of collective memory could as well become multilineal or polyphonic, or revert to managerialist center point.

CM3 Multilineal Collective Memory

CM3 a multilineal collective memory is transhistorical, and breaks with horizontal or vertical points. In 1996 Richard M. Kovacevich became CEO of

Norwest (charted in Minneapolis, MN), and began installing his 'store concept.' This is a significant language change: 'banks' become 'stores,' 'bankers' become 'store-managers.' The multilineal collective memory became realized in 1998 when Norwest acquired Wells Fargo bank's (chartered Sioux Falls, SD) 150 year history, and its stage coach logo, the tenth most recognizable corporate logo in the world.

In store concepts what's important is the 'cross-sell ratio.' In the US, the average consumer has 16 financial products across 8 institutions (its checking and saving in one, it's mortgage in another, its financial investments in another, its business banking elsewhere, etc).[4] Whereas the average cross-sell ratio for competitors is two products in the same 'store,' at Norwest/Wells Fargo it is at 4.6 (among highest in the industry) and their aim is 8. Norwest (store) and Wells Fargo (stagecoach) afford a composite or multilineal collective memory. What to do with the new 'bank' locations that Norwest/Wells Fargo acquire? During merger/acquisition mania, the composite memory of Norwest/Wells Fargo has absorbed some 2,000 independent banks.

In New Mexico, for example, in 1993 Norwest acquired First United Bank Group Inc. of Albuquerque New Mexico for $490 million. First National Bank of Don Ana, which was only recently acquired by First Security of Utah, became the combined purchase by Norwest/Wells Fargo to expand into Southern New Mexico.[5] Similarly United New Mexico bank was acquired by Norwest.

In 1998 Norwest's acquisition of Wells Fargo and conversion to 'Wells Fargo Logo', meant installing that multilineal memory onto all the recent and subsequent acquisitions. The collective memories of the acquired bank chains were purged, in order to install the Norwest 'store concept' and the Wells Fargo collective memory of the history of Wells Fargo in New Mexico. The composite Norwest/Wells Fargo collective memory was, as they put it 'flipped' onto subsequently acquired bank chains. People committed the Norwest/Wells Fargo language and memory to their identity, or were let go. In the various chain of 2,000 acquisitions, banks (stores) we studied had an 85% employee attrition rate.

What is ironic is in New Mexico and other western states, the Wells Fargo Stagecoach Empire was short lived. Henry Wells and William G. Fargo founded the enterprise that would become in 1850 the American Express Company. 18 March 1852 Wells Fargo and Company became a joint stock association to provide express and banking services to California, which was not regulated, and wide open. 'Anyone with a wagon and team of horses could open an express company and all it took to open a bank was a safe and a room to keep it in. Because of its late entry into the California market, Wells Fargo faced well established competition in both fields' (Wikipedia, ibid). In 1860 Pony Express was in deep financial trouble. From 1855 to 1865, came the glorious history of Wells Fargo, with its participation in Pony Express and overland stage routes

---

4 Wikipedia, accessed 16 Dec 2006 http://en.wikipedia.org/wiki/Wells_Fargo
5 Linda Mustachio Adorisio and I have been interviewing New Mexico banks tracing the history of mergers and collective memory transformations.

(taking over Overland Mail Company). In 1866 Wells Fargo consolidated under its logo and ownership operations of a mail route from Missouri River to the Pacific Ocean, dominating stagecoach lines in Western states (Wikipedia, ibid). With the 1998 Norwest/Wells Fargo collective memory multilineal composite, storytelling and image management became story-selling the stagecoach glory decade (1855–1865) as totality of Norwest/Wells Fargo history extended to the over 6,000 store locations. As of September 2005, Norwest/Wells Fargo has 6,250 locations it calls 'stores,' with 153,000 (store) employees, and 23 million (store) customers.

There is a problem here, in that, through its trajectory, antenarrative can change its attributes of meaning so much, that it is hardly fair to call it the same antenarrative. This seems to me to be a flaw or limit of the sequence based modeling of storytelling and social reality. Network models focus on flow, when they are longitudinal. Acts of counter-memory, mutations make points indiscernible. Still this duo, multilineal collective memory, is far from being polyphonic.

CM4 Polyphonic Collective Memory

Polyphonic collective memory does not operate in GLR (General Linear Reality), does not produce as much counter-memory, at least not in the moment of Being, the encounter of fully embodied beings. With Bakhtin (1973, 1981, 1991, 1993) we find an assumption that Abbott's GLR model does not address. That is, a story-based model of the dialogic social world, in which story is unfinished, the attributes are unmerged, and the act is in the moment of Being where sequential and network interpenetrate in acts of participation. Antenarrative, in the interpenetrated sequential and network models of reality, becomes a fluctuating entity that is intimately tied up to context and event-sequence. Antenarrative in polyphonic collective memory is not restricted to point-to-point transversal, to center-point revisionism, or duo-center point translation and reductionism, as in prior types. There is not the parodied, dissociated identity, or sacrificial subject (what Foucault calls counter-memory). The point of polyphonic collective memory is anti-memory. Instead of a collective memory detaching itself from context, polyphonic savors contextual ties. The storytelling keeps reterritorializing by not imitating or masquerading. The lines of polyphonic flight are towards context, antenarratives becoming context.

In sum managerialist collective memory relies almost exclusively on BME retro narrative, and assumes these narrative entities to be more coherent and monotonic in meaning over the course of point-to-point communicative connections to center-point memory. Antenarratives in this type of collective memory are very restricted. In BME there is insistence that a given story have one and only one meaning, and characters are expected to remain in their narrative persona. BME assumed whole fixed story entities, with sometimes variable (missing) attributes. Antenarratives assume stories merge, divide, move, appear, and disappear.

There is a difference in doing story network study at one time frame, versus doing story network study over time. In looking at combination of (Tamara) sequencing (from room to room) and networking (over time between audiences and tellers) it is possible to get away from linear transformations of GLR in more managerialist collective memory models. It would require getting away, as well, from assuming stories are fixed entities, with variable attribute manifestation (ie. terse told or full told stories assuming there is one full entity story to be told or that is understood by some participants).

In the antenarrative of Tamara storytelling studies (Boje, 1995), or multilineal collective memory, characters or agents change so much during the chase of antenarratives between rooms or locations of an organization, that it seems unfair to claim they are the same character.

In the case of polyphonic collective memory, recognition of the multiple meanings of story (as in Tamara's two people in same room having different meaning) is an example of Abbott's 'multivocality problem' (Abbott, 1988: 176). However, the difference with multilineal is that the antenarratives do not radically change the identity of characters, who are expected in Bakhtinian polyphonic theory to be fully embodied dialogic storytellers.

In general, my approach to collective memory and antenarrative is that meaning depends on context, and on situated performance of storytellers. This is why I prefer *in situ* study of story, either in simulation or in fieldwork, rather than semi-structured interviews. Interview, in most cases, is a rather contrived situation (but can yield results, when done phenomenologically, with repeated visits, rather than one-shot methods).

COLLECTIVE MEMORY DYNAMICS

Collective memory dynamics are defined as a multiplicity of valuative standpoints on past, present, and future, and are permeated with three kinds of memory: cognitive, aesthetic, and emotive-volitional (see sections that follow). Collective memory may be defined as the variegated, fragmented, discontinuous organizational processes for transforming and appropriating emergent story types into control narratives through modes of deliberation. As an adaptive process, emergent stories that survive excitation and deliberation may modify embedded, longstanding narrative and sensemaking registries (S1 to S8).

Retrospective BME whole sensemaking is most consonant with (D1) dialogs of positivity, and easy prey to managerialism. Emergent stories have the opportunity to restory legendary and archetypal mythic heroes and villains, and defining events in previously narrated history. Villain, hero, rogue, clown fool, martyr archetypes are set into play in S5 (BME) and oftentimes in what passes for D1 (dialog).

Retro fragments of sensemaking are most often contiguous with D2 debate, as a means of controlling subgroup rivalry and power. In some organizations D2 debate is according to rules and processes, long established. Archetypes here are around rivalry, transforming another groups' hero into fool. D2 is the interplay of in-group and out-group, as one groups' hero is made the villain, fool, clown, or rogue. Reflexivity fragments sensemaking is a level of complexity, already interactive in terms of polyphonic processes. While system thinking assumes hierarchy among complexity properties, in organizations, any holographic combination is possible.

I–we (or transcendental) reflexivity sensemaking is some sort of D3 dialectic, such as Kantian transcendental logic or Mead's 'I–we' dialectic sets. There seems a fit between dialectic deliberation process in a sort of social dialectics, where there can be reflexivity on relations of unconscious to conscious.

Emergent story occurs in a context of Systemicity complexity, and already embedded narrative expectations. Emergent story arises in a variety of types, but not in empty world. There is contextualized interplay of reflexive and retrospective sensemaking embedded in modes of deliberation on how to tame emergent stories.

Collective body memory theory assumes our physical and social body remembers the blows in ways of storytelling textuality, visuality, and orality. This is partly horsesense and emotive–ethical body memory. Work abuse is written onto the body memory. Carpal tunnel syndrome from typing, calluses of the farm worker, back pains of the garment worker, burns on the arms of the fry clerk, nasty bruises on the legs of stewardesses pushing carts down the aisle, and so forth are remembered. Storytelling Organization oppresses by collapsing and subordinating individual memories to one 'grand narrative,' often in BME progressive sequencing, such as managerialism.

I turn now to explicating three kinds of collective memory that are interpenetrating, not independent. Sensemaking registries are associated in three types of memory.

Aesthetic–Sensory Memory

Aesthetic–sensory memory is first, the collective body of individuals' memories, organizational archives of documents, films, videos, and websites record aesthetic–sensory memory (smell, taste, touch, visual, and acoustic.)

Cognitive–Rational Memory

Second, the cognitive–rational memory of whom, what, when, where, and why, set in retrospective memory. Cognitive–rational memory includes cognitive, more transactive memory processes. The collective storytelling acts encode, categorize, and associate in ways that specialize social memory capabilities. Expert teams, for example, may specialize who encodes, who categorizes, who is most likely to recognize emergent patterns that are task relevant.

Emotive–Ethical Memory

Third is emotive–ethical memory. In the Introduction, and again in Chapter 1, I spoke of a new type of sensemaking. I call it 'emotive–ethical memory.'

Emotive–ethical has its own special registry. Its individual and collective body memory is etched in emotions of bogey rumors (fear), pipedreams (hopes), wedgedrivers (distrust), and projection (stereotypes). Several sensemaking ways are about ethics. In dialectic I–we archetypes of oppression and injustice. In dialogic polypi, the three memories are an active architectonic, an intertextually in organization, societal, and global discourses about ethics of answerability. Bakhtin (1993: 42) defines it as 'an answerable act or deed is precisely that act which is performed on the basis of an acknowledgment of my obligative (ought-to-be) uniqueness'. For Bakhtin it is our unique standpoint in-the-moment of Being, in participation with others, where we have no alibi, since no other person is there to listen or tell, to make a valuation, and to act, to put signature to story. Ethic–emotive memory of the body is interpenetrated with inscriptions from contemporary as well as the past participatory collective body experience. All the horror, terror, and rage at the inequity, injustice survives. Story emergence enters the narrative prison of emotion memory. In Bakhtin's (1990, 1993) parlance, ethical questions interplay with retro-questions in emotion memory. *Who is answerable for the systemicity of oppression? What, when, and why did it happen? How did it feel to the senses?* For Foucault (1977b) it's *who's responsible for the panoptic imprisonment of the body in intersecting gaze?*

Bakhtin is not the only one to develop emotion memory. Working with actors' emotion memory, Stanislavski (1936: 156) taught 'emotion memory' exercises as a way to draw upon experiences of the body to utilize the 'theatrical archives of [their] mind.' Stanislavski says emotion memory expresses itself through time as it *'purifies, it also transmutes even painfully realistic memories into poetry'* (Stanislavski, 1936: 163, italics original). Organizations have a different archive. Blows to past generations are remembered in narratives, in collective memory. Body memory is imprinted upon the Storytelling Organization.

In the interplay of Aesthetic–Sensory, Cognitive–Rational, and Emotive–Ethical memories, a basic principle of Collective memory becomes apparent. *If you imprison emergent story in only cerebrally cognitive–rational memory, the storytelling is flat. It's retelling is without sensations and without emotion–ethical purchase.* Emotive–ethical memory embeds the aesthetic–sensory and cognitive–rational types of memory. Emotive–ethical memory, at a collective memory level, recalls the aesthetic–sensory, as well as the cognitive–rational (whom, what, when, where, and why). But, the reverse is not usually the case.

Managerialism issues from its standpoint a substitution for all other standpoints participating in collective memory. Managerialism is therefore the most disembodied narrative prison, a value judgment in the abstract, removed from concrete deeds if polyphonic participation. There is an ontological difference between managerialism as one of the polyphonic participants, and managerialist imposition of one standpoint over and above all others.

Collective memory is not unitary or singular. It is not a whole. It is tattered, an interplay of storytelling consciousnesses. From managerialism, there is no way to enter the world of performed storytelling acts located in the Tamara of dispersed rooms of telling and listening. In short, managerialism substitutes one standpoint for all participatory standpoints in storytelling organizations. There is no whole story in participatory storytelling. There are endless sides to participatory storytelling events of collective memory.

Each unique side is a standpoint, a center for obligatory answerability to others' sides of stories (Bakhtin, 1993). Active answerability is in the event-ness of Being, in the moments of participation in events of storytelling and story listening. Passive answerability is not compellent. It is an outsider, non-participant, or disinterested bystander act of storytelling.

STORY RIGHTS

Emergent stories are being erroneously called 'tacit-knowledge.' It's erroneous because if people can story, they are not being tacit. Workers are being interrogated, and examined, to extract their emergent stories. Story rights are being violated. Story rights are defined differently in oral tradition than property rights, since each story is assumed to be owned by a memory of a community, and can only be retold by another with explicit permission. Once in written form, and published on paper or online, it can be cited. Are story rights being appropriated by property rights of organizations?

Story Rights

According to Lang and Lang (1961: 71):

> Every story is 'owned' by a member of the community. Each story though known by many, may be recited only by the 'owner'; he may, however, present it to someone else by teaching that person and authorizing them to retell it.

Property Rights

In the manic search for 'knowledge assets,' story rights amount to nothing. Knowledge assets belong to an employee's company. At the societal level, story rights of all citizens belong to the institution of government. In a recent essay I challenged the ethics of denying people their story rights. Making phone, cell phone, and email traffic the object of 'spy' surveillance violates story rights (Boje, 2006a). The property rights of stories of Storytelling Organizations are also disputed around *who can profit from emergent story?* Is it the individual story-author, or the corporation?

The controversy is wrapped up in the knowledge management, knowledge reengineering and learning organization fads of story consulting. Emergent story is treated as an in-place metering device to apprehend 'tacit knowledge.' And, in a managerialist ideology, emergent story belongs to the corporation, and not to the individual employee. Since Taylorism, according to managerialist ideology, the purpose of organization was to transfer knowledge from the skilled worker to the 'system.' In Taylor's day, at the turn of the century, collective memory technology meant storing knowledge of workers in the planning offices using 'time and motion' studies of how workers did work.

Storymaker originated from New Zealand. It's the invention of Theodore Taptiklis. Taptiklis developed a process and supporting software that enables the storage and retrieval of stories by individuals wanting to share or exchange them with others, using cell phones and other portable devices for both recording and playback. In corporations in UK and New Zealand, workers and executives are recording their stories of professional experience and problem-solving into digital recorders, and are then able to access them from a central archive using Storymaker's software. This allows people to participate in the new contemporary architectonics of story storage and retrieval.

Taptiklis is also concerned with 'story rights'. That is, who gets to decide who has access to a story? Taptiklis favors giving the person who tells the story the right to determine access rights, and to pull a story if they feel their rights are violated. I talked to Theodore about the relation of antenarrative to collective memory:

> Once it becomes evident that knowledge lies in the transient connections between human beings, through a medium something like antenarrative, then it follows that knowledge is not any kind of separable or stable 'object', and the whole rationalist edifice with its assumption of humans as separate atomic beings comes crumbling down.[6] (Theodore Taptiklis)

Storymaker elicitors facilitate the initial set collection of stories in *one-to-one elicitation sessions*. It's not old stories that interest Taptiklis. It is emergent stories that are transcribed. Storymaker as an enterprise however does not release transcripts; only the *oral* story playback is permitted. The transcript serves as a way to do 'key word' searches, allowing the retrieval of the sentences before and after the keyword, across all of the stories of a particular storyteller, or all the stored stories of the entire 'storytelling organization'. Options for retrieval are by key words in the story, themes affixed to stories, or by the particular person.

Taptiklis privileges the oral over the written text and clearly makes an assumption that Plato and Aristotle had made. Written text is more subject to twisting and distorting by the reader than the oral performance.

The next chapters alert you to relationship of story and strategy.

---

6 Theodore Taptiklis, 24 Jan 2006 email correspondence, used with permission. For more on Storymaker see http://storymaker.org.

PART II
STORYTELLING ORGANIZATION STRATEGIES

Part II takes us in to application of key concepts, self-organizing opposition of narrative and story forces, interplay of narrative and story varieties of sense-making, such as dialogisms of emergence, and interacting collective memories that lead to the field of strategy. In the main, strategy has been all about narrative control to the exclusion of story generativity.

In Chapter 4, 'Polyphonic Strategy Stories' polyphony is defined as 'the plurality of independent and unmerged voices and consciousnesses' (Bakhtin, 1973: 4). A polyphonic strategy story is one collectively and generatively written, visualized or orally told by all the stakeholders to an organization. It is said to be the next frontier of strategy, but is so very rare, in comparison to monologic narrative. Story polyphony must be studied therefore with an attention to narrative noticing. For example, in strategy narrative forensics, we detect clues to notice bits of emergent story that survive despite narrative control. A strategy narrative has a motto (like Nike's Just Do It!), a founding plot (like Phil Knight's 1962 term paper-plot that low-priced shoe exports from Japan could replace Germany's domination over US running shoe industry), a mission (Nike designs, develops and markets high quality footwear, apparel, equipment and accessory products worldwide), a vision (like for every sport brand a team or sports legend to sell it), and a founding narrative (often mistaken as a founding story). In a Stanford small business class, Phil Knight conceived the game plan in a term paper. He chased down celebrities like Michael Jordan and Tiger Woods to endorse the plan. I show how writing polyphonic strategy story contributes to some 13 schools of strategy that are mainly about narrative order (ten posited by Mintzberg, and three he left out).

In Chapter 5, stylistic strategy stories are shown as an orchestration of image, or on occasion more a dialogism among oral, print and video media, websites, gesture-theatrics, décor and architecture modes of *image expression*. Stylistic dialogicality is defined as a plurality of multi-stylistic story and narrative modes of expression (orality, textuality and visuality of architectural and gesture expressivity). This has not been studied ever in organization strategy, only in marketing as branding, and there, not as multi-stylistic, not as dialogism.

In Chapter 6, chronotopic strategy story is the juxtaposition, or possible dialogism among several ways in which space and time are being narrated. Chronotope is defined by Bakhtin (1981) as the relativity of space and time in narrative. Chronotopes are embodied in ways of writing, visualizing, and telling strategic in stories and narratives. Chronotope becomes a dialogized manner of narrating when multiple chronotopes interact. The theory is that chronotopes are embodied in ways of writing, visualizing, and telling stories and narratives. I have sorted chronotopes into my own categories (adventure and folkloric). The theory is that adventure chronotopes are centripetal (monologic, centering), while more dialogic story chronotopes are centrifugal (chronotopically diverse, generative). Again, such a thing has never been studied in strategy.

In Chapter 7, architectonic strategy stories are an orchestration of ethics in relation to aesthetics and cognitive discourses. Story and narrative (along with trope and metaphor) are domains of discourse. For it to be dialogic, the three discourses become more fully answerable to one another, not just a pretense as in image management. Cognitive architectonic was invented by Immanuel Kant (1781/1900: 466): 'By the term Architectonic I mean the art of constructing a system...' and expanded by Bakhtin (1990, 1991) to the three discourses interanimating. Architectonic theatric inquiry method is what I read in Bakhtin as the interplay of the *Authors, Beholders* (spectators), *Characters* (i.e. heroes, villains), and *Directors*. It's a way of interrogating how strategy is not just cognitive, but makes ethical claims, and can be highly aesthetic. Again, my contribution is it has never been studied in strategy.

In Chapter 8, polypi strategy storying is the multi-dialogized complexity whereupon polyphonic, stylistic, chronotopic, and architectonic dialogism collide with monologic narrative order. It is unlikely to be something that is orchestratable. *Polypi* is defined as the dialogism of four types of dialogisms:

- Polyphonic dialogism of multiple voices in interactive moment of the event horizon
- Stylistic dialogism of types of telling (orality, textuality and visuality) that juxtapose
- Chronotopic dialogism of varied ways of narrating temporality and spatiality that interplay
- Architectonic dialogism, the interanimation vibrations of cognitive, aesthetic, and ethical social or societal discourses

Polypi dialogism allows us to look at how the concepts innovated in Part I (storytelling-sensemaking plurality, systemicity, dialogism, collective memory) play out in terms of a complexity understanding of strategy writing, telling, and visualizing, in interplay with strategy narratives.

The point of Part II is to show complexity and storytelling to be improvisationally interpenetrated. Ralph Stacey (2006) talks about it as improvisational, spontaneous strategy that allows for short-term flexibility, making those five year plans and designs quite the waste of corporate resources. He has not yet ventured into storytelling. And polypi like the individual dialogisms has yet to be studied empirically in strategy.

4

POLYPHONIC STRATEGY STORIES

A polyphonic strategy story is defined as one written, visualized or orally told by all the stakeholders to an organization. Very rare. More usual are monovocal narrative strategies written, etc. by one expert or a dominant coalition bitten by one logic, but not the entire set of stakeholders with diverse logics. This chapter looks at why Mintzberg et al. schools of strategy, plus a few others, pay so little attention to polyphonic strategy story. I make the case that most schools adopt a rather monovocal way of writing strategy, that there are more polyvocal ways, and both are intertwined with the Storytelling Organization.

HOW TO WRITE STRATEGY STORY

What is a Polyphonic Strategy Story?

A polyphonic strategy story is a construction by many embodied voices, logics, and perspectives. It can also be visual art, photos, décor or some oral telling. It takes strategy story forensics to interpret the traces of polyphonic deliberation in practice or in the schools of strategy we will explore. I want to begin with how to write one. My inspiration is the work of Gertrude Stein (1931). I will get to stylistics of visual, oral, as well as written strategy story in the next chapter.

How to Write Polyphonic Strategy Story

The simple answer is to get participants from every stakeholder group (in and around the organization, except perhaps competitors). Have them engage in Socratic story circle, where they allow each person's voice and logic to be fully enunciated, and subjected to questioning. It's where tellers are asked to do active story noticing, and then get down to the task of polyvocal writing. Polyvocal means many voices. Polyvocal writing hardly ever happens in strategy. It not a matter of technology of group writing. It's more than who gets invited to the table. The key questions are, do they speak in fully embodied voice, and is conversation generative of new ideas?

How to Write a Monophonic Strategy Narrative

The simple answer is only invite a story (more accurately, narrative) consultant who believes only a dominant coalition of strategy experts can write a strategy story. Monovocal means one voice. Monovocal strategy narrative is defined as what is told or written by an expert, or a dominant coalition of voices that are rather exclusionary of any wider stakeholder set of voices.

What is a Strategy Narrative?

For Gertrude Stein (1931), there is no difference between a short story and a paragraph. But, I think in the case of strategy, most of it is narrative, not story. A strategy narrative is a paragraph which has a logo and five sentences. One sentence each for motto, plot, mission, vision and founding story (which can be a paragraph, or longer):

1 **Logo** is defined as the symbol of the corporation, often not a sentence, but can be a letter or image (e.g. Nike's 'Checkmark' or 'SWOOSH' sound – in 1971 Knight paid Caroline Davidson, a student at Portland State University, $35 for the Swoosh logo; McDonald's: 'M' or 'Golden Arches'; IBM: just letters IBM).

2 **Motto** is defined as a sentence (sometimes a word or skaz-phrase) stating the moral sentiment that binds logo to the sentences that follow (e.g. Nike: 'Just Do It!'; McDonald's: 'I'm Lovin' It!', circa 2002; IBM: 'Think!' (Thomas J. Watson, Sr., circa 1914).

3 **Plot** is defined as a sentence stating sequence of events that will get enterprise from mission to vision (e.g. Nike: 'In 1962 Phil Knight wrote a term paper with the plot, low-priced shoe exports from Japan could replace Germany's domination over US running shoe industry,' Nike's strategy in 2006 10-K: 26[1]:

> Our strategy for building this portfolio is focused in four key areas:
>
> • Deepening our relationship with consumers;
> • Delivering superior, innovative products to the market place;
> • Making our supply chain a competitive advantage, through operational discipline and excellence; and
> • Accelerating growth through focused execution.

Also, McDonald's Annual Report 2005; 6: 'Strategy is Plan to Win', also known as 5 P's (pp. 10–11) – people, products, place, price, and promotion); and IBM's 2005 Annual Report; 14: 'Strategically, the company has exited commoditized businesses, increased its concentration in higher-value businesses and created a more balanced portfolio'.

4 **Mission** is defined as a sentence that answers the questions, who are our customers, why do we exist? (e.g. Nike's 2006 Annual Report: New CEO Mark Parker asks, 'what part of the Nike story should I focus on?' then mentions brand 8 times, Nike 2006 10-K: 26 'NIKE designs, develops and markets high quality footwear, apparel, equipment and accessory products worldwide,' or 'Our goal is to deliver value to our shareholders by building a profitable portfolio of global footwear, apparel, equipment and accessories brands'; McDonald's 2005 Annual Report 10: 'Our Brand Mission is to be our customer's favorite place and way to eat'; IBM's 2005 Annual Report: 43: 'The mission of Global Financing

---

1 All Nike items in this section are from http://www.nike.com/nikebiz/investors

is to generate a return on equity and to facilitate the client's acquisition of IBM hardware, software and services' (different mission for each division)).

4   **Vision** is defined as a sentence that answers the question, where are we going? (e. g. Nike: for every sport brand, a team or sports legend to sell it; McDonald's 2005 Annual Report 4: 'Our mission. Becoming our customers' favorite place and way to eat' (note their vision and mission are same); IBM's 2005 Annual Report: 10: 'vision ... "Innovation that matters"').

5   **Founding Narrative** (often called founding story), is defined as a sentence or para-graph (or longer) that answers the question, where did we come from? (e.g. Nike: In a Stanford small business class, Phil Knight conceived the game plan in a term paper. He chased down celebrities like Michael Jordan to endorse it. 'Nike founder Phil Knight shadowed [Tiger Woods] from hole to hole, appraising the young phenom's every smile the way a golf coach would his swing. "I hope we sign him," Knight said at the time. "If not, I hope he goes to medical school".'[2]; McDonald's: 'some say it was Ray Kroc who figured out the concepts behind assembly line fast food, invented fast food that tastes the same everywhere, in décor that looks the same everywhere, others say it was the McDonald's brothers founding story repackaged.[3]; IBM's predecessor was Computing-Tabulating-Recording Company (C-T-R), 15 June 1911).

The above examples are masterpieces of strategy writing. Most organizations write strategy narrative without co-locating logo, motto, plot, mission, vision, or founding story in one paragraph. Some leave out one or more of the elements in writing annual reports. Others write tersely. Some strategy paragraphs are as short as a motto word, for example IBM's 'Think.' Yet to those in the know, what is tersely told conveys much of the mission, vision, plot, and founding story. Nike's 'Just Do it' and McDonald's 'I'm Lovin' It' are a bit longer. Others are too long for a book. Most agree strategy and narrative go hand in hand.

Why is Strategy Narrative Important?

As IBM puts it:[4]

> The character of a company – the stamp it puts on its products, services and the marketplace – is shaped and defined over time. It evolves. It deepens. It is expressed in an ever-changing corporate culture, in transformational strategies, and in new and compelling offerings for customers.

---

2   Jackie Krentzman, *Stanford Magazine*, 'The Force Behind the Smile.' 1997 on line http://www. stanfordalumni.org/news/magazine/1997/janfeb/articles/knight.html

3   The official story of McDonald's founding from the McDonalds.com web site: In 1954 'Ray Kroc had never seen so many people served so quickly when he pulled up to take a look. Seizing the day, he pitched the idea of opening up several restaurants to the brothers Dick and Mac McDonald, convinced that he could sell eight of his Multimixers to each and every one. "Who could we get to open them for us?" Dick McDonald said. "Well," Kroc answered, "what about me?"...'

4   IBM History online http://www-03.ibm.com/ibm/history/history/history_intro.html

There are other organizations with carefully crafted strategy narrative vocabulary, and whole paragraphs, that do not do what they say their strategy is. Therefore, we need strategy story forensics.

STRATEGY NARRATIVE FORENSICS

Strategy narrative forensics is defined as detection of clues to solve a storytelling mystery. Clues are followed where they lead. Stein (1931: 386) puts it this way:

Now what is forensics.[5]
Forensics is eloquence and reduction.
... Forensics is a taught paragraph.

Can forensics help strategy paragraph writing? Every strategy paragraph is going through changes, often yearly. These changes leave a trace, clues in the writing.

One trace we already mentioned is who agreed to co-write the strategy? Whose voices are participating in the crafting of each sentence? Many stakeholders are not included in the strategy writing of the examples reviewed of Nike, McDonald's and IBM. Many are not allowed into the strategy scriptorium room. Strategy narrative forensics is about the trace of monovocal or polyvocal in the writing. Did a hired consultant write it? Who wrote this? A board? Was it a narrative drafted by a dominant coalition of executives, or some management committee? Whodunit? Was it any good?

The US Army solves the effectiveness problem with its *After Action Review*. Strategy narrative forensics compares theory espoused with the theory enacted in an *After Action Review*. It does more, asking who was involved in the writing. Some masterpieces of strategy are written without consciousness of forensic *After Action Review* (Stein, 1931: 390):

A masterpiece of strategy.
An argument of their deliberation
The forensics of above which has not been written.
No thought of their search.

Quarrels over strategy paragraph sentences, vocabulary, and grammar are quite common. Forensics traces the history written by an elite and the genealogy of those left out of history. The level of change going on makes forensics quite challenging. For example, take McDonald's motto.

Of course, since 2003, 'I'm Lovin' It' remains the staple, and is currently engraved beneath the 'M' logo. Forensics is retrospective sensemaking. The focus is in following clues. Do not ask forensics about the future. So forensics cannot

---

5 Stein does not use question marks or commas, a rebellion against narrative coherence.

TABLE 4.1   McDonald's mottoes over the years[6]

1954:	'K.I.S.S.' or 'Keep It Simple Stupid' by Ray Kroc. It was later replaced by a more politically correct motto. The sign in his office remained (1954 is an estimate).
1955:	'I believe in God, family and McDonald's – and in the office that order is reversed.' – Ray Kroc. Also not politically correct and was replaced.
1957:	McDonald's first official motto was 'QSC' (quality, service and cleanliness) in 1957; after 1957 it became QSC&V (adding 'value' to it)
1961:	'Look for the Golden Arches.' The same year, the 'All American Meal' campaign featured a ham burger, fries and milk.
1962:	'Go for the goodness at McDonald's'
1965:	'McDonald's – Where quality starts fresh every day'
1966:	'McDonald's – The closest thing to home'
1967:	'McDonald's is your kind of place'
1971:	'You deserve a break today – so get up and get away to McDonald's'
1974:	'Two all-beef patties special sauce lettuce cheese pickles onions on a sesame seed bun'
1975:	'We do it all for you'
1976:	'You, you're the one'
1979:	'Nobody can do it like McDonald's can'
1981:	McDonald's revived 'You deserve a break today,' its most successful campaign.
1984:	'It's a good time for the great taste of McDonald's'
1990:	'Food, folks and fun'
1992:	'What you want is what you get'
1995:	'Have you had your break today?'
1997:	'My McDonald's' and 'Did somebody say McDonald's?'
2000:	'We love to see you smile' and 'Welcome to La Famile' (Fiesta Menu motto).
2003:	'I'm lovin' it' – the first global ad campaign in McDonald's history
2005:	'Are you Mac enough?'

6 KISS motto came from http://www.darron.net/philosophy.html; Kroc's God, country, McD's motto is from http://www.mcspotlight.org/media/reports/trans.html; items after 1957 to 2003 – 14 Apr 2004 JS Online Milwaukee Journal Sentinel Fast-food icon's first franchise opened 49 years ago Thursday, by Jan Uebelherr, http://www.jsonline. com/story/index. aspx?id=222159; except for 2000; Fiesta motto - Where Are the Hamburgers – McDonald's new Fiesta menu *Los Angeles Business Journal*, 16 Oct 2000 by Merrill Shindler; 2005 'Are you Mac enough', http://www.urbanracer.com/articles/ anmviewer.asp?a=1287

be strategy. 'There is no argument in forensics' (Stein, 1931: 386). Forensics searches for cause, in the whodunit. Some clues are meant to be false leads. Others are meant to be overlooked by forensics.

Strategy forensics is defined as the search for clue traces of elaborated argument, high or low involvement of stakeholders, in notes left by strategy scribes (espoused), as compared to those left in strategy enacted. Forensics is careful not to be seduced by words in a line. They look in-between-the-lines for clues of omission. Forensics carefully examines words inserted, or left out.

There are differences, often subtle, between strategy writing done under each CEO, each new dominant coalition, each new change in technology can mean a significant turn. Forensics is a trace of differences (Derrida, 1991). Instead of IBM's 'Think' or Apple Computers' 'Think Differently,' Stein (1931: 389) says, 'Think forensically.'

In sum, strategy narrative can be one that fits an entire organization or more like a rose with each petal its own individuated strategy account. This still leaves the forensics a double question:

1   Who participated in the writing? The choices are managerialist collective memory (consult last chapter in this book):

   (a)   Managerial Collective Memory (Horizontal and vertical lines to retrospective center point)
   (b)   Punctual Collective Memory (Didactic silos, horizontal and diagonal, some feigning of multiplicity)
   (c)   Multilineal Collective Memory (Transhistorical, break with horizontal or vertical points)
   (d)   Polyphonic Collective Memory (Acts of anti-memory, mutations make points indiscernible)

2   What is the genealogy of the changes or metamorphoses of the strategy story, its collective pattern of deliberation and stakeholder participating, in relation to the above types of collective memory?

It's time to put strategy narrative forensics to work. We do so next in sorting out the strategy schools controversy. Each has its narrative. There is precious little story work. The ambition is to be polyphonically dialogical story strategy, but the schools do not quite get there.

STRATEGY SCHOOL CONTROVERSIES

The biggest controversy is determining how many strategy schools there are, followed in importance, by sorting out their genealogical roots (what exemplar authors are relied upon by each school), and which ones are linkable to strategy narrative writing done by practitioners (see Table 4.1). First we will present the controversy by showing three school approaches in one table (Table 4.2). This shows at a glance the inadequate school coverage of the three, as well as contradictory placement of exemplars. I will then show how Barry and Elmes (1997) strategy narrative model is an incomplete rendition of Bakhtin's ten chronotopes (a topic given more careful consideration and elaboration in a subsequent chapter).

Table 4.3 opens the question of which chronotopes fit each school's approach to strategy story writing, as well as what to do with emergence, novelty, and other areas that Bakhtin elaborates do not fit well in any of the school schemes. Table 4.4 will take us through the Mintzberg schools as they are, Table 4.5 will summarize my main critiques, and Table 4.6 will propose a number of school amendments (including omitted schools, moving exemplar authors and constructs to new positions, and defining several new school projects). Finally, Table 4.7 will look at Normann's (1977) work, a key exemplar in Mintzberg et al. (1998, 1999, 2003) of the so-called 'cultural school' of Scandinavia and Japan, whose adherents do spiritual strategy using anthropology. The problem is Normann is from Switzerland, was a devotee of Selznick (of Design School) and Chandler (of Configuration School). You can discern right away that such gross misclassification of Normann, Selznick, and Chandler is quite controversial. Let's begin with a contrast of three frameworks of strategy schools.

Contrasting Three Strategy School Frameworks

There is agreement, in Table 4.2, that Andrews' SWOT (Strengths, Weaknesses, Opportunities, and Threats) is an exemplar of the design school. Barry and Elmes (1997) view Andrews and design school (SWOT) as an epic narrative. Epic narrative is a collapse of Bakhtin's (1981) Greek romantic and chivalric adventures (see Table 4.3). The problem with their move is it is reductionistic, and does not allow us to look any longer at important differences between romantic and chivalric adventure in the strategy story writing, in particular the plot. Let's get to that a bit later.

Compare the number of schools in each framework. Five of Astley's seven schools are in Mintzberg et al. The new ones are the Strategic Choice School and the Social Ecology Strategy School. Four of Barry and Elmes' schools are in Mintzberg et al.'s framework. The new one is the Polyphonic Strategy School. That means, without redistricting, there ought to be 12 not 10 schools in the Mintzberg et al. framework. Astley offers one plan for redistricting. Schools are combined under his 4 C's. Constraint lumps Design and Contingency schools together. Choice lumps Planning and the new Strategic Choice schools together. Competition lumps Positioning and the Population Ecology schools together. Collaboration is a completely new kind of school, of which the new school of Social Ecology (new to Mintzberg et al.) is the main exemplar. For Barry and Elmes, Configuration and Positioning are lumped into the 'purist narrative' approach. The purist narrative is a particular chronotope which Bakhtin called (the down side of) 'historic inversion of realism.' Purist ends up being a combination of other chronotopes, including that abstract analytic aspects of Greek Romantic Adventure. In short, several chronotopes can be unpacked in the Barry and Elmes schema.

What is interesting to note before we move along, is that, Mintzberg et al. contain many schools and exemplar authors, not anticipated by Astley (very forgivable, since it was published about 15 years earlier), whereas Barry and Elmes' was only one year before the first Mintzberg et al. rendition (also forgivable). What was omitted? Of the schools five are overlooked: Entrepreneurial, Cognitive, Learning, Power, and Cultural are omitted by Astley (environment is reallocated into the districts: constrain, choice, competition and collaboration). Barry and Elmes omit seven schools: Planning, Entrepreneurial, Cognitive, Learning, Power, Cultural, and Environment schools altogether (a very long list). They also omit Astley's additions, Strategic Choice, and Social Ecology schools. All three frameworks omit the Resource Based View (RBV) and the Agent-Based Modeling schools.

We can look at one more aspect of Table 4.2 – how Astley's framework is a parsimonious, but too hierarchical way to classify schools: Constraint to Choice, but does not evolve to Competition or collaboration. Constraint and Choice schools are called 'egocentric' since they focus on how one organization strategically adapts to its task environments. Competition and Collaboration, by contrast, look at populations of organizations. Rather than simultaneous or cumulative forces, these are hierarchically theorized.

'Constraint' has a deterministic perspective: exogenous constraints delimit strategic behavior quite narrowly. Strategic 'Constraint' schools, such as design, contingency and configuration – are focused upon business strategy as goodness of fit of an organization with its environment. 'Choice' is more a matter of planning, of negotiating or creating a task environment. Astley's critique of contingency theory is that it ignores strategic choice, how an organization selects an environment. Unlike Mintzberg et al., Astley does not classify Pugh et al. (contingency model) as an environment school, treating contingency as a deterministic-Constraint approach. Child (1972) is characterized as someone challenging contingency theory assumptions, and giving firms more degrees of strategic choice. Managers can choose which clientele to serve, target markets, select technologies, etc. Porter's focus is cut-throat competition among industry rivals, while in population ecology (environment school) competition is natural selection. Astley excludes Schumpeter's creative destruction.

Astley's critique of population ecology and resource dependence (Hannan and Freeman; Aldrich) is that it ignores biological examples of collaboration among and between species. In other words, their population ecology model is based on the organic metaphor from biology, but only the competitive elements are being applied, the more collaborative elements of populations being ignored.

Astley's major contribution to the field is the reintroduction to a forgotten 'Collaborative' strategy school. His main exemplar is Emery and Trist's (1965) social ecology (open systems) model. Astley also cites Vickers (1965), Schon (1971), Michael (1973), Ackoff (1974), Metcalfe (1974) and his own work, as examples of theorists who adopt a more social ecologist perspective.

Let us look more closely at the Barry and Elmes framework. In Chapter 2 we looked at the various dialogisms (polyphonic, stylistic, chronotopic, architectonic, and polypi). While this chapter is about polyphonic strategy story writing, it is appropriate to remark briefly on Bakhtin's ten chronotopes, and how Barry and Elmes treat them.

TABLE 4.2   *Contrast of three frameworks of strategy schools*

Astley, 1984	Mintzberg and Lampel, 1998, 1999, 2003	Barry and Elmes, 1997
Q1 – Constraint: • Design School (Andrews) • Contingency School (Pugh et al.; Galbraith) **Q2 – Choice:** • Planning School (Ansoff) • New Strategic Choice • School (Child) **Q3 – Competition:** • Positioning School (Porter) • Population Ecology School (Aldrich; Hannan and Freeman) **Q4 – Collaboration:** • New Social Ecology School (Emery and Trist; Astley)	**1 – Design School:** • Selznick • Newman • Andrews **2 – Planning School:** • Ansoff **3 – Positioning School:** • Schendel • Hatten • Porter **4 – Entrepreneurial School:** • Schumpeter • Cole **5 – Cognitive School:** • March and Simon **6 – Learning School:** • Lindblom • Cyert and March • Weick • Quinn • Prahalad and Hamel **7 – Power School:** • Allison (micro bargaining strategies) • Pfeffer and Salancik • Astley (macro networks) **8 – Cultural School:** • Rhenman; Normann **9 – Environmental School:** • Hannan and Freeman (population ecology) • Pugh et al. (contingency) **10 – Configuration School:** • Chandler • Mintzberg • Miller • Miles and Snow	**1 – Epic Narrative:** • Design School (Andrews) **2 – Purist Narrative:** • Configuration-Archetype (Miles and Snow) • Positioning (Porter) **3 – Techno-Futurist Narrative:** • Configuration of roles and structures (Mintzberg) **4 – Polyphonic Story:** • Polyphony is direction strategy field is headed (Boje)

Barry and Elmes' (1997: 429) model of strategy narrative is a major contribution to the field. It posits several chronotopes, and in an interview Barry did with me, calls for polyphonic strategic story research. Barry and Elmes say too much attention is paid to monophonic narrative strategy, and not enough to polyphony. They observe, if "'storytelling is the preferred sensemaking currency of human relationships among internal and external stakeholders" (Boje, 1991: 106), then surely strategy must rank as one of the most prominent, influential, and costly stories told in organizations.'

TABLE 4.3 *Barry and Elmes, 1997, narrative types*

Barry and Elmes' four narrative types	Bakhtin's ten chronotypes
1 – Epic Narrative: • Design School, e.g. SWOT (Andrews) **2 – Purist Narrative:** • Configuration- Abstract Archetypes (Miles and Snow) • Positioning (Porter) **3 – Techno-Futurist Narrative:** • Configuration of roles and structures (Mintzberg) **4 – Polyphonic Story:** • Polyphony is direction strategy field is headed (Boje)	**ADVENTURE TYPES:** **1 – Greek Romance Narrative** (Barry and Elmes collapse it with number 3 below) **2 – Everyday Life** (chance and novelty that could be Barry and Elmes' 'Techno-Futurist') **3 – (Auto) Biography** (e.g. of CEOs or firms) **4 – Chivalric Romance** (Epic in Barry and Elmes collapses numbers 1 and 3 above) **FOLKLORISTIC TYPES:** **5 – Historic Inversion of Realism** (This is Barry and Elmes' Purist, abstract analytic) **6 – Rogue, Clown & Fool** (i.e. 3 masks) **7 – Rabelaisian Purge** (i.e. of superficiality) **8 – Folkloric Basis of Rabelaisian** (i.e. emergence in here-and-now of labor events) **9 – Idyllic** (i.e. unity of time/place fragments) **10 – Castle Room** (i.e. place/milieu affects narrative)

Bakhtin defines chronotope as the relativity of space and time in narrative. Chronotope becomes a dialogized manner of narrating when multiple chronotopes interact. Barry and Elmes sort a few schools of strategy into four types of narrative.

First is Bakhtin's epic chronotope (Andrews' SWOT school). SWOT, as Barry and Elmes argue, is CEO monologue-aspect of the design school, the dominant view of strategy into the 1970s. SWOT cases are complicated (shopping list) adventure narratives, but not very complex. To me they are Greek Romantic Adventure (GRA) chronotope. The GRA is an abstract, formal system of space and adventure time. Its link to space–time is more mechanistic than organic.

Second, purist type (Porter's five forces; Miles and Snow's archetypal role forms) is an analytic/abstract archetype. This is a collapse of the analytic/abstractness of GRA (the archetypes in particular) and reversal of historical realism chronotope (i.e. reversal of here-and-now space–time narrative into a futuristic ephemeral temporality narrative).

Third, techno-futurist (Mintzberg's 1978 adhocracy archetype), that for Mintzberg is an illustrative example of Configuration School (1 of 10 schools). What kind of chronotope is this? I would say it is most aligned with Everyday Adventure (which for Bakhtin has some aspects of GRA). What's different is in Everyday, the hero's life is embedded in metamorphosis of human identity, which a new technology will do, or a travel to some foreign land. As with the McDonalds brothers' invention of new technology of fast food, then Ray Kroc setting out on a global adventure to travel the world, putting up M-arches everywhere. McDonald's operates in diverse countries, avoiding local historical ties when possible, adapting the menu when absolutely unavoidable. This chronotope is about strategic emergence and adaptation of the grander narratives of McDonald's.

Fourth, they conclude by saying the polyphonic type is the cutting edge problem facing strategy (citing me as a prophetic source, thank you).

Barry and Elmes leave us to theorize and research the identity of seven more chronotopes in strategy narrative in the strategy schools (auto-biographical adventure, and all six folkloric chronotopes, where story is more apt to be prominent). The seminal contribution they make is in positing that strategy is stuck in narrative wholeness, and that story polyphony of multiple tellers doing something generative is the next frontier. They sketch the outline of a theory and leave us to pen it in. They posit two chronotopes, leave a third undefined. We will get to this task, but now it is time to sort out some major problems in the Mintzberg et al. framework.

For Mintzberg et al. (2003: 24–25), 'lines of literature' become strategy schools as they depose 'earlier schools.'

I went to the sources cited and read the originals. I looked at ways they narrated, and ways they approached Astley's 4 C's. This leads me to my critique of the Mintzberg et al. framework, which is about the controversial independence of schools assumption.

The Mintzberg et al. strategy school model is flawed for several important reasons. First, their framework assumes school independence, thus omitting genealogical or forensic study of the roots of schools with shared ancestry. As we look at individual authors, outside of Mintzberg et al.'s re-writing, their classification changes dramatically. Works of Normann, Selznick, Chandler, and Schumpeter seem to be misread by Mintzberg et al., or at best strangely summarized. To be blunt, the classification of exemplar-authors is an abomination of their writing. School exemplar authors readily borrow ideas from one another, sometimes, entire constructs, such as how Porter appropriates Andrews and Ansoff. Other exemplars are very misread, such as how Schumpeter, who hated entrepreneur-heroism, is the heroic champion of the Entrepreneur School (he preferred oligarchy and monopoly).

There is misrepresentation. There is nothing intuitive in the rational models of Schumpeter and Cole. Mintzberg et al. make a key assumption that the strategy schools are independent, rather than commutative or derivatively interdependent. For example, instead of 'intuition,' habits of thought are rationalized into socioeconomic infrastructure. While there is 'entrepreneurship' in creative destruction, it is the 'firm and the society,' not the entrepreneur-CEO doing this. Schumpeter's narrative is that 'capitalistic civilization is rationalistic, 'and anti-heroic'

TABLE 4.4   *Mintzberg et al.'s ten strategy schools and exemplars*

Strategy School	Exemplars	Base Discipline	Champions
Design	Selznick (1957) Newman (1951) Andrews (1965)	None (architecture as metaphor)	Case studies teachers (especially at or from Harvard University), leadership aficionados – especially in the United States
Planning	Ansoff (1965)	Some links to urban planning, systems theory, and cybernetics	'Professional' managers, MBAs, staff experts (especially in finance), consultants, and government controllers – especially in France and the United States
Positioning	Hatten and Schendel (1977) Porter (1980, 1985)	Economics (industrial organization) and military history	As in planning school, particularly analytical staff types, consulting 'boutiques,' and military writers – especially in the United States
Entrepreneurial	Schumpeter (1934, 1950) Cole (1959)	None (although early writings come from economists)	Popular business press, individualists, small business people everywhere, but most decidedly in Latin America and among overseas Chinese
Cognitive	Simon (1947) March and Simon (1958)	Psychology (cognitive)	Those with a psychological bent – pessimists in one wing, optimists in the other
Learning	Braybrooke and Lindblom (1963) Cyert and March (1963) Weick (1969) Quinn (1980) Prahalad and Hamel (1990)	None (perhaps some peripheral links to learning theory in psychology and education). Chaos theory in mathematics	People inclined to experimentation, ambiguity, adaptability – especially in Japan and Scandinavia
Power	Allison (1971) – (micro) Pfeffer and Salancik (1978) Astley (1984) – (macro)	Political science	People who like power, politics, and conspiracy – especially in France
Cultural	Rhenman (1973) Normann (1977)	Anthropology	People who like the social, the spiritual, the collective – especially in Scandinavia and Japan

(Continued)

TABLE 4.4   (Continued)

Strategy School	Exemplars	Base Discipline	Champions
Environmental	Hannan and Freeman (1977) Pugh et al. (1968)	Biology	Population ecologists, some organization theorists, splitters, and positivists in general – especially in the Anglo-Saxon countries
Configuration	Chandler (1962) Mintzberg (1979) Miller and Friesen (1984) Miles and Snow (1978)	History	Lumpers and integrators in general, as well as change agents. Configuration perhaps most popular in the Netherlands. Transformation most popular in the United States.

Source: Mintzberg et al. (1998); Mintzberg and Lampel (1999); Mintzberg et al. (2003)

(Schumpeter, 1942: 127). It's *not* the entrepreneur-heroic that Mintzberg et al. narrate, the CEO galloping on a fully armored stallion to wreak creative destruction on one out-dated industry after another. It's the 'unheroic oligarchy' that has its department of RandD coming up with new weaponry: new products, new technologies, new methods of production and organization. I think what Mintzberg et al. have done is confused lay (emic) understanding of the heroic CEO entrepreneur with Schumpeter's mechanistic theory of creative destruction, his defense of monopoly against government regulation and against neo-Marxist critique of the exploitation of labor but capitalism; making not the CEO but capitalism the hero.

Selznick is the more misread of all, certainly a reductionism to limit his generative roots to the Design School, and not see how most forensic detection of every school leads back to Selznick. Equally strange is Chandler, who is more deserving as founder of Historiography School, a predecessor to Genealogy School (see revised redistricting plan for Schools in Table 4.6).

Second, there are schools omitted. Though the model keeps reappearing in successive Mintzberg et al. editions, it ignores important new work, such as, RBV, agent-based modeling, and the more polyphonic aspects of story strategy, as well as multi-stylistic, architectonic (especially ethics), and critical strategy (see Table 4.6). Add to this list collaborative approaches cited by Astley, and several narrative approaches by Barry and Elmes. Note, all three schools framework (Mintzberg, Astley, Barry/Elmes) work only by exclusion of key works. Missing are not just new works, but ones contemporary to their framework: Emery and Trist's (1965) open system model multi-organization collaborative strategy, Child's (1972) strategy choice and Aldrich's (1979) resource dependence models. According to Mintzberg et al., positioning school stands on the shoulders of military strategy literature, dating as far back as Sun Tzu in 400 BC (see Sun Tzu, 1971). They do not include Sun Tzu in their table of schools. My

TABLE 4.5   *Critique of the Mintzberg et al.'s strategy schools framework*

Strategy School	Exemplars	Critique of Mintzberg et al.'s typology
Design	Selznick (1957) Newman (1951) Andrews (1965)	Andrews' SWOT has nothing in common with Newman or Selznick's work. Andrews' is a snapshot; Selznick's is an historical model of institutionalization and need of dominant coalition to address situation differences
Planning	Ansoff (1965)	Ansoff is foundational to Porter's work
Positioning	Hatten and Schendel 1977) Porter (1980, 1985)	Porter combines Andrews' SWOT with Ansoff's diversification and focus strategies
Entrepreneurial	Schumpeter (1934, 1950) Cole (1959)	Schumpeter and Cole are economic historians who look at entrepreneurship as 'creative destruction'
Cognitive	Simon (1947) March and Simon (1958)	Simon's early work and his later work with March pose different kinds of cognitive implications for strategy
Learning	Braybrooke and Lindblom (1963) Cyert and March (1963) Weick (1969) Quinn (1980) Prahalad and Hamel (1990)	Lindblom's 'science of muddling through' is not the same as Weick's retrospective-enactment, and both are different from the competency models posed by Quinn, and Prahalad and Hamel. Competency models owe debt to Selznick's 'distinctive competence' cognitive models and ways firms enact environments or muddle through, rather than responding directly
Power	Allison (1971) – (micro) Pfeffer and Salancik (1978) Astley (1984) – (macro)	Astley does a typology of strategy schools according to their approach to the environment; Pfeffer and Salancik have a resource dependency model of power ignored by Astley; Astley also ignores Mintzberg (1979); Allison's work in Model II builds upon cognitive and learning exemplars.
Cultural	Rhenman (1973) Normann (1977)	Normann integrates Selznick's life stage institutionalization, Chandler's multi-divisional form, contingency, cognitive, learning models with archetypes of dominant coalition roles that are fit or unfit to environmental situation factors; Rhenman and Normann's works are the most inter-school framework within the Mintzberg et al. ten schools
Environmental	Hannan and Freeman (1977) Pugh et al. (1968)	Pugh et al. is a contingency model, while Hannan and Freeman is a population ecology model mimicking Darwinian variation-selection-retention; as Astley points out, it is a population model of organization competition, not an egocentric contingency model; contingency and population ecology ignore collaborative inter-organizational models, such as Emery and Trist (1965), which Mintzberg et al. also exclude.

(Continued)

TABLE 4.5   (Continued)

Strategy School	Exemplars	Critique of Mintzberg et al.'s typology
Configuration	Chandler (1962) Mintzberg (1979) Miller and Friesen (1984) Miles and Snow (1978)	Chandler does comparative history; Mintzberg is not doing history, his is a next step in contingency, with five ideal archetypes of firms; Miles and Snow, and Miller and Freisen's are also a configuration of firm archetypes that are fit or unfit to environment contingencies. By contrast, Normann (cultural school) frames constellations of archetypes of dominant coalition within each firm, and their contingency fit/unfit to environmental situation, and life cycle (using or anticipating exemplars of all ten Mintzberg et al. schools)

strategy colleague Terry Adler (personal communication, 2006) tells me deception can also wear down, and use up a competitor's resources. He cites the example of advertising for executive positions, in order to entice competitors to mimic your resource investment, thereby enticing him to waste resources. Adler makes a point about the warfare among schools, in their various classification schemes (yes, this one too). Schools build upon other schools, their exemplars and works, but erase the roots, so as to appear to be the contemporary school, the one that tops all the others, the successor to the emperor's throne.

Third, the schools framework is dominated first by contingency thinking, and over time, by system thinking, especially more mechanistic and open systems organization and environment conceptions. The road to complexity thinking, particularly emergence, is not being taken. The open system thinking is very limiting. Porter is my very limited exemplar of an 'open system' strategy theorist. Open system combines the first two cybernetics: centripetal (first cybernetic of deviation-counteraction) and centrifugal (second cybernetic of deviation-amplification) to paraphrase Maruyama (2003). I agree with Mintzberg et al. (2003); Porter stresses the first more than the second cybernetic:

> Acceptance of Tom Peters's urgings – '"Don't think, do" is the phrase I favor' – could lead to the *centrifugal explosion* of the job, as it flies off in all directions, free of a strong frame anchoring it at the core. But acceptance of the spirit of Michael Porter's opposite writings – that what matters most is conception of the frame, especially of strategic positions – could produce a result no better '*centripetal implosion*, as the job closes in on itself cerebrally, free of the tangible connection to its outer actions'. (Mintzberg, cited in Mintzberg et al. 2003, bold italics, mine)

Fourth, their classification of exemplar authors is in too many schools, quite arbitrary, with the configuration school meaning acclaimed as successor to all other schools. For example, Hamel and Prahalad (1993: 80) exemplify the 'learning organization' school of strategy: 'Being a "learning organization" is not enough; a company must also be capable of learning more efficiently than its competitors.' Prahalad and Hamel (1990) incorporate frames at lower orders of complexity (SWOT, entrepreneurial, planning, positioning, and environment) with Selznick-appropriated, learning of core competencies: 'the real sources of advantage are to be found in management's ability to consolidate corporatewide technologies and production skills into competencies that empower individual businesses to adapt quickly to changing opportunities.'

Fifth, the two polyvocality questions are not being answered by their framework:

1 What is the collective memory (managerialist, punctual, multilineal, or poly-phonic) of each strategy school? One would expect Plan, Design, and Entrepreneurial to be managerialist; Cultural and Power to be punctual; and Cognitive Learning to be multilineal; and Configuration and Learning to be some-what polyphonic.
2 What is the genealogy of changes in each school, which ones are antecedent to others, which are independent emergence? Selznick, for example, is greatly appropriated and resituated by most school exemplar authors. Work by Selznick (1957) is foundational to many of the schools of strategy (cognitive, learning, power, cultural, environmental, and configuration).

In sum, strategy authors are rhizomatic, and intertextual, borrowing concepts and entire models from each other's written works (sometimes without citing them). Mintzberg et al. schools have become a colonizing regime of signs, taught widely throughout the planet. Mintzberg et al. has emerged as the more dominant framework (compared to Astley, or Barry and Elmes), and is the one taught in most strategy courses, in most MBA programs worldwide.

Table 4.6 reclassifies exemplars and schools into a more complexity-thinking model, as opposed to the open system thinking of the three frameworks reviewed. I interrelate Bakhtinian dialogisms to Boulding/Pondy levels in systems thinking, with a revision to the schools of strategy typologies that Astley, Mintzberg et al., and Barry and Elmes theorize. To make the case, that predominantly the schools framework are oriented to system thinking, I have put in the first column the system hierarchic levels suggested by Boulding. The second column lists the corresponding strategy schools. And the third column their complexity properties (that become holographic instead of hierarchical).

The top half of Table 4.6 is making the case (column 1) that levels 1 to 5A are more about system thinking.

Levels 5B to level 9, and a new level being Boulding's schema (Critical Strategy), gets more at a dialogic model, compatible with complexity thinking. In a dialogic model, such as Bakhtin's chronotopes, there is not a hierarchic order of system elements. Rather, each of the elements can embed in the others, thus a more holographic depiction is possible.

There is a grossly misrepresented, or misread exemplar in the Mintzberg et al. Schools Framework – the work of Normann who was so very devoted to Selznick, but obsessed with Contingency Strategy School. You can easily see that Normann is not really about Cultural Strategy, is more about Entrepreneur archetypes, and changing archetypes as the dominant coalition is supposed to match strategy narrative to contingency of organization and environment adaptation.

Normann (1977) incorporates or anticipates each of the ten Mintzberg et al. schools. Its dialogism is at the level of polyphony among the various schools, their logics and views. It is not at the level of direct face-to-face engagement or participation that could be called Socratic dialogue. It is more about cognitive mapping, and stakeholders of the mind, thus it is not a Bakhtinian polyphonic, more an imitation of polyvocality. One bright spot is ethics. As Normann says, strategy is 'also a question of ethics' (1977: 7). However, this too is not a dialogic construct, not anything that is architectonic. Normann's life stage model is in the language of cybernetics, system theory, not complexity thinking.

This is an ideological battle, a struggle of ideologies. In that struggle, Normann, the open system theorist, is concerned with 'centrifugal diversification' forces being in harmony with centripetal forces. More diversified (multidivisional, global) companies moving into simultaneous global businesses 'emerged in just this way from centrifugal diversification among an established business idea' (p. 146). Therefore, Normann concludes, 'total commitment to one central business ideas is a thing of the past' (p. 147). In the termination phase, if there is not a struggle among ideas, if a petrified narrative strategy idea is dominant, 'one of the functions of the growth culture is to seize upon tensions to relay it and resolve it' (p 152); more accurately instead of resolve it, to channel it in more centrifugal diversification.

There are instances (rare) of open systems thinking. The organization is an idea system in which the roles of *defender, political carrier, shield-maker, and conqueror* are opposed by the role of the '*variety-generator*' (pp. 127–35). The dominant coalition is in a state of dialogic tension. It is the variety-generator who insures that requisite variety is being organized, or else systemicity reverts to first order cybernetic complexity.

The key challenge for the dominant coalition is how to sustain any dialogism. I do not mean dialog, but instead I refer to the dialogism among ideas, embodied by powerful actors and less powerful stakeholders. Each established balance of power has its champions and defenders, as well as oppositional idea forces. Such conflict, for Selznick, is a matter of co-optation, whereas, for Normann, there is the definite influence of open systems thinking, and perhaps an invitation to something more dialogic and centrifugal.

Normann's model is polyphonic only at the egocentric level of focal organization, and is otherwise quite managerialist collective memory. Only executives and powerful managers voice and embody ideas and roles in the dominant coalition. As we examined in the last chapter, Normann combines Selznick's themes of life stages, institutional learning, dominant coalition archetypal roles, with requisite distinctive institutional competencies, and fit/misfit to contingent environmental situations. There is absolutely nothing new in Normann, except that he references available literature in the established and emerging ten Mintzberg et al. strategy schools, in a historical genealogy.

To Normann, ideas stem from 'critical events, often in the past' (p. 11). Normann's historian exemplars are Chandler, Selznick, and Crozier. Normann

TABLE 4.6 Part I: Reclassifying schools by system thinking levels

Boulding's System Hierarchic-Levels	Strategy Schools	Complexity properties that become holographic to one another, instead of hierarchic or successive
L1. Frameworks (frame metaphor/narrative)	SWOT-Design School	Every strategy school has a frame; frames vary by being branch (independence or succession assumed) or cumulative (subterranean rhizomatic roots interconnect schools). Andrews frame is SWOT: the heroic CEO uses firm's strengths and opportunities to overcome it's weaknesses and threats; I don't think Selznick belongs in Design school; I transfer him to L5B, and name a school after him (see Part II of table)
L2. Mechanistic (machine narrative)	Entrepreneurial/Cognitive School	Every school of strategy assumes entrepreneurial; differences are with making individuals, institutions, or part of role set of dominant coalition. Root metaphor is machine. March and Simon (1958) cognitive school, and various contingency fit/unfit models of strategy. Schumpeter (1934, 1950) and Cole's (1959) 'creative destruction' is institutional force, not heroic CEO narrative as Mintzberg et al. say. Rationality more mechanistic worldview of this school is reduced to archetype role
L3. Control (thermostat metaphor/ narrative)	Planning/Contingency Schools	1st order cybernetics is either goal directed teleology of purposive behavior, or backward glancing constructivism (as in retrospective, or feeling one's way). Ansoff's (1957: 113) control narrative: measuring profit potential of various product-market strategies by forecasting environment trends, assessing contingencies, and contrasting these with long-run objectives. In short, this is a highly (first) cybernetic control (i.e. rational goal) model of strategy; Pugh et al. contingency model; Mintzberg's (1978) configuration is a reformed contingency framework; not at level of open system; be glad I did not demote it to grade 1: framework

(Continued)

Boulding's System Hierarchic-Levels	Strategy Schools	Complexity properties that become holographic to one another, instead of hierarchic or successive
L4. Open (cell metaphor/narrative)	**Open System/Positioning/ Choice/RBV/Learning Schools**	1st order cybernetic is opposed by 2nd order cybernetic of variety building to be able to process complexity of task environments. Some schools loosen tight coupling of resource contingencies and environmental situations (i.e. RBV), to all for strategic choice, and even changing the environment through acts of collaboration (i.e. social ecology). RBV of the firm provided the second template for Strategy, with Penrose (1959) founding, then dissertations of Prahalad (1975), Doz (1976), Bartlett (1979) and Ghoshal (1986), then championed by Barney (1991). Learning: Lindblom (1959) 'science of muddling' and Weick's (1969) retro enactment. Porter's positioning is integration of Andrews and Ansoff, in five forces model of industry rivalry; Astley's selection of Emery and Trist (1965) collaborating organizations network to tame turbulent environments, plus Child's (1972) strategic choice. All ignore resource-based view (Penrose, 1959; Barney, 1991)
L5A. Organic (plant metaphor/narrative)	**Environmental School**	Instead of cell, the root metaphor is a plant, and how in populations of plants, there is variation-selection-retention; it takes a long time for strategy to get beyond organic metaphors (cell and plant, as well as animal packs). Emery and Trist (open system) collaborative model, is alternative to Hannon and Freeman's population ecology of competition; all previous exemplars and works are implicated, at population levels of complexity

TABLE 4.6 *Part II: Reclassifying schools by complexity thinking without levels*

Complexity schools of strategy rooted in dialectic or dialogism

L5B. Polyphonic dialogism manner of storytelling	Selznick's institutional life cycle is organic complexity, but his role theory of dominant coalition responding to environmental situations is more polyphonic. Cultural school (Rhenman; Normann) builds upon Selznick and Penrose, as well as cognitive, learning, power schools, but do not get at multi-stylistic or image management complexity; I relocate Quinn, Prahalad and Hamel here, their models of distinctive competency are derivative of Selznick; also move Miles and Snow (1978), Miller and Friesen (1984) archetype firm roles; and Mintzberg (1973) managerial roles.
The forgotten 'Selznick' School and Normann's only slightly dialogic school of schools	In Normann's (1977) revival of Selznick, there is a forgotten dialogic model of life stages; it is organic, but begins to be dialogic with cognitive, learning, symbol-history schools. It does not address image, symbol, etc. complexity properties; it remains polyphony of logics/ideas (see Table 4.7)
L6. Image (multi-stylistic story juxtaposition or dialogism)	
No Strategy Schools (We will call it Multi-stylistic Strategy School)	No strategy schools theorize multi-stylistic manner of image-story strategy. In short cognitive and learning schools do not theorize stylistic dialogism. Image narrative separates from the sign (archetype) polyphony and constellation/configuration/contingency/learning frames. This is multi-chronotopic: adventure travel globally, with learning which cognitive to associate with which situation.
L7. Symbol (multi-chronotopic story dialogism)	
No Strategy School covers (We will name it Genealogy School)	History becomes multiple ways of telling history. What was all sign-maps, or image management, now incorporates symbol in acts of self-reflection about the stories told. Selznick's ghost, Chandler, Schumpeter (1934, 1950), Cole (1959) do historical biography; not much self-reflexivity, but strategy escapes organic metaphorization; this school is still in mono-chronotope stage

(Continued)

Complexity schools of strategy rooted in dialectic or dialogism

L8. Network (architectonic story dialogism)	**Macro-Power Strategy School, but does not cover the ethics or aesthetic discourses**	Multiple discourses interanimate; not just the cognitive maps, nor stylistic-image management, but also an ethical discourse. These are societal discourse penetrating what an organization is expected to tell about itself. Pfeffer and Salancik; Allison; beginning of architectonic-societal discourse external control of organizations shaping firm's discursive strategy; not yet interanimating cognitive with more ethic and aesthetic discourses
L9. Transcendental (polypi story dialogism)	**No Strategy Schools (We will name it 'Polypi' School)**	Polypi is interanimation of several types of dialogism (polyphonic, stylistic, chronotopic, and architectonic). No strategy schools, or exemplars address transcendental challenges posed by Boulding in relation of knowable to unknowable. One suspects modernity has gone into relapse, allowing more spiritual/religiosity discourse into the idea culture, into strategy practice
L2. Critical Strategy School (dialectic, not dialogism)	**Not part of Astley, Barry and Elmes, or Mintzberg et al., (Called Critical Strategy School)**	Critical Strategy comes out of Critical Theory (Frankfurt School) and small 'ct' critical theories that came after (see reviews by Boje and Haley, 2008; Levy et al., 2003; seminal EJROT special issue with Booth (1998), Harfield (1998), Stoney (1998), and Thomas (1998). As Horkheimer and Adorno (1944/1972: 121) put it, 'the people at the top are no longer so interested in concealing monopoly: as its violence becomes more open, so its power grows.' Thus the critique of managerialist collective memory strategy for its pseudo stakeholder dialogues that is too monovocal

TABLE 4.7 Normann's life cycle of archetypes of dominant coalition

Life Stages	Associated Archetype Role Constellation	Systemicity Implications
1 Feelers	Entrepreneur (adaptive specialization into new ideas) mapmaker of environment	1st cybernetic constructivism; entrepreneur feels out lines of adaptive specialization and thereby maps the environment (as in science of muddle through and retrospective sensemaking)
2 Developmental	Variety pool builder; selector (morphogenesis)	2nd order cybernetic is necessary to build requisite variety (becomes open system); a dominant coalition of power legitimates one of the adaptive specializations
3 Exploitation and Stabilization	Conqueror; interpersonal process moderator (does variation on ideas)	A conquer may vary the dominating idea, but does not innovate. Since the dominant coalition has many roles, an important role is process moderator to manage conflicts
4 Market Penetration	Defender of the niche; steer the learning	The niche is well sorted out, and a defender role is needed to keep other competitors from coming into the niche. Steering the learning emerges as a role
5 Termination	Visioner; anticipatory adaptation; destroyer of old ideas	In decline, the dominating idea can no longer be varied, it must be destroyed, and a new anticipatory adaptation found; its back to new lines of flight: felling out a new growth idea, remapping the environment

finds contingency theory insufficient since it lacks a 'typology of growth' (p. 20). Yet he keeps falling back into it with incessant references to Woodard, Burns and Stalker, and Lawrence and Lorsch.

The organization is an idea system, more or less consonant with a power system of roles, and a distribution of distinctive competences that 'tends to pass through growth cycles' (p. 46). Normann posits one of the early models of a learning organization. However his exemplar for learning is Berger and Luckmann. Normann therefore defines a growth culture as an institution with strategic ideas embodied in signification actions of powerful actors in a learning process of socialization and 'knowledge-development' (p. 35).

Story Possibilities for Strategy   Very close to polyphonic dialogic is the way in which Normann theorizes the organization as a struggle of ideas among powerful actors, situated in growth stage, and environmental situation. Yet inevitably it's always a dominant power coalition that determines which growth ideas are strategic. It is always, for Normann, the environment contingencies (moderated by growth stage) that determine if the ideas are fit or misfit to the environment. To be more accurate, the prevailing or dominating ideas constitute the 'psychological-social reality of prevailing groups of significant action in the company' (p. 18) within a 'stakeholder' model of the environment (p. 83).

Normann (pp. 155–67) posits five options available, which I have paraphrased, and adapted to the current discussion about dialogism:

1 **Expulsion** – purge opposing views, ideas, or ideologies.
2 **Over-legitimation** – if they cannot be expelled, then make them marginal, a decoration, isolate them where they do not harm dominating idea forces; use repressive tolerance of co-optation.
3 **Compromise** – do some superficial integration within the dominant logic; sustain the hegemony of dominance, marginalization.
4 **Incongruence** – maintain a fundamental dualism between main opposing ideas; do not let them integrate beyond superficial compromise; instead of compromise, push them further apart.
5 **Synergy** – combines some aspects of each idea into an ensemble; out of the dialectic of opposing ideas, forces and roles emerge, in synthesis

Normann is also critical of Ansoff. He prefers more retrospective, feeling and muddling one's way, to the assumption that planning is rational goal teleology. Rather, for Norman the cognitive and learning schools succeed in convincing him that it is 'bounded' rationality process. Like Chandler, Selznick, Cole, and Schumpeter, Normann understands organizations to be products of history, and critical events, often in the past (pp. 1, 11).

There is an important insight in Normann (1977) about how polyphonic strategy story keeps falling back into managerialism. If organizations adapt to environmental shifts and to stages in life cycle by aligning power coalition roles, then there needs to be a way to manage struggling ideas. A variety pool builder, conqueror, or defender, can subvert the entrepreneurial process of environmental mapping. Power struggles among ideas, embodied in powerful actors, can veer away from the unseen hand of the environmental situation tipping which actors dominate the constellation of roles. Normann's key insight here is that as ideas accumulate, the wrong strategic growth idea can be in play at the wrong time.

The dialogic situation gets more severe as companies adopt decentralized multi-divisional forms. Normann questions Chandler's grand hypothesis that structure follows strategy. In his reading of Lindblom's (1959) 'science of muddling through' there is a lot of feeling one's way, then the building of requisite pool of competencies, resources, etc. becomes a 'major determinant of the possibility of finding a strategy' (p. 10). Normann's critique of Chandler is that 'he does not really discuss strategy formulation at all' (p. 10).

Gender Bias in Strategy   There are too many fathers of schools, and not enough mothers. The father of the 'resource based view of the firm' (RVB) is Jay Barney (1991, 1995). Yet his work clearly builds upon the mother's work, Edith Penrose (1959). Why is the school exemplar the father and not the mother? Only in Normann (1977) is Penrose the mother privileged in a resource view. More women scholars, notably Mary Parker Follett, the mother of strategy, are noticeably absent from the all male school deans, exemplary teachers, and written curriculum of works. I did it this way to make a point: strategy schools are chauvinistic. Why is the mother of contingency, Joan Woodward (1965) excluded from the classification of schools?

In sum, there is awareness of polyphonic strategy story, but in the main, most of the strategy schools are about monological narrative strategy. The next chapters explore how polyphonic dialogism, which is in its nascent form in strategy, begins to interact with other dialogisms: stylistic, chronotopic, and architectonic. It is here where the dialogized manner of story strategy begins to separate from linear narrative.

5

STYLISTIC STRATEGY STORIES

Stylistic Strategy Story is defined as orchestration of image, or more a dialogism, among oral, print and video media, websites, gesture-theatrics, décor and architecture modes of image expression. Stylistic strategy story orchestration is defined as juxtaposition of varied styles for image management. Stylistic strategy story dialogism is defined as the interactivity of various modes of expressing organization image in interplay with forces of narrative control. The contribution is to illustrate three stylistic strategies: hailing, dramaturgic, and triple-narrative control of emergent story.

McSTYLE

McDonald's Storytelling Organization orchestrates a monological stylistic strategy that attempts to control complexity, and contain emergent stories. Strategy schools have not theorized stylistic strategy, but it is obviously in wide practice. In France, McStyle is defined as an orchestrated juxtaposition of architectural and décor styles for McDonald's restaurants in France. There are ten classic styles of McDonald's restaurants, and three new thematics, to answer emergent story that McDonald's fails to meet high French aesthetic standards.

WHAT STRATEGY SCHOOLS SAY ABOUT STYLISTICS

Nothing. Stylistic strategy story orchestration in all its multi-modality is orchestrated, more or less successfully, by Storytelling Organizations, but not studied in strategy (more the province of marketing). Cognitive and learning schools of strategy ignore how stylistics must be re-contemporalized over time and across countries to keep up with *emergent fads*. Multi-stylistic *self-portraiture* is an extension of strategic narrative, a way to shape McDonald's identity as McStyled *image*. It is, if you will, a strategic stylistic competence. It's way past branding. *Branding* is defined as sensemaking control by centralizing and unifying coherence. The strategy field has not studied the ontic counter-forces of strategy and emergent story, already in organizational practice. I think this is because complexity in strategy theories has not progressed beyond organic sorts of narrative orders.

TABLE 5.1   *McStyles in French McDonald's[1]*

Classic McStyles	Newest Thematic McStyles
Automne (Autumn theme)	L'equipe (Sports)
Printemps (Spring theme)	Montagne (Mountain)
Eté (Summer theme)	Mer (Sea and Surf)
Rouge (Red color)	
Blues (as in music)	
Rouille (Rust color)	
Rothko (Rothkovitch 1903–1970, abstract expressionist painter)	
Nouveau Monde (New World)	
Amérique (New York look)	
Origine Des Plaines (1st Ray Kroc franchise opened in Des Plaines)	

ONTOLOGY OF STYLISTIC STRATEGIES

The meaningful analysis of stylistic strategy narrative control and emergent story calls for inquiry into the ontology of stylistic expression that is beyond open systems thinking. Much of narrative control is first cybernetic control by deviation-counteraction. Open system added second cybernetic complexity property of deviation-amplification (requisite variety storied in organizing to match variability in environments). I propose ontological study of the third cybernetic revolution by examining stylistic dialogism modes of strategic expression.

First a story to explain why I use Bakhtin's (1981) heteroglossic language theory of stylistic dialogism, to move beyond *Open Systems Theory*, instead of Derrida's work. My mentor Lou Pondy was reprimanded by Robert Cooper (1989) for adopting an antiquated information-processing approach. It was rooted in Shannon and Weaver's (1949) first cybernetic sender-message-receiver-feedback model. Pondy (1979, later with Mitroff, 1979) called for the move beyond first and second cybernetic (open system) models of organization. Cooper's critique did not address Pondy's (1978) substitution of Chomsky's language theory for the outdated first cybernetic model. Cooper would be correct in critiquing Pondy this substitution, as well as for not getting beyond open systems. Cooper uses Derrida's work on writing, as the better language model. However, I prefer Bakhtin's heteroglossia, that anticipated Derrida's play of

---

1 For McStyle see http://www.mcdonalds.fr/ and click 'Tout Sur McDo' then 'McStyle.'

differences, because of the theory of stylistics, and its compatibility with strategy ways of writing and speaking.

To understand what Boulding (1956) means by image, and Bakhtin by style, as orders of complexity, we can look to Erving Goffman (1959). Goffman wrote about the arts of image management. In staging its character, 'unmeant gestures' and 'gaffes' can jeopardize the image (1959: 208–9). Projected image, say in an annual report, is 'the polite appearance of consensus' between writers and readers (p. 210).

Bakhtin's stylistic dialogism has implications for strategy. Each narrative strategy stylistic constitutes part of a firm's identity. Besides gesture and oral styles of telling, there are many modes of writing styles that interact in ontological markings. Each strategy voice has its ontic coordinates. Annual reports, for example, constitute the ceremonial repetition of strategic narratives in an orchestration of increasingly dialogic writing stylistics among photos, graphics, letters, and numbers. The ontology of strategy stylistics, its repetition, is how one style interanimates another, or deviates from an old one. It involves the firm in strategy stylistic image management. The image narrative can be authentic style or part of deception, an illusion, or an impostor, as in Enron.

There is an order of stylistic complexity where narrative control and emergent-amplification are opposing forces of the Storytelling Organization. Orchestration of stylistic strategy narratives encounters, even spawns, resistance in a myriad of *rebellion* in emergent counter-stories (e.g. culture jamming). Orchestrating multi-stylistic modes of telling official strategy stylistic narrative is all about 'image' and the resistance to counter-image. The managerial control of corporate image can veer out of control. It's about the illusion of narrative control in the face of story emergence (see Chapter 3).

Stylistic strategy story orchestration is defined as the manner of influencing and orchestrating image in diverse stylistic modes of narrative control over emergent story. Organization and environment stylistic modes dialogically answer one another's way of telling.

Narrative inquiry into *stylistic maelstrom* generated by even one global firm is daunting. A global corporation puts outs hundreds of pages of annual reports. It proliferates hundreds of pages of press releases, brochures, and advertisements. Add to this, countless speeches by executives at annual meetings, training sessions, and press conferences, plus everyday expressive conversation and gesture. Organization's multi-stylistics dialogizes and redistributes, becoming more dialogic in news coverage, business cases, and other imitative image-expressivity of popular culture.

Stylistic strategy story dialogism includes the counter-story, the juxtaposition of styles, and their resistance, such as culture jamming when some graphic artist crafts meaning resistance to strategically orchestrated image management. One quickly realizes that strategically orchestrated stylistic dialogism expressivity spins narrative image control to be countered by emergent rumors of scandal. The problem is strategy schools have been theorizing written and verbal narrative utterances at conceptions of organic system complexity, but studying them as closed systems. Interpenetration between organization and environment strategic stylistic dialogism has been ignored.

Stylist strategy is in practice, but outside of strategy literature has yet to be studied. An exception is Yue Cai's (2006) study of the stylistic strategy of Motorola annual reports, finding that since the 1990s, stylistics are getting more dialogic.

Weick's (1995: 6) enactment sensemaking could be a way to look at stylistics: 'sensemaking is about such things as placement of items into frameworks, comprehending, redressing surprise, constructing meaning, interacting in pursuits of mutual understanding, and patterning.' This framing and reframing occurs in stylistics. Weick (1995: 127) cites Fisher's (1984) 'narrative paradigm theory' and Polkinghorne's (1988) survey of 'narrative knowledge' in the social sciences, but does not draw out the stylistic implications.

Fisher (1984) makes the point that people judge not on content, but on the narrative style. He addresses how people justify behavior (past or future) by telling a credible narrative, not by producing evidence, not by logical argument, but with style. Fisher proposes that the test of narrative rationality is 'coherence', a function of audience assessments of probability and fidelity. Strategy schools missed the most important aspect of Fisher's (1984, 1985a, 1985b, 1989) narrative paradigm theory. Audiences are assessing not only coherence, but also the subversive aspect of narrative style, *the lie*. Instead of assessing logic of formal arguments, a jury, for example, assesses stylistic *verisimilitude*. Fisher is critiqued for failing 'to specify how critics are to make their choices between narrative probability or fidelity, and provides no criteria for testing narrative probability.'[2]

Polkinghorne's (1988) theory of narrative knowledge also emphasizes veracity, the appearance of truth in narrative style. Fields of strategy, and Weick's reading of Polkinghorne and Fisher, seems to miss three postmodern implications of narrative style: subjectivity of narrative selectivity of some incidents, problems with truth claims when organizations manipulate their image, and problems multi-stylistics poses for which narrative representation to believe.[3] Postmodern critique of control narrative is advanced by Denzin (1989: 26), in how narrative performance in written texts inadequately depicts lived experience.

When the Storytelling Organization writes its biography, its annual reports, its press releases, etc. the writers and readers form a collusion, conspiring to create lives they write and read about, narrating lives of workers, investors, customers, communities, and so forth. There can be false claims and distortions in image stylistic management done in the writing and orality of stylistic strategy narratives.

---

2 Wikipedia Encyclopedia, accessed 20 February 2006 online at http://en.wikipedia.org/wiki/Narrative_paradigm

3 See Donna Alvermann's 2000 essay on Narrative approaches, online at http://www.readingonline.org/articles/handbook/alvermann/

We look at the interplay of image and veracity in three stylistic strategy examples: hailing, dramaturgy, and triple narrative.

HAILING AS STYLISTIC STRATEGY

Louis Pierre Althusser (1998: 302) defines *hailing* as a process by which the person being hailed recognizes themself as the subject of the hail, and knows to respond (it's me). Hailing in Goffman's dramaturgy is the way in which we are drawn into or accept or embody a role ('you mean me?'). Althusser uses the example of the police officer yelling, 'Hey you!' and you assume you are the addressee and subject of the hail, and know how to respond. And I think this is done through stylistic orchestration. In stylistic dialogism, the image narrative is deployed in an assemblage of stylistics likely to be unchallenged by the audience being hailed, and recruited into a role. In terms of narrative strategy, the audience is being 'hailed' by the stylistics, to participate in the image and ideological role narrated by the corporation (Althusser, 1998: 302).

McDonald's, for example, uses complex stylistic assemblages to recruit parents (parents, like you, prescribe an active lifestyle for our children, are concerned about nutrition, etc.). The stylistics hails the parents, recruiting them into the ideology of 'Go Active' narrative.

In one particular McDonald's flyer, parents are being hailed, recruited to play a dramaturgical role. Ronald McDonald uses everyday speech 'Choice and change your kids will love' and the image of Ronald is stylized as a visual hail, the text reading:

> This leaflet tells you about the nutritional content of the McDonald's Happy Meal, which gives your kids a choice of fun and tasty food and drinks. It also provides you with some useful information about your kids' diets.

The rest of the text invites parents to study nutritional information useful for their kids' diets. More scientific styled speech, such as lists of cholesterol, allergy information, etc. ascribed to institutional authorities is contained in the brochure.

When Morgan Spurlock's *Supersize Me* documentary began to accumulate film festival awards and was being released in theatres worldwide, McDonald's updated its strategic stylistics. The film offered audiences a glimpse behind the stylistically orchestrated image. A claim in the film was that many McDonald's restaurants did not indicate the nutritional risks of fast food diets. Another claim was that the Supersize portions of fries, burgers, and drinks were especially risky to one's health. McDonald's reacted by putting nutritional information on the back of trayliners, updating brochures, eliminating Supersize options, bringing in a line of salads, putting Ronald on a diet, and transforming him into a fitness coach, enrolling nutrition gurus, such as Bob Greene and fitness experts, such as Donna Richardson-Joyner to offer parents advice. Spurlock's documentary showed fat Americans getting fatter on fast food diets. McDonald's was successfully repelling lawsuits by parents claiming their children were being fattened up, and that the claims of nutrition and fitness constituted false and deceptive advertising.

In Goffman's (1959: 212) terms, to save face, the image of McDonald's had to be stylistically revised to accept 'certain moral obligations.' We can debate the veracity, but stylistically the images are ontologically there in every McDonald's restaurant. Narrative obligations were constructed in dramaturgical devices that are stylistic. *McStylistics* come in many genres from menu displays (salads, fruit and nuts, etc.), TV advertising, brochures, annual reports, press releases, publicity tours by corporate spokespersons such as Greene and Ronald, etc.

DRAMATURGY AS STYLISTIC STRATEGY

The stylistic assemblage sustains the image dramaturgically. The power of stylistic strategy is that the stylistics can deepen the 'working consensus of roles' between customers and corporation. Each styled image from *skaz* of everyday speech (e.g. McChicken, I'm Lovin it!), science speak in nutrition guides, photos of clowns with children, executive's press releases about health and fitness, to coloring books for toddlers, plays its part by masking any corporately calculative, instrumental, or manipulative moves. Each stylistic is managed so as to not commit unmeant gestures, faux pas disclosures of backstage secrets. Stylistic orchestration fits Weick's (1995) third-order control narrative: enrolling audience through sensemaking control.

The orchestration of sensemaking narratives of control is opposed by the more dialogic stylistics, which veer out of corporate control. Narrative control is the centripetal force. Stylistic dialogism among fragments can be a centrifugal amplifying force of heteroglossia. Narrative coherence and dialogic variety making, along with emergent story are intertextuality mutually implicated forces and counter-forces.

The Storytelling Organization, at this level of complexity, exploits dramaturgic opportunities, avoiding threats by selecting characters (spokespersons, clowns, executives, etc.) who are loyal, disciplined to perform their roles, and can be relied upon to be circumspect (not reveal secrets). Dramaturgic control is accomplished, as well, by inviting audiences to an annual meeting orchestrated to give the organization a minimum of trouble. Nike, for example, has had to move its annual meetings away from Oregon, away from activists. Reebok, when it does its annual Human Rights Awards event, only announces the location to select (embedded) reports; activists learn of the location only after the annual ceremony is concluded.

Stylistic dramaturgy maintains the kind of 'definition of the situation' (Goffman, 1959: 238) that affirms the Storytelling Organization's ideology. Orchestration of stylistic complexity can no longer be contained in narratives controlled by corporations to produce ideology hailing. An entire army of narrativists orchestrating stylistic hails, will find that emergent counter-stories unravel strategic secrets, giving the audience a glimpse of what is backstage. Control narrative and emergent story (gossip, rumor, rebellion) interplay in dialogic-stylistic-complexity. Gaffes in stylistic competency or by whistle blowing disclose strategic secrets.

Letting too many styles loose can set off risks to image control. An otherwise solemn, serious annual meeting, or a boring annual report stylistic narrative can self-deconstruct, as one stylistic accuses another of being insincere. This is the danger of E6 Innovation, Improv, and Quasi Object emergent types of story. A foolish mistake in an image stylistic becomes too obvious a hail. A claim to be concerned about nutrition, fitness, or the diet of children, can be read as an emergent ruse story, or as E4 propaganda. High variety stylistic diversity is dramaturgically risky business because it is here where emergent story self-organizes out-of-corporate-control.

Financial experts, looking for emergent stories of deception and misrepresentation, read stylistics critically. Stylistics is therefore a high stakes game of erecting an image that invites investors to trust the story strategy. If claims exaggerate the opportunities and under-report the threats, financial experts might just sound the alarm. To counter such risks, collusion is cultivated. This was apparent in the Enron scandal. Even as Enron slid into bankruptcy court, financial experts were advising their audience to buy. It is not that financial experts are deceived by glitz, sheen, gloss, and spectacle of financial statements. It is not that accounting and the SEC do not have rigid standards for reporting financial claims. In order to get away with a lie the dimension of an Enron, the image must be carefully managed. It's not just a photo shoot but people are choreographed, told what to wear, how to pose, how to hail the audience to give the most favorable impression. Corporations are under scrutiny, and express their image meticulously. They avoid risk of inadvertent disclosure by posing their characters, making each stylistic genre resonate with every other stylistic.

Any attempt to slander corporate image is met by dramaturgical correction. If the image of a corporation in the press is that it contracts to sweatshops, then the stylistics can be orchestrated strategically to give just the opposite impression. The corporation is converting sweatshops into model factories. Image is re-orchestrated to convey the reversal-veracity of the accusatory image.

The danger in second-order control (i.e. scripting the narrative tightly) is that the scripted performance when disrupted is not able to find its way back to the tightly coupled plotline (Goffman, 1959: 228). Therefore, a loose assemblage of styles is enacted so that the fragments can rearrange image, be adaptive in the face of negative press.

There are instances of what Goffman (1959: 232) calls 'tacit collusion.' Narrative collusion is relied upon. Collusion is defined as a defense technique of image management that seduces tacit agreement be maintained between audience and performers not to think too critically, and spoil the illusion. The audience is expected to not ask very difficult questions. As stylistics gets more pluralistic, third-order narrative controls (ideological hailing and theatrics) become risky stylistic strategies. There can be inadvertent disclosure. The tactic conclusion of investment experts, workers, and spokespersons is underestimated. Characters tactfully are invited to not see, to pay no inattention to the gaffes and faux pas. This sustains false image. At shareholder events, audiences enact a lively approval of corporate performance. Their applause is cultivated to enroll them, to demonstrate performance approval as dramaturgical fact of their collusion. 'A tacit agreement is maintained between performers and audience to act as if a given degree of opposition and of accord existed between them' (Goffman, 1959: 238).

Emergent story opposition to corporate claims, even by activists, will loose an audience if it is too rude, too impolite, without proper etiquette. The tacit *working consensus* between opposition, corporation, and audience, is not be too impolite. Corporations disclose just a little of its misrepresentation, but depend upon politeness to not read in-between-the-lines. Tactfulness is strategic stylistic. What they are being tactful about is not breaking the dramaturgic frame. Social etiquette is integral to collusion needed for the *mismanagement* of image. Any stylistic excuse will be read tactfully, giving protective narrative cover. Audiences are hailed, recruited to give dramaturgical assistance, to show inattention to stylistic traces, to co-operate with the frame.

Analytically, if one is willing to set etiquette aside, more accurately, to read etiquette critically as collusion, strategic secrets of dramaturgic exploitations are evident in the stylistic arrangement. My point is that there are dramaturgic aspects of the multi-stylistic image narrative interactive with emergent story opportunities that can be critically read. In the next section I focus on how annual reports can be studied critically by deciphering stylistic elements that manipulate the definition of the situation.

TRIPLE NARRATIVE AS STYLISTIC STRATEGY

As above, a multi-stylistic annual report is very hailing to a variety of readers, and carries the risk that an image inconsistent with managerial ideology is being constructed inadvertently, and will emerge in counter-story. This brings us to triple narrative, defined as when two or more orchestrated narratives (such as narrative rhetoric and surface stylistic narrative) give rise to a third, more emergently dialogized story of thick empirics. For example, an annual report is a triple narrative stylistic.

First it is empirics interpreted in narrative rhetoric about lists of assets, liabilities, acquisitions, and closings, 'just the facts.' Second, the double sells empirics-narrative with surface stylistics, photos, charts, testimonials, and letters. Third, one can critically read both the thick empirics, and the surface images narratives for a third type of narrative, traces of attempts to deceive (Cai, 2006). This third can be an emergent story left inadvertently, and sometimes by defectors, on purpose. The third emergent story, or implicated missing emergent story, is read in the clues, in the aberrations of the narrative control of the report.

The first and second narrative is simultaneous, using the same elements to tell, but tell quite differently. Each gives clues to the third narrative of over-control, the one that is missing, read in-between-the-lines.

Critical discourse analysis is defined as opening up the 'infinite space where doubles reverberate' (Foucault, 1977b: 59). And those doubles reverberate in ways that are telling about how a Storytelling Organization tricks self-destruct. Discourse is defined as 'the infinite play of differences in meanings mediated through socially constructed hegemonic practices, especially in stories (Boje, 1991: 107; Clegg, 1989: 178; Cooper and Burrell, 1988; Laclau, 1983, 1988)' (from Boje, 1995). Story is a domain of discourse (see critical discourse analysis).

I theorize an annual report can be read as a fictive protection against the death of the firm, one that is a plurality of three narrative controls. Narratives of heroic leader adventure, glorious inventions, exploits, and fortunes gained by the organization is one way to disarm death. The inevitable mortality of each leader and organization, its technologies, its cash cow products is postponed. The first control narrative, the official telling in the annual report official-speak, reestablishes the invincibility of the firm. In the second narrative, the orchestrated-image, there is mostly silence about the missing third narrative. There are traces of the defiance and of the evasion of death's inevitability.

This strategic stylistic orchestration of three narratives is an annual ritual that partially controls emergent story, while giving it opportunity to arise. The first type of strategy narrative, in each annual report, works to place infinity (all that is transcendental) outside itself. The second narrative type strategically uses multi-stylistics to craft fashionable image narrative of the organization's identity. The missing third is left in-between-the-lines.

Writing strategy narratives is a collaborative effort of accountants, publicists, executives, staff, and consultants. It takes forensics to ascertain if it is orchestrated (or random) juxtaposition or dialogism. The first narrative addresses itself to reporting the numbers, the lists of acquisitions, new products, investments in R&D, in new technologies, adventures in this or that country, going global, etc. Yet, even in the first narrative, there is also embellishment, the erection of stylistic image, in an 'endless murmuring we call literature' or strategy literature (Foucault, 1977b: 60). In the third, in the moment of expressivity 'a work whose only meaning resides in its being a self-enclosed expression of its glory is no longer possible' (p. 60).

Why? Because the second narrative, the one mostly told with silence, by omission, and those very telling denials, is all about the struggle to deny death her due. And we can trace clues in the first and second narrative to detect the missing third. Each narrative tries unsuccessfully to erase the other's sovereignty.

Ironically, the annual report claims to tell all, to prohibit exaggeration, to be authenticated by experts, etc. Yet, the annual report, especially recently, is full of testimonials, photos of happy customers, dedicated employees, and a lot of strangely constructed insertions of commentaries by many stakeholders. Triple narration by organization narrators narrating through appropriated voices, spliced into the report to appeal to some reader, can unravel. The Annual report is a strategically stylistically dialogic assemblage, a network of fragments, letters, footnotes, letters, exhibits, insertions, deletions, and all those lists of assets, liabilities, acquisitions, disposals, etc. repeated in this tedious and monotonous ceremony.

The juxtaposition of wildly different styles of writing and modes of expression, creates a pastiche where the sterilized exhaustive lists of facts and figures is set off against a less strict way of telling. The third narrative, mostly untold, is done with lots more transgressing, denying, expropriation, of others' voices. This is the point at which what is seemingly orchestrated (or random) can take on dialogic import. And yes, there is a conflict, a dialogic one, between the strict ways of telling, and the more unrestricted murmuring way of alluding, in acts of supplementarity, of second and third narrative manner of dialogic stylistic strategy.

In spite of appearances, the annual ceremony is a duel between the Good, Bad, and Ugly triple narrative stylistic strategy. These three ways of telling strategy use writer tricks, each a forked-tongue way of telling. And therein lies the complexity of juxtaposing all the laundry lists of income and expenses with the image-management narrative, and that missing third, that is alluded to in lists and the stylized images. Reports follow previous ones, and anticipate new ones, in the absolute 'law of increment' (Foucault, 1977b: 65), and Bakhtin's (1991: 1–4) 'answerability.' Each annual report, the accumulated succession of them, creates an annual mirror, more accurately a hall of mirrors, in the 'infinity of illusion' (Foucault, 1977b: 65).

In first narrative, by the thickness of the annual reports the docile reader is persuaded to give weight to quantity, to exhaustiveness. Over time, annual reports are longer, thicker, more multi-stylistic, and full of fragments. In its 'too-muchness' there is just all this ornamental superabundance, all the extensive footnotes, the certifications, the strange numbers (Foucault, 1977b: 65).

In second narrative, the thin surface of the image, the photos of diversity are there to persuade the same docile reader that the firm really does celebrate and value diversity. And there is, on most of the pages a different image story, one about ethics, doing no wrong, being absolutely transparent. Embedded is the obligatory CEO's letter telling us of an enchanted future, a future full of progress and risk free possibility.

Then there are traces of a third narrative. One in between the two ways of telling (too-muchness and allusions to image), where there is possibility of emergent story escaping death, of transcendence. In the plurality of stylistics, the photos, scientific-sounding jargon, the accounting tables, the letter from the CEO, and some quotes from customers, employees, and sometimes community folks, there is a terror of death, a fear of it. An example will help clarify the concept of triple story, in multi-stylistic narrative strategy writing.

McDONALD'S TRIPLE NARRATIVE

First Narrative

In the 2004 annual report, we are told:

> McDonald's operates and franchises more than 30,000 local restaurants in 119 countries on five continents... a leader in social responsibility... generate substantial amounts of cash... serve nearly 50 million customers a day... are 50 years young. McDonald's is a local business. We... are your neighborhood restaurant... are the crewperson who serves you... do business with local suppliers.... learn every day from our customers.... give back to the communities in which we do business. (McDonald's 2004 Summary Annual Report 2)[4]

Second Narrative

The second type of narrative control is accomplished with more visual styles, and accompanying captions, using more everyday language.

The first strategic narrative is supported with a second, with photos, graphs and charts, and various interpretations of numbers in footnotes and main text. On page 3 of the 2004 McDonald's Annual Report there is a photo of a young couple eating McDonald's French Fries. In the report, that photo takes up the entire page, with only the 'M' emblazoned on the French Fries wrapper to tell us something. How do they consume fries and stay so thin? The report has many such photos (a black couple riding bikes; a thin woman doing yoga; kids of different ethnicity hugging and eating their Happy Meals; teens playing beach volleyball; a young man leaping in the air with his guitar), and some storytelling that is about image, not about just the numbers.

On page 67 of the 2007 McDonald's Annual Report, an animated couple carrying their McDonald's fast food is as happy as can be[5]. On the cover two women are in conversation. One eats a slice of an apple, the other has a cheeseburger. On page 10 a young girl with braces eats a fruit salad. On page 14 two more women are smiling and eating. Page 16 has a pair of younger children, one with a McDonald's Milk Jug. The financial report does not start until page 21. The point is that these images are part of McDonald's strategy storytelling.

McDonald's global strategy is called 'Go Active!' referring to its strategy narrative, that eating fast food with exercise and informed choices is nutritional and

---

4 McDonald's 2004 Summary Annual Report at http://www.mcdonalds.com
5 Donald's 2007 Annual Report at www.mcdonalds.com/corp/invest/pub.html See also http://peaceaware.com/McD for similar images.

healthy: 'to be the leading restaurant promoting healthy, happy, active lifestyles everywhere we do business' (slide 17 in Kapica, 2004 presentation).[6] The first and second narrative are given weight authority: McDonald's Global Advisory Council consists of 16 leaders in nutrition, education, and fitness from 10 countries; the council works with 20 McDonald's staff members from a variety of disciplines to pursue the 'Go Active' strategy (slide 16, Kapica, 2004). Skinner emphasizes that 'promoting balanced, active lifestyles' will be an important part of McDonald's future:

> As the world's leading restaurant organization, McDonald's strives to make a difference. We believe leadership equals action, which is why we are addressing three critical areas—adding even more choice and variety to our menu, providing nutrition education and supporting physical activity. When it comes to advocating a balanced, active lifestyle, we plan to take positive actions on behalf of our customers. (Skinner in McDonald's 2004 Summary Annual Report: 12)

Ronald is changing.[7] If you compare the stylistic images of Ronald over time, several things can be deduced. First, Ronald is getting slimmer, and younger. If you compare the Ronald images in the 2004 Annual Report with the 2001 Annual Report, you can see the differences.[8]

We can read in-between-the-lines, and in-between-the-images an emergent story. Ronald has become a child-fitness coach, with the older, heavier Ronald no longer the fitting image of McDonald's. The change is strategic, in that it supports the new 'nutritious' McDonald's image.

After the leaping guitar player photo, is the caption

> I love music. It's a great escape from school work. Don't get me wrong. I like school, but I'm not that big on tests. After exams are over, my friends and I celebrate with a Big Mac and fries while we jam out. I guess you can say, 'i'm lovin' it' (2004 Annual Report: 17)

Likewise, on page 15:

> We also are connecting with customers by letting them express their individuality and their zest for life through our successful 'i'm lovin' it' theme. 'i'm lovin' it' is youthful, energetic, familiar, happy and modern—no matter

6 Cathy Kapica, 2004 'The role of quick serve restaurants in wellness', presentation of global corporate strategy to the American Overseas Dietitic conference, Nicosia, Cyprus, 27 March.
7 See http://peaceaware.com/McD for historical images of Ronald McDonald.
8 2001 Report p. 1 cover photo of Ronald at http://www.mcdonalds.com/corp/invest/pub/annual_rpt_archives/2001_annual.RowPar.0005.ContentPar.0001.ColumnPar.0002.File.tmp/mcdarpp14_28.pdf

what your age. Through 'i'm lovin' it,' customers express their individuality and celebrate their commonalities. They describe what they love about life and how McDonald's fits into it. They tell us we are inclusive... that they can be themselves with us... that they always feel comfortable and welcome at our restaurants.

The second narrative is something about life, about being active, *loving McDonald's*, for its fit into love about life.

Third Narrative

There are clues in the protestations about the 'Go Active' McDonald's lifestyle, to the missing narrative. There is confrontation with death throughout the report. There are more than the usual clues in 2004, because McDonald's has lost two CEOs to death, the kinds of death that are commonly associated with fast food diets. This circumstance is a threat to corporate image. Somehow the third narrative must be addressed, and its implications reversed. On page 5 of the 2004 McDonald's Summary Annual Report is a letter from the Chairman of the Board, about succession planning, and it speaks to the organization's encounters with death during the past year:

> Unfortunately, our preparedness was called upon twice last year when the McDonald's System was saddened by the untimely departures of two exceptional CEOs. Jim Cantalupo passed away unexpectedly last April, after just 16 months at the Company's helm. Seven months later, his successor, Charlie Bell, stepped down due to an illness that ultimately claimed his life.

The new CEO, Skinner (pp. 7–8), continues to tell the story of Jim Cantalupo's death, followed by Charlie Bell's story. Skinner tells the story of the 'I'm lovin' it' strategy and the 'battle with death': '... it was a year in which our performance thoroughly affirmed our strategic imperative—to grow by being better, not just bigger.' He then returns to the battle with death:

> But...if 2004 was a year of unparalleled achievement, it was also a year of unprecedented tragedy. This tragedy began in April, with the sudden and unexpected death of Jim Cantalupo at our Worldwide Owner/Operator Convention. Jim had led our Company for just 16 months, but in that time he created the foundation for the remarkable turnaround that continues today. And the Convention, which should have been one of Jim's finest hours, instead became one of the McDonald's Family's saddest moments. Just weeks later, Charlie Bell, Jim's talented successor as CEO, discovered he was suffering from colon cancer. Throughout 2004, we watched this vibrant leader wage a courageous battle against the disease, a battle that ended in January in his hometown of Sydney, Australia. Both Jim and Charlie worked their way to the top of our System through

passion, incredible hard work and great instinct. They were remarkable men. Today, with 2004 behind us, I am often asked...how did McDonald's do it? With all the misfortune, how did your Company post one of its most successful years ever?

Newest CEO Skinner, claims that McDonald's was highly successful, in the face of death, and the report itself ends with a eulogy to Jim Cantalupo and to Charlie Bell, and a rather ironic remark: 'Charlie gave his all to McDonald's' (p. 26). The clues to the missing emergent story are everywhere.

McDonald's Workers Resistance Annual Report (2002)[9] had these counter-narratives and emergent stories:

> 2002 saw McDonalds' apparently unstoppable expansion not just slowed but in certain places reversed – around the world McDonalds is closing restaurants and pulling out of some countries completely. Profits are down (although still enormous) and Jack Greenberg has been unceremoniously ditched as top honcho. In stark contrast, McDonalds Workers' Resistance (MWR) has progressed impressively during these twelve months. We have developed from a small group of agitators to a substantial network increasingly capable of affecting McDonalds' business.

In Australia a franchise owner (Rod Hackett) put up a website telling his counter-story of McDonald's cannibalism strategy: 'cannibalization being the encroachment on an existing restaurant's primary trading area by a new restaurant.' Hackett goes on to tell his counter-story:[10]

> I became aware of a review of the Australian Franchising Code of Conduct then being undertaken, and a request by the Federal Government for submissions from interested franchisees, in respect of the Review. I brought this information to the attention of McDonalds Victorian franchisee representatives in the belief they would bring it to the attention of the general franchisee community – regrettably they chose not to do so!

> I therefore felt compelled to alert the franchisees myself – two days before the government's closing deadline for the lodging of submissions. Thus I fell from grace.

> Subsequently, I was threatened, after Tat Cork (the Regional Director of the corporation) informed me: 'An officer of the corporation has recently said, 'When do we f**k Hackett?' And that not merely one, but two new McDonalds restaurants were now to be opened nearby, one of which was to be sited only about 400 meters away from my business's primary asset: my restaurant at Fountain Gate.

---

9 For McDonald's Workers Resistance Annual Report see http://www.mcspotlight.org/media/press/releases/mcspot120203.html

10 Ron Hockett's Franchisee Report is at http://www.licenseenews.com/ethics1.html

The point I am making is the strategy narrative in corporate annual reports is multi-stylistic, and dialogic not only within a report, but also intertextually the stylistic dialogism interacts with polyphonic dialogism among many stakeholders. Sometimes the more orchestrated stylistic narrative strategy leaves clues to emergent story.[11]

---

11 For more examples see McSpotlight fact sheet http://www.mcspotlight.org/case/ pretrial/factsheet_ref.html

6

CHRONOTOPIC STRATEGY STORIES

My focus is integrating systemicity theory and chronotopic dialogism with several traditional schools of strategy: history-design, configuration, and cultural. I identify ten chronotopes as they relate to McDonald's chronotopic strategy story. *Chronotopic Strategy Story* is defined as the juxtaposition, or possible dialogism among several ways in which space and time are being narrated. In the last chapter (stylistic dialogism) we learned that the variety of stylistic materials is inexhaustible, and there is much selectivity in which fragments are included or excluded.[1]

Chronotope is defined as relativity of time and space: 'the intrinsic connectedness of temporal and spatial relationships that are artistically expressed in literature' (Bakhtin, 1981: 84–5). He employs the term chronotope as an Einstein Theory of Relativity with time being the fourth dimension of space:

> Time, as it were, thickens, takes on flesh, becomes artistically visible; likewise space becomes charged and responsive to its movements of time, plot and history. (1981: 84)

I must challenge Bakhtin for his hierarchical system thinking. Bakhtin's ten chronotopes, unlike Boulding's levels (Chapter 1), are not successive-hierarchically ordered. The Idyllic (number 9), for example would carry forward the first eight chronotopes, but the chronotopes are more kaleidoscopic. Bakhtin's approach (once you get beyond its chronology) is a holographic rendition (chronotopes combine in any order). Idyllic, for example, could be part of an everyday adventure, but without several other folkloric or adventuristic chronotopes required for inclusion.

Historically, as chronotopes emerged, they became increasingly dialogic to one another. Contemporary strategy is not just multi-chronotopic. Strategy can be chronotopically dialogic. Table 6.1 is my summary definitions of ten chronotopes I find in Bakhtin's writing. The first four are adventure (elimination of brute heteroglossia by structuring some kind of centripetal, centering). The last six are folkloric (and are more centrifugal, diffusing or amplifying).

Chronotopic Dialogism then can be seen as a holographic relation of centering (centripetal of chronotopes 1 to 4) and amplifying (centrifugal of chronotopes

---

1 I am indebted to Randy Chulick, a rhetoric PhD student at New Mexico State for contributing editorial assistance on this chapter, discussing the ideas with me.

6 to 10) forces. In this chapter we continue our exploration of how multi-dialogism is related to strategy.

TABLE 6.1   *Ten Chronotopes[2]*

Centripetal Chronotopes:

1. Greek Romance Adventure
2. Adventure of everyday life
3. Biography & Autobiography Adventure
4. Chivalric Romance, the Epic Adventure

Centrifugal Chronotopes:

5. Reversal of Folkloric Historical Realism
6. Rogue, Clown & Fool Folkloric Archetypes
7. Folkloric of Rabelaisian purge
8. Folkloric Basis for Rabelaisian
9. Idyllic Folkloric (organic localism)
10. Castle Room Folkloric

STRATEGY CHRONOTOPES

The question arises, which chronotopes are manifest in schools and exemplars of strategy? Let me state five researchable propositions:

1 Strategy writers use different chronotopes.
2 Some writers use multiple chronotopes.
3 Strategy schools' typologies ignore the folkloric chronotopes.
4 There are more chronotopes in use than are theorized in strategy.
5 The dialogism of inter-chronotopic relationships has not been studied.

In reformulating the Mintzberg et al.'s, Barry and Elmes', and Astley's typologies in Chapter 4, I relocated part of the design school (notably, Selznick) into what Boulding would call Level 7 (symbolic). I asserted that the Configuration School of strategy (e.g. Chandler), which privileges history, has Level 7 chronotopic properties. Cole was an economic historian (as well as Schumpeter) whose work bridged into Level 7. And Normann was not just Cultural School. Indeed, the kaleidoscope (or rhizomatic subterranean) escaped Mintzberg et al.'s framework. The ten schools of strategy that Mintzberg et al., as well as alternative classifications by Barry and Elmes, and Astley, do not address the more

---

2 In Bakhtin (1981) chronotopes are developed chronologically according to when they are first used in writing. Chivalric in Bakhtin comes after Reversal of Folkloric Historical Realism. However, since Chivalric is adventure, I prefer to group it by type instead of chronologically. I am deeply appreciative of Randy Chulick for helping me sort this out.

TABLE 6.2 *Chronotopes and definitions*

Chronotope	Definition
1 **Greek Romance Adventure**	Systematicity of time and space; both time and space are interchangeable sequences of events, that leave no trace on the hero; hero travels through diverse geographic terrain and encounters characters different from themselves
2 **Adventure of Everyday Life**	Mix of adventure-time with everyday time; hero's life sheathed in context of metamorphosis of human identity brought about by trial, and revelation on the public square; type of metamorphosis is mythological cycle of crisis, so person becomes other than what she or he was by chance, accident and trial
3 **Biography and Autobiography Adventure**	(Auto) biographical time in energia, analytic and stoic subtypes; each subtype appeals to a circle of readers, and like the first chronotope, character metamorphosis is excluded. Historical time and spatial events are how a character discovers hidden character traits (that were there all along) and by laying one's life bare, illuminating it on public square in self-glorification
4 **Chivalric Romance, the Epic Adventure**	Hyperbolization of time with other-worldly verticality (descent); this is strange mix of (1) Greek Romance and (2) Adventure novel of everyday life; testing of heroes' fidelity to love or faith in chivalric code; fairy tale motifs linked to identity and enchantment; chance (number 2) of gods, fate rupture time of normal life with series of suddenlys, making the systematicalness of Greek romance fragment
5 **Historical Reversal of Folkloric Realism**	An inversion to folkloric fullness of here-and-now reality (folkloric realism) becomes transformed by trips into past (or mythic thought) to concretize otherwise ephemeral and fragmented future
6 **Rogue, Clown and Fool Folkloric Archetypes**	Out of depths of folklore pre-class structure are three medieval Folkloric Archetypes masks; mix of (4) folkloric and (2) everyday adventure and (3) public shared theatrics and (5) chivalric romance; right to be in the world and see falseness of every situation; metamorphosis of being in life, but not a part of it, making public the non-public sphere, and laying bare conventionality of feudal and institutional hypocritical in a theatrical space (public square).
7 **Folkloric of Rabelaisian Purge**	Rabelaisian Laughter has two phases (1) purge of transcendent worldview; and (2) laughter of renewal to create a more positive construction. It interacts with preceding chronotopes, e.g. purging romantic, false official ideology and false chivalric code/epic/religious/feudal using Rabelaisian laughter of the 3 masks and grotesque realism, to reverse the folkloric appropriation by modernity
8 **Folkloric Basis for Rabelaisian**	Time is collective and part of productive growth, measured by labor events; generative time is pregnant time and concrete here-and-now, a time sunk deeply in the earth, profoundly spatial and concrete, implanted in earth and ripening in it (metamorphosis); pre-class
9 **Idyllic Folkloric (organic localism)**	Idyllic folkloric time is agricultural and craft labor, it is family organically grafted to time events and spatiality (place), living organically in familiar territory, in unity of place; rhythm of life linked to nature and cyclic repetition that is separated from progress myth; not a stage of development; a rebirth; the idyllic fragments and disintegrates with advent of modernity
10 **Castle Room Folkloric**	The place and time of telling, such as a Castle Room, or a Salon, or a Fast Food Restaurant is its own chronotope

TABLE 6.3   *Ten chronotopes and strategy schools*

Adventure Chronotopes	Strategy Schools and Exemplars
1 **Greek Romantic**	Andrews' SWOT is epic adventure chronotope (combination of Greek Romance and Chivalric) in Barry and Elmes' (1997) schools framework
	Ansoff (1965) rational, abstract frame of goal focus and diversification
	Schumpeter (1942) and Cole (1959) at level of institutions (not its only chronotope)
2 **Everyday**	Selznick (1957) everyday adventure that is cyclic, the life-cycle of the institution faced with sudden crises adapts by preferring Fox or Lion leader-archetypes in the dominant coalition of power (not his only chronotope)
	Chandler's (1962) everyday travel adventure: organizations invent strategies that result in the decentralized multidivisional form (form follows strategy) as they move into multiple terrains
3 **Analytic Biographic**	Chandler's (1962) comparative history method is a variant of Bakhtin's analytic biography (well-defined rubrics or principles beneath biographic material)
4 **Chivalric**	Selznick (1957) institutional leader is chivalric, expected to be beyond opportunism and utopianism; uses self-reflexive self-knowledge
	Schumpeter (1942) and Cole (1959) – economic historians whose chivalric code is 'creative destruction' and defense of monopolistic capitalism. Neither author treats individuals as hero; rather institutions are heroes
Folkloric Chronotopes	
5 **Reversal of Historical Realism**	Miles and Snow (1978) and Miller and Friesen (1977) shun historical realism; they type organization perceptions of environment according to various symbol-archetypes, e.g. Miles and Snow: reactor, analyzer, defender, and prospector archetypes (from least to most adaptive). Both are contingency frameworks.
	Normann (1977) symbol-archetypes keyed to life cycle model of institutionalization, patterned after Selznick, and to most other schools in Mintzberg et al.'s scheme (particularly cognitive and learning) and others but with different exemplars (design, power, environmental, and configuration).
6 **Clown-Rogue-Fool**	McDonald's examples: Ronald-Hamburglar-Grimace
7 **Rabelaisian Purge**	McDonald's associations of fast food with hybrid food/human and food/animal characters to affirm comic death over real death
8 **Basis for Rabelaisian**	McDonald's strategic substitution of netherworld collective generative time for individual labor and consumptive fast food time

(Continued)

TABLE 6.3   (Continued)

Adventure Chronotopes	Strategy Schools and Exemplars
9 **Idyllic**	McDonald's strategically manages local and global life as idylls that meet in unity in their home away from home.
10 **Castle Room**	McDonald's is a place where families meet, a substitute for playgrounds cities no longer fund

(centrifugal-oriented) folkloric chronotopes.[3] Bakhtin's chronotopes are non-hierarchical, and can interact in any order. There is therefore no theory of strategic multi-chronotopicity.

An alternative way to assign strategy writers is by chronotope. It allows us to theorize the type of narrative control in interconnected sensemaking relationships. The point to keep in mind is that, in theory, a higher order Boulding level of complexity is interactive and implicated with lower properties, but with the Bakhtinian approach, the possibility of interaction is not confined to a linear sequence of imaginary levels. One can find an interaction in Everyday with Idyllic. Chivalric can be in interplay with Greek and Everyday, etc.

ADVENTURE CHRONOTOPES

Adventure chronotopes are highly popular in strategy writing. They occur singly or in combination.

Greek Romantic Adventure

Greek Romantic Adventure is defined as an abstract, formal system of space and time in adventure. Andrews' SWOT is an example of Greek Romantic adventure chronotope. A heroic CEO battles environmental threats, overcomes weaknesses of the firm, plays on firm's strengths to exploit environmental opportunities. The link to time/space in SWOT frame is more mechanistic than organic. Time, for example, can be sped up to overcome spatial distance and alien worlds. Platonic forms, abstract ideas of SWOT drive strategic response. Adventure time is systemic. Globalizing a large space with diverse countries, while obliterating ties to place or local history. It is ahistorical adventure. The rational planning Ansoff school appears to be more of a romantic adventure narrative chronotope, an abstract formal system.

Schumpeter (1942) and Cole (1959) are abstract-systemic chronotope, at the level of institutions. We also looked at Arthur Cole (1959) an economic historian who ran a center at Harvard and a journal focused upon entrepreneurial strategy. What chronotopes does Cole deploy in his history of entrepreneurial strategy? Cole, I asserted in the last chapter, builds upon Schumpeter (1942).

---

3 See Chapter 4, in this book, for listing of schools of strategy in relations to Boulding/Pondy levels of systemic complexity

The systemic-abstract of McDonald's is well known, as is the romantic adventure telling of Ray Kroc's founding of the franchise expansion. Kroc was successor to the McDonald brothers who invented the abstract-system of fast food Taylorism. McDonald's operates in global space of diverse countries, avoiding local historical ties when possible, adapting the menu when it must. Heroes in Greek Romantic adventures have Aristotle's 'energia', which means their dramatic personae does not change, traits are merely discovered. Energia is consistent with Kroc's (1977) autobiography.

Everyday Adventure

Everyday Adventure is a mix of everyday time of suddenlys and accident with previous adventure chronotope. Unlike Aristotelian energia (Greek Romantic Adventure chronotope), in Everyday Adventure, the hero becomes other than what she or he was by close encounters with the suddenlys of emergent chance and accident. I therefore categorize it as emergent story, up to the instant it is imprisoned by control narratives. The hero's life is a metamorphosis of human identity emergence. However, it is interactive with other more controlling narrative chronotopes. It is less abstract and linear than the first chronotope. As a mythological cycle of crisis and recovery, it can easily fall into narrative expectation, of what should emerge next. Emergence arises in the chance encounters. Bakhtin argues it is organizational: 'A real-life chronotope of meeting is constantly present in organizations of social and governmental life' (Bakhtin, 1981: 99). The course of the hero's life corresponds to travel and wandering the world, where one meets foreign cultures.

I read Philip Selznick as adopting more of an everyday chronotope, but still rooted as well in the romantic adventure chronotope. Selznick (1957) is a sociologist, who places strategy in historical context by constructing a life-cycle narrative. For Selznick the everyday adventure is cyclic, the institution, its growth patterns, how it behaves under socioeconomic conditions of stability versus sudden emergencies. Institutions have the cycle of birth, maturation, and death. Selznick's life-cycle model draws upon social psychologist Daniel Katz. Katz (1951: 144) presents more of a romantic adventure cycle with definite stopping points:

> A rapidly developing organization which has certain goals to achieve under emergency time-pressures presents an entirely different time pattern from a stable organization which may have passed the peak of its power. In the former case, the leadership pattern may emphasize initiative, creativity, daring and, to some extent, a rejection of traditional pathways to goals and even a reformulation of organizational goals… In the latter case of the older, even declining, institution, the pattern may be one of conformity to tradition, an emphasis upon conventional pathways to conventional goals and even a change from the goal of the organization to the goal of efficiency as such.

For Selznick (1957: 103), Katz's 'remarks suggest the need to place the interpretation of organizational behavior in historical perspective.' While Selznick adopts the 'language of evolution or life-cycle' he also finds it to be 'misleading when applied to organizations' but uses it just the same to 'call attention to the developmental problems that arise in organizational experience' (Selznick, 1957: 103). Romantic adventure cycle is counted by emergence of everyday suddenlys, here-and-now problems that call for organizational changes of leadership. In Selznick's (1957: 104) phrasing, 'The early phase of an institution's life is marked by a scrutiny of its own capabilities, and of its environment, to discover where its resources are and on whom it is dependent.' And 'as these commitments evolve, the organization loses its purity as an abstractly or ideally envisioned entity; it assumes a definite role in a living community; it becomes institutionalized.' What was emergent becomes institutionalized, and what is institutionalized will need to change. Emergence, for Selznick, is imprisoned in narrative life cycle. 'In fact, of course, we must see an organization in its historical context, as an institution' and **not take the life-cycle narrative of chronological phases too literally** (Selznick, 1957: 111, bold emphasis mine). Rather, sudden crises emerge and a new stage of development is demanded from the elites of an enterprise. Machiavelli and Pareto's leader types are invoked: sometimes the historical context demands the 'Foxes,' the innovator types devising new programs and techniques, and other situations call for 'Lions' who 'take over complete control, trimming innovations to meet the needs of survival' (Selznick, 1957: 112).

Emergent suddenlys, and internal and external conflicts unify narrated experiences into the organization's 'special identity' (ibid, p. 106). In strategy terms, at each stage of the organization's life cycle the organization develops its institutional core, i.e. its core competencies. Each phase in the organization's life-history cycle calls forth a different leadership, a different developmental problem, and therefore different core competencies that are historically sensitive to sudden changes in the market, technology, etc. that call for a different strategic orientation.

The Fox and the Lion-leaders archetypes are a basic organization-history-situation contingency-cycle narrative. Each leader type limits adaptation of an institution to new historical conditions and contexts. Foxes de-standardize, de-formalize, and de-centralize. Lions standardize, formalize and centralize. The model sets up a heteroglossia. The centering (deviation-counteracting, centripetal) Lion is countered by decentering (deviation-amplifying, centrifugal) Fox. When the situation shifts, the conformity and rigidity of the Lion or the adaptive innovating of the Fox, is mismatched to the institution's environment. In the life-cycle historical narrative, these leaders are never simultaneous. The problem of leadership and institutional change is that over time an organization becomes infused with values, traditions, and particular methods that are institutionalized as organizational identity and 'distinctive competence,' and this handicaps subsequent adaptive response to shifts in the historical situation (ibid, p. 139).

Analytic Biographic

I met Alfred Chandler, Jr. when he came to present to the strategy faculty at UCLA in the 1980s. Chandler's (1962) comparative history method is multi-chronotopic: Romantic, Everyday emergence, Chivalric, and Biographical. Chandler (1962: 1) uses 'comparative business history' as his biographical approach to examine how du Pont, GM, Standard Oil, and Sears, without mimicking one another *emerged* the decentralized, multi-divisional form, around the same time in the 1920s.

Chandler (1962: vii, 284) builds upon entrepreneur historian Cole and Schumpeter's 'creative response concept.' Chandler does not directly cite Selznick, but the role of administration, as an institutional theory is evident. Like Selznick (1957: 111), Chandler (1962: 130–3) narrates the biography of GM executive Billy Durant as akin to Selznick's Fox, and Alfred Sloan to the Lion. Durant was the marketer-builder of empire, who left the administrative-system-engineering details to Sloan. Chandler does not make the CEO the hero. His quest is for the origin, the birth of an administrative institution, the M-form (decentralized, multi-divisional firm).

Instead of Selznick's more evolutionary life cycle model, Chandler is studying a different complexity property. It is not a matter of firm's youth or maturation (as in Selznick's life cycle), but of the global reach. 'Until the volume or technological complexity of an enterprise's economic activities had so grown as to demand an increasing division of labor within the firm, little time needed to be spent on administrative work' or 'specialization' (Chandler, 1962: 13). It is not an alteration of Fox and Lion to exploit environmental fit. Chandler's frame is quite different. Business institution's administration can focus simultaneously upon co-ordinating, appraising, and planning long-term as well as more immediate unexpected contingencies or crises by adopting the decentralized form (Chandler, 1962: 9).

Chandler tells emergent 'story of how each of the four innovators met its firm's changing administrative needs and problems which resulted from the expansion of its business' and tells it 'from the point of view of the busy men responsible for the destiny of their enterprise' (pp. 6–7). For Chandler, it is in the firm's executives becoming reflexively aware of a change in conditions. Awareness of emergent conditions becomes coherent strategy that necessitates change in administrative plan, then into M-form (p. 299).

Chandler imprisons complexity awareness in chronological narratives (form follows strategy). This makes the enterprise histories comparable. Chandler narrates broad historical developments clearly, coherently, and precisely. Chandler's historical construction is highly detailed, and exhaustive. He reviews and summarizes thousands of pages of text: annual reports, memorandum, and biographies. This is supplemented by interviews. Chandler assembles texts and events in time series. The history of four corporations is reduced to a particular and limited problem, emergence of M-form in Chandler's 'whole' monograph.

Chandler is what Collingwood (1993: 121) calls a 'spectator' to the 'spectacle' of economic history. Like Marx, an 'anti-historical naturalism' infects much of Chandler's idea of history (Collingwood, 1993: 123). Consciousness follows shifts in natural dominion (in material conditions).

Chandler's positivistic conception of history derived from evolutionary naturalism turns into contingency model. Chandler's conception of history is one of managerial progress of the administrative race toward rationality; it's progress of M-form over other forms to better-fit environmental conditions. Once M-form emerged, it took on a universal aspect, being imitated by fourscore and more firms facing similar situations. His analytic biographic chronotope is rooted in positivistic naturalism and managerialist progress mythos.

Chandler writes a single narrative (S1) to bind the M-form up whole, in a plot about one event, emergence of M-form. In Collingwood's (1993: 472) terms, this event is a complex thing, consisting of a plurality of many parts. Chandler enumerated and composed corporate narrative brilliantly. It's the history of the *American Industrial Enterprise*, as Chandler's (1962) title suggests.

Chandler's (S1) narrative whole is a chain of causes and effects, one event being the cause of the one after, and the effect of the one before. Chandler has fallen into an error, assuming leaders to be rational beings that act on the same universal principles.

Rather than causal determination in an historical narrated sequence of event chains, Collingwood (1993: 475) argues 'every event ... is an expression of human thought, is a conscious reaction to a situation, not the effect of a cause.' It's like a 'symphony.' Bakhtin's term is polyphonic symphony of voices and logics. Strategy orchestrates the rhythm, the timing of each instrument. In more dialogized history, threads crisscross with many diverse, and polyphonic narratives. A more dialogized narrative does not collapse the multi-chronotopicity into one.

Chandler's chronotope is a narrative of progress, more accurately, the gradual narrative consolidation of M-form into ideal form. Narratives of progress rest on the metaphysical illusion that the world is getting better and better. A counter-narrative is each period has its ideals. Sometimes it's progress. Other times it's the chaos of Enron and WorldCom. The emergence of M-form is produced through a particular struggle of forces, in a battle against conditions, in a 'hazardous play of dominations' to install a 'system of rules and thus proceeds from domination to domination' (Foucault, 1977b: 148, 151). Foucault (1977b: 146) proposes a more Nietzchean genealogy of emergence and complexity. Genealogy follows a complex course of emergent dispersions, everyday accidents and suddenlys, with lots of errors and reversals, and no metaphysical truth of being lies behind what we know. History is written by conflicts of social class and racial disorder (ibid, pp. 144–5).

Schumpeter, Cole, Selznick, and Chandler are historians supplying managerial prototypes. Schumpeter and Cole use the romantic chronotopic, providing the entrepreneur with knights' armor. Selznick combines the knight with everyday adventure and with chivalry code. Chandler uses analytic biography chronotope to transform knights of industry into what Foucault calls 'monumental history' (1977b: 161). A monumental history is defined as 'a history given to the recovery of works, actions, and creations through the monogram of their personal essence' (p. 161).

We can read a dialogized narrative of differences in-between-the-lines of unity. Chandler (1962: 317) notes that du Pont and GM reformed their bureaucratic hierarchies with ease, while Jersey (Oil) and Sears struggled. In three of the four companies (Sears, du Point, and GM), organizational changes were accomplished by men who arrived shortly after sweeping changes in top management and were not socialized or 'identified with one certain pattern or role of action' (ibid, pp. 319–20). Most executives (Pierre du Pont, Alfred Sloan at GM, James Barker at Sears) were MIT graduates, common socialization in rationalism of engineering. At MIT managers learned Taylor's scientific management techniques. Chandler argues that each of the four firms had 'differences in the ethos or personality' (p. 319), and 'delays in initiating or completing the new structure (decentralized multi-divisional form) usually resulted from the failure of the senior executives to appreciate the administrative needs created by expansion into new markets... too enmeshed in day-to-day operating activities to realize' the new needs were administrative, and not just marketing, finance, production, etc. (p. 323). Rumelt (1974: 76–77) found the opposite relationship between strategy and form. Strategy follows divisionalization (i.e., more divisionalization of form encourages a strategy of still further diversification).

Chandler's monumental history becomes monophonic narrative imprisoning the more dialogic genealogy of the 'concerted carnival' of narrative variety (Foucault, 1977b: 161). It's carnival that Bakhtin (1968) dedicated his life to set free from narrative control. Carnival is dialogized plurality. Carnival opens into the remaining folkloric chronotopic dialogism.

Chivalric Chronotope and Self-Reflexivity

What about self-knowledge? It is here that Selznick moves beyond mere Greek Romance and Everyday chronotopes, and invokes the Chivalric Adventure. Leaders are to pursue a chivalric code, and put the survival of the enterprise ahead of themselves. For Selznick (1957: 143) reflexivity is a matter of 'self-*knowledge* ... an understanding not only of the leader's own weaknesses and potentialities but of those of enterprise itself... yielding the will to know and the will to act in accordance with the requirements of institutional survival and fulfillment.' Self-knowledge for Selznick is the avoidance of opportunism as well as utopianism.

Opportunism gets caught up in short-term immediate gains or exigencies, and misses long-run temporal effects of history upon organization identity. There is still a hint of romantic SWOT: 'The leader's job is to *test* the environment to find out which demands can become truly effective threats, to *change* the environment by finding allies and outer sources of external support, and to gird his organization by creating the means and the will to withstand attacks' (Selznick 1957: 145). And adventure! Opportunism can also be an 'adventurism ... willingness to commit the organization as a whole on the basis of a partial assessment of the situation derived from a particular technological perspective, such as that of the propagandist in foreign affairs or the engineer or designer in industry' (p. 149). Utopianism is 'wishful thinking,' a romantic 'flight to abstractions,' 'a retreat to technology,' and the '*overgeneralization of purpose*' such as 'making profit,' 'quick returns' etc. (ibid, p. 147–9). It is the chivalric, responsible leader who steers a course historically, between opportunism and utopianism, but with continuity of identity and core competency. Selznick seems to transcend the romantic adventure, and bridge the everyday with the chivalric chronotopes.

Cole and Schumpeter are multi-chronotopic, combining Romantic and Chivalric adventure. They present rationalistic and mechanistic ideas of history. Schumpeter (1942) and Cole (1959) are economic historians. Their chivalric code is 'creative destruction' and narrative defense of monopolistic capitalism. Neither author treats individuals as heroes. Rather institutions are heroes. Cole's socioeconomic history of entrepreneurship is a mechanistic account, where entrepreneurship is a 'device for the seizing of opportunities' and 'a mattress on which unwise adventurers may fall' (Cole, 1959: 81). It is historical narration, not of CEO-heroes, but of abstract and formal socioeconomic forces. Cole's socioeconomic forces shape the business enterprise in an 'entrepreneurial stream' (Cole, 1959: 77–8). Like Schumpeter, Cole presents a defense of monopolistic capitalism, where institutions, the state, large corporations, the business school, etc. contribute to entrepreneurial performance. In short, different strategy writers use quite different chronotopes.

FOLKLORIC CHRONOTOPES

Folkloric chronotopes are prevalent in strategy writing, but not labeled. They can be rescued in Mintzberg et al., Barry and Elmes, and Astley. The rescued chronotopes are therefore fruitful for future research.

When we investigate the folkloric chronotope, Bakhtin's (1981) insight is that the historic axis of the adventure chronotopes (especially with chivalric romance) moves to a vertical axis (becomes perpendicular to the horizontal axis of time, and is about ascending-descending). These are the chronotopes that are more apt to be centrifugal.

Reversal of Historical Folkloric Realism

There is trans-positioning in this chronotope, an inversion of time, into *mythic Past* to realize a less *ephemeral Future*. In a sense the mythic overcomes the present. Folklore did not know time or space separated from embodiment in emergent here-and-now. Future time is ephemeral, present time 'is' and past time 'was.' Ephemeral future is not as concrete, dense or weighty as past time. By taking the archetype route a mythic past becomes the basis to concretize the future, and bring them into the present.

It appears to me that Mintzberg's techno-futurist strategy and the 'purist strategy' of archetypes and positioning (in Barry and Elmes) is what Bakhtin (1981) calls the chronotopic 'reversal of folkloric' time and space. Some exemplars are not using adventure chronotopes or any historical analysis to define their archetypes, and just accent the reversal (i.e. Miles and Snow; Miller and Friesen). That means what was emergent in the fullness of here-and-now (folkloric) reality becomes inverted by trips into mythic archetypal-thought to concretize the future. Miles and Snow (1978), and Miller and Friesen (1977) shun historical realism of the biographical chronotope. They type organization perceptions of environment according to various symbol-archetypes. Miles and Snow's archetypes are reactor, analyzer, defender, and prospector (ordered from least to most adaptive). As with Mintzberg, these are contingency frameworks.

Normann's (1977) symbol-archetypes are keyed to the life cycle model of institutionalization, and patterned after Selznick. Normann anticipated most other schools in Mintzberg et al.'s Schools typology (particularly cognitive and learning, design, power, environmental, and contingency/configuration). Normann also builds on Chandler's global reach spatialization, M-form dispersion to multiple countries.

In archetype theories of strategy the present seems to lose its integrity, to break down, into seemingly abstract configurations or conglomerations of mythic archetypes. Configuration school, in general, is a process of metamorphosis, a debasement of the kind of realist positivistic historicity that Chandler did. It's no longer the Fox versus Lion archetype of control or amplification, it is an entire constellation of mythic archetypes that define and dominate the configuration school of strategy. Historic inversion frameworks of archetypes succeed Chandler's attention to the materiality of history. The differences in the configuration archetype schemes are over the question of radical or more gradual transformation. The future is bled dry. The archetypes reenergize a presumed future with symbols of the material past that divine what to do in the here-and-now.

The archetype wing of the configuration school shuns historical realism. Mintzberg et al. attempt to revitalize contingency frameworks calling them configuration (Woodward, 1958; Burns and Stalker, 1961; Pugh et al., 1968). Mintzberg (1979), Miles and Snow (1978), and Miller and Friesen (1977) approach configuration in different ways, but all develop a wrinkle in the contingency school by posing their model of archetypes. For Mintzberg configuration is archetypes of structure; for the others, configuration is archetypes of strategies (defenders, entrepreneurs, etc.).

We can trace a transition in Mintzberg's perspective on configuration archetypes and their contingent relations to environment, from his earliest to most recent writing. Mintzberg's (1973) first book, *Nature of Managerial Work*, was a heretic's challenge to the then dominant Fayol principles and functions of management. Fayol's was an organic metaphor, the organization as a tree with functional branches. Mintzberg observed the activities of senior managers, and found they did not fit Fayol's managerial principles and that functions (plan, organize, command, control, lead etc.) were coherent, more about verbal behaviors than writing or analyzing. Mintzberg found managerial work to be highly fragmented, full of brevity, dominated by verbal behaviors rather than writing behaviors, and high variety, with so many interruptions that behaviors changed quickly. Rather than Fayol's organic functions and principals, Mintzberg defined ten archetypal roles and rules. In other words, instead of Fayol's organic tree metaphor, Mintzberg's metaphor was roles in a theatre play. Role was defined as 'a set of certain behavioral rules associated with a concrete organization or post' (Mintzberg, 1973: 36). Fayol's organic framework conceived of achieving organization goals by phases, whereas Mintzberg's theatric framework theorized fragmented, simultaneous, enactment of multiple archetypal roles.

Mintzberg's ten archetypal roles were conceived as universal to all practising managers: *informational roles* (figurehead, leader, and liaison) link all managerial work together; *interpersonal roles* (monitor, disseminator, and spokesperson) ensure that information is provided. The *decisional roles* (entrepreneur, disturbance handler, resource allocator, and negotiator) make significant use of the information. Fayol's functions and Mintzberg's roles differ. For example, Fayol's planning function became an assemblage of roles such as liaison, disseminator, entrepreneur, and negotiator; organizing implies roles such as liaison, representative, disturbance handler; motivation connects to roles of leader, resource allocator; control takes in roles of figurehead, monitor, and disturbance handler. Fayol's organic functions were more about writing, reviewing and analyzing documents, whereas Mintzberg's roles were more about interacting with people in a high interruption context.

Mintzberg's *The Structuring of Organizations* (1979) assembled a typology of five ideal and pure types of organizations: simple structure (organic entrepreneurial mode), machine bureaucracy (i.e., Weberian), professional bureaucracy, divisionalized form (i.e., Chandler's decentralized, multi-divisional form and Weick's loosely coupled form), and adhocracy (i.e., Toffler's highly organic form). Mintzberg (1979: 299) argued that '**various coordinating mechanisms, design parameters, and contingency factors – all seem to fall into natural clusters, or configurations**' (bold in original). Mintzberg cautions these are ideal types, and that configuration is a theoretical framework (1979: 46–9). In other words, the ten archetypal roles of managers become design parameters in the ideal archetypes of structural configuration.

Mintzberg then relates the dual-archetype (configuration) framework to contingency theory. In his contingency–configuration ideal type framework, simple structure and machine bureaucracy are fit for simple and stable environments; professional bureaucracy is moderately adaptive to higher variety environments, whereas divisionalized form and adhocracy are more suited to complex environments with disparate forces. The five configurations form a 'pentagon' that bounds 'a reality within which real structures can be found... some real structures fall into position close to one node – one of the pure structures – while others fall between two or more, as hybrids, perhaps in transition from one pure form to another' (p. 469). Since Mintzberg and Lampel (1999), configuration as a school of strategy is differentiated from contingency. The above review gives you some idea of what a sleight of hand that is, how inextricably intertwined they are in these texts.

Mintzberg and colleagues (2003) contemporalize the configuration-archetype framework in the constructivist paradigm. It is a move that further camouflages the roots of configuration in contingency theory. For me, constructivism has roots in Immanuel Kant (1724–1804). According to Mahoney (2006) 'five basic themes pervade the diversity of theories expressing constructivism. These themes are (1) active agency, (2) order, (3) self, (4) social-symbolic relatedness, and (5) lifespan development.'⁴ People are embedded in symbolic systems, such as the archetypes that we are reviewing. The archetypes constitute the world socially constructed symbolically.

Miles and Snow (1978), on the other hand, construct a different framework of configurational archetypes. They are firmly rooted in contingency, not constructivism. Theirs is not about managerial roles or ideal structures, but about strategy archetypes that they correlate with environmental, structural, and technology contingencies. They type organization perceptions of environment according to reactor, analyzer, defender, and prospector archetypes (from least to most adaptive strategies). Archetypes are theorized to be strategic orientations reflective of an organization's adaptation to challenges/problems of entrepreneurial, engineering, and administrative spheres. Contingency instead of Mintzberg's (pull) is for Miles and Snow the 'fit' between organization's strategy and environmental context.

Miller and Friesen (1977) are not that different than Miles and Snow; it is still rooted in contingency theory, not in constructivism. There are just more archetypes. They used Q-sort factor analysis to empirically derive ten archetypes from 81 case studies: six archetypes of successful strategy and four archetypes of failed strategy. The approach is to use causal models derived from survey research to label archetypes of strategy in a typology of contexts. Successful strategies include: adaptive moderate dynamism, adaptive extreme dynamism, dominant firm, giant under fire, entrepreneurial firm, and lucky innovator. Failure strategies include: impulsive firm, stagnant bureaucracy, headless giant, and swimming upstream.

Archetype is a highly debatable metaphor drawn by strategy-configuration school from the field of Jungian psychology, and then assigned to factor structures to be correlated with contingencies of the environment. Archetypes have a metaphoric or symbolic relation to the world. Contingency models of the relation between organization size, structure (or configuration), choices of technology, and the fit to environment context tend to be as Mintzberg (1979: 223) argues 'cross-sectional studies,' and find mixed results. In complexity, Stacey (1992: 124) argues against contingency/archetype theory: 'most of nature's systems are nonlinear feedback ones' exhibiting chaotic patterns 'far from equilibrium' (p. 11). Feminist, postmodern, and postcolonial theories reject contingency/configuration theory because it ignores the subordination of women and minority races in unequal distributions of power (Ferguson, 1991; Mills and Tancred, 1992; Calas and Smircich, 1996). Rather than complexity being about positivist relations between size, technology, structure, strategy, and environment, it is a matter of politics and power among subgroups. Finally, contingency- configuration frameworks sidetrack consideration

---

4 Michael Mahoney's web page, 'What is constructivism and why it is growing,' accessed 2 March 2006 at http://www.constructivism123.com/What_Is/What_is_constructivism. htm

of ethics, how regimes of (male, white) power formulate abstract models of structures, technology, size, environmental markets, etc. that dim our awareness of the relationship between strategies of power and poverty, inequality, etc.

The remaining folkloric chronotopes have not been theorized in strategy. They are to be found in practice.

Rogue-Clown-Fool

'The rogue, the clown and the fool create around themselves their own little world, their own chronotope' (Bakhtin, 1981: 159). Rogue has ties to real life but the clown and fool are 'not of this world' (p. 159).

We have studied McDonald's strategy of narrative humor, in particular Hamburglar-Ronald-Grimace as the Rogue-Clown-Fool chronotope (Boje and Cai, 2004, 2005; Boje and Rhodes, 2005a,b; Boje et al., 2005a). We even produced a play to explore this chronotope (Boje et al., 2007). Part of the work was for me to transcribe six films starring the trio. As before, this chronotope of the three most ancient masks enters into a dialogic relationship with the other chronotopes we have examined thus far. Hamburglar, for example, lies, steals burgers, and sometimes plays cruel pranks on his friends. Ronald also enacts roguish deception by parodying the high language of religion, priest, god, confessor, and miracle-worker. Grimace is pre-modern, from a folk island culture that does not embrace technology. He can unleash chaos.

Rabelaisian Purge

Rabelaisian purge is a cleansing of spatial and temporal world of remnants of transcendental. It is a grotesque method using laughter to degrade, debase, and descend and then to renew, rejuvenate, and redeem. This serves to reduce historical inversion of folkloric realism by modernity. Rabelaisian laughter has two phases (1) grotesque laughter in order to purge rival chronotopes that do not achieve pull potential and authenticity in temporal and spatial terms, such as the purge of transcendent worldview, the mask of conventionality, and (2) laughter of renewal to create a more positive construction. In the here-and-now world are to be found transcendental associations reinforced by tradition, religion, and ideology (Bakhtin, 1981: 169, para).

McDonald's uses grotesque humor to associate food and drink with the lofty and spiritual antics of Hamburglar-Ronald-Grimace. For example, using parodic humor Ronald does one of his transmutation miracles. He pulls a tire pump from his pants and inflates a cheeseburger to the size of a coffin, Ronald and his gang climb between the buns, and are swallowed whole by a female T-Rex. It is a parody of Jonah and the Whale bible narrative. McDonald's cartoon films frequently serve up religious concepts and symbols to billingsgate (i.e. foul language), evoking a transcendent aesthetic. The films bring fast food into direct contact with transcendental images of comic death and rebirth (note that Rabelaisian humor was meant to purge this sort of transcendence). In each episode, Ronald dives from this world into the underworld, and returns at the end. Characters such as Hamburglar, Grimace, Birdie, etc. are grotesque hybrids of human/fast food or animal/fast food. What is strategic? Get children to associate fast food with spiritual, to associate comic death, instead of slaughterhouse death of animals.

Basis for Rabelaisian

Folkloric bases for Rabelaisian chronotope are in generative time, in pre-class agricultural society. Folkloric is everyday time, in ceremony, holiday, and the labor cycle of day-night, and seasons. Everything exists in time cycle at collective level, before individual time. 'Both labor and consuming of things are collective' (p. 207). It is a 'sense of time' that 'works itself out in a collective battle of labor against nature.' 'Generative time is a pregnant time, a fruit-bearing time, a birthing time and a time that conceives again' (p. 207). Generative time is '*profoundly spatial and concrete*' (p. 208). Individual lifetime is post-folkloric. Private lives do not exist. All is emergence, and there is a 'decline of material available for narrative events' (p. 209). In McDonald's Grimace is folkloric time. Trips to Grimace Island are pre-class tribal state of human society. McDonald's work time is on the clock, with alarms timing everything. Breakfast is served till 10AM. Fast food time is clock time, not generative collective time. McDonaldland serves as a counterbalance to McDonald's corporate time. Fast food abandons the folkloric chronotope of pre-class collective life. Fast food is humdrum and coarse without the magic of the netherworld, McDonaldland. Fast food is resymbolized strategically as the very basis of communal life. McDonaldland substitutes the family life of grotesque food/human food/animal characters for labor and consumption time. The folkloric collective bases of time undergo fundamental strategic changes. The concrete time of human labor and consumption life is sent to netherworld.

Idyllic

Family, agricultural labor, and craftwork are idylls. Idyll space and time is 'an organic fastening-down, a grafting of life and its events to a place, to a familiar territory with all its nooks and crannies, its familiar mountains, valleys, fields, rivers and forests, and one's own home' (p. 225).

McDonald's sells itself strategically as idyllic, where the generations localize, and globalize without limit. Globalization and localization meet at McDonald's. Globalizations weaken and blur temporal boundaries between places on the planet. The same little 'home away from home.' Everyone just loving it. McDonald's strategy has been to globalize its menu, but allow for local variations. New Mexico serves green chile. New York and California, Netherlands, and India get veggie burgers. 'Strictly speaking, the idyll does not know the trivial details of everyday life' (p. 226). The Idyllic is a sublimated form, a way to conjoin local human life with global life, and posit the unity of their rhythm. Local disintegrates global, demanding accommodations. Global disintegrates local, as people have fewer choices.

Castle Room

Bakhtin (1973) calls the Castle Room an historic and folkloric chronotope. In novels of Stendhal and Balzac appear places inside the castle, the living room and salon where the dialogs become exceptionally important and where the characters, ideas and passions of the heroes are reveled. 'It is in here where a visible and concrete form of the omnipresent power of the new owner of life is reveled: money.' (Bakhtin, 1981: 456). It is possible to say in contemporary life, instead of rooms in castles we have fast food places to meet. In neighborhoods without parks, mothers take their children to McPlayplace. In China, the elderly gather to have McPlace to go. The meeting place to discuss makes a difference on the quality of the discourse. The ambiance of a salon or coffee house in Denmark is one of cozy-warmth. McDonald's is so garish, plastic, and harsh, one wants to run screaming from the place. McDonald's plastic meeting place along life's journey is opposed by the Slow Food movement, that is a place of conversation and conviviality (Ritzer, 1993/2002).

The field of strategy is dialogically chronotopic. Various ways of temporalizing and spatializing are strategically orchestrated in the adventure chronotopes that are monological (more centripetal). The field of strategy has been about these rather limiting adventure chronotopes. The folkloric chronotopes are in practice by mega-corporations who revitalized their image, and manage the interface of emergent scandal with narrative control. They have to cope with increasingly divergent folkloric (centrifugal) chronotopes that take them into more dialogical strategy processes. The chronotopes therefore provide the basis of emergent self-organization, the coherence force of adventure on its historic axis, and the differentiation of the folkloric appeal to the mythic axis.

7

ARCHITECTONIC STRATEGY STORIES

Architectonic Strategy Story is defined as orchestration of ethics in relation to aesthetic and cognitive aspects of storytelling. For it to be dialogic, the three discourses become more fully answerable to one another, not just image management. Bakhtin's (1990, 1991) work on architectonics is only recently translated to English. Its impact on social sciences (in English speaking communities) is only beginning to be felt. Applied to strategy, the architectonic dialogism is the interaction of several societal discourses that affects firm's narrating. One of the key developments in our post-Enron world is MBA students are expected not only to be cognitively analytic, but ethical. Organizations and their strategy makers are being held answerable. In this chapter we look at two types of architectonics. First, the architectonics of how authors are cited or not among strategy schools. Second, how architectonics work in organization strategy practice, beyond academic schools.

Three authors, Immanuel Kant, Mikhail Bakhtin, and Michel Foucault write about architectonics in different ways. Like Kant (1781) and Bakhtin (1981), Foucault (1977b) treats architectonics as societal discourse. From there they diverge.

Kant invented cognitive architectonic (*Critique of Reason*, 1781/1900: 466): 'By the term Architectonic I mean the art of constructing a system... Reason cannot permit our knowledge to remain in an unconnected and rhapsodistic state, but requires that the sum of our cognitions should constitute a system.' For Kant architectonics is cognitive, and is deeply implicated in constructing systemicity.

Bakhtin preferred the term 'consummation' to construction, and was careful to not assume a monophonic, monologic, or mono-languaged system. He preferred to look at the unmergedness, the unfinalizability of system, or what I define throughout as *systemicity*. Bakhtin (1990) added ethical and aesthetic discourses to Kant's cognitive architectonic discourse. Ethics here is the very notion of *answerability* (defined as how one domain of discourses answers another). Ethics, here, is defined as being about how, and for whom, systemicity is consummated. For example, we conducted architectonic narrative research looking at how McDonald's inhabits Wal-Mart, at the aesthetic, cognitive, as well as ethical discourses (Boje, Enríquez et al., 2005).

Ethics is reanimated in aesthetic and cognitive domains of discourse, in which story and narrative belong, along with metaphor and trope. Keep in mind the polypi of dialogisms are interrelated, so that ethic and cognitive resonate in aesthetic stylistics, as well as in polyphonics.

Of the polypi of dialogisms we are exploring, architectonic dialogism is a more complex *manner of narrative, systemicity and strategy*. Architectonics is a higher order of complexity, as well as strategy, because it takes us to the level of societal discursive plurality.

Architectonic Dialogism is defined as the interanimation of cognitive, aesthetic, and ethical discourses in 'mutual answerability' (Bakhtin, 1990: 2).

> Cognition does not accept ethical evaluatedness and the aesthetic formedness of being, but thrusts itself away from them. (Bakhtin, 1990: 276)

Polyphonic strategic narrative does not relieve organizational responsibility for architectonic answerability (Bakhtin, 1990: 2). Architectonic questions involve more than the pluralism of polyphonic dialogism, or the stylistic dialogism among various modes of expressivity.

- Who is speaking?
- Who is speaking for whom?
- Who authored, directs, and consummates the systemicity complexity one works or shops within?
- How is tentative wholeness consummated?
- What is my answerability if I hear a story?

Answerability is an intertextual, inter-discourse network of authoring and co-authoring, speaking and writing, where others narrate us, more or less strategically.

Architectonic Strategy is defined as 'aesthetic visions' cognition of actions to transform 'aesthetic environment' (Bakhtin, 1990: 279–80) and ethical discursive environment. Organizations enter, and evolve in, an already aestheticized, cognized, and ethically diverse environment. Emergent story and control narratives find an already aesthetically ordered socioeconomic world.

Bakhtin (1990: 84–97) develops a *Architectonic Theatric Inquiry Method*, a dramaturgical architectonic method defined as the interplay of *Authors, Beholders* (spectators), *Characters* (i.e. heroes, villains), and *Directors*. Characters' image is created by Authors, as actors read scripted lines before a mirror, and while on stage get cues from Directors, whilst relating to Beholders.

- Author (A) 'The author's consciousness, on the other hand, just like epistemological consciousness is incapable of being consummated' (p. 89).
- Beholder (B) is an 'active spectator' (p. 78)
- Character (C) is not 'someone who *expresses*, but someone who is *expressed*' (p. 84). Character 'as artistic constituent is transgredient to the consciousness of the ones who characterized' (p. 77). Character is aesthetically creative when they author their own lines. C as actor does not express their own life, only the life ABD scripts for them.
- Director (D) is the director of the stage and scripts (p. 77). Director coaches the expressive form of Character, per Author's intent.

Unless any wears two or more hats, each has their own stock of life experience. Combinations are possible, such as Beholder/Character: spectator (Beholder) who becomes also actor (Character), in what Boal terms 'spectactor.' Or an Author can become participant observer (Beholder), but usually not Director. Authors, Beholders, Characters, and Directors consummate organization theatrics, and transorganization theatrics. As researcher, I am Author, and Beholder using contemplative gaze. I am Author of theory and research, but not the Director of organization's scripted practices.

Foucault does not reference either Kant or Bakhtin's theories of architectonics. For Foucault (1977b: 137) architectonics is a kind of historical (genealogical) analysis of the function of authors, how their works (i.e. texts) delimit by inclusion/exclusion, grouping together several authors and works into what we have been calling, school. Foucault (1977b: 118) explores how naming an author, and links of certain works to an author, has 'its architectonic forms.' This would apply to naming strategy schools, linking authors and works. The strategy schools frameworks have been slow to address societal discourse and their architectonics. Yet, in practice, organizations strategically change societal discourse.

We will address architectonics of strategy schools and authors, answering other authors, and look at what is consummated. Then we will look at strategy practice.

ARCHITECTONICS OF STRATEGY SCHOOLS

Narrative Strategy, Emergent Story, and Systemicity Complexity now enter the labyrinth of architectonic dialogism. For Foucault schools compete in ways that architectonically self-destruct. For Bakhtin, it's a matter of schools as closed philosophical systems infinitely open internally, without finalizability of unity.

> Even a philosophical system is closed and consummated only externally whereas internally it is open and infinite, for the unity of cognition is always achieved a yet-to-be-achieved unity. (Bakhtin, 1990: 210)

We will begin with Boulding, then look at Open System, and Power Schools. There is scant mention of ethics or aesthetics. It's pretty cognitive, but beneath the surface, the other discourses are making their transformations.

Complexity of Schools

Boulding's (1956) level eight property of complexity is the network of social organizations, and their interface with societal discourses. This is the level where I theorize Bakhtin's (1990) architectonic focus on how cognitive, aesthetic, and ethical discourses interanimate each another seems compatible with Boulding's. Both models are cumulative, interactive properties, rather than succession. In this chapter we explore how complexity properties of systemicity and architectonic discourse interface with narrative strategy schools.

Beyond Open System

In looking at the environment school, Astley points to the missing chair for Emery and Trist. Emery and Trist (1965) saw a return to fundamental shared values, or new ones, as ways to counter the trend of 'maladaptive' open systems responses to turbulent environment. Emery chooses Aristotelian aesthetic values, along with Ackoff's teleological purpose, to tame the turbulent environment of interorganizational relations (Emery, 1977; Ackoff and Emery, 1972). Emery (1977) advocated four harmony values: homonomy (belongingness), nurturance, humanity, and beauty. This lets in not only aesthetics, but opens the door to 'humanity' as part of ethical discourse.

Open system theory ignores power competitive relations, in favor of the harmony co-operative values. Emery criticized Von Bertalanffy's (1956) *General Systems Theory* for focusing upon extrinsic values instead of his harmonious values. For Bakhtin, harmony values and purpose-seeking teleology are examples of Aristotle's vitalism aesthetics of Devine design (1990: 269).

Purely from an architectonic perspective, Open system theory's error is to be monophonic, to enclose 'open' in a 'single consciousness of self-experience,' language, and logic (Bakhtin, 1990: 80). Emery brought in his 'researcher's lived experience of aesthetic contemplation, but it is brought in quite uncritically and without any awareness of the methodological significance of doing so' (Bakhtin, 1990: 268). What is uncritical about it? His declared artistic values will tame turbulent environment represents closed system philosophy.

Emery's method of aesthetic contemplation denied the already aestheticized environment of organizations. Emery's aesthetic values are alien to the embedded aesthetic values and architectonic dialogism of discourses of organization and environments. Organizations have their own strategies to influence architectonic dialogism. Organizations have multiple authors, beholders, characters, and directors, as do their environments. Beyond the observer effect beholding has on the phenomenon being observed, Emery's contemplation of harmony values cannot nihilate the theatrics already in play. One might argue that his participative democracy changes character's roles with his directing. This still does not preclude that there are architectonics already in play in organizations and environments.

The disclosure by Astley that Emery and Trist (1965) were being ignored in strategy because it is a collaborative multi-organization model, whereas strategy schools, in Mintzberg et al., privilege competition. The call for polyphony in Barry and Elmes' classification opens the door to ethical discourse and part of the strategy narrative discourse. Emery and Trist, for example, are read as social ecology, as a collaborative strategy model by Astley, in ways that take them beyond what Boulding called open system. But where does Astley take Emery and Trist? Not into configuration, contingency, or competition models. I think it's into how organizations and societies shape each other's discourses, into values and ethics of democratized versus hierarchical governance.

If Emery and Trist are open system (level 4 in Boulding), then can they also be level 8 (social network)? If there are multiple and incommensurate models and frameworks of strategy writers and their writings, then it would seem we have crossed over from an open system logic to not only social networks, but gone beyond mere polyphonic dialogism. We are dealing here with a higher order of complexity, the incommensurability of logics, worldviews, and ideologies among strategy authors, and their bids to frame schools.

Before we get to the other schools with anything to say about architectonics, some remarks. In Chapter 4, we contrasted three typologies of schools of strategies (i.e., Astley, Barry and Elmes, and Mintzberg et al.). I thought this book would be easy to write, a simple matter of looking at the interrelationship of schools of strategy, story, and systemicity properties. What a monumental task it is proving to be. We began by looking at how Barry and Elmes (1997) classification of strategy schools by narrative chronotopes left out several Bakhtin chronotopes, and many schools. Astley's (1984) strategy by four C's (constraint, choice, competition, and collaboration) left out many. Mintzberg et al., when viewed by narrative strategy or by the systemicity complexity model, misclassified many important writers and left others out completely. The three typologies were selective in their choice of exemplars.

Power School

We shall need to complete our exploration of the power school of strategy that Mintzberg et al. classify. I have saved this exploration until now because it is the power schools, more than the others (except for Selznick, Cole, or Schumpeter) that addresses societal discourse, and its role in shaping strategy of collaborating firms, as well as its network structure of interorganizational relationships.

The power school does more at a cognitive architectonic level, ignoring ethic and aesthetic architectonic discourses. Normann (1977) does address ethical discourse, as an idea force in the dominant coalition, but at a micro-level of power. Normann's aesthetic is rooted in a theory of harmony or as he terms it 'consonance.' He does not succeed in interanimating ethics with cognitive framing of contingencies, and an aesthetic consonance. Consonance is folded back into contingency frameworking, and ethics gets mentioned once. His 'principle of consonance' is that subsystems are interdependent (economic recourses, production, reward, power, status, and cognitive are subsystems). Consonance, as an aesthetic is fit and unfit relations among parts. Consonance becomes a narrative of the internal coherence of the ensemble of roles and competencies to the stage and situation. The organization is a subsystem of ideas (pp. 17–18). His approach is cognitive as well, 'in future I shall refer to the victors in this struggle as the company's *dominating ideas*' (p. 18), embodied in the social situation, 'embodied in the people who work there' (p. 27). In short, Normann is not looking at architectonic dialogism, it is polyphony.

In social sciences the cognitive discourse remains more pronounced than ethic or aesthetic discourse. Stylistics is becoming quite strategic to give the 'image' of being ethical in organization identity. Societal discourse of ethics is asserting more influence upon how organizations are expected to narrate themselves. In the last chapter we reviewed apparent shifts in stylistics in annual reports. Organizations consummate their strategy narratives with more attention to transparency and ethical codes.

How has narrative strategy, as a domain of societal discourse, been addressed in the power school? Mintzberg et al. (1998, 1999, 2003) assert that Pfeffer and Salancik, Astley, as well as Allison are exemplars of the power school of strategy. I will assert that it is the power school of strategy, more than the others, that appears to focus most directly upon societal discourse. Therefore, the discourse theory of architectonic dialogism is an appropriate way to theorize the dynamic relationships between strategy, control narrative, story emergence, and systemicity.

I was just finishing my PhD at University of Illinois. Jerry Salancik was one of my mentors, so I can recite many of his articles, and much of his book with Pfeffer. Pfeffer and Salancik (1978: 234) tried to break free of strategic-contingency, by redefining open system theory with a more Weickian twist, enactment: '... the environment does not come knocking on the organization's door announcing its critical contingencies ... participants must enact and interpret their environment and its effects on the organization.' Pfeffer and Salancik assert that indeterminacy between enacted environment and strategic contingencies is mediated by power that is institutionalized and by social embeddedness in interorganizational networks. 'One source of institutionalization of power is the definition of organizational contingencies and problems' (Pfeffer and Salancik, 1978: 234).

Pfeffer and Salancik theorized 'resource dependence perspective' in relation to 'external control of organizations.' Their framework combines Emery and Trist's (1965) 'open systems theory,' approach (turbulent environment is multiple organizations) with (Pugh et al.'s) strategic-contingencies and Weick's enactment theory. The triplicity result is cross-school (environment, contingency, and learning) focus upon how environment as a network of organizations become 'known to the organization through a process of enactment' (xii). For Pfeffer and Salancik (1978: 65), 'The important contribution of Emery and Trist was the recognition of a distinction between the set of transacting organizations, the organization set... and the larger social context within which both the organization and its organization set are embedded.'

Mintzberg et al. place Pfeffer and Salancik in the power school of strategy, rather than in the configuration, learning, or environment schools. Configuration and environment schools (particularly Pugh et al.) are dominated by strategic contingency models. Learning school, for Mintzberg et al., is dominated by Weick's enactment sensemaking perspective.

What is excluded in typologies of schools of strategy speaks volumes. Mintzberg et al. exclude Emery and Trist (1965) from their schools framework scheme. This could be because institutionalization of power combined with Weick's (1969) enactment idea, weakens any direct link between environment enactment and strategic contingency. Subunits coping with critical strategic contingencies attempt to enact task environments favorable to their subunit. Pfeffer and Salancik (1978: 260) assert, 'enactments of dependencies, contingencies, and external demands are in part determined by organizational structures, information systems, and the distribution of power and control within organizations.'

Pfeffer and Salancik do not discuss narrative or storytelling directly. Rather they focus upon conflict in loosely coupled interorganizational networks as firms compete under conditions of resource scarcity. Network is an external constraint upon the organization's (and subunit's) ability to sustain resources. It is Salancik and Pfeffer's approach to enactment theory that points us in the direction of societal demands for corporate narrative.

> If environments are enacted, then there are as many environments as there are enactors, which may explain why there are so many typologies of organizational environments, as well as why different organizations and even different individuals within each may react differently to what appears to be the same context. (Pfeffer and Salancik, 1978: 73).

The implication is that the environment is enacted in narratives, which are increasingly dialogic, especially in more turbulent environments.

Pfeffer and Salancik, still stuck in configuration and contingency models of strategy, organization, and environment, do not get at the dialogized manner of architectonics. There are implications of architectonic dialogism that they do not address.

For example, I theorize narratives as involved in the enactment process in five ways. First, narratives enact a social selectivity, reconstructing select images, while forgetting or ignoring others (see earlier chapter on collective memory). Secondly, narratives enact a recreation of the past in a retrospective backward glance (Weick, 1969: 65). Narratives can also be a forward glance, and is more chronotopically diverse than just retrospection (i.e. more than Bakhtin's folkloric reversal). Thirdly, people perceive visual and auditory information from the environment, which they represent in narratives. They respond to enacted representations instead of directly (or mechanistically or organically) to contingencies or to emergent story. People narrate images and illusions, and sometimes premeditate and construct deceptions strategically. Fourthly, environment is not only networks of organizations, but networks of control narratives organizations tell, and rules enacted by institutions to control how organizations narrate. Finally, organizations are selectively attentive to societal discourses, and do attempt (sometimes successfully) to shape societal discourse using ad campaigns. Narrative and story as domains of societal discourse is being shaped by organizations. The price of participation in societal discourse is the organization has to watch how it strategically narrates its identity and how the environment of other organizations is storying about them.

I have given you an extensive review of the interrelation of enactment with the power theory of external control that Pfeffer and Salancik developed, since

Mintzberg et al.'s framework of schools treats Weick as a learning school exemplar, while Pfeffer and Salancik are classified as just power school. What is clear is that Pfeffer and Salancik's contribution is to intersect three schools of strategy (power, environment, learning).

Astley (1984) has a different framework for classifying schools of strategy from what Mintzberg et al., erect. Mintzberg et al. lump Astley into the power school, rather than into environment school. Both classification schemes (see Chapter 4 for review) are selective, and present quite different histories of the field of strategy. Astley conspicuously ignores several schools Mintzberg believes important (configuration, entrepreneurship, cognitive, learning, and culture), and combines exemplars across schools.

How Foucault's Architectonics Treats Schools and Authors

Applying Foucault (1977b: 116), there is a practice of 'slights' in whose exemplars gets included or excluded. It's school versus school put downs, and slights that become the framework of interiority. Instead of analyzing the writing and speaking by people in organizations, we are witness to the sign-warfare games among academics. The writing game is to make academics heroes, while leaving the working staff voiceless. And now I am caught playing the game.

Strategy schools constitute a monstrous family accomplished with practices of inclusion and exclusion. There's a reversal. Instead of leaders, managers, organizations, or institutions being classified, it is academic writers who are the heroes being erected in family genealogies. Academics are spared the necessity of addressing architectonic expressive narrative practices of organizations, as well as workers, leaders, managers, vendors, customers, investors, and regulators. Working people are marginalized, and so is the Storytelling Organization.

As the dead authors and traces in works accumulate, the traces of traces get reassembled into schools. There is increasing architectonic dialogism among strategy discourses. Societal discourses interplay to keep redefining schools of strategy. In post-Enron, the pressure is on to bring out ethical strategic discourse. This may be due to death of the author.

Are authors dead? If dead, why does their name keep being used, as a place marker, or sign to identify strategy school? Foucault (1977b: 123) wants to raise authors from the dead, and look at how the name of an author is being used to group several texts together, and differentiate them from other texts. I am concerned with how the author and their works are reconstructed in 'architectonic forms' (Foucault, 1977b: 118). If the author is dead, 'what are we to make of those things he [or she] has written or said, left among his [or her] papers or communicated to others?' (Foucault, p. 118, additions, mine). Killing authors is important to the game of immortality of one's written works.

When a work had the duty of creating immortality, it now attains the right to kill, to become the murderer of its author. (Foucault, 1977b: 117)

For Foucault the inclusion or exclusion of authors and their works, such as in or out of schools problematizes the functions of author (and works) in classification schemes. The problematic issue of 'death of the author' is that someone is writing. Someone is classifying dead authors and works, and these ways of writing frame schools quite differently. Authors falling into disfavor are treated to silence. Making academics the heroes is a way of silencing the authors of stories and narratives that make up the cases academics classify. Worse, we exclude the authors of corporate strategy, in practice, from research.

The function of naming authors and works is the 'circulation and operations of certain discourse within a society' (Foucault, 1977b: 124). Games of naming interrelations of structure, environment, system, and strategy is how the business school responds to societal discourses. In particular in a post-Enron world, the societal plea to teach ethics in the business school interanimates with the aesthetics of the writing and the frameworks emerging in the field of strategy.

In the wars between schools, including and slighting schools, there is a 'total effacement of the individual characteristics of the writer' and there is 'quibbling and confrontations' that serve to 'cancel out the signs of his [or her] particular individuality' (p. 117, additions in brackets, mine). The killing of them is the murder of silence. Then there is the suicide of the author not having voice in their writing.

Foucault argues that each 'work' of an author 'can be extracted from millions of traces left by an individual after his death' (p. 119). The three frameworks are selective about what traces left by dead (and living) authors are included and excluded. Further, there are traces of authors cited, and uncited in each exemplar's works. The traces left by other authors are consecrated into exemplars.

For example, Porter, as an exemplar, is an integration of Andrews as well as Ansoff. Writing (or spoken) 'work' by 'author' as trace of traces becomes problematic; 'school' also becomes problematic because the supposed unity of a given school disintegrates. It disintegrates into a disappearance of traces of murdered authors, and traces rebirth in the works of other dead authors to posit the various succession frames of classification. In each (branch) instance we avoid confronting the specific events that make it possible to 'reserve the existence of the author' and authors' works (Foucault, 1977b: 117).

Foucault names this problematic 'écriture' (p. 117). Ecriture is defined as acts of writing and authoring that make a work of writing as well as authors a metaphysical event of the interplay of presence and absence. The écriture of frameworks is the interplay of presence and absence of authors and works, to erect and classify schools, to slight with silence and lack of invitation. By erasing the traces of authors, traces of dead authors' ideas can be transposed into privileged schools in a process of 'transcendental anonymity' (Foucault, 1977b: 120), a religious belief in 'fixed and continuous tradition or the aesthetic principle that proclaims the survival of the work is a kind of enigmatic supplement of the author beyond his own death.' Here Foucault bridges a Derridian use of supplementarity with Bakhtinian architectonics, the dialogism of cognitive and aesthetic discourses. The death of the author is held in check by an appeal to a transcendental aesthetic principle of fixed continuity of a work. Attaching a number of author's names and works to a school implies what Foucault (1977b: 123) calls homogeneity, reciprocal explanation, and common utilization. Yet, there is not much that is fixed or continuous about authors, works, or how multiple authors and works are expropriated to construct schools. This is certainly true of my tables in earlier chapters that collapse schools of story/narrative or strategy schools into Boulding/Pondy systemic or narrative framework.

In each work academic authors, works, and traces are conspicuously absent, in a bid for succession. The bid by Astley is that collaboration can overcome contingency, choice, and competition strategy models. The bid by Mintzberg et al: is that configuration school recombines traces of the other nine schools in a way that keeps the contingency model alive. The bid by Barry and Elmes is that ways of narrating define strategy schools, and these schools are becoming more polyphonic. Yet, what if the complexity is more than just stylistic differences in narrating, and more that just polyphonic incommensurate logics – what if we are entering the space of architectonic dialogism?

The implication in contrasting the strategy school frameworks is that slotting authors and works into schools is not a simple act of hierarchic classification. A plurality of strategy ideologies make bids for commonality and homogeneity, but cannot attain reciprocal explanation because the architectonics is dialogic. The authors' names and works become signs, representations for classification, but the disputes among discourses are not fiction, it is a war of all against all. It is dialogic warfare, and it is architectonic, not just polyphonic dialogism.

The first implication is that authors of strategies have become a form of property to various business schools. Copyright laws attest to the sovereignty of the author. School, however, is not just academic curriculum in a given university; it is the property of publishing houses, the practices of consulting firms, in an active appropriation of power. The role of authors or works turns into a sign, the author disappears as a definer of the sovereignty of a school.

Secondly, the ways of writing stories and narratives of strategy get 'accepted, circulated, and valorized' within the identity of schools. An obvious example is how integral the Harvard case method is to writing strategy. A text or fiction in a Harvard case does not reflect upon the circumstance of the writing. The meaning of the writing depends upon its demonstration of a school of strategy in recurring textual motifs or narrative styles. A less obvious example is how integral free market capitalism is to strategy. This explains by democratic governance models, such as in Emery and Trist or Marx, are incommensurate with entrepreneurial (creative destruction) models of Schumpeter. As a school makes its authors more symbolic referents, and the authors become more anonymous, the conceptual framework of a school becomes more legitimated as social science.

Thirdly, the author gets (re) constructed as a 'rational entity' in each of the strategy school frameworks we reviewed (Foucault, 1977b: 127). Each school framework extracts traits as pertinent, assigns continuities, and makes exclusions.

Finally, in terms of architectonic dialogism, the moves by schools vary by historic period, in reply to societal discourses. Authors are eliminated from schools when their works are no longer defined as consistent with the doctrine expressed. As the number of viewpoints accumulates, a given school can come undone. Schools can be evolutionary or revolutionary to one another. A sub-curriculum can break away and become a school that combines sub-curriculums of other schools. A new manner of stylistic or architectonic expression can redefine a school, so although the name is the same, what is being written is quite different. For example, early Mintzberg (1973) is about the theatrics of archetypal roles to supplant Fayol's principles. Mintzberg (1978) is about the pentagon configuration of ideal forces. Mintzberg et al. (1998, 1999) try to save contingency, by inventing configuration. Mintzberg et al. (2003) seeks to reframe configuration into constructivism. What is 'Mintzberg' author, in changes in his school from decade to decade?

Each school has become a plurality of discourses, and a simultaneous dispersion of egos and works into schools. One hears the voice of Caesar assembling a position out of traces. The direction we Cai (2006) and I took was to focus on the exemplars, instead of the schools, by looking at systemicity and narrative approaches.

ARCHITECTONIC DIALOGISM IN STRATEGY PRACTICE

We've looked at architectonics of school rivalries. What about practice? Practice is being inundated by societal demands to invoke ethical discourse.

In post-Enron late capitalism, there are societal demands for more ethical discourse. The polyphonic dialogism is instructed to include an ethical voice. The stylistic dialogism has embraced aesthetic expressivity, as an image management strategy. As cognitive, aesthetic, and ethical discourses accumulate, and juxtapose, Bakhtin (1990) argues they begin to interanimate, to show up in one another, to express one through the other. Image management, at stylistic level, has met the societal call for more ethical discourse by national and global companies. However, there is some evidence that stylistic orchestration of images is not succeeding always in erecting the mask of transparency in front of what too many of us have seen backstage. At some point ethical discourse will be the result of changing the Storytelling Organization from its image management, to tell stories based in substantive changes in material conditions of work.

Architectonic dialogism is subject to impression management, as well as to expulsion, over-legitimation (co-optation), compromise (consensus), incongruence (duality), or sometimes to synergy. Bringing ethics into the cognitive discourse (rational contingency, configuration, and constellation frameworks) is being actively resisted.

It is easier to interanimate ethical expression through stylistics and impression management than for ethics to invade the sanctum of production or change the rewards for labor from poverty to living wages. The rhetoric of story substitutes for substantive change in human relationships.

ENTER TRANSPARENCY 101

My mother told me 'if you can't say anything nice, don't say anything at all.' Let me take her advice to heart. Nike has perhaps the most elaborate Storytelling Organization in existence to deal with emergent stories from the anti-sweat-shop movement (see Chapter 3 for definitions):

E1 Gossip

E2 Rumor

E3 Fad

E4 Propaganda

E5 Rebellion

E6 Innovation

E7 Improv

E8 Quasi Object

Nike's architectonic strategies have been very effective. In terms of 'architectonic strategy' Nike uses cognitive-aesthetic narrative strategy to put forth ethical claims. In a 2003 press release, Nike announced it won the 'Hong Kong Caring Company Award.'[1] Won it again in 2004. In 2005, Nike jumped to number 13 from 31 on the *Business Ethics Magazine* list of *100 Best Corporate Citizens*.[2] These awards are very impressive when you consider that a network of unions, campus groups, reporters, and over 100 academics have alleged Nike is among the least ethical companies.[3]

Transparency in Jean-Jacques Rousseau's philosophy implies openness, clarity of communication, and accountability.[4] Transparency has gone through several phases

1   Denial: There are sweatshops but that is as it should be according to Nike Index, which says that when Nike enters a low-wage country, the workers organize, even unionize. When Nike leaves, the country enters next phase of economic development. That means Nike is part of nation's economic development. So no problem.
2   Blame contractors: There are isolated cases of sweatshops in Nike contract factories. This is being monitored by reputable Ernst & Young accounting firm. Nike holds them accountable to ethical code, and demands perpetrators mend their ways, or lose their contracts.

---

1   1 June 2003 press release from Nike, Inc; 'Nike Wins Hong Kong Caring Company Award' accessed 5 June 2006 at: http://www.csrwire.com/article.cgi/1496.html
2   *Business Ethics Magazine*, Spring 2006, 20(#1), see Nike press release, accessed 5 June 2006 at http://www.nike.com/nikebiz
3   For a listing of 106 Nike studies see http://cbae.nmsu.edu/~dboje/AA/academics studyingwriting.htm
4   I owe a debt to philosopher Frits Schipper. We are working on a chapter on Transparency 100 and Rousseau.

3 Damage control: Minimize emergent stories of sweatshop abuse by taking action against critics, such as 'War Room' strategies of surveillance and releasing press packets with counter-stories.

4 Reassert control over damaged corporate image: Strategies include spectacles of positivity; celebrity endorsement studies such as by former Ambassador Andrew Young, etc.

5 Transparency 101: Release locations of some 700 Nike factories, do independent monitoring by Fair Labor Association (FLA) and trusted independent local monitors.

Transparency phases are tied to systemicity complexity. In phases, the strategy is to organize requisite variety (second cybernetic, level 3 Control) as well as networks (level 8) of response to counter the emergent stories (E1 to E8) that the anti-sweatshop network puts forth.

Phase 1 Denial

Effective Storytelling Organization architectonic strategies change with the situation. Nike's most effective counter-story has to be the Nike Index. Quoting Nike's website:

> Nike Index tracks a developing economy's economic development by Nike's activity in each country. Economic development starts when Nike products are starting to be manufactured there (Indonesia, 1989; Vietnam, 1996). The economy hits the second stage – development at a level where per capita income indicates labor flowing from basic industries like footwear and textiles to advanced industries like electronics and cars (Hong Kong, 1985; Korea, 1990); and an economy is fully developed when Nike has developed that country as a major market (Singapore, 1991; Japan, 1984; Korea, 1994). (Nike FAQ website)[5]

The fabula of Nike Index is that when you trace where Nike has been, that nation's economy is doing far better. Nike enters a nation with low wages and poor working conditions. The workers organize, the wages go up, and Nike leaves to find a country in need of development.

Phase 2 Blame Contractors

This phase of transparency strategy was prevalent from Nike's inception until 1997 when Ernest & Young's audits of factory compliance to Nike's code of

---

5 See copy of archived 1997 Nike FAQ at http://business.nmsu.edu/~dboje/NIK faqcompensation.html. See Nike Index explained at: http://business.nmsu.edu/~dboje/ conferences/nikeJustInTimeGAMEBOARD.htm

ethics was discredited widely by the media. In 1992 Levi-Strauss and Wal-Mart developed first Code of Conduct – Nike followed in 1993. These forms of transparency claim the corporation's ethical accountability.

Phase 3 Damage Control

Damage control to fallout escalated after 1997, when Ernst & Young's audits were discredited. A celebrity was hired, former Ambassador Andrew Young, to do a quick personal tour of Asian factories to insure nothing was going on. That tactic quickly backfired when the emergent story appeared throughout the media that Nike hired his translators. Nike's 'war room' was ramped up to deal with this and other crises, and continues to this day.[6] It monitors emergent stories of anti-sweatshop movement activity, deploys staff members to distribute press packets to press, sends Nike representatives to speak at academic conferences or universities where Nike is being critiqued. Writers are recruited by the 'war room' to put out more appreciative counter-stories (Boje, 2000b). War room receives collaboration from university athletic programs to be on look out for carnivalesque student rebellion (Boje, 2001b).

Phase 4 Reassert Control Over Damaged Corporate Image

A highly effective strategy is to run spectacle of positivity to drown out any negative emergent stories. Annual meetings, for example, are often star-studded, with celebrity sports pep rallies, with legends such as Michael Jordon, Tiger Woods, and other NBA favorites (Boje, 2001a). Phil Knight sometimes leads 'Just Do It' to thunderous applause at shareholder meetings. In 1997 and 1998 Nike's 'Frequently Asked Questions' website was almost completely devoted to answering political questions about labor rights, not questions about its shoes or key endorsers such as Tiger Woods and Michael Jordan.[7] Emergent stories included the 1996 CBS News program '48 hours,' and the 1997 'Vietnam Labor Watch's' study of working conditions in Nike's contract factories.[8] 1997 is also when Social Accountability 8000 standards were being trumpeted.

Phase 5 Transparency 101

This architectonic strategy produces and disseminates ethical discourse. It's undergone several changes. It began in 1999 with the release of some 700

---

6 *Workforce Magazine* Oct 2005 issue accessed on 14 Jan 2006 at http://www.work force.com/archive/article/24/17/96.php
7 See Boje's compilation of Nike stories at
   http://business.nmsu.edu/~dboje/nikestockstories.html or main site
   http://business.nmsu.edu/~dboje/nike/nikemain1.html
8 Vietnam Labor Watch Reports site accessed 5 June 2006 at http://www.saigon.com/ ~nike/report.html

factory locations to the Fair Labor Association (FLA).[9] Nike, Reebok, Adidas, and a host of other garment manufacturers, such as Liz Claiborne organized FLA to monitor their ethical codes. The FLA network arose to counter the damage caused by the Kathie Lee Gifford Scandal to the entire industry. On 29 April 1996 Charles Kernaghan made Kathie Lee cry on national TV. He accused her of employing girls in sweatshops, paid 31 cents an hour, working 75-hour weeks, to make her clothing line. In 1998, United Students Against Sweatshops began to organize 'Workers Right Consortiums' (WRC) on the same university campuses that had joined the FLA network. That meant FLA and WRC were competing to sign up the same population. My university, New Mexico State, for example, belongs to both.

In 2002, Nike removed Transparency 101 website material when Nike was petitioned to the US Supreme Court to hear the Kasky vs. Nike First Amendment case. It was an embarrassing setback. Nike had been claiming 'transparency' in its ads, and that it had learned from mistakes, and had cleaned up sweatshop practices. Nike's defense was not to deny the charges. Instead Nike claimed 'corporate free speech rights' were protected under the First Amendment of the US Constitution. *The Supposed Right to Lie* is the subtitle of Kant's (1785/1993) book on the difference between practical (lie if situation demands) ethics, and categorical ethics (never ever lie).

Transparency 101 was rehistoricized to being just about disclosure of factory sites, removing most claims that sweatshops were getting better. Nike's website still has a few:

> We've evolved from outsourcing labor monitoring to relying on a trained team of internal monitors and support for common monitoring platforms such as the Fair Labor Association... We are evolving from an exclusive focus on factory floor impact to an exploration of ways to help change the industry through *transparency and multi-stakeholder collaborations* [emphasis, mine][10]

Is there a missing story in the transparency and rights violated?

Where are the story rights of workers in Transparency 101? Workers' emergent stories of their own experience and reflexivity, so essential to fermenting rebellion and revolution in the garment and shoe industry are noticeably missing from Transparency 101. Multiple authors, beholders, and directors give expression to characters (workers) as hero or victim from outside the factories. Others plot and consummate, then narrate workers' lives. Nike and FLA narratively control workers'

---

9 Nike press release 13 Apr 2005, 'Nike issues FY04 corporate responsibility report highlighting multi-stakeholder engagement and new levels of transparency', accessed 5 June at 2006 at http://www.nike.com/nikebiz/news/pressrelease.jhtml

10 NikeBiz 2004 website accessed 5 June 2006 at http://www.nike.com/nikebiz/gc/r/fy04/docs/workers_factories.pdf

living emergent stories (E1, E2, E5). Workers are asked questions by commissioned monitors, but their stories are not recorded on the narrative templates. Responses are summed and totaled into charts and graphs. Transparency would be realized if and only if workers told their own stories.

Suppose the workers had the opportunities to story themselves, and become authors, and perhaps directors, not just characters others narrate. The worker storying herself, consummating herself aesthetically, cognitively, and ethically is the architectonics of liberation. That liberation would achieve ethics still-to-be-fulfilled (Bakhtin 1990: 134). Workers would be storying themselves instead of being under other's narrative control.

Nike's Transparency 101 is answerable for being a narrative control of aesthetic construction that substitutes for ethical inquiry. Transparency 101 is constructed of narratives of 'artistic verisimilitude' that substitute for workers' story rights (Bakhtin, 1990: 200). Lack of worker story rights is a 'sign of a crisis in the domain of aesthetic creation' of transparency (pp. 202–3).

Architectonic aesthetic strategies of Transparency 101 are realized in the composition, disposition, and consummation of written narratives, and not vice versa (p. 197). Inquiry into ethical value starts with performed actions, not the fibula of transparency.

Ethical inquiry could begin by looking at the architectonic question of answerability. Who is answerable for the sweatshop productive systemicity? Workers do not negotiate the speed of the line, the day's quota, the hours of unpaid overtime, or working conditions.

Transparency 101 may be accused of being 'the creation of a plastic-pictorial axiological image of the hero' (Bakhtin, 1990: 32, 77). Yet it's a darn effective strategy. Reading the fabula-plot of Transparency 100: Nike as hero hires Sheriff-monitors, to pursue the villain contract-factories, thereby saving victims, young women workers. Nike directs, authors, beholds, and stars in its own narrative-theatric production. My mother's advice aside, to quote an old proverb, Transparency 101 is 'a spoonful of honey in a barrelful of pitch' (p. 69).

ENTER SARBANES-OXLEY

The biggest change in architectonic relations of cognitive, aesthetic, and ethical discourses, has to be the Sarbanes-Oxley Act.[11] Behind the mask of (bounded) rational discourse, in the post-Enron era, demand for transparent ethical strategy is becoming more critical. An example of the interaction of networks of organizations with societal discourses is Sarbanes-Oxley. Congress responded to

---

11 SEC commissioner Roel C Campos' speech on 11 Jun 2003 in Brussels, Belgium was titled 'Embracing International Business in the Post-Enron Era' at http://www.sec.gov/news/speech/spch061103rcc.htm

Enron, WorldCom, Arthur Andersen, and an outbreak of other scandals with the Sarbanes-Oxley Act. Before these scandals, lobbying networks of collaborating firm agents were able to deflect any serious external controls. One of the things Sarbanes-Oxley does is develop new regulations concerning audit committees, internal controls and enhanced reporting.

Section 404 of the Sarbanes-Oxley Act of 2002 changes the way companies write up their annual report in several ways that changes narrative expectation. Authors of annual reports must include:

> Statement of management's responsibility for establishing and maintaining adequate internal control over financial reporting for the company; management's assessment of the effectiveness of the company's internal control over financial reporting as of the end of the company's most recent fiscal year; a statement identifying the framework used by management to evaluate the effectiveness of the company's internal control over financial reporting ...[12]

The effect of the Sarbanes-Oxley Act has been to invite investor confidence, by cracking down on fraud and malfeasance in how firms narrate. Various associations and academies have put their institutional pressure on the Business School to change its curriculum and pedagogy, to turn out MBAs that are not only analytically competent, but ethical. Much of this is aesthetic and cosmetic.

While there have been increases in arrests of white-collar executive and management criminals, the changes in annual reporting are still rhetorical moves. There's media spectacle of CEOs being handcuffed. The image narrative is a theatrics to regain the confidence of the audience in Wall Street, the SEC, the accounting profession, the business school, and public administration. Yet, there is some shift in emphasis in architectonics, with ethics getting more play than aesthetic style, but the ordering of importance of societal discourses from cognitive, aesthetic-image management, to ethical rhetoric remains hegemonically embedded. The upshot for architectonic dialogism is that organizations are incorporating an ethical strategic narrative, more than ever.

---

12 Quote is from SEC text of rule 33-8238, final decision, effective 14 August 2003 at http://www.sec.gov/rules/final/33-8238.htm

8

POLYPI STRATEGY STORIES

This chapter's focus is on the more transcendental strategy that interplays with the polypi of dialogisms. I will show how Wilber's integral, and Kantian approaches to transcendental relates to Bakhtinian dialogism. I am concerned here with storying that is multi-dialogic. Storying is defined as the more or less continuous behavior of getting story realized, getting others to take roles, to be part of either a managed and directed story, or one that is more emergent and even collectively enacted.

Transcendental Strategy is defined here as all reflexive strategy that is not derived from retrospective sensemaking of experience. Polypi and transcendental strategies interplay. It's rather a mode of cognizing that is a priori.

Story emergence occurs within modes of narrative expectation. Emergent story is apt to be under narrative control before its instant of emergent is fully realized. Acts of retrospection and reflexivity have their impact upon emergent story knowledge.

In the Introduction we explored how Weick's (1995) theory of narrative sensemaking chapter 'The Substance of Sensemaking' applies to Perrow's (1986) three orders of control. First order control is direct supervision. Second order control is programs or scripts of behavior. Third order control is 'assumptions and definitions that are taken as given' (Weick, 1995: 113). Weick (1995: 129) uses the words story and narrative interchangeably, but his way of talking about story is through its imprisonment in narratives of control: retrospective 'stories transmit and reinforce third-order controls by conveying shared values and meaning' of sense experience. There is a more pluralistic/retrospective sensemaking.

Retrospective narrative assimilates fragments into a unity-seeking form of sensemaking that over-persuades local knowledge. Its mode of control is by debate and rivalry. More polyphonic approaches, such as intuition furnish a priori knowledge in variety making manner of story. In the chapter on polyphonic dialogism, we examined how it takes forensic work to trace the marginal voices that speak back to power as idea-forces. Polyphony is overcoming control for inclusion of marginalized voices and ideas. It's about argumentation among fully embodied ideologies or points of view that increase variety.

Not all knowledge arises from retrospective sensemaking on experience dialectic mode of knowledge that makes synthetic or unity judgments and apperceptions a priori to retro sensemaking. Boulding's (1956) ninth level of systemic complexity is transcendental, the relation between knowable and unknowable. There are few transcendental a priori models of strategy narrative. Transcendental aesthetic strategy narratives are defined as beyond retro-narratives of whole linear sequence, such as managerial third-order control.

I want to get more rigorous about transcendental, by turning to Kant's transcendental. Kant (1781/1900: 67) addresses a second mode of knowledge that is a priori, such as the 'unity of the theme in a play, an oration, or a story' that is beyond retrospective empirical sense-knowledge. Kant's project, *Critique of Pure Reason*, is to find a way to unify the dualism of materialism of retro-sense-experience and the idealism plaguing transcendental metaphysics. The dualism is between a priori and a posteriori. As Kant (p. 44) puts it, 'only pure intuitions and pure conception are only possible *a priori*; the empirical only *a posteriori*.' Kant develops several types of transcendental pure reason. Two that are particularly relevant are 'transcendental logic' and 'transcendental aesthetic.'

Transcendental logic or 'Pure Reason' is defined by Kant (1781/1900: 15) as 'the faculty which contains the principles of cognizing anything absolutely *a priori*.' Kant critiques Hume for only partially demonstrating that ideas are not innate, and instead arise in reflection (retrospection) upon sense-experience (p. vii). Beyond retrospective sensemaking there is 'pure reason,' which for Kant is transcendental and antecedent to retrospective sensemaking knowledge, and is instead a 'super-sensible sphere, where experience affords us neither instruction nor guidance' (p. 4). Kant (1781/1900: 15) defines 'transcendental' as 'all knowledge which is not so much occupied with objects as with the mode of our cognition of these objects, so far as this mode of cognition is *a priori*.' Kant sketches Pure Reason 'architectonically' (p. 16). Bakhtin develops a more dialogic architectonic. Transcendental logic gives synthetic unity to diversity of *a priori* judgments about quantities, qualities, relations, and modalities of existence. Each is a transcendental, not an empirical deduction of experience. Rather than cause-effect retrospection, it is rather an a priori understanding of parts in relation to whole.

The second transcendental is our sense of space–time. Transcendental logic and transcdendental aesthetic are related. Transcendental logic stands in relationship for Kant to transcendental aesthetic:

> Transcendental logic has lying before it the manifold content of a priori sensibility, which the transcendental aesthetic presents in order to give matter to the pure conceptions of the understanding, without which transcendental logic would have no content, and be therefore utterly void. (1781/1900: 60).

Transcendental conceptions of space and time are not derived from retrospective reflections upon outward experiences. Conceptions of space and time are a priori or antecedent to sensemaking. Space and time, for Kant (pp. 25, 27), are 'synthetical a priori' pure intuitions: 'space has only three dimensions' is not an empirical reflection; it is a 'transcendental ideality.' Spatial conceptions, such as ascending to heaven, or descending to the netherworld are transcendental idealities, for many of us, not empirical sensemaking of experience. Kant (p. 27) illustrates just this; we do not know hell by sight (sensations of color), hearing (sounds of the screams), reeling (sensations of heat), smelling (the rotting flesh), or tasting (the flames). Hell is unknown to us by our sense experience. Time as well for Kant (p. 28) 'is not an empirical conception' and there are a multiplicity of temporal conceptions beyond the kind of sequencing or linear succession. Our intuition of time can 'represent the course of time by a line progressing to infinity' (Kant, p. 30) but that is a transcendental ideation that is dialogic to other cyclical, spiral, and out of joint conceptions beyond sensemaking intuition. 'Time and space are, therefore' to Kant (p. 33), 'two sources of knowledge, from which, *a priori*, various synthetical cognitions can be drawn.'

POLYPI STRATEGY STORYING

Bakhtin (1981) did not give a name to the dialogism of the four dialogisms (polyphony, stylistics, chronotopicity, and architectonics). I named it polypi (Boje, forthcoming: 362). Polypi is inter-dialogism of polyphonic, stylistic, chronotopic, and architectonic. Polypi strategy storying is defined as multi-dialogized complexity whereupon polyphonic, stylistic, chronotopic, and architectonic dialogism collide. It is unlikely to be a something that is orchestratable.

The multiple dialogisms theorized by Bakhtin seem to be about variety making (centrifugal deviation-amplification). Yet, there is still control. Stylistic orchestration of styles is a form of image management and control. It can also affect variety making when the juxtaposed styles of verbal, written, gestural (in dramaturgic sense), and architectural telling challenge each other's ideas.

Bakhtin's (1981) chronotopic dialogism is relevant to Kant's transcendental aesthetic. For Bakhtin, chronotopicity is the dialogic relativism of time and space. Time–space representations antecede and transcend sense-experience, but are none the less shared in single-chronotope narrative and the more dialogic manner of story (with pluralistic chronotopicity). If one tries to define chronotopic dialogism (relativity of time/space) from whole (BME) or fragmented retrospective sense-experience, it becomes an empty and useless role for empirical intuition in strategy. What gets lost in retrospective sensemaking approach is the 'transcendental distinction' of what after sense-experience remains 'utterly unknown' (Kant, p. 37). Also lost is intertextual discourse of multi-dialogisms.

Bakhtin's architectonic dialogism builds upon Kant's transcendental aesthetic. Kant (1781/1900: 466) limited architectonic to the transcendental logic or Pure Reason. Kant (p. 466) defines 'Architectonic' as 'the art of constructing a system', which he specifies as a 'systematic unity of knowledge.' Kant prefers a unity of various cognitions under one theme or idea.

For Bakhtin, architectonic dialogism is the interanimation of cognitive, aesthetic, and ethic discourses. Kant's ethics is not 'based on anthropological or other empirical consideration', it is purely transcendental (p. 472). One is ethical categorically. For Bakhtin (1990) ethics is a matter of answerability for systemicity. Who are the authors, beholders, characters, and directors of systems? Systemicity is unmergedness of parts, and unfinished whole, not unity or whole.

Polypi strategy cultivates transcendental complexity properties among the colony of dialogisms. Polypi's literal meaning is a colony of hydra. Hans Christian Andersen used it in his tale of *The Little Mermaid* when describing the guardians of the Enchantress. Disney is representative of corporate storying of pre-modern religious and spiritual practices, Disneyfying them. Polypi dialogism is also defined as more transcendental complexity, 'third cybernetics', one that is about re-enchantment of what has been Disneyfied (Boje and Khadija, 2005; Boje and Baskin, 2005; Luhman and Boje, 2001).

First cybernetics was control (deviation-counteraction). Second cybernetics was the open system (deviation-amplification), and third cybernetics is on the order of language, dialogized story of dynamic transcendentalism. Third order cybernetics, at its most complex level, is about the polypi colony of dialogisms (polyphonic, stylistic, chronotopic, and architectonic) that is in critical interplay with dialectic or dialogic reflexivity of spiritualities and religiosities at work.

I wrote a tale about my grandmother Wilda to explore polypi dialogism (Boje, 2005e, f). Wilda is the name of my grandmother, on my mother's side. Wilda is an enchantress. I put Wilda and capitalism into a rendition of Andersen's classic tale. It is a polyphonic story with voices of '*Mer-people*,' people, air angels, and if one listens, there is Andersen's voice, my own voice, and the voice of native traditions stupefied in Disneyfication. My tale is multi-stylistic, with interviews with family members, snippets of diaries, etc. It is also multi-chronotopic (Romantic, Chivalric, Biographic, and the Fortuna of Everyday adventure). It is also architectonic dialogism among cognitive presentations about Bakhtin, Kierkegaard, and Andersen, as well as an aesthetic expression, and an ethical critique of capitalism. Several colleagues wrote commentaries about my Wilda tale, and *Journal of Management Spirituality and Religion* provided us with space for us to do a Special Feature on 'Wilda' and commentaries (Boje, 2005; commentaries by Barrera, Hopfl, Hansen, Barry, Biberman, Matthews, and Bakke).

Polypi reinscribes transcendence spirituality that became Disneyfied out of Hans Christian Andersen's 'The Little Mermaid.' Polypi dialogism is a manner of story that is not a tidy coherent narrative with linear presentation of beginning, middle, and end. Early 1800s was still a time when mermaids and animal spirits were part of everyday reality. Modernity made such 'reality' unreal.

> Polypi colony will hunt when hungry by immobilizing prey with stinging cells at the tip of arms that feed its mouth; it will retreat when fearful, shrinking into the connective tissue of the colony... it can bud and reproduce without sexual intercourse. Cut one up into fragments and each part will grow into a full polypus. (Boje, 2005: 360–1).

HOW POLYPI STRATEGY WORKS IN PRACTICE

Organizations and their environments are spiritual/religiosity admixtures of transcendental logic and transcendental aesthetics. If transcendental is cultivated among worker ethics or in choosing market niches, then it is strategic. We have only begun to explore layers of spiritual archaeology and genealogy in story-telling organizations, their people, strategies, enacted environments, and systemic complexities. Capitalism, with McDonaldization, Wal-Martization, and Disneyfication is increasingly an evangelical capitalism rooted in transcendental logic and aesthetics (Boje and Cai, 2004). In terms of transcendental aesthetics of space, evangelical capitalism uses imperialism and empire to colonize corporate spiritualism in one global conquest after another. As management tries to enact story strategy and system, what happens is polyphony can arrest spirituality and religion as one more control of the story fabric.

Some of us resist retrospective-managerial-control narratives, we know that what is going on is a whole lot more fragmented, scattered, partial, and dialectic indeterminate, and unknowable. Organization leaders want managerialist adventure strategies to be on an epic scale. Yet, what we work and live in is the multi-dialogism of polypi.

We work and live within networks of organizations that put each of us into emergent story unplotted lines, and many defined narrative cycles, so plotted in religions that we sometimes resist because they are counter to inner spiritual beliefs. As people throughout organizations and their environments try to resist some organization narrative control and establish counter-story and counter-narratives, there is a profound dialogism that needs to be explored, studied, and understood.

The Storytelling Organization can get out of balance, or more probably, was never in any balance in the first place. Diversity of perspective can turn into monologic prison. Polyphony dialogism can degenerate to an exercise in consensus. Or worse, some form of managerialist tyranny persists that overturns polyphony.

Stylistic dialogism can degenerate into the managerial orchestration of image, a way to pull the wool over the eyes of employees, consumers, investors, or SEC regulators.

Chronotopic dialogism can devolve into mono-chronotopicity. For example, an adventure chronotope can become too much an attempt to relive the past, or a bit too techno-futurist. An organic or mechanistic metaphorization can take over dialogic imagination. Architectonic dialogism can decompose into just cognitive ruling over all other discourses. The counter-view is that there is ethical and spiritual progress, as people bring their religious and spiritual values into corporate strategy.

POLYPI, TRANSCENDENTAL, AND INTEGRAL

Nancy Landrum and Carolyn Gardner, whose dissertations I was honored to chair, did a groundbreaking article in the *Journal of Organizational Change Management*. It is the first article that interrelates business strategy and Wilber's transcendental practices. Landrum and Gardner (2005) argue that Ken Wilber's (1996) all-quadrant (AQAL) integral approach can be applied to business strategy. I follow Landrum and Gardner in making revisions to the AQAL integral model, which I lay out in Table 8.1. This revised quadrant model stresses the diagonal intersects that are genealogical among the quadrants.

TABLE 8.1   *A revised four transcendental quadrant model*

Q1: EGO-CENTRIC – 'I'	Q2: ECO-CENTRIC – 'IT'
Shift from Self-centered to Emerging ethic; from first voice of 'I' internalized monologue of sensemaking to internalized 'Other' (second voice) dialog with other races, ethnicities, gender, or nature.	Shift from Slash and Burn to merging Other Eco-ethic; from I (1st voice), Other (2nd voice), or We (3rd voice ethical consciousness) – to voice of the voiceless (4th voice of enchantment)
Stories about self-development, self-realization, and then internalizing the voice of the Other in Q2, Q3, or Q4.	Stories about taking a stand on the environment, being species oriented instead of privileging just human species (e.g. Deep Ecology; Ecofeminism), and hearing voices of the voiceless
Q4: SPIRIT-CENTRIC 'WE'	**Q3: CORPORATE-CENTRIC – 'ITs'**
Shift from Rival-Fundamentalism to Emerging Transcendental ethic.	Shift from greedy profiteering to Emerging Humanity (as end unto itself) ethic.
Stories about netherworld, about moving from Q1 (mind) to Q4 (heart); finding a 'middle way' between Q3 and Q4; moving to a Q4 stewardship or re-enchantment of nature.	Stories about rediscovering Q4 humanity ethic, Q2 re-enchantment, or Q1 shift to Otherness at level of Q2 corporate networks controlling 'We' or 'It' or 'I.'

Q1 is ego-centric imprisonment of emergent story in narrative retrospective sensemaking about coherence, and linear-developmental chronology. It's also the second-order control (scripts and program routines), and third-order control over situation defined by sense-experience that Weick (1995) writes about.

Q2 begins with a slash and burn spirituality, and becomes increasingly eco-centric. The index here is from disenchanted elements of nature to enchanted nature that is highly symbolic complexity. Eco-centric would be a cross between dialectic and dialogic reflexivity, and be all about eco-ethics. Re-enchantment re-establishes the animism spirit-centric view of Q4. Q3 invokes a transcendental logic of re-enchantment that is a priori.

Q3 in Wilber dominates the other three quadrants in late postmodern and global capitalism. Max Weber called it a rationalistic spirit of capitalism, interconnected to Q4 since the dawn of capitalism. Corporate-centric logic has emerged after several shifts: from greedy profiteering and tribal ethnocentricity to nation-centric (imperialism) and corporate-centric global empire; there are differences of opinion with regard to the shift toward a humanity ethic. One view is the shifts need not be progressive on this yardstick. Some of us see empire with its network of corporate sovereignty, devolving into nation-imperialism. Worse, recent moves by empire re-establish Social Darwinian spiritual ethics.

Q4 extends from simple to the complexity of plurality of spiritualities and religiosities. This can be related to polypi of dialogisms, as well as to retro-narrative fragmentation.

There are differences in whether to treat Q4 as netherworld or the New Age transpersonal, or to take a less radical approach and see it as some sort of re-emergence of collective culture or collective consciousness (modified Q1).

In Integral theory, when you cross between quadrants historically or genealogically, interesting hybrids emerge. Evangelical capitalism is a cross of ego-centric with corporate-centric. The work of deep ecology and ecofeminism intersects Q4 spirit-centric with Q2 eco-centric, in a call to re-enchant nature. Some postmodernists want to cross Q2 (eco-centric) with Q1 (ego- centric) science, to get a more sustainable approach to natural science, or to counter the devolution seen in Biotech Century, with its genetic re-engineering, patenting of DNA, patenting of indigenous seed practices, etc.

In strategy, social ecology (Emery and Trist, 1965) seems to me to cross Q2 (eco-centric) with Q3 (corporate-centric) ethics, in ways different from evangelical capitalism; with social ecology there is more of a focus on democratic participation, as well as community participation, whereas in evangelical capitalism there is a call for conquest, either imperial or empire.

In the crossing of Q3 (corporate-centric) with Q4 (spirit-centric), there is a strong movement to allow people to admit they bring their religiosity and spirituality to work, that some of the ethical actions stem from the embodiment of spiritual/religious ideas by people working in organizations. If the balance in Q3 dominates Q4, there are narratives about how being spiritual helps the bottom line through an attention to quality, productivity, and doing what one is told. If Q4 dominates Q3, then productivity is not the most important criteria for decisions, or strategy.

A genealogic perspective looks at dialogism between quadrants, without presuming a developmental narrative of progress, synthesis, or integration. There are four ways to look at the relations among the quadrants.

First, we could adopt a strict Weberian perspective, and note that Q4 has been inextricably related with Q3 since its earliest days. Weber's (1904) thesis was that religious beliefs and practices constituted a rationality in the Protestant Ethic he called 'the spirit of capitalism.' For Weber 'spirit of capitalism' is an historical concept, tied to the development of rationalism worked out in religious practices. Weber's evidence comes from what he reads as Calvinist ethics in writings by Benjamin Franklin. Weber's thesis is that since the Reformation, the more ascetic Protestant (or Calvinist) religious values were instrumental in the rise of capitalism, whereas more Catholic and all Eastern values were not consonant with rationalization.

Secondly, several scholars have modified Weber's thesis pointing out that other western religions, as well as eastern religions had beliefs and practices that led to the 'spirit of capitalism.' Weber rejected eastern cultures for their lack of rationalization, observing that they did not have an Aristotelian systemic method in their science, music, architecture, or commerce. Calvinists, on the other hand, for Weber displayed the classic capitalistic entrepreneurial ethic, seeking profit rationally and systematically. Numerous critics argue either that capitalism took roots before the Reformation, or that during the time of the Reformation, there were no dramatic differences between Catholicism and Protestantism (both saw work occupations as divine callings). Sombart's thesis was that the "impersonal, rational, 'materialistic commercialism'" characteristic of the capitalistic spirit of Protestants, could be traced back to Jewish religious texts. Contemporary scholars note that Jewish texts posited a less rationalistic, and more mystical way of knowing that were excluded by Sombart. Nevaskar's (1971) review of Weber's thesis, argues that several eastern religions, in particular, Jainism have a spirituality that expresses itself in more capitalistic enterprise. In other words various religiosities and spiritualities 'played a role in the genesis of the spirit of capitalism' (Nevaskar, 1971: 56). What we witness in late modern global capitalism is the latest iteration.

Thirdly, neo-Marxist theorists reject even the modified Weberian thesis. Rather the spiritual or religious ethics changed to suit political economy conditions. To neo-Marxists, appeals to religion and spirituality values is another way for capitalists to obtain a labor force 'willing to work very hard for low wages' to demonstrate their calling or asceticism (Nevaskar, 1971: 46). Various intellectual movements that had nothing to do with religious or spiritual values were formidable in the rise of capitalism, such as the Machiavellian ethic, had been ignored by Weber.

Fourthly, more contemporary scholars theorize that the rationality of capitalism and spirituality/religiosity discourses mutually shape one another, in ways that change and adapt one to the other across the millennia. Early Calvinists and Puritans possessed social and commercial ethics vastly different from later ones. Tawney (1926) argues that religions adopted the hard work, risk-taking, rational organization, and profit-making ethics of capitalism, rather than the other way around, as Weber posited. Whether one sides with the chicken or the egg, the point is that the forces are mutual in contemporary times.

TRANSCENDENTAL STRATEGY CASES

Landrum and Gardner (2005) assert that there are no business cases in which all four quadrants and all levels (AQAL) are applied in strategy. They review cases involving Ben and Jerry's, the Body Shop, and Patagonia.

Jainism Business Transcendental Strategy

As a Jain, I meditate, do not wear leather, silk, and practise a vegetarian (actually vegan) diet. In Jain spiritual philosophy, business owners are discouraged from having anything to do with the meat and dairy industries. It is not a matter of retrospective sensemaking; it is a transcendental logic. Hotel owners with restaurants do not serve meat in their dining facilities. Shoe manufacturers do not use leather; cosmetics do not use animal products or rely on animal testing. Jains do not enter into business occupations that involve the taking of sentient life. Jains are vegetarian. They believe in rebirth, and living in ways that disentangle one from karmic influences, lest one devolve in the next life.

Transcendental aesthetics includes temporality as cycles of rebirth. Transcendental logics include ahimsa (non-violence and reverence for all life). Jainism is very pluralist, with many gods and goddesses; however these are considered finite, not infinite beings. Gods and goddesses are not superior to human beings in Jain philosophy. There are also 'sacred animals, trees, places, emblems, temples, idols, and sacred scriptures' (Nevaskar, 1971: 171). Part of Jainism is renouncing vices of lying speech as well as greed or stealing. In short, there is a good deal of asceticism in Jainism that carries over into business strategy, into the choice of business, and its conduct. Jains became traders, since it is easier to practice ahimsa. Jains also took up money lending and banking, since, as traders they need to do something with the accumulation of capital. Jainism's transcendental logic encourages commercial values of honesty and frugality, as well as private ownership of property and means of production and distribution (Nevaskar, 1971: 207).

Tom's of Maine – Integrating Bottom Line and Transcendental Logics

Tom Chappell, after four years of Harvard Divinity School, founded Tom's of Maine with his wife. Their transcendental logic includes frequent reference to the Quakers: 'do well by doing good' (Chappell, 1994: 25), although Tom says he learned 'many religious views' and 'the balancing act between the spiritual and the practical, the divine and everyday.' This includes the Buddhist, finding the Middle Way, and Hebrew mystics, finding the Good Way. In short, a plurality of spiritual/religious traditions informs Tom's transcendental strategy logic. Tom's mission is to seek financial success while behaving in a socially responsible and environmentally sensitive way. Tom and Kate were the first to introduce toothpaste made wholly from natural ingredients. A line of natural personal care products, some available in health-food stores, followed. The balancing act between transcendental strategy and more practical business strategy was OK between 1973 and 1980. However, between 1980 and 1986, the couple noted that 'growth and profit dominated business planning' (p. 26). The couple decided to conduct strategy sessions that would renew their more transcendental values. As Tom says, 'I wanted to turn the conventional business planning process inside out and upside down' (p. 27). Tom continues, by describing the more stylistic image approach we described in the theory section:

> Typically, companies meet in strategy sessions to formulate a business plan, then tack on some values to legitimate it. (Chappell, 1994: 28)

Another way to put it, in terms of Table 8.1, is to move from 'It' to 'We' values.

Relevant to Table 8.1, Tom gave members sections that, by my reading, come from Kant's (1781/1900) writings about transcendental logic to overcome self-interest, and Kant's (1785/1993) *Grounding for the Metaphysics of Morals* concerning transcendental ethics. The later focuses on humanity being treated as an end unto themselves, not as a means. Richard Niebuhr of Harvard Divinity School gave a talk on how management could free themselves from business habits, 'their obsession with discipline, control, focus, their maximization, and profit' (p. 30).

In terms of Table 8.1, the result was a shift from Q1 and Q3 to Q2 and Q4. The result of the strategy retreat was to integrate relationships 'to the customer, the employee, the environment, *and* the bottom line' (p. 30). Ten percent of pretax profits went to charity and worthy causes; employees would receive childcare subsidies and get time off to volunteer within the community.

I want to assert here that Tom's of Maine, as well as Body Shop, Patagonia, and Ben and Jerry's are not the only businesses that ascribe to transcendental logic and transcendental aesthetics. One can look to western Christian writers who advocated a more transcendental strategy for business. These would include Norman Vincent Peale (1952), Napoleon Hill (1960) and W. Clement Stone (1960, 1987). In the 1950s and 1960s their books were the staple of many, if not most US corporations. If one could master one's business attitude, then their economic fate was assured. For example, in Hill's (1928) three volume work 'Law of Success' the transcendental logic of positive mental attitude: 'we translate into physical reality the thoughts and attitudes which we hold in our minds' (cited in Hill, 1960: 8). Attitude became the invisible talisman for business people. Belief in a Divine Power would help people with the power of their mind, which would ordain their business destiny. This was the way of the 'cosmic habit force' (Hill, 1960: 74). There was faith in 'transmutation of desire into its physical, or monetary equivalent' (Hill, 1960: 49).

Sexual and Creative Energy

Hill (1960) believed that sexual energy could be sublimated into creative energy: 'sex transmutation is simple and easily explained. It means the switching of the mind from thoughts of physical expression, to thoughts of some other nature' (p. 176). Sex is the most powerful drive and can be transmuted into creative energy of imagination and will power. The sixth sense is 'creative imagination' (p. 179), the source of business intuition or hunches. According to Hill, mates, such as Josephine, to higher spheres of thought, stimulated leaders with over active sex energy, such as Napoleon Bonaparte. Hills puts it this way, '*There never has been and never will be a great leader, builder, or artist lacking in this driving force of sex*' (p. 184, italics in original). Another way to say all this is that sexual energy was sublimated into ascetic practices, the energy transmuted to creative imagination and action. For Hill (1960: 188) leaders lacking in sex energy were a 'flop.' Hill constructs a theory of sex, love, and romance. Sex is biological, while love and romance are spiritual (p. 193). The energy of sex and positive thinking, however, is not all there is to transcendental. Marcuse (1964) calls this approach 'one-dimensional', a refusal to think or act critically. In our terms, BME coherence and positivity.

Pittron and the Beneath-the-Open-Hearth Chapel

A case that is more integrative of the two modes of knowledge – retrospective sensemaking and a priori transcendental – is Pittron. It occurred just outside of Pittsburgh, in a steel company in Glassport, named Pittron. Pittron is one of two

hundred companies in the Textron Corporation. It happened in 21 months of
1973–4, when Wayne Alderson (1980) became VP of operations at Pittron, just
after an extended bitter 84-day strike that began 26 October 1972. Wayne
began a strategy he called 'Operation Turnaround.' As you will discover,
Operation Turnaround became a journey of not just economic transformation,
but spiritual action. In 21 months the company became one of the most profitable in the US. Here are the results after 21 months of Operation Turnaround
Strategy (Alderson, 1980: 72–3):

1 Sales up 400%
2 Profits rose from deficit of $6 million to profit of $6 million (shift is $12 million)
3 Employment up 300% (from 300 workers to over 1,000)
4 Productivity rose 64%
5 Labor grievances declined from 12 per week to one per year
6 Chronic absenteeism disappeared
7 Quality of production became best in company's history

Alderson began Operation Turnaround with a series of small symbolic actions.
He describes Operation Turnaround as an 'operational strategy' of responsibility and reconciliation in relationships that had taken a 'downward spiral'
(pp. 56, 60). These are the symbolic first steps.

In 1972, long before Tom Peters coined the term 'managing by wandering
around' (MBWA), Wayne did it. Wayne's MBWA was to wander each day
through the areas of the foundry, learn the names of its 300 workers, and sometimes stop to see what it was like to work hard, doing one of their jobs.

In a place where everyone wore hard helmets, with the boss wearing the symbolic white helmet, and workers wearing dark blue or brown, Wayne had his helmet painted black. The symbolic action was to remove one of the dualities; he did
not adopt the blue-collar uniform, and stayed with his white shirt and tie.

In a consummate act of symbolism, Wayne had his safety helmet painted
black. The simple gesture had a galvanizing effect on the men. Ultimately,
the hat was treated like a religious relic, enshrined in a case under an open
hearth. (Alderson, 1980: 62)

Wayne observed what while the manager's office had wood paneling, the
union steward's office was drab concrete. The symbolic action was to get him
paneling to show respect for human dignity.

Wayne began greeting workers at the gate when their shift ended. Workers did
get the symbolic message that Wayne was behaving just like a preacher greeting the
flock after service. Most ignored his extended hand; they were union, and Wayne,
even with a black helmet, was the enemy. Over time the effect of these symbolic
gestures was cumulative, and some 30% began to wave or shake his hand. The next
stage of symbolic actions amplified the religious/spiritual symbolism.

Joking around, the shop steward began to tease Wayne about his preacher-
symbolic gestures. The union representative asked Wayne, 'where's your bible?'

Wayne stuffed a small bible in his jacket pocket, and pulled it out. The shop steward and the VP of operations began to debate some scripture. A crowd of workers crowded about them. The next taunt was 'what about a bible study?' Wayne gave in after the third request. A bible study was arranged for Wednesday during lunch hour. The bible study was non-denominational including Baptists, Methodists, Pentecostals, Presbyterians, Roman Catholics, Jews, and quite a few agnostics and atheists. Attendance was strictly voluntary. What is amazing is Wayne Alderson had no interest in theology, and often his speech was salted with curse words, but was not profane (p. 74). A steel foundry and mill is a tough place to manage or work in. It is not the usual setting for a spiritual transformation journey.

The Bible study grew, and a larger place had to be found; the place was under the Open Hearth, in a catacomb, that became known first as 'chapel' and then as 'Chapel-Under-the-Open-Hearth' (p. 79). Workers and managers assembled to engage in more transcendental discourse. The foundry and steel company was undergoing a 'spiritual renaissance' (p. 84). 'The chapel became the most visible symbol of Operation Turnaround. God was in the plant' (p. 86). More religious symbols were added. Workers forged bookend sized praying hands. There were enough forged for the workers, then more had to be forged, as family members wanted their own. On Sunday, 20 January, 1974, 2,000 people assembled in the chapel to celebrate the anniversary of the strike. There was resistance. News of the chapel spread to the community and industry. People wanted to know what was going on. Seven thousand people attended the first Value of the Person Seminar (a 3 day event) – the Communist Party had picketers outside accusing management of using spirituality to exploit workers (p. 102).

A spiritual philosophy emerged, symbolized in the slogan, 'Love, Dignity, and Respect' (p. 64); this later became known as 'Value of the Person' by treating them with love, dignity, and respect. Symbolic transformation, and the spiritual ideals became embodied in persons: Wayne was nicknamed the 'Preacher' and Lefty, the union representative, became known around the plant as 'Friar Tuck' (p. 98).

The emergent story spread to the media. There was a gas shortage in 1972. People lined up for gas in stations that often ran out, leading to fights. Meanwhile Pittron hoarded its gas, needing it to keep production running. Wayne argued with the management committee that Value of the Person meant sharing the gas with the workers. Not only did that mean giving it to them for free, so they could get to and from work, but worse, Wayne wanted an honor system, where workers could pump what they needed. The plan was considered outrageous, but finally a majority agreed. News leaked out:

> The news media showed up in time to see Wayne pumping gas into the employee's cars. One of them shouted, 'Why are you doing this?' 'Why not? Wayne replied. The answer became a buzzword in the plant. Robert Kennedy's slogan became a reality at Pittron: 'Some men look at challenges and ask 'why? "Others look and ask, "why not?"'' (Alderson, 1980: 66)

'Why not?' treat a worker with dignity became a symbol. This led to supervisors ceasing to use the racist 'N-word' as well as dropping ethnic slurs such as 'Dago,' 'Pollock,' etc. A worker was late getting back from going home to lunch with his wife. Wayne saw him duck into the plant gate, and confronted the worker, but not for being late, 'How could you do that? If she were still here I'd make you go back there and kiss her goodbye... Don't ever think your job is more important than your wives' (p. 71). It was not just respect for workers. A manager's wife called Wayne to complain that her husband was rarely at home and had become a workaholic. Wayne cut back his hours, and asked him to spend more time at home. These symbolic actions became symbolic stories that spread rapidly through the plant and the community.

In the midst of Pittron's spiritual renaissance, a fire broke out 9 November 1973. It was not just a fire, but more accurately, an explosive inferno. Twelve men were in the vicinity of thousands of gallons of molten metal spilling onto the shop floor. The fact that all 12 escaped without injury was considered a miracle, and was written up that way in the media. Another relic was added to the display case in the chapel-under-the-hearth. It was a bible, which had survived unscathed while everything else in the path of the lava-like molten metal and explosions had been destroyed.

No good deed goes unpunished   Rumors began to circulate in the summer of 1974 that Textron Corporation was going to shut down 'Project Turnaround,' despite its dramatic record of profit, productivity, quality, and morale. An article describing the chapel and bible study at Pittron was circulating at Textron Headquarters. Executives were joking that Pittron had become a 'Sunday School' and that Wayne had some kind of 'Messiah Complex' (p. 112). Another rumor spread that Textron was selling Pittron to a conglomerate. Wayne returned from vacation in Europe to Textron, and offered to buy the plant; his offer was refused. Textron sold Pittron to Bucyrus-Erie Corporations (makers of strip-mining crane and earth-moving equipment) for $18 million. The President of Pittron went to Alderson's home, 'You don't have a job anymore, Wayne. You're finished. You're too close to the men. You're emotionally involved. I told you this would happen. We've been sold, it's over. Please come in and talk to the men' (p. 120). Wayne, at the urging of managers, union representatives, and workers called Bucyrus-Erie Corporation, to verify what he had heard from Pittron's President. Chairperson Berg said no final decision had been reached about Wayne's future employment. Wayne flew to Milwaukee for a meeting with Chairperson Berg.

Berg thanked Wayne for turning around the foundry, and making it profitable. He communicated his problems with Wayne's style of leadership.

> Wayne, I think what you are doing is a good thing. The world needs it. But we're not quite ready for it yet. I'm afraid you're a little bit ahead of the times. Would you be willing to give up your involvement with the men and the chapel-under-the-open-hearth? The men would still be free to meet there

on their own time, but I want you to get out of it ... Wayne replied, 'No sir, I will not give it up'. (pp. 123–4)

Instead, Wayne began his practice as a special consultant to management and union relations. Wayne and his daughter went on to found and establish the Value of the Person Seminar. There was a documentary film made by Robin Miller, titled 'Miracle of Pittron' which had its official debut 27 October 1975 to a crowd of 2,000 people in a school auditorium: 'All the memories of the days of Operation Turnaround were rekindled as they watched themselves in action on the silver screen. Viewers were at times disturbed by the audience weeping in the room' (p. 136). The film ended with two standing ovations. There was a preview, prior to the first showing in the White House by President Gerald Ford, who sent a very enthusiastic letter (p. 137).

Critique of Pittron Case 'Value of the Person' presentations also received their share of criticism. In a workshop for mediators and arbitrators in New York, the film Miracle of Pittron received critical comments: 'What are you trying to pull?' You're peddling religion! What about the Jews? What about people who don't buy into all this Christian stuff? This is no place for preaching' (p. 178). Wayne's reply, 'but I'm not here to peddle Christianity. I'm pushing the Value of the Person... The very thing you hate and fight against – prejudice – is what you are spitting out right now' (p. 179). Reactions from a Marxist publication, Daily World (formerly Daily Worker) on 7 December 1978 were more severe; the headline read, 'Bosses launch cult – labor cult' and 'Alderson pseudo-religious productivity cult' (p. 193 in Alderson, 1980). Alderson's (1980: 195) reply is that he is a 'qualified capitalist' who 'rejects both the virulent form of *unrestrained laissez faire capitalism*' and '*socialist capitalism.*' Alderson defines his approach according to the 'Stewardship Principle' where private ownership is permitted by 10 commandments.

Alderson and his daughter Nancy Alderson McDonnell (1994) wrote a version of Theory of the Person to accompany their seminars. They toned down the spiritual and religious aspects. Whereas Alderson (1980) is explicit about the role of prayer, bible study, as well as spiritual regeneration strategy in relation to turnaround and productivity, the more recent book is more of a human relations seminar manual. There are very mentions of the Bible (e.g. p. 142, 239) and these are to illustrate human relation points about building teams, or promoting quality.

I went to a 'Value of the Person' seminar conducted by Wayne and Nancy in Pittsburgh in about 1997. There were representatives of labor and management from dozens of Fortune 100 firms. Wayne and Lefty, one of the union leaders at the Pittron foundry told stories about the chapel, the bible study, the reaction from the corporation. My wife's father (Phil Rosile) and several of her uncles (Tony, Ed, Nunzio) are People of the Person graduates. They have applied the principles of love, dignity, and respect in their own organizations. They do not install chapels or Bible studies. Rather, they bring their religious/spiritual philosophy to bear on their management of people. For example, when Phil Rosile sold his food distribution wholesale company, he dismissed several offers, settling on one that would protect the workers' job security and benefits.

Critical Spirituality? Critical spirituality is an ethnomethodology. It is defined as the study of how people at work engage the transcendental. It assumes that various religions and spiritualities define transcendental quite differently. The word 'critical' refers to critical theory and critical postmodern theory. Critical Theory of the Frankfurt School (i.e., Benjamin, Horkheimer, Adorno, Marcuse, and Fromm) rejects organizational religious or spiritual metaphysics and classifies these as ideology used to exploit the consumer culture industry. Adorno (1951/1974: 231), for example, says:

> Metaphysical categories are not merely an ideology concealing the social system; at the same time they express its nature, the truth about it, and in their changes are precipitated those in its most experiences.'

Critical postmodern theory is skeptical of the appropriation of metaphysics into strategy practices, fearful it is one more example of Social Darwinism. Social Darwinism is a corporate reading of transcendental forces of an invisible hand of competition that sorts the rich from the poor.

Making spirituality/religiosity values and beliefs strategic, raises problematic issues studied in 'critical spirituality' theory. For example, Steingard and Fitzgibbons (1995) argue that global capitalism is a spiritually flawed discourse that is not ecologically sustainable. Butts (1997) is outraged at the selfishness, greed, and mean-spirited, winner-take-all scapegoating (class warfare) inflicted on the working class and other disfranchised social groups. Walck (1995) is cautious about spirituality, reminding us that our global discourse ignores the 'spirituality' of the poor. Mitroff and Denton (1999) surveyed 230 managers and top executives: 92% would like to include spiritual principles in their organization, but refrain from doing so for various reasons: no models for doing so, not wanting to appear new age, not wanting to step on others' religious or spiritual practices, etc. In short there are reasons for a critical spirituality discipline.

Critical spiritually is an inquiry into the dark side of managerialism and our late (post) modern global capitalism. A critical spirituality asks Nietzsche's (1990, #4: 35) question: is capitalism 'life-advancing, life-preserving, species-preserving, perhaps even species-breeding?' Bakhtin's (1968) works are about a critical spirituality, about the carnival of resistance of one religiosity or spirituality to another. For example, one could read Bakhtin (1990) for its exploration of not only the architectonic interanimation of cognitive, aesthetic, and ethical discourses, but as an exploration of spirituality and religiosity that enters dialogism.

PART III

CONSULTING TO STORYTELLING ORGANIZATIONS

Part III applies key concepts of Part I (storytelling-sensemaking, dialogisms of emergence, and interacting collective memories) to how story consulting is done, and could be done. Part III answers two questions of how to consult to storytelling organizations and how to consult transorganization storytelling organizations?

Instead of buying into guru story consulting, or getting fairy tales read to you, why not notice the embedded fabric of narrative and story in real time Storytelling Organizations? And, not just oral stories, but those embedded in written documents, in photos, and décor, even in architecture itself, as forms of collective memory. Instead of buying all the snake oil in charlatan story consulting that is all the rage, why not look at restorying. Restorying is a new kind of consulting, one not as rooted in managerialism or in monological conceptions of whole-system theory. In (White and Epston, 1990) narrative therapy the process is one of constructing a new narrative, renarrating one that is fashioned out of marginalized or peripheral episodes in an individual's life history. The new story becomes an alternative interpretation of the individual narrative possibility. Restorying the complexity of multiple dialogisms (introduced in Part I, and applied in Part II to strategy) in storytelling organizations is beyond the capability of snake oil story consulting. Restorying intervenes in the variety making of collective memory, the complex fabric of real time and space systemicity, and traces the interplay of sensemaking of storytelling. It's not some 90 second or two minute springy-elevator pitch narrative. A behavioral storytelling approach to story consulting means interventions that change story and narrative practices in the organization not in some off-site retreat about archetypes using focus groups called story circles (that are anything but). Restorying, by contrast, is a more dialogic process of multi-story, multi-plot deconstruction that is antecedent to sensemaking retrospection of experience. It takes more grounded ethnography and antenarrative inquiry into the complexity of sensemaking. While there are scores of books on story consulting to organizations, most of these are rooted in the narrative prison view of 'proper' story, not in doing the story noticing, seeing story emergence.

Transorganizational Development (TD) is planned change in the collective relationships of a variety of stakeholders, transforming networks of Storytelling Organizations, to accomplish something beyond the capability of any single organization or stakeholder (adapted from Culbert et al., 1972). Here too it's a matter of convening stakeholders of a network of Storytelling Organizations to restory, to improvise a story that is a new plot, to break the hegemony of any dominant narrative sensemaking that is keeping things from getting any better. It's not just retrospection on history or founding stories, its prospective, tracing antenarratives, doing the work of setting up collaborative search conferences, as Emerys call them, or doing the work of socioeconomic networking among organizations using the kinds of theatre inquiry that Henri Savall addresses. Chapter 10 contrasts a dozen transorganizational story consulting approaches, with particular attention to the grass-root activism of Alinsky. In my thesis, many of these TD story consulting approaches put emerging story into narrative prison by orchestrating or steering dialog, debate, dialectic, or dialogisms. The breakout comes in deprogramming.

9

CONSULTING TO STORYTELLING ORGANIZATIONS

This chapter is about how story consulting is too much about 90 second springy-control narratives (elevator pitches) and not enough about emergent story webs, to be very practical or useful. It introduces *story turn* of reflexivity and transcendental that interacts with what is well known as the *narrative turn* of representation. The distinction is made between dialog, debate, dialectic, and dialogism in development practice.

Figure 9.1 is about the interplay of D1 (dialogs) of retrospective narrative convergence, D2 debates among retro-narrative-fragments, D3 dialectic reflexivity, D4 transcendental dialogisms beyond polyphonic, and Dⵔ (demonstrative) here-and-now story sensemaking. All five modes interpenetrate one another.

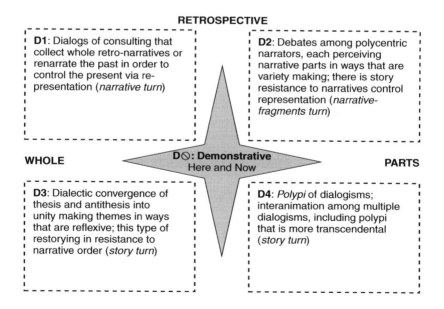

RETROSPECTIVE

D1: Dialogs of consulting that collect whole retro-narratives or renarrate the past in order to control the present via re-presentation (*narrative turn*)

D2: Debates among polycentric narrators, each perceiving narrative parts in ways that are variety making; there is story resistance to narratives control representation (*narrative-fragments turn*)

WHOLE

Dⵔ: Demonstrative Here and Now

PARTS

D3: Dialectic convergence of thesis and antithesis into unity making themes in ways that are reflexive; this type of restorying in resistance to narrative order (*story turn*)

D4: *Polypi* of dialogisms; interanimation among multiple dialogisms, including polypi that is more transcendental (*story turn*)

FIGURE 9.1   *Four ways practice* develops *storytelling organization*[1]

---

1 Dⵔ (Demonstrative) is defined as the interplay of narrative and storyist turn in the here-and-now of emergence. It can be understood as not-story, or not-yet story.

STORY TURN

Story Turn is, I believe, a new paradigm. One finds lots written about the Narrativist Turn (Lyotard, 1984; Polkinghorne, 1988). If we take Bakhtin's dialogisms (i.e. dialogic manner of story), Derrida's distrust of narrative, Stein's aversion to developmental narrative, and Benjamin's preference for story competencies seriously, then it makes sense to posit a Story Turn that is beyond (or before) the Narrative Turn. In previous parts of this book, I have distinguished 'narrative,' defined in Aristotelian ways that has over the course of modernity become representationalism, and a more 'Story Turn' that is more about reflexivity and transcendental metaphysics.

My distinction between narrative and story turns rests on this point: narrative genres are encased in a linear, monological framework (Bakhtin, 1973: 13) that has become representation, detached from living story life. Renarrating is used as a device to unify diverse fields of vision into managerialist homophony discourse into dead representations, general archetypes, and abstract models. I take the radical position that retrospective sensemaking narratives renarrate experience into centripetal force of heteroglossia, while ignoring the more centrifugal forces of story. This results in the narrative fiction of 'systematic monological philosophical finalizedness' (Bakhtin, 1973: 26). The counter-force, of multi-story dialogism is the more centrifugal force of difference or divarication. The narrative turn, in sum, is D1 → D2, from mono-logocentric dialogue to polycentric debate. A story turn is more about D$\emptyset$, D3, and D4.

How would a narrative turn and story turn differ in terms of ontology, epistemology, methodology, and praxis? Ontology of D1 narrativist is monologic, monovocality. Ontology of D2 narrative turn is polylogical, here and there, polyvocal. Both are all about retrospective sensemaking of experience.

Story turn is defined as a priori, transcendental logic and transcendental aesthetics. That is the important difference between Weickian narrative control and Kantian/Bakhtinian manner of story dialogicality. In other words, on many levels narrative and story are similar, but on the dialogisms they are different. Weickian retrospective sensemaking knowledge of experience is different from Kantian knowledge of pure reason derived a priori in the inner sense of thought and idea. By praxis I mean interventions into systemicity.

D1 narrativist praxis is at the level of 'micro dialogue' (Bakhtin, 1973: 33). It is about people doing story as part of meetings and conversations (be they in the same room, or more virtual, such as by Internet). Dialogue, can be broadly defined as, one person addressing themselves orally, in writing, or in (theatric) gesture to another person, to a third person. In managerialism, what passes for dialogue, is more accurately monologue. Debate takes us into polycentrality, and sometimes (rarely) into polyphonic dialogism. Polyphony is this 'multivoicedness [that] reveals the variety of life and the complexity of the human experience' (Bakhtin, 1973: 36).

Story praxis is about storying and restorying that is dialogical. D$\emptyset$ is more about the ways retro and ante, and reflexive and transcendental collide in the here-and-now. D$\emptyset$ story is several unmerged, unfinalized, contemporary, and traditional stories, arising side-by-side, in the moment of Being.

Complex Responsive Processes (CRP)

Clearly, a more comprehensive theory of story complexity and change is needed than current managerialist-functionalist approaches that claim narrative turn (Boje, 2006b). I would like to propose an integration of Ralph Stacey's (2006) latest rendition of Complexity Theory with the story turn. Stacey's (2006: 124) Complex Responsive Processes (CRP) argue for a complex adaptive heterogeneity rooted in the 'wider improvisational processes' of writing and talking about organizations that is heart of emergence.

CRP Theory is relatable to all five modalities of story consulting in Figure 9.1. Stacey (2006) never uses the term 'story,' and only mentions 'narrative' once in passing, and in a derogatory way. I will therefore have to translate story into complexity. Because there are no wholes, and no boundaries to complexity systems, Stacey (2006: 128) rejects the mechanistic and organic models of system theory. Stacey (2006: 126) mentions Kant as introducing the notion that system is a useful metaphor, but cautioned applying the concept directly to human action. Kant (1781/1900: 466) says, 'by the term *Architectonic* I mean the art of constructing a system' which is useful for constructing science, but a human storytelling systemicity is 'an aggregate, and not a system.' Stacey (2006) is close to what I mean by 'systemicity': the unmergedness and unfinalizedness of parts. If systemicity is the interplay of parts, 'there is then no need to think in terms of systems or wholes' (p. 125). Local story interaction in organization systemicity is more of a rhapsodic, emergence. Yet, emergence is only rhapsodic for a moment, and then one or more mode of story control stops it.

Emergent story can be improvisational and spontaneous, and in the 'here-and-now' is demonstrative of emergence. Central to CRP Theory is the 'notion of emergence' (Stacey, 2006: 139); 'global patterns continually emerge in local interaction.' As we saw in the collective memory chapter, this one would be called highly polyphonic, in the moment of Being that is face-to-face direct participation by a wide range of stakeholders, where answerable action could be noticed among participants.

Emergence comes about in the absence of, or despite the four forms of deliberation and governance (D1 to D4). However, story emergence vanishes in the moment when its improvised and spontaneous performance becomes a repetitive pattern, an ordered narrative re-presentation. And this is the one place that Stacey (2006: 137) mentions 'narrative form' as something that controls. As Stein (1935) argues, the continuous presents of instants is not a beginning, middle, and end linear narrative; nor is it a developmental story. In each suceeding present instance complexity emerges and re-emerges in interactive story that is out-of-narrative-control. DO Demonstrative improvisation quickly falls prey to one or several forms of story control (D1 to D4).

D1 (Dialogue) is more about managerialist collective memory monologue. Global patterns are assumed to change system-wholeness, as the result of some totalized managerialist-derived global story, outside the local, in-the-moment, interaction of storytellers. The only dialogue is a managerial one (stakeholders of mind reading what monologue is expected here), which all others must imitate or pay the consequences of their resistance. In strategy, dialogue is the interaction of managerialist planners to create a strategic plan or design in advance of its implementation. The assumption is the strategy story comes before implementation. If one assumes the managerial narrative-consulting model, then the global narrative (in its two-minute elevator pitch) concocted by management will control the whole (its more systems thinking, more arrogance and hubris). The narrative assumption is problematic, because with authoritarian rule over story, there emerges passive, sometimes active resistance to monologue passing itself off as dialogue. Many narrative-consulting methods that call themselves by the name 'dialogue' do outlaw debate. Or in the case of Denning (2005) teach executives how to use humor to overcome resistance to their two-minute springboard narratives.

D2 (Debate) is more about more multi-lineal collective memory, perhaps some punctual. Stacey posits a radical shift in what is the dynamic complexity of the Storytelling Organization. In story terms, there is a myriad of local storytellers interacting, in various parts of the organization. The story improvisation is not a matter of programming some kind of master narrative from the top, and inculcating it throughout, as in D1. What is story improvisation in this mode of sensemaking? Here, story noticing comes from taking into account the wider interests of powerful subgroups, one of which is certainly D1 managerial story control, but it is also noticing the emergent patterns. Debate is the rivalry among distributed local groups of narrative and storytellers who debate representation and interpretation, and what account will become some collective story. Positing a whole system is a distraction when groups of storytellers debate what is and what is not. The shift in thinking in CRP theory is to pay attention to local storytellers. It is naïve, Stacey argues, to small segments of local communicators to follow rules analogous to digital agents in some computer simulation of complexity. The distinctive complexity property of a Tamara Storytelling Organization is that living storytellers (and narrators) are locally interacting all at the same time in different rooms (Boje, 1995). Since storytelling is fundamentally a social process, and not only retrospective, but also reflexive, then there is another form of story control beside rivalry.

D3 (Dialectic) is definitely a collision of two collective memories, sometimes more. Stacey reaches for his George Herbert Mead (1934) book. Mead's theory is that there are many 'Generalized Others' that serve to control one's communicative interactions. In the Storying Turn, this translates to reflexivity upon how others will receive the story you tell. Foucault (1977a) would call it the 'internalized gaze.' Those generalized others survey our telling of a story, its contents, implications, and the way we tell it. For Stacey (2006: 126), the communicative agents are capable of what is 'essentially reflexive and reflective' sensemaking and do not follow 'mechanistic rules.' Storytellers are reflexively conscious and self-conscious, and sometimes unconscious of their generalized others, who watch them, tell and not tell. The generalized other is a more powerful form of social control than managerial dialogue, and the debate among factions. A story interpretation of Mead (1934) is that the many generalized others are the 'Me' of a story reflected upon by tellers and listeners. The 'I' is our independent voice. This sets up the classic

"I-Me' dialectic" that Stacey (2006: 130) posits are socially formed whilst forming the social complexity of organizations in acts of reflection and reflexivity. The 'I-Me' dialectic is not some face-to-face dialogue, nor is it a debate among storytellers distributed in different divisions. The storyteller's 'I' is the subject of the man 'Me's', the apperceptions of Others (i.e. groups, organizations, community, societies, and even the transcendental Others). This is the 'I'-'Me' dialectic of interacting selves of the social in stories told by storytellers in the Storytelling Organization. It is a radical shift away from the sender-message-receiver-feedback model of first order cybernetic system theory (Shannon and Weaver, 1949). The 'I' and 'Me' are socially constructed in 'we' storytelling animals. One cannot story independently of social control of the generalized others internalized as 'Me's.' 'I' inhabits a society of social selves. Inside each teller and listener there are a society of social selves doing a reflexivity role play, and many of the 'Me's' are disembodied others that haunt our conversation. Like at Disney where one asked, and still asks, 'What would Walt do?' Or at Wal-Mart where people always ask, 'What would Sam do?' (Boje and Rosile, 2008). Or at McDonald's, 'What would Kroc do?' (Boje and Rhodes, 2005a, b). Social control in storying turn, is exactly the 'role play/silent conversation of a body with itself, and the social' and the 'public vocal interaction or conversation between bodies' (Stacey, 2006: 130). But the storyteller's interaction forms and is formed by the social in one more way.

D4 (Dialogic) is directly participatory and it can be at the level of polyphonic collective memory. The social control of story is intertextuality of multiple discourses that are dialogic to one another. As we saw in the stylistic strategy chapter, the dialogism can be orchestrated, image management. Following Bakhtin (1981), we can posit an internal dialogism of the selves (analogous to Mead's internalized social selves) that this is interplay with external dialogism of multiple discourses. (Boje and Khadija) 2005a. Stacey (2006: 135) does not use the term dialogic, but does write about how groups do struggle 'frequently about which discourse is to dominate.' Bakhtin (1990) extends Kant's theory of architectonics, as the interanimation of not only cognitive appreciation of transcendental (as in multiple selves in Mead's theory) but also the interplay with aesthetic and ethical discourse. In the dialogic manner of storytelling, multiple discourses are intertextual to one another.

Multiplicity

The implication for the 'story turn' is that the important interaction among storytellers is at the local level. At the local level, telling is communicative interaction in ways that are self-organizing emergent processes. However, there is still 'story control' going on. Out of the local interaction, global patterns of 'coherence' are produced but in the absence of some 'global programme or plan' (p. 125). There is emergence without the imposition of narrative control from the top (or center), such as by a managerialist group. More accurately CRP theory recognizes several social control forms that are applicable to Figure 9.1.

I therefore theorize five interactive forces (D0 to D4) of retrospective and reflexive, as well as whole narrative and more fragment (part) story practices. Figure 9.1

is not to be read as a two-by-two. Rather, the multiple ways of storying are interactive, sometimes simultaneous, other times iterative, and not in any particular order.

DⓋ *demonstrative* is here-and-now, but can devolve to other types. Demonstrative means that all that is not story is being evinced. DⓋ is not story. Heidegger (1962) says, 'If we are to understand the problems of Being, our first philosophical step consists in … "not telling a story".' DⓋ enters in the middle telling; it is not yet story. Story threatens to emerge, but can unravel into antenarrative fragments. DⓋ forsakes developmental telling of D1 (e.g. Denning) or D2 (collecting and typing story fragments, e.g. Snowden). DⓋ is in-between teller and listener: Stein says 'the narrative in itself is not what is in your mind but what is in somebody else's.' (*A Transatlantic Interview*, cited in Ryan, 1984: 55) What does it mean to not story? Bakhtin (1929/1973: 44–5) cites a segment of *A Gentle Creature* where Dostoevsky says: 'The point is that this is not a story and not a sketch.' The teller is distraught, does not concoct story or narrative, and keeps at the emergent level, until story emerged.

My *theory of storyability* is that story turns event into experience, and shapes that into collective memory. This makes a major contribution to Weickian enactment and retrospective sensemaking theory. In retrospective sensemaking it is assumed that there is no difference between event and experience, that event just becomes experience by application of sensory perception. Second, sensemaking theorists assume that there is no important difference between retrospective narrative, re-enactment, and more prospective antenarrative theory. Finally, there is no role for emotion, as a way of sensemaking, a way to recover from trauma, where one just keeps re-enacting, and not storying, not being in control to willfully story. I argue that re-enactment and storyability sensemaking are quite different.

Figure 9.2 gives a summary of a storyability model, which I hypothesize is compatible with complexity and trauma theory. According to storyability theory not every event in complexity or in life trauma is storyable into experience.

Re-enactment Looping   The theory is that events only become experience when we willfully story event into experience. Research into Holocaust, genocide, war, rape, child abuse, accident, loss of loved ones, and other severe trauma events suggests that trauma is initially just re-enactment without storyability into experience or memory (Bal, 1999; Hirsch, 1999). In what I call 're-enactment looping' trauma victims dissociate (number 1 in Figure 9.2) from the trauma event by splitting of the self to compartmentalize, by annihilating the self (number 2), by acting out (number 3, such as reliving past events of trauma, triggered by resonance in the presence), and by repressing (number 4) the events that can leak into discourse in, for example, pregnant pauses and by Freudian slips (as the unconscious struggles to break into consciousness).

Restorying   The theory that it is possible to help trauma victims to overcome a dominant story that is hegemonic, and invent a new story if it becomes supportable by an individual's circle of relationships (White and Epston, 1990). However, in the case of re-enactment looping, the events have not become

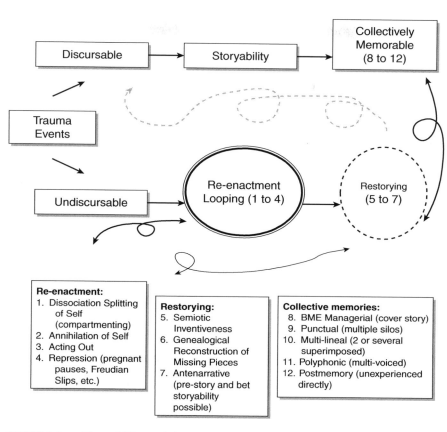

FIGURE 9.2   *Storyability model*

storyable into experiences or memory. Therefore I propose several new steps. Semiotic inventiveness (number 5) recognizes that to story is only possible in discourse (be it gesture, oral, or textual). It takes symbols and images in the hermeneutic sense of storying, to create plots, or replot. To restory trauma means to engage in the genealogical reconstruction of missing pieces (number 6). The genealogical method (Nietzsche, Foucault, Adorno) has not been used in conjunction with restorying (or as it's called in clinical social psychology, narrative therapy). Finally, before story, there is what I have invented as antenarrative (number 7, antenarrative bet that prestory can lead to storyability).

Collective Memories   The more complex case is more polyphonic collective memory (number 11) where the collective memories are fully embodied by different actors (persons and their groups), and these interact to negotiate collective storyability, and the restorying, as well as antenarrating possibilities. Finally, in trauma research, there is what Hirsch (1999) terms 'postmemory' (number 12). Postmemory is definable as collective memory that was never directly experienced by the person having the memory. For example, going to work and hearing a founder's story, or historical saga, to which you never had any direct participation with the events. Or, in the case of trauma, the subject of this essay, when you study sweatshops, but never actually worked in one (unless you call universities sweatshops, but that is a stretch).

What Stein (1935) adds, is an answer to Gabriel's (2000) question, where does story reside? It resides in-between tellers and spectators (or readers). For Heidegger, to get at Being means to not story. It suggests that story consulting may be finding coherence where life is in disarray. I tell fragments of some story I only partially understand, interrupting it with exposition, and contradiction, and leaving lots of blanks, pauses, and spaces which you, the reader, fill in, or take off into some story fill-in that has litter and maybe nothing to do with the story I am telling tersely. Gabriel (2000: 5) and I (Boje, 2001a), for example, agree that 'Not all stories are good stories, nor are all individuals effective storytellers.' I can agree with his point. Yet, I disagree with the next part of his charge '... in particular, factual or descriptive accounts of events that aspire at objectivity rather than emotional effect must not be treated as stories' (Gabriel, 2000: 5).

In storyability, there is much that is not yet storied, or antenarratives, that are not yet narrative.

D1 dialogue consulting can achieve *renarrating*, but has not been conceived at the (D4) level of dialogism that is *restorying*. Renarrating moves from one coherence narrative to another. Restorying is defined as deconstructing any dominant story, in order to develop a story out of fragments that can be liberatory from oppression (White and Epston, 1990). D3 and D4 represent two types for restorying that involve reflexivity, rather than retrospection. D3 is reflexive about transcendental or unconscious ways of telling. Story reflexivity is also attaining awareness of stories we are telling that we do not know we are telling (like the tells in a Poker game, or the blind spot in JoHari Window). Secondly, D4 restorying is reflexivity in a different way. D4 storytelling is through multi-dialogisms (beyond just polyphonic); the tellings are intertextual in ways that require reflexivity (i.e. multi-stylistics, multi-chronotopicities, and multi-architectonics). In D4, each type of dialogism is reflexive on multiples stories of other people that are beyond the plasticity of dialogue interventions at the level of narrative metaphorization or debates among fragmented narrativists. In particular, D1 and D2 focus on the narrative turn, while D3 and D4 are more concerned with what I would like to call the story turn.

Heteroglossia is polyphony and carnivalesque. Both are relevant to organizational development (OD) because they are about the forces of renewal and contemporalization. For example, polyphony is 'imbued with a carnival attitude to the world' (Bakhtin, 1973: 87) as well as the 'life-giving power to transform' (p. 89). In modernity or postmodernity, 'a critical ear always perceives even the most distant echoes of the carnival attitude to the world' (1973: 88). Dialogism is the juxtaposition of carnivalesque and more managerial points of view. Carnival provokes these viewpoints in the words of interlocutors. Carnival is about renewal through a pathos of change that facilitates 'misalliances' (1973: 101), such as sacred with profane, lofty with low, etc. in a jolly relativity that brings hierarchy down to earth, into the zone of familiar contact with carnivalesque laughter. 'In the act of carnival laughter death and rebirth, negation (ridicule) and affirmation (joyful laughter) are combined' (p. 104).

A polyphonic praxis of OD breaks down the character masks of monological unity, destroys finalized conceptions of whole system thinking, goes beyond closed philosophy of managerialism, breaks with narratives of the dialectic as well as with organic stages of evolutions. Rather than system wholeness, finalizedness, or merged parts, the focus is on unmergedness and unfinalizedness of systemicity.

D1 Dialogue is not the same as (D2 or D4) dialogicality. Dialogue consulting interventions lack critical and carnivalesque realism; there is not enough dialogic imagination. Dialogue consulting does not achieve the complexity level of D2 fragmented logics (polylogic), or D4 multi-dialogisms. We will review various stakeholder, search conference, and learning organization approaches to dialogue in Chapters 10, 11, and 12. Each dialogue approach claims to move beyond managerialism through interventions in dialogue. Yet the dialogue interventions re-enact chamber masquerade of more managerialist plasticity. Dialogue is not carnival enough to be dialogic; it lacks the free flow of misalliances of thoughts, images, and ideas. There is too little street language, too much archetype abstraction, and too much retrospection to allow more carnivalesque forces to take place. I imagine here a new OD, one that changes the 'dialogical angle' (1981: 150) of consciousnesses, and their ideas, in acts of juxtaposition. It is OD beyond the narrative canon.

MANAGERIALIST NARRATIVE OD

Sometimes story control is quite necessary. D1 narrativist dialogue consulting reduces dialogic complexity to a single plane, usually, managerialism renarrating in metaphoralizations of frames, machine, cell or plant organicism. That can be a necessary focus, a way to bring people together. More often consulting promises D2, but delivers more D1. The more D2 polyphonic dialogism is not achieved because the intervention does not transcend this plasticity with what is life-generating, and life-affirming. This still leaves D3 and D4 (story turn) to theorize.

Managerial consensus sacrifices elements of the diversity of locality idea-forces in ways that subvert complexity (D2 → D1 or D4→ D1). The danger to organizations is that monologic centripetal conditions of managerialism occur where alternative and multiple points of view are driven out by convergent renarration. Local voices are co-opted into marginality. There are situations when a more polyphonic organization is not ideal, when a more monoglotic organization is appropriate. The downside of annihilating localism, or renarrating diverse local idea-forces into just the one narrative identity, is the demise of polyphonic organization that could have been the requisite variety to make more complex sense of turbulent environments.

D3 and D4 are reflexive. Imagine, if you will, an organization that is something like a Dostoevsky novel (Bakhtin, 1981: 60): 'multi-generic, multi-styled, mercilessly critical, soberly mocking, reflective, in all its fullness the heteroglossia and multiple voices of a given culture, people and epoch.' Heteroglossia is the interplay of centripetal (centering) forces and centrifugal (decentering) forces of language. Heteroglossic manner of story is complexity in storytelling organizations.

D1 renarrating and D3 restorying are centripetal forces that get the better of more centrifugal forces of D2 fragmentation and D4 antenarration in dialogic manner of restorying. This suggests that narrative turn forces D1 are centripetal, whereas D2 narrative turn forces are centrifugal. In story turn, D3 is unity making (centripetal), while D4 is variety making (centrifugal). In short, the order of complexity of narrative and story turns each have force and counter-force.

There are several reasons why managerialism has not been given a clear-cut narrative-theoretical basis. First, managerialism, even in dialogue, is a 'philosophical monolog' posing as dialog that thwarts the dialogic 'plurality of unmerged consciousnesses' (Bakhtin, 1973: 22). Managerialism degenerates and destroys the dialogized 'fabric of the story' (1973: 44). In multi-story we glimpse the fabric's unfinalizability, indeterminacy, and its interaction with unmerged consciousnesses. Claims on the present are placed along side unresolved claims of the past and future.

Secondly, dialogism is not about the dialectic narrative 'reduced to thesis, antithesis and synthesis' (Bakhtin, 1973: 22). Rather, dialogism is 'not evolution, but coexistence and interaction' (p. 23). Nor is dialogism a retrospective sense-making. Much of organizational development (OD) is about narrating organizations in stages of development and retrospective sensemaking narratives of experience. A dialogic approach focuses upon juxtaposition, putting memories of the past side-by-side with the unfolding present, such as an 'unexplicated sin or crime, an unforgiven insult' (Bakhtin, 1973: 24). Juxtaposition is not retrospective; its focus is coexistence of divarication, not stages of organizational development. Divarication is the branching into differing viewpoints and thoughts that constitute contradictory philosophies. In dialogism there is a move beyond 'systematic monological philosophical finalizedness' (Bakhtin, 1973: 26). The intersection of unmerged consciousness in the sphere of ideas, multiple styles, multiple conceptions of space and time defies the 'finalized monological whole' of retrospective-coherence narrative (p. 34).

Thirdly, in antenarrative, the pre-story is a bet that a coherent narrative or a multi-story dialogism will be forthcoming. Antenarrative is antecedent to retrospective sensemaking. Antenarrative is full of stops and starts, and meanderings; antenarratives unfold in the present, picking up and depositing context as they traverse the social (Boje, 2001a). Antenarrative is too confused and erratic a form to meet the dictates of proper narrative cannon.

Finally, we can bring antenarrative, narrative, and dialogism together to understand the interaction of managerialism with other philosophies. Managerialism refracts one voice through the verbal or textual verbiage of some other person's milieu (Bakhtin, 1973: 166). Failing such acts of co-optation, there is either expulsion of non-managerial philosophies, or negotiations to limit the full force of more dialogic philosophies. In all these approaches the result is hegemony of managerialism. Dialogism, by contrast, allows for the life of multi-story, in unrefracted, unfinalized, and unmergedness. Absentee interlocutors enter into dialogic collusion (Bakhtin, 1973: 170). There is a 'zone of dialogical contact' that is beyond dialogue (Bakhtin, 1981: 45). In dialogic consulting, multiple ideologies interanimate each other instead of moving to consensus.

RENARRATING STORYTELLING ORGANIZATION

Rosile and Boje (2002) applied White and Epson's (1990) *Narrative Means to Therapeutic Ends*, to organization change. White and Epson call it 'restorying', but I will argue it is more accurately called 'renarrating.' These are the basic renarrating steps:

1   Characterize: Describe the organization at its best, if it were functioning perfectly and living up to all its ideals. An influence map will expose relevant persons and problems keeping a dominant narrative in play.
2   Externalize: What is the problem, viewed as separate from any individual, as an external entity? A problem, not individual (s) is the problem, for example, What does a 'power struggle' look like? who does power report to? who does power hang with?
3   Sympathize: What benefits does the organization derive from the problem? In deconstruction, it is finding the dualism, and exploring each side of each dualism.
4   Revise: Disadvantages of the problem, benefits foregone, and reasons to change. In deconstructing dualisms, the limitations of dualisms are stressed.
5   Strategize: Find a 'unique outcome' from the past, even a potential, which allowed the organization to defeat the problem. These exceptions to what the dominant narrative posits, become basis for authoring a new narrative, for example, when did you speak back to power?
6   Re-historicize: Make the 'unique outcome' the rule (instead of the exception) in a NEW narrative of freedom from the problem.
7   Publicize: Enlist support for the new narrative. Use letters, ceremony, etc. to socially reinforce and concretize the new narrative.

What I think is needed is to move from renarrating organizations, to restorying organizations in the more dialogic manner of a story turn approach to change and organizational development. I think what is pioneering in White and Epston's (1990) narrative family therapy is that it works at a systemic level, and combines deconstruction with narrative and renarrating. What renarrating lacks is a dialogic theory and praxis of antenarrative, story and restory.

RESTORYING AND DIALOGISM

I would like to sketch the basics of a dialogic restorying model. Narrative therapy is deconstructing the dominant narrative, by externalizing the problem from people characterizations, sympathizing, revising and strategizing to reverse the dualities, rehistoricizing to find examples when the dominant narrative did not have its death grip on the identity of the individual, and finally publicizing to reinforce the renarrative change in the family network. Restorying organizations that are theorized as unmergedness of parts, unfinalized wholes, with multi-level orders of systemicity complexity is beyond simple renarrating.

Readers of Weick (1995: 127–9) without exception took sensemaking to be about emergence of variety rather than control. They were blind to the Aristotelian premises about narrative coherence: causal chain, with wholeness of beginning, middle, and end. If the one cultural situation aimed at is story control, then the assumed story emergence of complexity is nowhere to be found in Weick's often cited section. A myth has been created about stories only being about retrospective sensemaking of emergence.

Reflexivity inaugurates self-examination. Retrospection is about a romantic view of sensemaking stories during an era when control by executives has begun to erode. Retrospective story control is an Emersonian perfectionist model of self-realization through heroic emulation. Selling sensemaking control in springboard stories appeals to executives who are out-of-control of their complexity organizations. Structural/functionalist stories makes executives the hero, able to regain control that eluded them. Executives are given an Aristotelian formula of story control. Executives have only to apply the will of their creative imagination. Story control is nothing more than Nietzsche's (1967) will to power.

A neglected source of sense emergence is the mass of people whose stories are marginalized by managerial control over their story by some executive eager to hear their own voice and no one else's. They cry out against narrative control, and their loss of voice.

The important question is how to listen to the variety of narratives and stories already in motion in Storytelling Organization. It is time to look beyond executive's will to power in reducing story variety to narrative control. It subverts the emergence forces of complexity.

How Polyphony is used in Organization Studies

Mumby (1994) accused management research texts of being monophonic; he stresses that in polyphonic text each voice is equally valid. There has been writing that imagines something called 'polyphonic organization' (Hazen, 1993, 1994; Boje, 1995; Mumby, 1994). Bate (1997, 2000) picks up Hazen's call for 'polyphonic organization' in a study of change in a hospital, from hierarchy to networked community. Methodologically, he does not study the way the voices (heard) are dialogically dynamically intertextual in situ to one another. Instead Bate collects a plurality of sub-culture voices, and culls out emotion schemas within the narratives/stories he collects.

Can polyphony get beyond managerialist control? My research looked at the polyphonic aspects of dominant (official) narrative and marginalized counter-stories at Disney (Boje, 1995). Oswick et al. (2000) looked at how polyphony gets subverted, how a team player developed consensus around a univocal narrative in a hegemonic exercise of power. More accurately, it was not only mono-logic but also homologic. A homophonic text is one where 'all aspects of plot, dialogue and characterization are subordinated to the monologic will of the author' (Gardiner, 1992: 27).

Barry and Elmes' (1997: 442) polyphony challenge was 'strategists adopting this method [that] would be less focused on promoting their own strategy and more concerned with surfacing, legitimizing, and juxtaposing differing organizational stories.' They cited Semler' (1993), Boje's (1995), and Smircich et al.'s (1992 a, b) ways to juxtapose dialogically linked views/stories.

Not every strategist is sure that polyphony is best. Ng and de Cock (2002) argue that they do not want to give a polyphonic interpretation to collected boardroom (strategic) narratives, since it would compromise the story they (as researchers and omniscient-narrators) prefer to tell. This seems to replace one hegemony with another. One possibility is suggested by Roth and Kleiner (1998), who view Van Maanen's 'jointly-told tale' as polyphonic fieldwork, 'sharing authorship' and giving 'equal validity' to two (or more) meaning systems.

Polyphony too often becomes used as a metaphor by consultants and practitioners. Using polyphony as a metaphor serves to colonize and entrench dominant narrative. Palmer and Dunford (1996), for example, focus on ways that authorities stylize dialog by reframing context in order to sustain managerialist influence over business practices. Along this vein, Phillips (1995: 628–9) explores an example of how a dominant character in a text can bring in another point of view without the sense of closure of an omnipotent author. Payne and Calton (2002) apply dialogic to stakeholder theory using a polyphonic approach; the challenge in dialogic research is to move from theories of one (stakeholder) consciousness (be it omniscient narrator or research) reading various other consciousnesses. In sum, polyphonic studies are finding that stakeholder dialogues are hegemonic, and polyphony is applied metaphorically without attention to equal rights of participation.

How do we theorize an OD practice at the level of polyphony? First, I think, one must distinguish between stakeholder dialogue approaches, and what Bakhtin theorizes as more dialogic manner of story. Dialogue consulting interventions focus on surfacing warrants and points of disagreement among stakeholders in order to achieve consensus. Processes such as Future Search (Weisbord, 1992) and Social Ecology (Emery and Trist, 1965; Emery, 1993, 1994, 1997) and Dialogue Coaching (Senge, 1992).

A Futures Search can take up to three days, but includes stakeholders such as executives, staff, managers, employees, and external constituencies.

Social Ecology (also called search conference) takes a year to several years, involving a jury process to identify stakeholders who will move changes into place, plus a structured approach to environmental scanning, and ways to bracket and put aside disagreements as common ground is forged among participants.

The emphasis in Dialogue Coaching is on the pursuit of order, often defined as overcoming resistance to change through active listening, and attaining consensus. Consensus as a goal of such dialogue processes has been criticized for creating a monologic consulting intervention (Deetz, 2000). People are trained by dialogue consultants to actively listen, to tell better narratives, and to understand metaphor creativity, but not to address the systemic level of language.

Too much organizational change work centers on increasing participation in dialogue, but in ways that remains quite monologic (one logic). Even when a diversity of points of view interact in dialogue, the stress is placed upon achieving consensus, or in utilizing rhetorics of persuasion to negotiate a common ground for all. In Future Search, Social Ecology and Dialogue Coaching, this keeps contentious points of view on the margin, and allows the majority to trudge forward. These ideas are pursued more systematically in Chapter 10 (Consulting Transorganization Storytelling Organizations).

AGAINST CONSENSUS

Volosinov's (1929/1973) *Marxism and the Philosophy of Language* and Bakhtin's (1986) *Speech Genres*[2] both argue that the utterance is the product of the immediate social situation, history, and the broader social milieu. Bakhtin (1981: 272) theorized two counter-forces, one centrifugal (deviation amplifying) and the other centripetal (deviation counteracting) that defined language systems. In a given dialogue, in an utterance of that dialogue, there is a dialogic conflict of multiple points of view being expressed by any given participant, and more dialogic points of view by the social milieu constructing rebuttals and submitting what has been shared to their own reading of the facts. In short, from a dialogic theory perspective, 'language lives' (Bakhtin, 1984: 183). The utterance of change is not just about dialog – it also includes the more systemic qualities of utterance of change that are dialogic at levels of systemic complexity. Meaning and change is not only generated through dialog interaction with other stakeholders, it is a dialogic interpretive process that is systemically embedded in the organization and its social milieu. A monologic consensus process can masquerade as a dialogue. On the other hand, what sounds like 'single-voiced discourse' (Bakhtin, 1984: 189) can be multi-voiced dialogic, expression, even out of the mouth of one participant. People double-narrate, and speak with double-voices (not in the sense of forked tongue).

RESTORYING POLYPHONIC DIALOGISM

> The essence of polyphony is precisely in the fact that the voices remain independent and as such, are combined in a unity of a higher order than in homophony. (Bakhtin, 1973: 17) ... Such would be the polyphonic manner of the story... [This] dialogical field of vision'. (p. 60)

The polyphonic dialogic manner of story is beyond managerialist or retrospective narratives of control. It is outside the dominant field of vision of retrospection; it is more what Kant calls apperception, but with Bakhtin this is from a dialogized plurality of points of view. Further renarrative centering (centripetal) and restorying divarication (centrifugal) are part of the heteroglossic force and counter-force of language (of which narrative and story are domains).

Apperception of organization and environment from a plurality of points of view is not the same as retrospective sensemaking that dominates much of OD work. Rather, the past, present, and future, as well as local and global are set side-by-side in dialogic juxtaposition, that I am calling a priori apperception. My thesis is that polyphonic

---

2 Volosinov's (1929/1973) Marxism and the Philosophy of Language written in Russian in 1929 (English in 1973) is widely thought to be 90% the work of Bakhtin. During his commune period (late 1920s) a Bakhtin Circle was formed and authorship by the individual was subtexted in favor of communal writing works. For more on this see Holquist's introduction to Dialogic Imagination (1981).

dialogicality consulting the monological scenes of managerialism can be deconstructed and reconstructed to be dialogically pluralized through acts of juxtaposition. Further, what passes for polyphony consulting is mostly at the level of micro-dialogue, that does not escape the '*Weltanschauung*' of 'systematic-monological' managerialism (Bakhtin, 1973: 64). Micro-dialogue is not the same as dialogism. Next, I will give a condensed review of how polyphony has been addressed in organization theory.

Renarrating Polyphonic Dialogism

Renarrating polyphonic dialogism is firstly changing the balance of dominant narratives and marginalized forces of storied-ideas, points of view, ideologies, or philosophies. Secondly, renarrating polyphony changes the complexity of participation and governance from managerial consensus monologues masquerading as dialogue to polyphony of idea forces. Polyphony is defined as 'the plurality of independent and unmerged voices and consciousnesses' (Bakhtin, 1973: 4). Polyphony is 'destruction of the organic unity of the ... narrative fabric'; it is the multi-story 'whirlwind movement of events' (p. 11). Polyphonic dialogism of multi-narrative fragments is at a higher order of complexity than monologic narrative convergence.

Restorying Transcendental

Restorying that is dialectic, is thesis that is opposed by an opposite antithesis. The logic of this world is reversed in the logic of the underworld. The rational meets a more carnivalesque netherworld of masks. Our subconscious desires spill onto the stage of everyday life.

Restorying Stylistic Dialogism

A second type of restorying sets the transcendental in interplay with multiple-dialogic forces. Whereas D3 dialectic is unity making, the multiplicity of discourses introduces a level of complexity that is multi-dialogic. Restorying stylistics, for example, moves beyond orchestration of diverse stylistic modes of telling for image management, to a pluralistic stylistic. Organization change and development theory and praxis have been completely deaf to 'dialogized style' (Bakhtin, 1981: 274). The dialogue of face-to-face style has been thought to be no different from dialogic intercourse that is not face-to-face (i.e. written, visual, or theatric-gestures). A stylistically dialogic analysis of a corporation would focus on the points of intersection of the dialogized styles.

Restorying Chronotopic Dialogism

Restorying chronotopicities moves beyond being stuck in mono-chronotopic monologue to more relativistic plurality of space and time conceptions. Traditional organization change and development theory and praxis is wedded to developmental narratives of temporality in ways that ignore other chronotopicities. In chronotopic dialogism, we enter the 'complex unity of an Einstein universe' with its jolly relativity (Bakhtin, 1973: 12).

Restorying Architectonic Dialogism

Restorying architectonics resituates the interanimation of cognitive, aesthetic, and ethical discourses. Narrative and Story are subdomains of societal discourses. This restorying is a resituation of societal, organizational, and individual ways of narrating and storying.

Polypi Dialogism of Dialogisms

Restorying at this order of systemicity complexity involves the interrelations of knowable and unknowable. Specifically, it is the interrelation between what is retrospectively knowable by sensemaking of experience, and the a priori apperception of transcendental logic and transcendental aesthetic.

The question I want to pursue in this chapter is what is restorying polyphonic dialogism? Subsequent chapters will look at theory and praxis of organizational change and development that involve the interactivity of the other dialogisms, in respective orders of complexity.

IDEA-FORCES

Storytelling Organization theory, research, and consulting practice began with the idea that stories are situated within systems of communication and relationship (Boje, 1991, 1995; Gephart, 1991; Boyce, 1995; Kaye, 1996). A storytelling organization is constantly adding stories to its collective memory bank, while deleting stories or just forgetting some by choice or attrition. Each new event sets off vibratory energy dynamics into collective memory of storytelling organizations. Each new event sets off revisions and transformations to collective memory, to story space. Old stories linger on obstinately, antenarratives (pre-stories) seek to gain a foothold, but many old stories cannot be swept away. In this way collective memory evolves. While the individual can change their inner life story through meditation and narrative therapy, transforming the life story of a storytelling organization is a different level of analysis, something where restorying at a dialogic level of intervention must take place in praxis (Kaye, 1996).

One approach that is promising in OD is the mirroring of one's consciousness through others' consciousnesses. Bakhtin (1973: 43) gives this example: 'he looks in all the mirrors of others' consciousnesses and knows all the possible refractions of his own image in those mirrors.... His self-consciousness lives on its unfinalizedness, its openendedness and indeterminacy.' This seems to me to be at the level of self-reflection, self-elucidation, and self- revelations, an internal dialogism with internalized voices of others and conversations with the other, refracting your own ideas.

Polyphonically conceived organizations are more about the dialogism of ideas than about retrospective narratives of experience or narratives of evolution in growth stages. Juxtaposition sets human consciousnesses, embodied ideas, side-by-side to defeat ideological monologisms. This move frees the sphere of pluralistic ideas from finalizedness and determinacy.

> The idea begins to live, i.e. to take shape, to develop, to find and renew its verbal expression, and to give birth to new ideas only when it enters into genuine dialogical relationships with other, *foreign* ideas. (Bakhtin, 1973: 71).

Stylistic dialogism, by contrast is about the juxtaposition of multiple images of the ideas. In the struggle among ideas, there is assumed to be absentee interlocutors. Diatribe is 'conversation with a character who is absent' (Bakhtin, 1973: 129) such as the invisible stenographer or some invisible inquisitor. Boje and Rhodes (2005 a, b) look at the diatribe with dead CEOs, how their idea-forces live on. The many styles and voices exist as 'idea-forces' (Bakhtin, 1973: 73). The danger to organizations is that ideas become self-enclosed in managerialist idea-forces, which drive out other *foreign* ideas. It is time to imagine a consulting praxis where the 'vertex of dialogically intersecting consciousnesses' (1973: 74) is considered a creative force. Retrospective sensemaking of experience can be helpful in generating empirical evidence of ways the idea-force or some coalition idea-forces is appropriate to the environment. The implication is that the vertex of dialogically intersecting different ideas affects strategy as well as strategic change. Most OD praxis, focused on consensus or negotiation, serves to reduce dialogic complexity and plurality.

A polyphonically dialogic approach to OD would explore the labyrinth of voices, points of view, philosophies, and consciousnesses. The result could be a polyphonic organization of 'mutually illuminating consciousnesses' (Bakhtin, 1973: 80). Dostoevsky called for a method of 'integral contrapositions' (Bakhtin, 1973: 78–80) that could be the basis for this new approach to OD. I have asserted that the contrapositions are a priori, rather than retrospective, and praxis that looks at juxtapositions could break out of narrative petrification one finds in stage-growth models. Instead of plotting organizations in the Aristotelian framework of tragedy, comedy, satire or romance, an integral contraposition method would focus upon multi-story, multi-plot, multi-stylistics, and multiple unmerged consciousnesses.

In sum, polyphonic dialogic contrapositions cultivates the multi-story of multiple independent wills, philosophical views, and ideas that get reduced to monological singularity in dialogue consulting and stakeholder conference models. Stories have idea-force that belongs to someone, is embedded in socioeconomic context. Antenarrative traces interact with full-fledged narratives, and more dialogic manner of story, in the complex fabric of storytelling organizations.

10

CONSULTING
TRANSORGANIZATION STORYTELLING
ORGANIZATIONS

There are 16 major schools of large system change I term Transorganization Development (TD). Each TD school has its exemplary authors, texts, methods, and devoted practitioners. My thesis is that TD approaches put emerging story into narrative prison by orchestrating or steering dialog, debate, dialectic, or dialogisms. The breakout comes in deprogramming.

Transorganization Development History

In 1972 UCLA Management School professors wrote a manifesto on *Transorganization Development*, going beyond traditional *Organization Development*. They defined Transorganizational Development (TD) as planned change in the collective relationships of a variety of stakeholders to accomplish something beyond the capability of any single organization or individual (Culbert et al., 1972). My first professor job was at UCLA, where the stage was set for TD (Motamedi, 1978; Boje, 1979; Cummings, 1984; Boje and Wolfe, 1989; Boje and Hillon, 2008).

In 1998, I began studying similarities and differences in TD schools by developing a website, with TD schools as my focus.[1] Each TD school has different exemplars, and models of praxis; they engage in rivalry according to implicit rules, or what we call the TD Gameboard (Boje and Rosile, 2003b). I was particularly interested in deprogramming TD approaches that were guru fads without much substance. I turned to David Collins' (1998) work for sociological critique. Since then other critical theory books on consulting have emerged. Clark and Fincham's (2002: 14) critique for example, boils down to: 'stories [told by consultants] are also a medium through which gurus can establish their own status within the broader business community by associating their ideas with highly regarded and successful people and/or organizations.'

---

1 TD Gameboard website at http://business.nmsu.edu/~dboje

1 DEBATE: Alinsky/ Cortez COMMUNITY ORGANIZING	2 DEBATE: Emery PDPD (Participative Design for Participative Democracy); SEARCH CONFERENCE	3 DIALOG: Davis and Weisbord STS (Sociotechnical Systems) and FUTURE SEARCH	4 DIALOGIC: Savall SEAM (SocioEconomic Approach to Management)	5 DIALECTIC: Argyris, Torbert, Reason ACTION RESEARCH, ACTION SCIENCE, and ACTION INQUIRY
16 DIALECTIC: Collins CRITICAL THEORY SOCIOLOGY				6 DIALOG: Cooperrider and Srivastra; Georges APPRECIATIVE INQUIRY
15 DIALOG: Chisholm NETWORK ORGANIZATI ONS	**TD GAMEBOARD RULES** 1 Develop a TD system change model; 2 Defend from all other models on the TD gameboard; 3 Launch a training seminar for consultant instruction in narrative control; 4 Build a following of PhD consultants 5 Conduct research to confirm your model's findings; 6 Loop up to game rule 1; or 7 Attend deprogramming classes *Source*: adapted from Boje and Rosile, 2003b: 11			7 DIALOG: Hammer and Champy REENGINERING
14 DEBATE: Boal; Boje, Rosile and Saner POSTMODEN THEATRE (organization is theatre approach)				8 DEBATE: Goffman FRAMEWORKS (metaphoric approach to theatre) 9 DIALOG: Owens OPEN SPACES
13 DIALOGIC: Bakhtin; DIALECTIC: Debord; Best and Kellner CARNIVAL, SPECTACLE THEATRICS	12 DEBATE: Culbert et al.; Boje, Wolfe, Motamedi, Cummings TRANS- ORGANIZATION DEVELOPMENT	11 DIALECTIC: White and Epston; Barry, Boje and Rosile; Kaye, Boyce RESTORYING/ NARRATIVE THERAPY	10 DIALOG: Senge; Schein, Boisot DIALECTIC: LEARNING ORGANIZATION/ KNOWLEDGE/ NETWORKS	

FIGURE 10.1   *TD gameboard © David M. Boje 16 Sept 1999[2]*

2 This TD Gameboard is updated from the original by positing which TD approaches are more about Dialog, Debate, Dialectic, or Dialogic

Various universities package and sell consulting stories. Moving clock-wise around the TD Gameboard, Emery's PDPD is taught in Queensland University in Australia, as well as in workshops at New Mexico State University. Davis' approach to large system STS was taught for two decades at UCLA, until he retired. Savall's approach is taught at Lyon University in France, as well as at New Mexico State University (by joint MOU agreement between our universities). Argyris' Action Science is taught at Harvard. Torbert's Action Research is taught at Boston College. Reason's community program is taught in the UK. Appreciative Inquiry (AI) is taught at Case Western Reserve and at Benedictine Univeristy. Senge's dialog learning organization approach is taught at MIT. Culbert et al. (1972) and my own work in TD, as well as that of Motamedi began at UCLA. Motamedi continues it in the Pepperdine program. Collins' (1998) critical theory approach is taught at Leicester University in the UK. Other approaches are taught in various institutes or consulting firms without any university affiliation or partnership. Table 10.1 gives brief descriptions of the schools.

TD schools can be analyzed by their story/narrative practices and their affinity and resistance to debate. I distinguish in Figure 10.2 between approaches which privilege dialogue (without debate), debate, dialectic, and dialogic. At center the star, D⊘ (Demonstrative), indicates emergence of story in the here-and-now. My theory is that story emergence is trapped in the narrative prisons of D1 to D4. I propose an integrative approach.

D1 Positive Dialog

The first narrative prison is positive-only dialog. Sometimes story control by narrative is very important and useful. Dialog is the positive harmonious, win-win, side of harmony. Senge's (1990, 1994) Learning Organization dualizes dialog and debate. With negative debate, negotiation is banished.

Teams learn to switch between discussion and dialogue. The purpose is to share mental models and find their convergence. Senge argues that it is not individuals, but networks of people and organizations that transform how large systems work. Yet, for Senge (1990: 346), the 'purpose stories' of managers is 'the overarching explanation of why they do what they do, how their organization needs to evolve, and how that evolution is part of something larger.' Managerial purpose stories are stressed, not polyphony (Senge 1990: 351).

Edgar Schein (1996: 19) also adopts a collaborative dialog approach to secure shared mental models. Like Senge, Schein (1993: 41) stresses dialog, 'the evolution of shared mental models . . . [makes] dialogue a necessary first

TABLE 10.1　*TD schools*

TD Schools	Exemplars	Descriptions
1 Grassroots Community Organizing	Saul Alinsky, 1946, 1971; Ernesto Cortez	Alinsky brings community organizations together to change their relation to a target network of organizations through activism, until a renegotiation occurs; Cortez developed a more spiritual, less activist approach. Most similar to 2 and 4; most dissimilar to 7
2 Search Conference PDPD	Fred Emery and Eric Trist, 1965; Merrelyn Emery, 1993	Rooted in sociotechnical systems approach; Fred Emery's wife Merrelyn does multi-organizational *Participative Design for Participative Democracy* (PDPD) search conferences. Scenarios apply Pepper's (1942) contextualist world hypothesis. Most similar to 1, but without the activism; dissimilar to all others
3 Future Search	Weisbord, 1992	Weisbord, one of Emery's students, does 3 day format of large group conferencing; participants put ideas onto large post-it notes
4 SEAM	Henri Savall et al., 2000	Savall's version of STS is detailed qualitative study of metascript and metatheatrics that extends STS into accounting and economics, as well as strategy. Most similar to 1 and 2; most dissimilar to 3, 6 and 7
5 Action Science/ Action Inquiry/ Action Research	Argyris & Schön, 1974, 1978, 1996; Torbert; Reason	Collaborative approaches to joint research between academic scholars and practitioners
6 Appreciative Inquiry	Cooperidder and Srivastva, 1987	AI applies retrospective narrative methods of Gergen (1994) and Weick (1995) to create collectively authored positive stories of change possibility; Benedictine and Case Western doctoral programs.
7 Reengineering	Hammer and Champy, 1993	Reengineering helps CEOs concoct a legitimating narrative of the downsizing
8 Frameworks	Goffman, 1959, 1974	Dramaturgical approach that is being applied to TD networks (see Boje et al., 1994)
9 Open Spaces	Owens, 1995	Non-structured self-organizing of agenda and task groups

(Continued)

TABLE 10.1   (Continued)

TD Schools	Exemplars	Descriptions
10 Learning and Knowledge Organizations/ Knowledge Networks	Senge, 1990, 1994; Schein, 1984, 1993, 1996; Boisot, 1995, 1998	Senge (1990) describes mental story as cognitive mental maps: 'the images, assumptions and stories that we carry in our mind of ourselves, other people, institutions, and every aspect of the world'; for Schein (1984: 13) stories evolve over time in organization's life cycle, or become petrified and do not change with time; Schein (1993) looks at culture as shared assumptions and values. Boisot maps tacit knowledge narratives into 3 dimensions of I-space
11 Restorying	Barry, 1997; Rosile and Boje, 2002; White and Epston, 1990	Barry argues that narrating and renarrating past stories is a major aspect of organizational change. White and Epston's work is more accurately, renarrating; Rosile and Boje's work on restorying.
12 Transorganization	Culbert et al 1972; Boje and Wolfe, 1989; Motamedi, 1978; Cummings, 1984	This is founding work in an explicitly TD approach to changing networks of organization
13 Spectacle, Festival and Carnival	Bakhtin, 1968; Boje, 2001b; Debord, 1967	Theatrics of Capitalism approach looks at interplay of carnival, festival, and spectacle of late modern capitalism
14 Postmodern Theatre	Boal, 1979, 1992, 1995; Boje and Rosile, 2002	Boal uses theatre for social change, as form of community activism; Boje and Rosile extends Savall's SEAM approach of metascript by looking at the more Tamara or Metatheatre aspects
15 Network Organization	Chisholm, 1998	Chisholm applies Action Research and STS background to the problem of Network Organizations. He uses Search Conference we have reviewed in the Emery and non-Emery approaches, as well as the Davis STS Design Team approach of large system change
16 Critical Theory	Collins, 1998	A critical theory approach to large system change. A way to deprogram

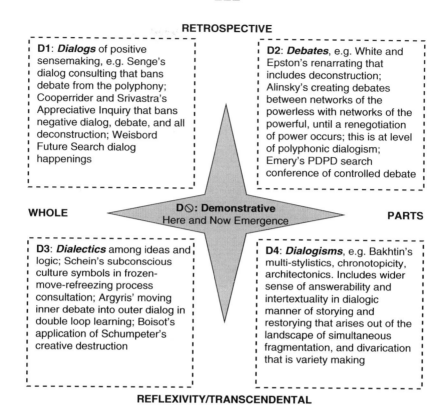

RETROSPECTIVE

D1: *Dialogs* of positive sensemaking, e.g. Senge's dialog consulting that bans debate from the polyphony; Cooperrider and Srivastra's Appreciative Inquiry that bans negative dialog, debate, and all deconstruction; Weisbord Future Search dialog happenings

D2: *Debates*, e.g. White and Epston's renarrating that includes deconstruction; Alinsky's creating debates between networks of the powerless with networks of the powerful, until a renegotiation of power occurs; this is at level of polyphonic dialogism; Emery's PDPD search conference of controlled debate

WHOLE   **DØ: Demonstrative** Here and Now Emergence   **PARTS**

D3: *Dialectics* among ideas and logic; Schein's subconscious culture symbols in frozen-move-refreezing process consultation; Argyris' moving inner debate into outer dialog in double loop learning; Boisot's application of Schumpeter's creative destruction

D4: *Dialogisms*, e.g. Bakhtin's multi-stylistics, chronotopicity, architectonics. Includes wider sense of answerability and intertextuality in dialogic manner of storying and restorying that arises out of the landscape of simultaneous fragmentation, and divarication that is variety making

REFLEXIVITY/TRANSCENDENTAL

FIGURE 10.2   *Model of narrative control of emergent storying in TD praxis[3]*

step in learning' (p. 41).[4] Scheins' Learning Organization is read differently by different authors. Schein's theory of culture and learning organization is critiqued by Collins (1998), but celebrated by Clark and Fincham (2002), and somewhat less so by Chan (2000). Of the three, Collins presents a more devastating critique.

Chan (2000: 13) applauds Schein (1985, 1999) for not conflating a signified (corporate culture) for its referent (social integration that increases productivity). Clark and Fincham's (2002: 5) celebrate Schein (1969) for 'encouragement of management learning, and the avoidance of defensiveness and denial.' They include Schein as a contributor, and label Schein *critical consultant* because he questions 'advice' consulting that can make them

---

3 DØ (Demonstrative) is defined as the interplay of narrative and storyist turn in the here-and-now of story emergence. It can be understood as not-story, or not-yet story.

4 N. Craig Hayden (no date given), 'Organizational Learning, Team Learning and Dialogue as the Foundation of Educational Reform', Masters thesis, online at http://www.collections canada.ca/obj/s4/f2/dsk1/tape7/PQDD_0029/MQ47454.pdf

dependent. Alvesson and Johansson (2002: 229) critique Schein (1969) for presenting an 'idealistic picture, portraying the consultant as a competent professional embracing integrity and self-control, and possessing unquestionable expertise suitable for solving different kinds of management problems.' Schein and others' texts are 'not particularly research-oriented' (p. 229). Schein's famous 'process' versus 'expert' dichotomy breaks down, since both types of consultant 'sells tools for producing meaning' in ways that control social action, and in the helper role, the client, not the consultant is responsible for resolving organization problems (Alvesson and Johansson, 2002: 236).

Collins (1998), by contrast, is highly critical of Schein on many more levels than rhetorical prowess of substituting helper for advice-giver. Collins (1998) joins Feldman (1986) in critiquing Schein's (1985) concept of 'culture' as reserved for deeper levels of basic assumptions and beliefs that are either taken for granted or unconscious. In particular, Schein locates culture not in a place, but in (pre) linguistic, unconscious, mental phenomena (Feldman, 1986: 87; Collins, 1998: 122). Schein's trauma method of 'learning, thinking and action is based on a narrow range of previously negative experiences' (Collins, p. 116). It's a negative feedback cybernetic loop. When environment shifts, the form of thinking changes. Collins also challenges Schein's culture thesis of unconscious taken-for-granted assumptions: 'It seems clear that each of us is able to operate, in some way with a negotiated version of dominant or mainstream values which suits our own aims and orientations' (p. 118). The 'basic assumptions' are not, for Collins, rooted in the unconsciousness of deep culture or deep antecedent 'psychological predilections' (p. 120). Feldman and Collins argue that patterns of behavior are cultural phenomena, and are not hidden in the unconscious, locked in mental models. One can think and reflect upon one's ideas and thoughts using narratives and stories. Their location of culture in the mind is inconsistent with Schein's helper-role of assisting clients to do empirical investigation of cultural artifacts. Artifacts like story/narrative. If culture is located in pre-linguistic subconscious, then Schein's advice that founders or subsequent 'managers can *create* cultures' [e.g. founding stories] is contradictory (Collins, 1998: 124). In anthropology, cultures are noted for being highly resistant to change. In folkloristics, oral story cultures are also noted for being resilient.

Cooperrider and Srivastra's (1987) *Appreciative Inquiry* (AI) does the same thing. Positive dialog is valued, and the debate among points of view is marginalized. I once co-chaired a showcase Academy of Management session where AI was compared to Narrative Therapy (NT). In AI the positive dialog produces a positive narrative of some networks of organizations doing global good. In NT, dominant narratives are deconstructed, and then, like AI, people engage in some liberatory storytelling to get beyond oppression of the oppressive global organizations. In short, as my colleague Cliff Oswick puts it, what AI needs is DI, 'Depreciative Inquiry!'

Harrison Owens' (1995: 12–13) book provides an example of Open Space. Forest Service Managers get a 15-minute briefing by Owens. He tells the story of how 420 teachers, school board members and administrators in less than an hour created 85 workshops and then ran a 2-day conference. The Forest Service hosted 224 people representing 65 organizations from Sierra Club to National Nude Sunbathing Society. As the story goes, 'in less than an hour, they created 62 task forces and managed the conference themselves' and as Owens says,' About the only thing they had in common was the issue at hand and their antagonism for each other' (ibid, pp. 12–13). My impression from Owen's Open Space is that it is an emergent process (structure is a happening). Yet, at its core I find lots of flip chart writing and post-it notes collaging stems from Owens' story. But where is the debate producing a critical story, and where is the evaluation of these task forces? I have been through Open Space approach. Most recent was an Organization Theatre Summit meeting of 35 theatre-consulting experts, in Copenhagen. We did the speak out. We put up a lot of one liners on flip charts that became the basis for task groups. We pretty much left Open Spaces behind and did theatric and story performances. Another encounter I had was with a New Mexico county that had brought in an Open Space consultant, but the intervention broke down into factions, and general chaos. Merrlyn Emery came with her Social Ecology (PDPD), and the county did a search conference, a form of debate we cover in the next section.

Various approaches to STS (but not all) set up dialog among action research experts, and action teams of practitioners. Lou Davis (an apprentice of the Emerys) takes a more analytic approach to Sociotechnical Systems (STS), and stayed with a form of social theory and technology analysis, that Fred Emery later abandoned. In the late 1970s and early 1980s, Lou along with James Taylor, worked at UCLA. They did some great projects that built co-operative relationships between unions, workers, and management, as part of the Quality of Working Life (QWL). QWL flourished in the 1970s and 1980s but with the downsizing and re-engineering mania of the 1990s fell on hard times.

As luck would have it, as a young UCLA professor, I got to teach the STS and environments of STS courses when Lou took a sabbatical. I had been teaching TD and a story ethnography seminar, and noted some of the differences, with STS, as Lou Davis taught it. Lou was focused on combining a social system model based on Parsons (1964) with a standard variance analysis charting of system waste and breakdown. Parson's model was highly functionalist, that a system is composed of subsystems, performing functions for the whole or entire system.

When I moved to New Mexico State, Merrelyn Emery was teaching a Search Conference seminar that seemed to resemble STS. I told Merrelyn I had worked with Lou Davis at UCLA; I got some lectures. She described Davis as the father of STS (sociotechnical systems) in the USA. But then added that when Davis apprenticed with Fred Emery at Tavistock, in the early days, he left before all the experiments had been completed. Davis kept doing the variance analysis of the technical, and Parsonian social analysis as the basis of STS in the USA, but Emery moved away from both. STS says J.C. Spender (1996) 'is unsuitable as the basis for a theory of the firm because it adopt[s] too naive a view of social systems and ignore[s] economic interactions' (p.55). STS does not move 'beyond the open systems' approach (Pondy, 1979) to get at higher levels of complexity (Boulding, 1956: 200–7).

The second STS student of Emery was Marvin Weisbord. Both do something called Search Conference. They focus on design principles, but have some major differences. The Weisbord *Future Search Conference* has these steps:

- Stage 1 – review the past with different methods
- Stage 2 – map the present
- Stage 3 – create a range of different scenarios
- Stage 4 – identify the common group
- Stage 5 – develop action plans

It is the work with Past, Present, and Future stories and scenarios that connects the approach to story/narrative. A steering committee and the consultant-facilitators manage Future Search Conference process. Large rolls of paper are unrolled and taped to the four walls of the room. The large group acts as a group mind to work through the stages (there is also small group work). Weisbord (1992: 325) is cited by Emery (1993: 228) as mixing 'focused searching with experiential learning exercises, training modules, "ice breakers," expert lectures, question and answer sessions, and any group activity that takes people away from the central tasks they have come to do.' I'd like to see some empirical evidence of the differences and similarities of Emery, Davis, Weisbord, and the Savall approach to STS (see dialogic).

There is no more negative use of monologue pretending to be dialog than reengineering. Boje et al. (1997) looked at how reengineers use retrospective narrative as part of their training in several ways. De Cock (1999) also provides a critique of reengineering rhetorical tactics. We analyzed how consultants tell narratives of past reengineering successes, and coach CEOs how to tell the story of the impending reengineering, characterizing those to be downsized as the 'fat' to be trimmed or the 'casualties' of the war on global quality. CEOs and managers are trained how to narrate and spin press releases, and how to structure the roll-out of the reengineering change as a narrative with several acts.

Max Boisot is after 'knowledge assets.' He is the hero of knowledge management and knowledge reengineering fad. This translates to getting tacit knowledge from narratives and emergent stories. Fortunately or unfortunately, things are not so simple. Transferring tacit knowledge (i.e. stories) is problematic for all the obvious reasons cited in this book. Even Boisot (1998: 57) points out, once you abstract, reduce, codify knowledge (i.e. tacit skill stories), you shed the concrete context. Narrative fragments that get diffused to another person no longer make sense to the end user. As he puts it, 'unfortunately data-structuring strategies designed to enhance communicate reaches, often unwittingly sacrifice communicative depth in the process' (p. 57). Worse, only to the extent that stories can be standardized, are they deemed efficient for meaning transport, and result in economic utility in other contexts. Boisot (1998: 93) points out how tacit knowledge gets hierarchically themed, organized, and stored into (story) data-bases. Boisot (1998: 219) argues that we typically view networks (markets or clans) as an alternative to the hierarchical relationships in bureaucracies and fiefdoms. 'One example of the market form of networking is the Internet' (p. 219). Boisot's model is highly problematic. It is true that stories are rooted in concrete experiential practices, but when one reengineers them in acts of data reduction, shedding, and standardization, there is not much understanding remaining; the knowledge asset has been destroyed. Further, a critical issue that knowledge engineers ignore is that when creating transferable knowledge, you cannot just do away with thorny legal issues of story ownership rights (i.e. stories are an intellectual property of the individual as well as of the enterprise).

Finally, in the new global knowledge economy, a tacit knowledge practice communicated in stories of skilled labor of one country is being abstracted, cod-ified, and diffused to less skilled, lower paid labor in Third World factories. That's deskilling, a narrative-interrogation to extract surplus knowledge value, then fire the worker. Narrative interrogation can make workers victims of the global knowledge economy.

Debate and all manner of deconstruction are dismissed from the social dialog playing field because such critical issues are highly problematic to managerial-ist control.

D2 Debate

The second story control by narrative is how one cannot just say anything. One takes account of local powerholders. Saul Alinsky was born in 1909 and died in 1972. The Grassroots Community Organizing Model is the earliest form of democratic TD consulting. On 14 July 1939 Alinsky held the first 'Back-of-the-Yards Council' meeting. He began fresh out of college working in the same (Back-of-the-Stockyards) neighborhood in Chicago that Upton Sinclair (1901, *The Jungle*). Alinsky pioneered 'organization of organizations' TD network com-posed of all sectors of the community: small business owners, labor union lead-ers such as Herb March of Congress of Industrial Organizations, Bishop Bernard Sheil of the Catholic Church, and leaders of ethnic groups (Serbs, Croatians, Czechs, Poles, Lithuanians, and Slovaks). The aim was to fight against poverty and unfair labor practices by calling for social and economic justice.[5]

Alinsky saw debate and protest as a way to bring the power organizations into negotiation with the poor. In 1940, he formed the Industrial Areas Foundation (IAF), a TD consulting organization to build TD networks throughout the US. Alinsky was mentored by CIO President John L. Lewis. Alinsky's (1946)

---

5 This section on Alinsky's history is a summary of 'the Life of Saul Alinsky,' Wikepeida and 'Progress Report' web documents at http://www.itvs.org/democraticpromise/alinsky.html http://en.wikipedia.org/wiki/Saul_Alinsky and http://www.progress.org/ alinsky.htm

bestselling book, *Reveille for Radicals*, was a manifesto calling upon the poor to create TD networks to reclaim US democracy.[6] In 1959 Alinsky began to organize TD networks in black communities, co-founding The Woodlawn Organization (TWO) in Chicago's south side, a challenge to Mayor Richard Daley's political machine. He extended church participation from Catholic to Protestant. In 1965 Alinsky organized a TD network of organizations to challenge Eastman Kodak's racial hiring practices in Rochester, NY. In 1969 Alinsky set up a training institute for student organizers, and wrote *Rules for Radicals*. The focus of the book was on getting beyond rhetoric, and getting students into poor neighborhoods, to become organizers, and reclaim democracy from politicians and corporations. Alinsky would march a band of poor people, church and non-governmental leaders into a corporate board meeting, or onto the front lawn of a CEO's home, in order to get them to negotiate.

Alinsky's methods inspired ACORN (Association of Community Organizations for Reform Now). After the Second World War, Fred Ross, Sr. began working in California to form Community Service Organization (CSO), mostly in Mexican American communities, and trained Cesar Chavez as an organizer. Unlike a TD model of organizing organizations into networks of action, CSO focused on 'direct membership' and was a precursor to the ACORN model initiated by Wade Rathke. ACORN is US's largest community organization of low- and moderate-income families, working together for social justice and stronger communities. ACORN was founded in 1970 by Wade Rathke in Little Rock, Arkansas. ACORN works in over 75 cities to improve housing conditions for the economically disadvantaged, increase community safety, secure living wages for all workers and improve the quality of local schools (Delgado, 1986).

Alinsky wanted to organize the middle class, fearing they were turning conservative in their politics. He challenged owners of stock in publicly traded corporations to lend their votes to 'proxies' so that social justice ballots could take place at annual shareholders meetings. On 12 June 1972 Alinsky died suddenly of a heart attack.

IAF continues to this day, with over 50 TD networks of inter-faith, inter-racial community-based, and small business organizations from NY to LA, reclaiming democracy, entering it with grassroots participation for social and economic justice. Alinsky's successor, Ed Chambers began to rebuild IAF as a training institute for organizers. Ernesto Cortéz Jr., a young organizer, began to develop a faith-based model of organizing. Cortéz recruited lay leaders, mostly female, in Hispanic Catholic parishes of San Antonio. Combining political organizing with faith traditions became a theology of organizing.

In 1996, I moved to New Mexico State University and met Merrelyn Emery. It is more about a controlled form of debate than Alinsky or Cortez. Participants

---

6 List of Alinsky Rules for Radicals, summary from http://www.geocities.com/WallStreet/ 8925/alinsky.htm

TABLE 10.2   *NGRMC President's frames*

The NGRMC 'Build Community' frame from 1989 to 1992 First NGRMC President
'Resident management and ownership will boost the self-esteem of "Housing Development X" thousands of residents, create a sense of neighborhood in a place now mired by fear, and provide a piece of the American dream to families that have given up hope.' (Marc, Lacey, 'Watts Residents Go Public on Privatization", *Los Angeles Times*, 14 July 1992: B1/
The NGRMC 'Move Out' Frame from 1992 to 1996 Second NGRMC President
'My American dream is not to own a unit in public housing – come on... I want a white fence and a Jacuzzi. A housing project is not the American dream. It's not even the African-American dream'... (*LA Times*, 14 December 1992: B1, B12)
(See pp. 207–8 in Boje et al, 1994).

in the Emery TD approach build a democratically participative 'learning planning community' (Emery, 1993: 242). For the Emerys, two design principles are essential (Emery, 1993: 3, 11):

- DP1 – redundancy of parts
- DP2 – redundancy of functions

It's more structured than Open Spaces or Future Search. At the community or industry level, the first phase includes nominations (Jury System) to the main Search Conference. 'The jury system is expected to yield a valid representation of what the community feels and thinks or wants in terms of justice, fair play and decency' (F. Emery in Emery, 1993: 207). As in the American tradition of the jury system, a cross section of the community is assembled, and it is these people that engage in the main TD Search Conference. It is the Search Conference participants who design and implement the actual change projects in the network of organizations (and for large programs, networks of communities).

Another form of debate is among frame-holders. Goffman's (1974: 133) frame analysis addresses the 'dramatic scripting' of 'everyday activity' according to knowledge people and organizations have about why events happen. If narratives are retrospective sensemaking of experiences, then Goffman's dramaturgical narratives are framing debates among stakeholders. Stories and narratives convey frames. Boje et al (1994) applied Goffman's (1974) frame approach to theatre to the networks of organizations involved in public housing in South Central Los Angeles. For my part, Alinsky inspired my eight years working with a Watts organization, the Nickerson Gardens Resident Management Corporation (NGRMC), where I was a volunteer consultant between 1989 and 1996. We worked with the Federal, State, County, and Community organizations that interacted with NGRMC. Two major frames were evident (Table 10.2). Our fieldwork identified frames of consultants working with particular organizations (Boje, et al. 1994: 208–9) (see Table 10.3).

TABLE 10.3   *Seven transorganization frames*

1   HUD/HACLA brought in someone from outside the state to train residents for Economic
Empowerment in phase one (Resident Advisory Councils) and phase two (Resident
Management Corporations). RMC by-laws were copied from their approach, for example,
'I have established resident management in my own housing development in another city.
I can show you the way. I am paid by HUD/HACLA' (*Source* : HA Annual Report 1991).

2   Someone with an MBA degree Frame authored the Economic Empowerment Grant for
$400,000 for this RMC, for example, 'I have MBA training and can show you how to
write grants, conduct your affairs like a business, and take on the Housing Authority.'
(*Source*: First RMC President Speech, January 1993 presentation at inauguration of
Second RMC President, Nickerson Gym).

3   Chief consultant Frame worked for First RMC President until January 1993 when Second
President took office, for example, 'I can work with you on teamwork, communication,
and resident empowerment.' (*Source*: interview, 1993).

4   Boje Frame – worked as strategy consultant, grant writer (e.g. Peace Corps Fellows
Grant) and got 1992 Dual Management One for First RMC President and worked with
1994 Dual Management Two for the Second RMC President. Second training was done
with combination of RMC, staff and University faculty, for example, 'I will negotiate
contracts, on behalf of the residents with the Housing Authority and work with both First
and Second RMC President.' (*Source*: field notes, 1993).

5   Various Consultants working for the Housing Authority, City of XX Frame for example, 'I
work for the Housing Authority to train residents to conduct Resident Management
Corporations according to the HA policy and procedure.' (for example, consultants
mentioned in HA Annual Report 1993).

6   A congressperson's lawyer has a Frame – this consultant/lawyer favored 'I represent
the congress person in this.' (Note: favored the 'Move Out' Residents Frame above)
(*Source*: videotaped RMC meeting Friday, 8 January 1993).

7   Consultant to a division of the RMC until January 1993. Did staff training, selection,
and in-house consulting to Transportation Staff, for example, 'I work for First RMC
President and do what she/he tells me to do. I am a professional.' (*Source*: interview,
January 1993).

Our fieldwork identifled frames of consultant working with particular organizations (Boje et al., 1994: 208–9)

Implications. First, there is consulting rivalry among frames in the 'real' world.
Secondly, it takes time to understand the multiplicity of frames and the complex context of public housing. Thirdly, when one president of an RMC is succeeded by another, and when the board also turns over, the staff relations are in
a mess; a new consultant is brought in, often with yet another frame. Fourthly,
each president has such a different frame. Fifthly, there is a great deal of stress
and chaos to make sense of; and mostly that is through storytelling. For example, where I consulted, the locks were changed four times in one month. When
consultants and Presidents with different frames gain control of the RMC and
board, they dismantle the opponents' programs and initiatives. It's a cycle that
seems to recur in many sites I have consulted with.

There are several differences between Alinsky Community Organizing,
Goffman's Frame Consulting, and what the Emerys do. First, in community

development (as prastised by Alinsky followers), the point is to disrupt the target system and bring them into negotiation. Secondly, the jury system of the Emery approach, as a sampling of people is more stratified, and less a matter of who is willing to pay the consulting fee to bring in the community development activists. Thirdly, the community development approach has a wider focus on what constitutes participative democracy. For example, for F. Emery, governance of the firm is outside the board room: 'I do not think' says F. Emery, 'that the functions of the board are best served by increasing management participation on the board. That sort of participation (by workers) threatens too many other wider and longer term social interests' (additions mine, F. Emery as cited in Emery, 1993: 190). Emery looked at workers' councils and other forms of worker control, and decided they were a failure. I need to point out that other approaches, particularly the more postmodern (e.g. Theatrics and Spectacle) and critical theory ones, do not share this view.

D3 Dialectic

A third means of control is what Mead (1934) calls the 'I-me' dialectic. The 'me' is all those internalized generalized Others we are socialized to be aware of when we tell stories: our parents, our organization, society, nation, and so forth. I used to teach Argyris and Schön's (1974, 1978, 1996) double loop learning to professional engineers who had become managers. In single loop learning, goals and strategies are selected and operationalized without critical reflection. The dialectic is between what we don't say aloud and what we let be said. The internal conversation is analogous to Mead's 'I-we' dialectic. There is only error correction (first cybernetic control, as in thermostat); Argyris and Schön (1978: 2–3) talk about it as thermostat control.[7] In double loop learning our a priori ways of framing goals and strategies are questioned. The difference between single and double loop learning recalls Aristotle's distinction between technical (preset routines) and practical (reflecting on what is good) thought. On the left side of the page, they wrote what they said to each other (single loop of technical thought); on the right side they wrote what they said to themselves (double loop of self-reflection and questioning what is good). Argyris and Schön seem to work with dialog, the inner debate, and set up dialectic to yield a synthesis.

Schein's approach can be re-read as a different dialectic. Schein's (1984, 1993, 1996) process consultation assumes there are two types of learning: tough and tougher. Tough to learn to change surface artifacts of culture, tougher to learn are deeper subconscious patterns of thought. The tougher learning is through coercion (e.g. boot camp) and even indoctrination (e.g. nunneries) to transform resolute patterns of thought (antecedent transcendental, in Kant's term) into new

7 See online Infed.org encyclopedia entry on single-double loop learning at http://www.infed.org/thinkers/argyris.htm

configurations of thought. Schein argues that the deep stuff of culture is in the a priori taken-for-granted symbolism, buried in our subconscious.

Collins (1998) is a Sociology of OD, that includes a dialectic Marxist approach. Collins' (1998) critique of Schein's definition of culture is that it locates culture in the subconscious (or deep level), but asks people to manipulate the artifacts (or surface level). Schein is caught up in the unfreeze, move, refreeze metaphorization of the coercive learning paradigm. Collins advocates a more critical theory perspective, noting that people can articulate the cultural fabric, and make liberating choices. Schein is more focused on the transcendental a priori symbolic constellations, while Collins, like Alinsky, is more focused on an open debate, one that leads to negotiation of points of view, and changes the balance of power of the haves and have-nots.

D4 Dialogic

The fourth way narrative controls story is through intertextuality limits on what one tells. There is always answerability, telling in ways that answers past ways of telling or anticipated ways not-yet told. It is apparent that if you exclude polyphony (in dialog or debate form), that there are few large system consulting models focused upon the remaining dialogisms (multi-stylistics, chronotopicity, or multi-architectonics). There are single styles, single chronotopes, and cognitive transcendental logic (in Kantian sense), but not variety or dialogism among the variants. I will suggest how one or two approaches are dialogic. They are not the usual one or two day, or weeklong workshops. These approaches take years to implement, and are based on collecting text, and showing intertextual relationships throughout the organization, and in-between networks of organizations, in the case of TD. I do not want to leave the impression that the polypi of dialogisms is being changed. It is one step beyond polyphonic, and that is about all.

First, Mikhail Bakhtin's work in dialogisms. While I do not know of a polypi of dialogism approach, I want to sketch out some possibilities. Bakhtin (1968: 11) points out that 'all the symbols of the carnival idiom are filled with the pathos of change and renewal, with the sense of the gay relativity of prevailing truths and authorities.' Carnival is not only the parody and mockery of spectacle power of crown and clergy, or the satire of the grotesque oppression of (post) modern times, it is life itself finding a way to revive and renew the community; life finds a way to break through, to liberate. Heteroglossia (its polyphony and carnivalesque elements) has two forces that collide, the centrifugal (expanding) and the centripetal (enclosing).

I contend that centripetality (collapsing and centralizing) forces and centrifugality (expanding and decentralizing) forces of heteroglossia result in the hybrid of monological and polylogical oppositions that occur in complex organizations and in TD networks. The hybrid mixing of monological and dialogical forces of linguistic consciousnesses and speech acts are oftentimes widely separated and fragmented in time and the storied space of TD. In addition whatever 'authoritative discourse' (Bakhtin, 1981: 342) becomes centered among the multiplicity, is subject to being dethroned by rivals.

Second is the SEAM approach, which I am discovering is theatrical, ethnographic, and intertextual, as well as interdisciplinary (inter-discourse). Henri Savall is the founder and director of the Socio-Economic Approach to Management (SEAM). As in various action research initiatives, these are cooperatively designed and executed interventions. The approach is much more inter-disciplinary and cross' disciplinary than most others on the TD Gameboard. SEAM interpenetrates strategy, information systems, marketing, operations, production, organization, compensation, human resources, accounting, and theatrics. The implementation changes accounting, strategy, HR, and quality practices. Savall and Bonnett were vehemently opposed to the re-engineering craze of the 1990s. They did not get sucked into the re-engineering fad; they remained skeptical of an intervention that was premised on destroying the social capacity of the firm in order to reap what they saw as temporary and short-term gains.

The major difference between these STS approaches is that, in France PhD candidates are trained in the use of qualitative analysis, not just in OD process consultation. PhD students spend a minimum of three years in the field under supervised apprenticeship doing semi-structured and unstructured interviews and observation of scripts and metascripts, as part of their training. The process of metascripts collection and diagnosis begins with employees, managers, and customers to explore areas of common and divergent. This is a careful and methodical diagnosis followed by a confrontation meeting called 'Mirror Effect.' In these mirror effect sessions, verbatim scripts of different stakeholder groups are compared, such as between management and workers, technicians and customers, etc. This is followed by collaboratively designed and measured experiments to effect changes in the relationship between Social, Technical and Economic. The firm goes through an extensive external and internal strategic planning and action planning initiative in the early phase in order to change the balance of power and authority to be consistent with the emerging strategic plans and their implementation. Policies and the allocations of training resources as well as areas of participation are re-negotiated among the stakeholders of the firm. In short, this is not a 3-day Future Search retreat.

SEAM has been 'validated by thorough experimentation of long duration in 1000 companies since more than 26 years, in 30 countries on 4 continents.' 'I have been going to Lyon, France and working with the ISEOR program (Institut de Socio-Economie des Entreprises et Organizations Centre de Recherche) since 2001. Savall combined STS with economics and accounting, in a socioeconomic approach. It took a few years of working with Savall and SEAM, before he disclosed, 'Organization is theatre.' Organizations are many scripts, enacted by many authors, editors, and actors to constitute a confused 'metascript.' At the July 2001 meetings of the EGOS conference in Lyon, France, I asked Savall and associates to explain the connection of SEAM to psychoanalytic theory. Their reply was the psychoanalytic approach to SEAM is focused on the archetypes revealed in the *Metascript* of the organization. Metascript is defined as the multiplicity of scripts (mostly unwritten ones) that define the field of actions, where strategies are plotted, characters get trained in their lines, and many feel con-scripted (imprisoned) in their character roles.[8] By comparing the metascript of the managers, staff, customers, vendors, and workers, it is usually the case that people are not working from the same script, and that many script revisions are in progress.

Marc Bonnet and Vincent Crisallini (2003) take a TD approach: 'Enhancing the efficiency of networks in an urban area through management consulting interventions.' They worked with the government organizations in a city of 250,000 to apply SEAM to a transorganizational context. They involved organizations from the public, private, education and labor section. They gathered the metascript fragments in over 100 interviews and hundreds of hours of observation. After the diagnostic phase, the 'Mirror Effect' results were fed back from those interviews and observations to participants. The data set consisted of 1,500 interviewee observations. People from throughout the network assembled to review their metascript, and suggest script changes. By sustaining a dysfunctional metascript (lack of effective dialog and performance) among the network players, there were measured economic costs to the city in terms of theft, damage to building and equipment, medical rehab costs from alcoholism, and lost revenues. During the Mirror Effect meeting, the costs and lost revenues were presented to the participants, so they could evaluate the result and do collective problem solving. How could a more effective network take place between key players in the city? The intervention was to have key players funded by the Municipal Authority work on an integration of their respective organizational processes. The players in the network identified the key processes of network interdependency that they needed to collectively co-ordinate. This involved not only logistic, but political and long term strategy decisions.

D⊘ Demonstrative

As reviewed in Chapter 9, there are some OD practices beginning to stress here-and-now, 'working live' in the continuous present (Stacey, 2006). My students and I did a 'working live' theatre intervention with a network of county agencies. The problem was that as the permitting process had many different agencies involved, as well as County Commissioners, no one could articulate or map what was the beginning-middle-and-end of it. We got people trained in some Augusto Boal theatre exercises, and helped them to act out the key problems. Then they collectively mapped and remapped their own system, until it made sense. We did not assume that there was a whole system; rather as systemicity, it was continuously under revision, and forever unfinalized, and unmerged. That's life in County government.

---

8 Taped interviews with Henri Savall, Veronique Zardet, and Marc Bonnet were conducted at the July 2001 EGOS conference in Lyon, France, and follow-up interviews were done at the August 2001 Academy of Management meeting in Washington D.C. with this same group.

PART IV

STORY METHOD

Part IV examines frontier issues of living story method, and closes the book with a Socratic story symposium. We conclude with answering two questions: How to move beyond text to living story method and whom would you invite to a Socratic storytelling symposium?

No doubt about it, story methods are dominated by textuality. One way out is living story method. *Living Story Theory* is defined in Chapter 11 as the emergence, trajectory, and morphing of living story from antenarrative-conception to the death of decomposition and forgetting to tell anymore (Boje, 2007b). Living story is neither being nor non-being. It is a form of haunting. The living story is in-between dead and alive, between forgotten fragments and revitalizing those into one's own life. I explore living story method in a narrative inquiry into how a transorganization network defines my Aunt Dorothy's murder, or is it really suicide? It means addressing story fabric. *Story fabric* is defined by four qualities along landscape and temporal dimensions: simultaneity, fragmentation, trajectory, and morphing. Finally, it's a way to explore *Critical Antenarratology*, a method to trace and pre-deconstruct an ongoing interweaving living story narrating and antenarrating that is always composing and self-deconstructing. Some deconstructed living stories die a quick death. There is no end to Aunt Dorothy's story, which is the point of looking at it.

In Chapter 12 I invited Mikhail Bakhtin, Fyodor Dostoevsky, Martin Heidegger, Paul Ricoeur, Jean Paul Sartre, and Gertrude Stein to a Socratic storytelling symposium. We discuss this book, and try to poke some fun at it. One frontier issue is how to engage one another in polyvocal storylistening? Socratic storytelling symposium is a way to explore what a face-to-face meeting with story ghosts would look like, and a way to see how meeting to do something besides managerialism could be consummated.

Acts of retrospection, reflexivity and emergence are interanimating in the day-to-day communicative interaction of people in the Storytelling Organization. While there have been many interview studies interrogating people about their narratives of complexity, system, strategy, and change – there is a far less ethnographic *in situ* study of story. Story noticing means tuning into ways narrative has yet to order story. Fragments of retrospective sensemaking are situated in localities distributed across the organization and its environment as a polyphonically dialogized landscape. Yet, there is also the landscape of the dialogical imagination. It is fraught with reflexivity and transcendental. We study organizations as less complex, more coherent, too linear narratives. We do not have the lenses to do story noticing. I am hopeful about a more Socratic investigation of the Storytelling Organization, that awakens our story noticing.

11

MOVING BEYOND TEXT TO LIVING STORY METHOD[1]

To study living emergent stories takes us out of the interview situation, and into the field of socioeconomic action, into a more complex transorganization and inter-individual systemicity than previous methods of storytelling have explored. This chapter is an autoethnography method tracing the interplay of dead narratives with living emergent stories. I tell the emergent stories as they arise in context of dead narrative fragments.

ʔ

Me We

Who 357 Her

Told Aunt Boje Dead

Track Clues Story Takes Being

Gentle Victim Passed Emerge Beyond Blanks

Dorothy Suicide Between Tellers Stories Sheriff Mystery

Catholic Memorial Mourning Executes Services Deceased Precinct Democrat

Relatives Daughters Disagreed Reporters Reporting Imbalance Homemaker Narrative Fragments

Mortuary Cremated Hormonal Creature Produced Emergent Storying Nothing

Restory Archive Records Coroner Decided Against Autopsy

Church Ritual Burial Family Mental Female

Death Ashes David Blame Uncle

Time Gaps Line Lost

Did She Gun

Or He

I

Why did I decide to pursue Aunt Dorothy's narratives and stories? I will italicize words in my poem that are reflexivities. As *I* get older, *Death* surrounds *Me*. My grandparents died in the 1970s. No one *told me*. My dad (Daniel) *Passed* away a few years ago. *I* had him *Cremated*. It's still too soon to decide what to

---

1 Ideas for this chapter reflected my Keynote presentation at 9:30 a.m. on Friday 30 June 2006 to the ninth Annual Storytelling Seminar: 'Careering across boundaries – storytelling perspectives', 29–30 June, organized by Norwich usiness School at UEA.

do with his *Ashes*. My ex-wife *Passed* months ago. *I* went to her viewing *Memorial*. *Death Ashes* is one reason why *I* started *Restorying* about my *Aunt Dorothy Boje* and my *Uncle* Vernon, deputy *Sheriff.*

I was reading Dostoevsky's (1876/1955a) *A Gentle Creature: A Fantastic Story* to answer Yiannis Gabriel's question. Gabriel (2000: 20) asked if Boje's (1991) terse stories are distributed in systemicity, and people can tell a story by saying 'you know the story,' then *where is story? What is its being?* What makes these both *fantastic stories* – neither is a very coherent narrative. There are many asides, lots of stuff a good editor would delete from the telling. In both, the authors (Dostoevsky and I) are in a state of confusion, trying to explain what *emerges* to themselves. 'Little by little' writes Dostoevsky (1876/1955a: 241, italics original), 'he really does *explain* the whole thing to himself and 'gathers his thoughts to a point.''

I want use to autoethnography to explore the ontology of story. Bakhtin (1929/1973: 44) says, what is fantastic about Dostoevsky's *A Gentle Creature* is that 'this is not a story.' Bakhtin (1929/1973: 44–5) cites a segment of *A Gentle Creature* where Dostoevsky says:

> The point is that this is not a story and not a sketch. Imagine a husband whose wife, a suicide who several hours earlier have thrown herself out a window, is laid out on a table before him. He is distraught and has not yet had time to gather his thoughts. He paces to and from one room to another trying to comprehend what has taken place, to 'get his thoughts together...

My English translation of Dostoevsky's (1876/1955a: 241–98) *A Gentle Creature*, does not say, 'this is not a story':

> The point is that it is neither fiction nor biography. Imagine a husband whose wife had committed suicide a few hours before by throwing herself out of a window and whose dead body is lying on the table ...

After my telling, I will provide other parallels between 'what is not a story' in Dostoevsky and my *Gentle Creatures*.

Finally, integrating narrative control and story emergence is my approach to Storytelling Organization. Systemicity complexity intertwines with five modes of sensemaking:

Whole narrative retrospection
Parts narrative retrospection
Unity narrative reflexivity
Parts narrative reflexivity
Story emergence

In organization studies we miss out on the interplay of multiple modes of sensemaking, such as whole, petrified narratives, more terse antenarratives, and emergent stories keep restorying. When we do inquiry into storytelling we err in looking for only one kind of sensemaking. It is equally possible that all or several of these sensemaking modes can be co-present and interactive within, among, and in-between Storytelling Organizations, individuals, and their families.

Whole Retrospection Sensemaking Narrative

This sensemaking is but one of four cells of the *Narrative Prison*. This began with Aristotle's definition of narrative:

> Narrative requires 'imitation of an action that is complete in itself, as a whole of some magnitude... Now a whole is that which has beginning, middle, and end' the definition of coherent narrative. (Aristotle, 350 BCE: 1450b: 25, p. 233)

There are several organization narratives of Dorothy pretending wholeness, coherence, with a causally ordered sequence. I shall tell them as they emerged in this writing.

On 17 May 2006 (10:30 a.m.) I made inquiry to the Spokane County Medical Examiner as to the availability of any records regarding the death of Dorothy Boje. Their website has a hot link to the Spokane County Sheriff's Office.[2] I called the Medical Examiner and was told records after 1991 were digitized. Old cases were sent to the State Archive. I called around, and finally got to the right archive location. Dorothy's case was at University Archives and Special Collection, at Eastern Washington University. A clerk said the Cover Record Form is public domain, but contents of the file are next-of-kin only. They checked with their boss, just to be sure. Next day he sent me a scanned copy. No story rights ethical issues thus far. I just began to theorize how many different organizations were producing narratives that differed in material ways from narratives and emergent stories circulating in my extended family since 1982.

> Coroner's Record Form Case no. 82–296
> Boje, Dorothy Elizabeth Deceased Age **54** Sex F Color **White**
> Date of Death **June 15, 1982** Cause **GSW to Head - SUICIDE** Place **Home**
> Personal Description (by Bertillon System)
> Single, Married, Widowed or Divorced **Married**
> Occupation **Homemaker-Own Home** Birthplace **Washington 9-26-27**
> Father's Name Charles Davis Mother's Maiden name Rose Schwangler
> Relatives or Friends **Vernon L. Boje, husband** Their Address **same**
> Disposition of Body **Date 6-15-82**
> Delivered to **Hazen Jaeger Valley Funeral Home**
> Result of Inquest and Copy of Verdict (or investigation)

2 Spokane County Medical Examiner, accessed 17 May 2006 at http://www.spokane county.org/medexaminer/

Victim in good health until she had a hysterectomy
Victim then had severe hormonal imbalance and mental problems
Recently seemed better, but told family she wished to be cremated.
It is obvious in reflecting back, she had made her decision and was at peace with it.
GSW to right temple with a .357.
IMP: Self-inflicted GSW to head.

– (signed) Lois Ryan Shanks, M.D. Coroner

The 'Result of Inquest …' narrative is retold as a linear sequence of highly selective elements, strung together to draw causal inferences. The beginning is a fragment: 'Victim in good health until she had a hysterectomy.' Then comes, 'Victim then had severe hormonal imbalance and mental problems.' Dorothy 'recently seemed better, but told family she wished to be cremated.' I can fill-in-the-blanks and tell you the Bojes are quite a Catholic family, with roots back to Denmark or Germany.[3]

In the Old Catholic tradition, cremation was not allowed. So to say 'she wished to be cremated' back in 1982, is pregnant with impression meaning. The next sentence identifies retrospective sensemaking: 'It is obvious reflecting back, she had made her decision and was at peace with it.' To what does 'peace' refer? Does it mean that she was at *peace* with her cremation decision, or that in retrospect she was at *peace* with her decision to commit suicide?

Then the climax: 'GSW to right temple with a .357.' This is followed by the Corner, stating 'IMP: Self-inflicted GSW to head.' You probably know what '.357' means. It's the caliber of the bullet used. What you may not know is that the bullet was from my uncle Vernon's .357 Gun. He was once Deputy Sheriff of Spokane County, Washington.

Do you know what 'IMP' means? Me neither. I called the JFK Library in Cheney, Washington where her record is stored. I wanted to find out, what does 'IMP' mean? A different archivist answered and did not know either. She had someone call the Medical Examiner Office. She called back. It seems Coroner's Reports use 'IMP' to mean 'impression.' That is 'for legal reasons, they never say it's the definitive cause.' I theorize *impression* is the *nothingness* of story *in-between-the-lines* of the narrative. That is its *being*. I will explain this theory shortly. First, I want to look at other organization narratives.

On 17 May 2006, 10:20 a.m., I called the *Spokesman Review Newspaper* archivist to see if she could look up the obituary and any news items regarding Dorothy Boje. There is a research fee since the records prior to 1992 are not electronic. She found a news article. She mailed it to me. The Newspaper narrative, from the *Spokesman Review* (15 June 1982: 13), arrived Monday 22 May 2006:

---

3 This is disputed. My cousins say Bojes descend from Denmark; my cousins have proof we are of German origin.

Woman takes own life[4]

The body of a 54-year old Otis Orchards woman was found at her home this morning, the victim of an apparent suicide, sheriff's deputies reported.

Deputies said the body of Dorothy E. Boje, N Road, was discovered about 7:30 a.m. by her husband, Vernon Boje, a former deputy sheriff.

The body was found on a couch in a back room at the house. The woman had suffered a .357-caliber gunshot wound to her head, deputies said.

A gun was found near the body but no note was found, deputies reported.

On 17 June 1982, two days after the 'apparent suicide' the *Spokesman Review* (Section 13) printed another narrative about the funeral.

OBITUARY: Boje, Dorothy E. - - Passed away June 15, 1982 at her home in Otis Orchards, Wa. Wife of Vernon L. Boje, at the home. Mother of Mrs. Keith W. (Cynthia j.) Bly; Otis Orchards, Mrs Tom (Mona Lea) Alfrey, Pierce, ID' Susan Boje, Spokane Valley; two grandsons. Sister of C. Jean Ogle, Bellingham, Wa; Mrs. Gene (Shirley) Miller, Renton, Wa; numerous nieces and nephews. Resident for 36 yrs. Member of St. Joseph Catholic Church, Trentwood, Precinct Committee Person for Otis Precinct of Democratic Party. Memorial Rosary Thursday, June 17 at 7:30 p.m. at St. Joseph Catholic Church. Memorial Mass, Friday, June 18, at 7 a.m. St. Joseph Catholic Church, Trentwood. Rev. Charles DePiere, officiating… Hazen & Jaeger Valley Funeral Home, N 1306 Pines Rd …

I have three official organization narrative sensemakings that tell Dorothy's 'alleged suicide' differently. The Coroner's Record and news article mention 'suicide.' The Obituary says 'passed away … at her home.' The news article says there is 'no note,' that Vernon was 'former Deputy Sheriff,' and that 'Sheriff's deputies' gave accounts to the reporter.

S2 Parts Retrospective Sensemaking Narratives

In terse fragmented, distributed retro sensemaking (Boje, 1991), a few lines of spoken or written narrative leave much unspoken and unwritten *in-between-the-lines*. In the Coroner's Record, there are words that become terse narrative codes: 'SUICIDE,' '82–296.' But then, what is the ontology of these narratives that are not story? For me, it's the relationships people and organizations make, between fragments.

I went in search of other narrative fragments. I don't think I will find the whole story. I decided to read the blanks in the Coroner's Record. The cover page, or cover narrative, has multiple blanks. For example, after 'At the request of' the word 'family' is typed in. But, there are only blanks after the ensuing spaces for 'Inquest held at,' 'date' and 'by', and no names listed of 'Foreman,' 'Juror' or 'Witnesses.' Reading these blanks 'between-the-lines' of typed narrative lines, it appears no inquest was held, no foreman or jurors or witnesses were called. The

---

4 There's an error in the address printed in the paper. It's 3705 Lynden.

tersely told narrative says that she 'told family she wished to be cremated.' We don't know which member of the family said this, or who provided the information to the Coroner about her 'hysterectomy,' 'hormonal imbalance and mental problems.' It is not clear who is 'reflecting back'? The file is legally sealed, and cannot be reopened. My story rights are to the cover. I sent an inquiry back to the University's archivists to find out if I was interpreting the blanks correctly: *Was there no autopsy?* On 18 May 2006, I received an email response.

EMAIL FROM STATE ARCHIVE

Dear Sir,

What I can tell you for sure is that there was no autopsy. There are other documents relating to the report, but they simply appear to be the reports of the first responder, the first police officer on the scene and a representative of the ME (or perhaps a detective) that came to the scene before the body was released to the mortuary. I sincerely doubt that there's anything in those records that would shed much more light on the situation. I did not read the other records in any detail other than to confirm the sources of the records and that there was not any follow-on inquest, so I may be incorrect in my opinion that they don't contain anything significant, however. I will certainly be happy to copy them for you, if you get permission from the authorized next of kin.

'ME' refers to Medical Examiner. I contacted an authorized next of kin. Of interest to me, there is more to the narrative than the official cover narrative fragments, but won't shed light on the situation. I was glad the State is protecting story rights.

There is an ontology of narrative that is institutionally realized, but it is constructed in ways that do not answer my basic driving question: *Whodunit it?* The News Report, Obituary, and Coroner's Record construct several co-present pasts: *Which is it?*

I decided to fill in more blanks. I did some research about hysterectomy and hormonal imbalance that could prompt suicide. 'It's estimated that, by the age of 55, one in five women will have had their womb (uterus) removed. This operation is called a hysterectomy...'.[5] There are several reasons given for having a hysterectomy: heavy bleeding is the most common reason, followed by painful periods, PMS, Prolapse (a 'dropped womb'), and cancer. From what I can gather, there are thoughts of suicide with hormonal imbalance. I am still researching.

I found Dorothy's plot, and those of my grandparents, and granduncle, on the Web. Dorothy's body, or its cremation, is buried at St Joseph Cemetery in plots next to my grandparents. But why so far away from my grandfather's brother,

---

5 Women's Health London, accessed 18 May 2006 at http://www.womenshealth london.org.uk/leaflets/hysterectomy/hysterectomy.html

Ernest Boje?[6] I was told, when I was old enough to be told, Ernest was not buried near his parents because he was gay. Others say he was just poor. Where is another brother, named Edward Boje buried? He married a Native American, and his name was written out of the family bible before I was born. No one knows her name anymore. I have Pullalup and possibly Yakima, and Cheyenne tribal relatives I would like to meet (Boje, 2005e,f).

> St Joseph Cemetery Plots[7]
> Boje, August Michael, b. 1894, d. Jan 16, 1974, SH-7-10/1, s/w ~~Catherene~~
> Boje, ~~Catherene~~/ E., b. 1900, d. Aug 16, 1972, SH-7-9/1, s/w August M.
> Boje, Dorothy, b. Sep 26, 1927, d. Jun 15, 1982, SH-7-9/2, w/o Vernon
> Boje, Ernest T., b. Sep 17, 1904, d. Nov 24, 1986, C-76-12/1, US Army

Why is this interesting to me? From the grave numbers, (SH-7), Dorothy, the alleged suicide, is right alongside my grandparents. The '/2' means Catherine is buried on top of Grandma. Ernest (C-76) is not nearby. Edward is not there at all.

My mind reels with *'Emerge Beyond Blanks.'* I am interrupted by other retrospections that ooze reflexivity. I recall that when I was in Spokane City Jail, a rebellious teenager just turned 18, my uncle Vernon came to see me. He used his influence to take me on a tour of the County Sheriff's Jail, where he was jailor. He showed me a cell so small one could not stand in it. Half-naked prisoners caged like rabbits, made me glad I was in the larger cell in the City Jail. My uncle returned me to City Jail, and asked them to give me a second night in the drunk-tank. I was sober. The stench of the puke, the urine of the drunks, and that lidless toilet that rose up like a throne was without paper, in the middle of the large cell. It was foul degradation. That biases my retrospective detective work.

More retrospections nibble. This was not my last visit to City Jail. I rebelled. I flipped off a judge at trial. I got sentenced to forever. I turned 19 in City Jail. My Dad got me out. I went in handcuffs to say good-bye to my mom, two brothers, and sister. In cuffs and squad car I was driven to the airport, out on the runway. On that runway, I signed a contract with the State of Washington attesting I would never ever return, for the rest of my life. I got amazing stares as I boarded. I was flown to New York to begin anew. That is why I never saw Dorothy again.

After I did a tour in Vietnam, I went to college, first in my family tree. I called back to the Police Department, to see if I could get a pass to see my mother, sister, brothers, cousins, uncles and aunts. I said, 'I have my PhD. I have not been in any trouble, since 1967.' The officer said, 'hold the phone.' I waited quite awhile. When he came back, he said, 'Look we computerized our office back in 1979. Everything before that went to the State Archives. So my guess

---

6 Trentwood Cemetery listing of Boje plots, accessed 17 May 2006: http://www. interment.net/data/us/wa/spokane/stjoe/st_joseph_ac.htm
7 There's an error on the St Joseph's website. Correct spelling is Catherine.

is you could come back, because there is no computer record.' I recalled how in the Army, at Whitehall Street in New York, the lady said, 'you have some rap sheet. I'll tear it up and you can start again in the Army. What's it going to be, Vietnam or more of life you have been screwing up?' Maybe that too contributed to it. I went back just after Dorothy was buried.

This next retro fragment is about to unravel, as I nest it in what I just shared. It was told to me by one of the three daughters of Dorothy and Vernon, when I visited Spokane, in 1982. What I said in my working document of *Family History* (14 May 05) was that 'Rumor has it that Deputy Sheriff Vernon (allegedly) shot his wife. His version is suicide.' I have no way of knowing if this is not suicide. Several organizations conclude it is suicide. Why do I story it differently?

Several points. There is no whole narrative. And Gabriel, the story ontology resides in me. Narrative fragments reside among various organizations and family members. Each has a rubric, a way people are trained to narrate. As I restory, I am nihilating the lines of narrative with what is in-between-the-lines, inside me.

Reflexive Narrative Unity

There are several transcendentals to explore. First is Mead's (1934) 'I-me' dialectic of a crowd of internalized 'Generalized Others' who exercise some control on how I narrate. In Narrative Therapy (White and Epston, 1990), this dialectic is between my unconscious and a conscious living story. There are two that Kant (1781/1900) calls transcendental logic, and transcendental aesthetics of apperception of space and time.

These dialectic dispersions and separations constitute their own complexity dynamics of reflexivity with retrospection. In real life, retrospection and reflexivity are inseparable. I am also complicit. My 'Generalized Others,' the dialectic 'I-Me' is the State, my Relatives, Jails, Sage Book editors, etc. In S2 fragment-retrospection, I am also being reflexive, at S3 level.

In the story of Dorothy told in the Coroner's Record, Dorothy was at peace with some decision. One 'IMP' is this is the decision to be cremated, which triggers my own sense of being and not being Catholic, and whether I had the right to cremate my Dad. The Catholic Church teaches:

> ... Every spiritual soul is created immediately by God – it is not 'produced' by the parents – and also that it is immortal: it does not perish when it separates from the body at death, and it will be reunited with the BODY at the final Resurrection[Cf. Pius XII, Humani generis: DS 3896; Paul VI, CPC # 8; Lateran Council V (1513): DS 1440.]... The Church permits cremation, provided that it does not demonstrate a denial of faith in the Resurrection of the body [Cf. CIC, can. 1176 # 3.] [8]

8 Father Pat's website, accessed 18 May 2006 at http://frpat.com/cremation.htm

I reflected. There was a viewing of the body of my ex-wife who was not cremated, but not my dad, who was. My younger brother wanted that viewing. My two brothers, my sister, and Dad's two ex-wives have not come to an agreement about what to do with his ashes. In time, that decision will happen. We still process our grief. For now, as the eldest child, dad's ashes are with me.

I do not know if Dorothy got her wish and was cremated. I cannot imagine that after a .357 Magnum GSW to her head, there would be a viewing. I could call the mortuary and find out, but it is not a question I am curious about. I prefer my last memory of Dorothy, standing in her new family room, at their farm, standing beside her new fireplace. Dorothy had an amazing smile, and was by all accounts a *Gentle Creature*. Our extended family has been shattered since her death in 1982.

Like Gabriel (2000: 20), I am not convinced that every narrative reflexivity is a story. What is not narrative, is in-between-the-lines, and a nothingness. I explore this ontology of question, next in more detail.

Retrospective Parts of Narrative/Discourse

Retrospective parts of narrative/discourse is polyphonic dialogism. There is as well, stylistic, chronotopic, and architectonic dialogisms that are in interanimation. The dialogisms interanimate with one another, at the level of the *polypi*. Polypi explores the multitude of dialogisms, beyond just any one of them.

At higher orders of Letiche's (2000) phenomenal complexity, and Stacey's (2006) emergent complexity, I think polypi is consistent with Kenneth Boulding's (1956) theory, the complexity properties are cumulative, rather than successive. In cumulative all the lower orders of phenomenal complexity intermingle with higher orders of complexity. For example, at S4, we would expect to find more complex orders of dialogisms interacting, but still find lower orders of complexity, such as polyphonic dialogisms as well as fragmented antenarratives, and petrified narratives that follow Aristotelian strictures about wholeness and coherence of beginning, middle, and end in storytelling.

In recent years, Karl Weick and his students have examined story and complexity in organizations from our respective vantage points. Weick (1995) stresses the retrospective sensemaking of experience and narrative-plots of coherence and control by which people story current experience to fit into past meaning structures. Weick's (1969) earlier work is about enactment processes. I emphasize the variety making and fragmenting aspects of story as people seek to transform their current experience into meaning structures that may be new. Yet, as we have explored, with variety making and sensemaking, there is still control.

I believe the combination of control narrative and emergent story perspectives offers a revolutionary breakthrough in complexity thinking. It not only is compatible with phenomenal complexity theory, but gets at a way to overcome a major schism.

Synchronous and diachronous approaches to storytelling organization need to be integrated. A synchronic approach looks at storytelling organization at a particular point in time, rather than over time. A diachronous approach looks at storytelling organization in historical development. My radical assertion is that synchronic and diachronic are oppositional storytelling organization forces.

If there is such a phenomenon as the polypi, then it would be among, and in-between, the dialogisms of Dorothy. The lines of one discourse (such as that of Coroner, Sheriff, Funeral Home, Journalism, etc.), of which narrative/ story is a domain, beckon to answer to other discourses. I am complicit in the answering.

I started reflecting about Dorothy's narrative fragment 'SUICIDE,' when I was reading the story by Dostoevsky of a 'Gentle Creature' that in Bakhtin's (1929/1973: 44) translation says 'it is not a story.' Both stories emerge out of nothingness, and are, ontologically speaking, as Dostoevsky (1876/1955a: 241) says, 'eminently realistic.'

I am conscious of a cleavage in being, a haunting of my being. I review my psychic life. I assemble her narratives into emergent stories guardedly as if telling it to judge, jury and stenographer. But, here's the revelation. I am no longer 18, standing in front of that Judge. I am 58, in front of a jury, at an *Inquiry*, which of course, never took place.

Like Dostoevsky's husband telling about death, Vernon and I are husbands, accused of death of wives. All these stories do not end with closure.

Our tellings are a 'muddled telling' (Dostoevsky, 1876/1955a: 247). There is reflexivity of impression as well as retrospective memory, all mixed up in the storying.

Two wives are said to have had a sudden impulse to suicide, and to have acted upon it. All three wives are described as *Gentle Creatures* by survivors. Two husbands (Pawn Broker and former Sheriff) had loaded guns in their house as a consequence of their occupation. After Dorothy, I never allowed them in mine.

The suicides could be just a 'horrible senseless accident' (Dostoevsky, 1876/1955: 292). Another five minutes and the impulses, one that of the teenager who was 16, and one the woman who was 54, could have subsided. In two, 'why she dies is still a mystery' (p. 291). The Pawnbroker if he had come home five minutes earlier, might have dissuaded his wife from leaping out a window. If her husband, Vernon, did not forget his gun, or returned five minutes earlier, would Dorothy live?

Emergent Stories Here-And-Now

There is in emergent story a relationship to retro and reflexive narrative complexity. Narrative and emergent story is the interplay of Sartre's (1943) *being and nothingness*. There are lines of narrative being that are surrounded by emergent story nothingness of what 'is' unsaid *between-the-lines*. But I think it is not just collapsible into whole or fragmented (part) narrative. It is not just S3 or S4 reflexivity. I think what is important is the emergent interplay.

Sartre (1943/1956: 137) gives three ekstatic dimensions, which I theorize are applicable to the five modes of story sensemaking. As Sartre does not discuss story or narrative, I have rewritten his lines slightly:

1   Story that is not being what Narrative is
2   Story that is being what Narrative is not
3   Story that is being what Narrative is not and not being what Narrative is

I explain *being* and *nothing* of narrative and story, as what is in the lines of the narrative and what is nothingness in-between-the-lines of story. There is nothingness between the lines narrative, yet we fill the lines in, the blanks invite us to fill in the void. Behind-the-lines of the narrative is the story that is not in-being, and behind the lines of untold story is the narrative lines that are written or spoken. A narrative that is being in-the-lines what story is not and not being what story is between-the-lines is at the heart of narrative/story complexity. These ekstatic dimensions are the heart of the complexity of narrative retrospective and reflexive in relation to story emergence, the part and whole sensemaking modalities.

My emergent stories of Aunt Dorothy's are imprisoned in retrospective and reflexivity sensemaking narratives told by several organizations, including the Coroner's Office, Sheriff's Department, State Archive of Records, Newspaper, Funeral Parlor, Catholic Church as well as other family members. My emergent stories and antenarratives of Aunt Dorothy are imprisoned in retrospective (representational) sensemaking narratives being told, and sedimented by several organizations, including the Coroner's Office, Sheriff's Department, State Archive of Records, Newspaper, Funeral Parlor, and Catholic Church. Family members recite some of these, or are reading between the lines. At the point of story emergence, I think that Dostoevsky's *A Gentle Creature* is both retrospection and reflexivity, in the moment of being, where coherence is not yet achieved, and may never be. There are only reflexivity-impressions, and the question at issue here, 'is this a story'.

I imagine that Gabriel, as well, will say of my emergent storying of Dorothy, 'this is not a story.' Is it a sliver of a narrative, or an antenarrative thought about the nothingness of Dorothy's emergent story? I mean to ask him when I see him next.

I called my mother (17 May 2006, 1:30 p.m.). Her 'IMP' or 'impression is as follows:

Mom's 'IMP'

There was fighting amongst the girls and their dad. As to whether he shot her or she committed suicide. I cannot picture him shooting her or her committing suicide. She was always so stable. She majored in home economics, was a good cook and did lots of sewing.

Being a good cook and housekeeper rank very high with my mother.

'Mom, did the daughters dispute what happened amongst themselves?' I asked. 'There was dispute amongst the daughters. Some took his side, some hers. He was deputy sheriff and I think the Sheriff's Office did not look that closely.' I asked my sister Karen to tell me her 'IMP' (21 May 2006):

Sister's 'IMP':

> She was bi-polar, and had a down phase and wasn't taking her meds. All three girls believe Vernon shot Dorothy, and have not spoken to him since. He hooked up with a new lady just months after Dorothy was killed. That in itself is very suspicious. Grieving husband of several months jumps into new relationship. It's very suspicious about the gun. He never went anywhere without his gun. He was [once] Sheriff, and did not leave home without that gun. It's like your keys. You put your keys and gun in the same place, and take them when you leave. With girls at home he locks the gun away in a safe place. On this one particular day he left his gun home. He forgot his gun, and Dorothy picked this one day to shoot herself. Its suspicious, very suspicious. The sisters told me, he never forgot his gun. Not ever!

OK, let's be clear. These are not the emergent stories. These are more reflexive/ retrospective fragments.

Emergent story is happening in this moment. Its ontology resides in me. My Uncle Vernon became a Generalized Other. I am restorying him. My uncle Vernon did me a favor, taking a punk, snot-nose juvenile delinquent to see what my future could look like. I have no way of knowing whose version of narrative or emergent story is true. If I add up the overlaps, I still don't know.

Several relatives at my ex-wife's funeral insinuated, would she not have died of an 'enlarged heart' if you David had not divorced? The other side of these tellings is, each could have been waiting for any next opportunity to die. If I am innocent, then are Uncle Vernon and Dostoevsky's Pawnbroker innocent?

On Saturday 3 June 2006, 3 p.m, my cousin Cynthia (Dorothy and Vernon's daughter) called me back. We had not spoken in 40 years. We caught up on whom our kids married, and what happened to our siblings. She is a year younger than I. She said she was doing family history. I said I was too. I asked, 'can we talk about your mom?' She said, 'sure.' I explained about Dostoevsky's *A Gentle Creature*. Cynthia told me it was definitely suicide, but that the daughters for many personal reasons had nothing to do with their dad. She gave me permission to tell this side.

> About Dorothy 'her step father had passed away and her mom had come to live with her after having a stroke. She had to take care of her mom, and over-taxed herself. Mom caught pneumonia and was at home in bed. I believe she also had an impacted tooth that had to be pulled at the same time. And her mother had gone into the hospital after another major stroke and succumbed to the stroke. My mom became depressed, overtaxed, and her mother passed

away, and she had other personal issues. Since you already know of the hysterectomy, I can now feel comfortable using those words. There were also some estate issues that she had to deal with regarding my Grandmother's estate as she was the oldest child and named as Grandma's personal representative. She had way too many problems on her plate.

Anyway, and ah, un, ah [long pause 3 seconds] and [another pause with crying, 5 seconds] ended up taking her own life with dad's service revolver. No question as to whether it is suicide or not.

I apologized for bringing it up.

That's Ok [*she replied*]. It's coming up on 15th June. Anyway, I was thinking about it the other day.

Cynthia and I talked some more, exchanged email addresses. She explained about Vernon had married his fourth wife. I told her my dad had three wives. His second was not yet 18 years old. After his third, he went to be a hermit in the forests of Oregon. 'We've had some dysfunctions within the Boje family. But all families have had some stuff happening' Cynthia said. She agreed to read over this chapter and make changes.

On 5 June 2006, 9:04 p.m. Cynthia sent additions to this chapter. To my sensemaking, they are emergent stories that unravel organization narratives, as well as my own.

News Report: There was a short note on top of the freezer. I do not know what happened to it.

Obituary: 'Passed away' or something similar is used a lot in obituaries for suicide cases. So the wording is not unusual. Many families do not want it known that their family member is a victim of suicide.

Cremation: I believe all of her immediate family members knew of her wishes, including my husband Keith. The information on the hysterectomy came from Dad, Keith or me.

St. Joseph's Cemetery Record: My Mother's *grave stone* is located at St Joseph's on the *same* plot as Grandma and Grandpa's. Dad said you are allowed to bury either 2 or 3 people in the same grave on top of each other. So a second marker (for Mom and Dad) is on Grandma and Grandpa's grave. Mom is not buried there. Her ashes were spread (per her wishes) at my parents 'ranch' by Blanchard, Idaho by Dad, my 2 sisters, my husband and me. Dad managed St Joseph's for several years and supposedly dug up the dirt where Mom's ashes were spread and transported them to Grandma and Grandpa's grave. Then placed Mom and Dad's marker on the grave. About Ernest: His parents were buried on the WA coast. He died in Spokane, so I am assuming that's why he was buried there. Don't know if Dad had anything to do with getting him a grave at St Josephs. About Edward: I will send a copy of a document cousin Linda has that lists Edward as one of Fred Henry's children. I never heard that he was 'written out of the family bible'.

Coroner's Record: Mom's statement about cremation was not related to her depression. She had simply told us that when she died she wanted to be cremated and her ashes spread at Mom and Dad's 'ranch'. What she *did* say to the family during depression was that she wanted to Kill herself. When her mental health counselor asked her how, she said with a gun. The family was then told that we should remove all guns from the house.

Dad said that Mom had promised him that if he locked all the guns in his gun cabinet, she would not open the cabinet. So he did not remove all the guns from the house.

The weekend before Mom died, she and Dad went to the ranch for the weekend as they did lots. Mom liked it there!! Dad had Mom put his gun in her purse (as they normally did because of bears, etc.) while they were at the ranch. For whatever reason, he did not have her remove it from her purse when they returned home.

At the time Dad was working as a night security guard for the Spokesman Review. He went to work Monday night and when he came home Tuesday morning, he found Mom sitting/leaning on a twin bed in the back bedroom. He immediately called me and told me Mom had shot herself. I was getting ready to leave for work. I asked him if he would be able to call for help and drove the 5 or 6 miles to their house at about 90 mph.

He was so totally lost without Mom that he married in less than 5 months after her death. He is unable to live alone for any period of time. With this marriage, he pretty much estranged himself from his daughters.

Karen's Narrative: I take exception to some of Karen's statements, but as they are her story, I will not edit the remarks. I will however comment. Mom was not bi-polar. She was seeing a counselor at the Spokane Community Mental Health Center for depression. I know because I helped get her set up for counseling and spoke with the counselor on more than one occasion. I was able to speak with the counselor after asking Mom to give the center permission to talk to me about her condition and treatment. And I carry the guilt of not having her hospitalized when the doctor asked me if I thought she should be hospitalized. I told him I thought that being hospitalized against her wishes would kill her. What a choice of words. Words that still haunt me. If I had let them hospitalize her, she might still be alive today. So as you can see, there is plenty of blame to go around.

Not all 3 girls felt he shot her.

He did not forget to take his gun with him Monday night when he went to work at the *Spokesman Review*. He was not allowed to take his *large* hand gun to work. I don't remember whether he had no gun at work or a smaller pistol.

Dad was working as a security guard because Mom (who did the family financial bookwork) felt his retirement pay was not enough for them to live on. They were in debt and in her depression, she was unable to see how they could get out of debt. I had to help them write checks to pay their bills because she was unable to perform that task for a while and Dad had never paid bills. I remember going over to their house after work on my birthday (3 May) to write checks and set up a budget for them. I tried to show Mom that with the budget they would be able to get their bills paid off, hoping that would make her feel better. That was 6 weeks before she died. So you can see the depression went on for quite a while.

Dénouement

I have a main point in this integration of narrative and story. Control narratives and emergent stories are everywhere around us. I am part of the telling, writing, and rehistoricizing. I resurrect fragments of a gaggle of organizations' partial narrative-control of Dorothy's posthumous identities. I investigated the sphere of interorganizational narrative complexity as well as unfinished ever-emergent story complexity of me and my extended family. I experience Dorothy emergent stories as a 'pure multiplicity' (Sartre, 1943/1956: 133). I am a beholder, a spectator, and a Boalian spect-actor on Dorothy's landscape as it interanimates with the transorganizational narratives.

Dorothy is listed in the Coroner's record as 'occupation: homemaker.' The death of her life journey is imprisoned in various organizational narratives. In the terse narrative of the Coroner's Record, Dorothy is homemaker and the impression of suicide is the cause of her death. In the obituary in the newspaper, she is a woman who gave birth to three daughters, who gave her two grandsons, and she had numerous nieces and nephews. My autoethnography is not a story. It is in-between biography and my impressions. In the dynamic boundaryless organizational world are the retrospective fragments of Aunt Dorothy. Organizations plan, manage, and develop the 'petrified narratives' of her life, career and death (Czarniawska, 2004). I recover her working-home-life journey in emergent storytelling, in ways of telling that are very telling, not-yet story.

A network of organizations constructs narratives alongside stories of Dorothy that continue to emerge in my family. In this polypi of dialogisms polyphonic logics struggle, multiple stylistics of verbal and written styles juxtapose, multiple chronotopes of varying temporalities and spatialities diverge, and the ethical discourse of architectonic questions reverberates into many other discourses. There is a complexity about Dorothy narratives and emergent stories, about various ways to get to the bottom or to the top of her story. It keeps unfolding and refolding. Always, there is another way of telling.

I hope I have provoked some interest in the being and nothingness of narrative and story. I wanted to explore story rights and ethics. I have answerability for what I Narrative and story crisscross ethical boundaries. In every emergent Present story impression or our life and career, the Past and the Future are ready to be imprisoned in various organizational narratives, and my own narrative prison. Restorying, for me, releases not only Vernon, but also me.

LIVING STORY THEORY

Living story theory is defined here as the emergence, trajectory, and morphing of living story from antenarrative conception to the death of decomposition and forgetting to tell anymore (Boje, 2007b). Living story is neither being nor non-being; it is a form of haunting. The living story is in-between dead and alive, between forgotten fragments and revitalizing those into one's own life. Living story is collective ongoing, simultaneous, fragmented, and distributive storying and restorying by all the storytellers reshaping, rehistoricizing, and contemporalizing. The living story fabric is a complex collective-weave of many storytellers and listeners who together are co-constructing (along with researchers) the dynamics that reduce living story opposed by antenarrative forces of more amplifying-transformation.

Kaylynn TwoTrees (1997), a Lakota storyteller, taught me elements of living story. 'What is the Lakota penalty for changing a story, telling a story wrong or without permission?' I asked. 'It is death,' TwoTrees replied, 'Because, the story in an oral culture is the entire living history of the community.' *'I'm glad I'm not Lakota'*. She stresses three aspects: first, living stories not only have relativistic temporality (i.e., bridging past into present), there are times when a story can be told (e.g., seasons). Secondly, living stories have a place and places have their own story to tell. Finally, living stories have owners, and one needs permission to tell another's story of a time or a place.

Story fabric is defined by four qualities along landscape and temporal dimensions: simultaneity, fragmentation, trajectory, and morphing. Strands of narrative and antenarrative are interwoven, raveling and deraveling, weaving and unweaving in families and Storytelling Organizations and in societal discourse. Stories are being told simultaneously across the landscape of here-and-now. People tell more fragmented stories than the more coherent form. People rarely tell full-blown stories from beginning, middle to end. It's fragmented since tellers leave most of the story to the imagination of listeners. Listeners fill in blanks, pauses, and silences with stories of their own. Listeners tune out a teller getting carried away with telling a story to themselves (Stein, 1935).

Fragmented antenarrative is also simultaneous with more coherent story production. Given the simultaneity and fragmentation in a storytelling system, the collective dynamics give rise to what I am calling trajectory. Antenarratives morph along trajectories, which is what makes them living stories. Trajectory is the passageway of an emergent antenarrative as it picks up and sheds meaning along different places and across different temporalities.

Morphing of living stories has rarely been studied. Studies can trace the morphing of living story elements (choice of incidents, characterizations, implications) that change from one performance site in the landscape to the next. Living story is about spin, about telling it in ways that garners legitimation. Morphing is also what happens when each new occurrence in the present prompts storytellers to restory reminiscences of the past in order to highlight values, persons, or episodes differently (Rosile, 1998; White and Epston, 1990). There is a drifting of content as new elements are emphasized, some jettisoned or skipped over. Morphing is part of the constant ebb and flux of rehistoricizing. It is what makes living story transformative to context. Spins and counter-spins set up the story fabric of organization. Simultaneity, fragmentation, trajectory, and morphing are qualities of living story fabric that are centrifugal, and opposed to more narrative forces that reduce story to linear developed beginning, middle, and end.

Dead narratives can be resurrected. Living story is not necessarily positive. Loving story can be a living hell. Some utopic stories of organizations are living hell. We get caught up in living stories that control our lives.

Each living story is related to many dead narratives. A living body of stories remains part of day-to-day discourse. Dead stories are the forgotten ways of telling. These ways of telling cease to exist. Remnants and fragments of dead ways of telling may be recoverable in archives. We can contact retirees or people who just left. Beneath the flowing lines of living stories in conversation there are these dead stories. Dead stories are like old bones poking through the skin.

To study living story we can investigate the underbelly of dead stories. We can penetrate the partially remembered stories, the ones long forgotten. We can invite people before our time, to tell their stories. Forerunners to contemporary story chatter were once living in day-to-day discourse; or stories were retrospectively imagined to have been told. There is a good deal of ambiguity and relativism with living stories. The living sensemaking currency of stories will eventually fail to circulate, and pass from collective memory. Dead stories are forgotten. When a person dies, all that remains are story fragments, some notes, an obituary, and some scrapbooks. The dead are kept alive in stories retold by friends and enemies, until they too pass away.

To suppose that anything remotely resembling a whole coherent story with beginning, middle, and end that occurred in a place is non-sense. Whole stories are products of organizational fiction, something concocted by press agents and managerial story consultants. We encounter living story fragments that occur here-and-there, now-and-then. Living story fragments suggest beginnings long forgotten, or purged from collective memory. Endings are illusions. Stories are more apt to begin in the middle, and die before they end. Story fragments clearly appear in organization dialogue, debate, dialectics, and discourses. The fragments can be related to earlier less recalled, or collectively forgotten story fragments. The living and the dead story fragments are interdependent. They are simultaneous. Dead stories are background to what is foreground in living ways of telling. There is a world of forgotten story fragments inseparable from living retrospective ways of telling. Living story inquiry is not just about recollection, it is about taking a critical view to antenarration.

CRITICAL ANTENARRATIVE

Critical Antenarratology is defined as a method to trace and pre-deconstruct an ongoing interweaving living story narrating and antenarrating that is always composing and self-deconstructing. Some deconstructed living stories die a quick death. There has been increasing interest in antenarrative theory and research (Barge 2002; Boje, 2001a, 2002, 2007a; Boje et al., 2004; Collins and Rainwater, 2005; Vickers, 2005). Critical antenarratology is rooted in Critical Theory work of Marcuse, Adorno, Horkheimer, Fromm, and critical theorists who have followed them, such as Clegg, Willmott, Knight, Parker, Jones, Hussard, Oswick, Alvesson, Grimes, Nord, and others. There is quite a long list of folks ('critters') attending conferences such as Critical Management Studies, Critical Discourse conference, and the Standing Conference for Management and Organization Inquiry (sc'MOI).

Narratology had a *story-as-text* focus, whereas critical antenarratology is inquiry into living story's collective storytelling processes. Archival research and interviewing the departed but still living, is a way to recover dead stories. There is important knowledge in dead stories. Dead stories may have been about failed ways of solving problems. Dead stories can be the failed strategies of an executive that was replaced by a succession of other executives. Their dead stories are layered one atop the other forming the context for some new executive adventure, some new quest for transformation. We do not recover whole accounts. Not usually. We cannot recover whole stories, if mostly they never existed. There have been few studies of the intertextuality of living stories (O'Conner, 2002). Yet, in answerability theory, each story is an answer to a previous or an anticipated telling. It is the dead ways of telling that are very telling. There is also a strange juxtaposition of living story to the background of dead stories not being told that speaks to answerability.

To study living and dead story requires attending to the authors, beholders (readers), characters, and directors of living and dead story production, distribution, and consumption. Living story research sorts out the variety of story practices of various people distributed in places and times. The story-as-text approach has oftentimes engaged in narrative-reduction to what has survived. The researcher reports a more coherent narrative than occurs in organization day-to-day action. The fragments get trimmed away; disappear in the edits. More attention is needed to *in situ* ways that coherence is sought, but not always, not even usually, achieved.

Critical antenarratology method looks at the interplay of managerial control narrative over more emancipatory forms of emergent story. Sometimes this emancipation is found in dead stories, in ways employees tell the stories, ways that are not officially sanctioned. The old cliché that those with the sword write history has merit. More polyphonic family history can be the topic of investigation, as counterpoint to totalized organization history. Little people's stories get cut from the official narrative, to become more dead stories.

Organization history is oftentimes a few coherent living stories retold by a dominant power coalition. It is the dead stories that matter! History is rehistoricized with changes in that dominant coalition. In managerialist history studies the power of tellers to spin or slant stories is ignored. Much of managerialist story research has focused on recirculating heroic stories of elite organization participants. Other heroes become dead stories. Stories of the little people have been marginalized, and get killed off. Managerialist story research serves to further marginalize the less powerful tellers.

12

WHOM WOULD YOU INVITE TO A SOCRATIC STORYTELLING SYMPOSIUM?

I integrate emergent story and narrative control in a Socratic Storytelling Symposium. I invited Mikhail Bakhtin (1895–1975), Fyodor Dostoevsky (1821–1881), Martin Heidegger (1889–1976), Paul Ricoeur (1913–2005), Jean Paul Sartre (1905–1980), and Gertrude Stein (1874–1946). The basis of the symposium is from my reading of Bakhtin's various writings,[1] Dostoevsky's *A Gentle Creature* (1876/1955a), Heidegger's (1927/1962) *Being and Time*, Ricoeur's (1983/1984) *Time and Narrative*, Sartre's (1943/1956) *Being and Nothingness*, and Stein's (1935) lectures against narrative. Our topic is forensic methods for studying living story and dead narrative fragments. The frontier issue is how to engage one another in polyvocal storylistening. The contribution is to explore dialogic imagination.

SOCRATIC SYMPOSIUM ON STORY AND NARRATIVE[2]

Dostoevsky:	Boje you're a spiteful man! You're an unpleasant man! Why did you bring us back from the dead? It's vulgar and horrific!
Boje:	I saw your *Gentle Creature* as an emergent story. I invited you to return from your graves so we might discuss integrating emergent story and narratives. I want to also talk about methods. I would like to start with what Martin Heidegger had to say about story and narratives in my Aunt Dorothy tellings.
Heidegger:	If your method is to use story to study being, I think you should stop. To understand the problem of Being, our

---

1 Bakhtin's imagined discourse comes from my reading of his early (1990) writing from the 1920s on architectonics as compared to later work (1973, 1981, 1984) written in the 1930s and 1940s.

2 Socratic Story Symposium refers to the experiments described in the Introduction to this book that took place in October 2006 in Las Cruces New Mexico.

first philosophical step consists in ... not 'telling a story.'[3] Boje your premise of 'Telling a story' continues two millennia of Aristotelian dogma about dramatic narrative structure. Like Bergson's account of time as durée you too are under Aristotle's shadow.[4] Rather than 'telling a story' we need more forensic methods that attend to what is present-at-hand. Otherwise we go about constructing story and narrative out of nothingness.

Stein: I thought the point of Dorothy in Boje's living story was to get away from Aristotle's beginning, middle, and end linear narrative. By staying in the continuous present, Boje's method got away from developmental narrative of various organizations. I think juxtaposing many ways of organizations' telling Dorothy narratives is stylistically flawed. I would have styled it much differently. What Boje tells and does not tell, and the way he tells and does not tell is rather telling.

Bakhtin: First off, I am elated to be here. Dorothy is more polyphonic manner of story in dialogic relation to narrative stylistic fragments. I will not bore you with the details.

Boje: I'm a fan. Say more.

Bakhtin: Obviously. Suffice it to say in Dostoevsky I saw a way of storying that allowed multiple voices. The organizations telling Dorothy stories are in embodied logics that are dialogic to one another, as well as to family members. Each voice is an ideological force. Boje, you talk in your book about reflectivity, but not about the two types of refraction.[5] First, each organization in the Dorothy tellings refracts a stylistic context. Second, each telling refracts a socioeconomic base.

Boje: Each antenarrative fragment reflects and refracts the ideological purview of each organization. Other fragments refract ideology of various family members. Heidegger, you talk about Being as something to 'bring forth.' Can emergent story be something brought forth, not as a technical device, but as a emanation veiled by Coroner, Sheriff, Church, Funeral Home, and so forth?[6]

Heidegger: If I understand you, what narratives organizations brought forth are about the nothingness in-between the

---

3   This is a direct quote from Heidegger (1927/1962: 26). It is followed by paraphrasing.

4   See reference to Bergson in Heidegger (1927/1962: 49).

5   This comes from Medvedov (1928/1978: 18). Bakhtin is silent co-author to the book and/or it's based on Bakhtin's notebooks from the 1920s.

6   See Heidegger (1927/1962: 50–2) for his concepts of 'technical devices' and 'bringing forth' as emanation.

	lines. Pre-ontological lines are implied, but not written into a text. The story remains hidden like some sort of ghost. Perhaps Sartre's work on nothingness is more appropriate.
Sartre:	It's good to be able to see again.[7] Boje is lost in the alienating world of institutions. Story is in between the beingness in some kind of discourse and nothingness. 'Telling a story' of Dorothy is what Heidegger might call pre-ontological. What is it for others?
Ricoeur:	My focus is on the hermeneutic spiral. What Boje calls story or antenarrative is what I call first mimetic moment, a kind of pre-story understanding of language, symbols and culture necessary to interpret the second mimetic moment of emplotment. And to understand emplotment, we are in the third mimetic moment of ways of interpreting plot that are socially available.
Boje:	Do I understand you correctly? Your approach to second mimesis is rooted in Aristotle's plot. You extend that approach by looking at pre-understanding of story, and after plot by being able to interpret new configurations in the order of action.[8] Your approach to Time is from Augustine, yet it is retrospective, as in Aristotle. The being of time is to have taken place, is no longer, or is not yet. It seems to be the experience of actions.
Ricoeur:	Narration implies retrospective memory, but can also imply prediction of expectation. Perhaps it is in pre-story of Dorothy that you find more expectation than memory.[9] Story can an proclaim event, and is therefore a way to control events.
Boje:	To me it's about narrative expectation. Each organization, as well as departments within them, and specialties, has their own rubric.[10] Each rubric is a kind of fill-in-the-blanks, like the Coroner's Record or Police Report. What gets collectively remembered about Dorothy is only the narrative expectations in their rubrics. Families want more than that.

---

7 Sartre lost his eyesight in the 1970s.

8 Ricoeur (1983/1984: 3) discusses his work as linked to Aristotle and Augustine. On p. 66 Ricoeur makes specific reference to plot as 'grasping together' being a Kantian conception of teleological judgment and configuration.

9 See Ricoeur (1983/1984: 10–11) for his theory of memory, prediction, and expectation. As with Kant (1781/1900), Ricoeur (p. 11) looks at 'pre-conception' on p. 17 Ricoeur is explicit about 'retrospection' and memory that appeals to the senses or what Weick (1995) calls sensemaking. See pp. 54–76 for Ricoeur's explanation of the three mimetic moments.

10 This insight about 'organization rubrics' of narratives comes from my conversations with Jo Tyler (May 2006), after my telling of Dorothy.

Ricoeur:	What you call 'collective memory' and 'narrative expectation' is dialectical. Memory of things past interacts with the present and future that is not yet. It's Augustine's temporal triplicity, the three-fold present.[11] I'm not in Aristotle's shadow. It's more than what Aristotle imagined.
Heidegger:	I did not mean to offend. Please continue.
Ricoeur:	Augustine believes that every experience leaves an impression on one's memory that does not cease to be. Like Aristotle, Augustine conceived of the future being absorbed into the whole that becomes the Past. However, for Augustine it is the mind that regulates the process of the future coming into the present, and being absorbed into the Past. The mind regulates the process by its threefold intention. There is expectation that a whole narrative is relegated from present narrative performance into one's memory, and there is expectation of what one has still to narrate, what is coming into the Present, then becoming the Past.
Sartre:	If you don't mind my saying so, your approach seems too Aristotelian. What you call narrative hermeneutics is nothing but linearity of pre-story, narrative present, and expectation of the narrative that is not yet finished.
Ricoeur:	I don't think I'm being understood. I mean it as dialectic of memory, attention, and expectation. Pre-story means having a pre-understanding of the temporal structures that call for narration.
Boje:	It seems you are making reference to Kant's work on transcendental a priori understanding, what he calls transcendental aesthetics of spatial and temporal conception. You also seem to stay with Aristotle that story must have a narrative plot that extracts a configuration from a succession of events.
Ricoeur:	Actually I mean Heidegger's *Being and Time* and his concept of *Dasein*. Kant does provide a basis for plot as a grasping together. However, I am not focused on dasein as place. Why would I not stick with Aristotle's poetics?[12]
Heidegger:	*Dasein* means entity. It is not about story. To get at Being, as I said at the outset, means to explore being by 'not telling a story.' The linear succession of time is a rather vulgar conception. Of this I am sure everyone here is well

---

11 See Ricoeur (1983/1984: 16) for concise statement of three-fold present. On p. 17 Ricoeur covers what Augustine thought about memory and retrospection. See p. 20 for Augustine's example of threefold intention.

12 See Ricoeur (1983/1984: 60–3) for his discussion of Heidegger's concepts.

aware. The way we story about temporality or about the landscape, depends upon Care. We story about what we care about. We take time for the things we care about. We make space for what we care about.

Boje: Would there be agreement that we need to be skeptical about story. Often it's just another linear narrative plot of very selective elements? My Dorothy storying and restorying is very selective about elements.

Heidegger: Your Dorothy story is very selective about what events get included. You narrate selectively, crafting her story, positing a certain sequence of a few events. But I am not sure we can get at Being through stories.

Sartre: In Aristotle's retrospective act of linear plot sequencing we are no longer dealing with reflection. Reflection, instead of Aristotelian mimetic dimensions has three ecstatic dimensions separated by nothingness. Story can be being what it is not, and not being what it is. The flow of Boje's emergent storying of Dorothy reaches toward being. There are existential methods to study emergent stories of family members and the kinds of narrative historicity posed by various organizations.[13]

Boje: Can narrative retrospection or a pre-ontological comprehension of some kind of antenarrative before story be about emerging into being? Tellings can be being-for-itself or being-in-itself. Is there pre-reflective or what Kant calls transcendental manner of story that is antecedent to retrospection?

Sartre: Kant reduces the world to consciousness. He is more like Husserl phenomenology of the mind than Heidegger who is more concerned with man-in-the-world of entities. That is why a Kantian transcendental view of story is going to be quite different from a story-in-the-world view of Heidegger.[14] Martin, correct me if I am not reading your mammoth work correctly. It seems to me to be the non-being of story that you object to, because you want to study being in-the-world. Outside of being-in-the-world, 'to tell a story' is just nothing, or non-being.

Dostoevsky: In Russian, consciousness means cognitive and ethics. Kant wrote about both.

---

13 See Sartre (1943/1956: 158–60) for discussion of psychic reflections that include jealousies, grudges, suggestions, struggles, ruses, etc. Psyphic temporality is also revealed by reflection. On p. lxiii is a discussion of relation of Heidegger to Sartre.

14 Sartre's (1943/1956) comments about Heidegger and Husserl are from pp. 4–5.

Bakhtin:	This is why I amended Kant. I wanted an architectonics that interanimated not only cognitive and ethical, but aesthetics.
Boje:	This is a good moment to ask about story rights and narrative ethics.
Bakhtin:	Perhaps you can put the question in the context of your models. You seem to have two. One is all those sense-making types. Another has lots of D's.
Boje:	The ways of sensemaking differ between BME (begin-ning, middle, end) retrospective linear narratives and more prospective antenarratives. The welling up of frag-ments into new patterns is the ground for organization complexity properties. The ground is set of possible story emergence. The various D's are about what Stein calls forensics, figuring out how stories were liberated in monologue posing as dialogue, debate among fragments, dialectic oppositions, and more dialogical telling. I try to follow all your writings and differentiate between dialogs of positivity, debates among poly-phonic voices and logics, the various forms of dialectic, and more complex dialogisms, such as stylistics, chronotopicity, and architectonics.
Heidegger:	Can you link these together more directly with collective memory?
Boje:	I can try. Dialogue gives preferences to retrospective sensemaking, but within dialogs of positivity we find so often in managerialist collective memory. This sensemak-ing forges a tentative wholeness, a totalized BME within a narrow viewpoint of those in power. More multilineal col-lective memory models get out of the general linear real-ity mode, into a collision of temporal orderings, be it in debate or dialectic. In Herbert Marcuse's 1964 book...
Stein:	I think Dostoevsky was dead by 1964.
Dostoevsky:	So were you. Can we continue?
Boje:	Anyway Marcuse objected to positivity discourse because it rejected critical thinking about the socioeconomic cir-cumstances of power. In many consulting projects, only positivity is allowed. Too often Dialogue is everyone going along with managerialist monolog, a single logic prevails. Debate is retrospective sensemaking of narrative frag-ments in a context that localizes. Voices are less likely to be marginalized, but the debate can turn from polyphony to cacophony. Dialectic has its own tendency toward fan-tasy about teleology. This reflexivity can ignore the geneal-ogy of material conditions. Alien archetypes can become more important than what Stein calls forensics. Dialogism

is situated in what I call the polypi of several dialogisms including polyphony, and more, such as chronotopicity, multi-stylistics, and architectonics. It is its own complexity property. Demonstrative is the complexity sensemaking of emergent story.

Stein: Too many D's. You have another D, Dorothy. I liked the Dorothy narratives and story, but too many D's leaves me cold. I don't think you can take continuous movement across the landscape of disrupted acts of narrative and lock it into a narrative prison.

Bakhtin: Disrupted is one more D. I thought Boje was going to talk about narrative ethics and story rights.

Boje: It is a relevant question for method. Dorothy, to me is a living story. The various organizations use rather narrow, self-serving narrative templates. For families seeking answers to existential questions, their narratives don't help much. There are story rights issues. My uncle, and my cousins, and their families, may dispute my way of telling, my sister or my mother's way. I got permission from my mother, cousin, and sister to tell. As a consumer, I purchased the obituary, news story, and Coroner's Record cover form from the various organizations. For the email, I got rid of identifying markers.

Dostoevsky: What about the narrative ethics?

Boje: I see narrative ethics as a method of inquiry. I think it fits Bakhtin's writings about answerability. Newton talks about it as responsibility.[15] We are responsible for what narratives we write, but also for the ones we read. We are answerable for what we narrate. I am answerable for what I narrate about the Other. Yet, I am also answerable, once I listen to or read some narrative fragment to answer. Dorothy's organization memory seemed to me a collective fiction because of the various ways she was being narrated. Bauman is concerned with how a stranger is being narrated. Dorothy to me is not a stranger. Newton, like Bakhtin believes that to hear a narrative or an emergent story is to bear some answerability or responsibility for how that person is being storied.

Stein: Are you saying I read or hear some narrative or story and I am answerable?

15 Bakhtin (1990) introduces answerability in his earliest published essay, 1919. The book is that essay plus surviving 1920s notebooks. Baumann (1993) is the specific reference to postmodern ethics. Newton (1995) is more universalism ethicist than Baumann who is all about local. Newton is less dialogical than Bakhtin. Newton (1995: 45) uses the words 'addressed and thus answerable' building upon what Bakhtin and Baumann are saying.

Boje:	Yes. It is how I co-ordinated my inquiry. I felt I was answerable for how I storied my Uncle, as well as how I storied Aunt Dorothy. I also felt a responsibility to reply to the narrations of the various organizations.
Bakhtin:	Answerability entails guilt. One has liability to blame.[16] Boje is answerable for the vulgar prose of the various organizations about his Aunt. We must become answerable to the core of our being. The narrative fragments must not only fit in some temporal sequence to make up Dorothy's life. They also interpenetrate each other with a unity of guilt and answerability. It's just to easy to create narratives while not answering for life.
Dostoevsky:	In *A Gentle Creature*, while it's neither fiction nor biography, I imagined I was telling it to a court stenographer, and making arguments to a jury.
Bakhtin:	Absolutely. I got the idea for answerability from your work. Architectonics is a method. It's a method of how discourses are put together socially and individually. Here its narrative ethics interanimating with the aesthetics of emerging story as well as cognitive elements of narrative fragments. One discourse interanimates the other. It's how whole is made out of the chaos of parts.[17]
Stein:	Emergent story is wild and while.[18] Its emergence is in an instant then that aesthetic is overtaking by all those narrative expectations. It falls once again under Aristotle's shadow.
Boje:	I am also interested in how emergent story comes into being out of fragments of ways of narrating, and out of nothingness. As I understand your work Sartre, there is another way of conceiving beingness of living story and the nothingness of dead story as complements to each other. In Hegel's conception a story emerges out of story-thesis and antithesis of counter-story, and what was story and counter-story passes into nothingness when there is synthesis. Sartre, you want to emphasize the reciprocal forces of repulsion of living-story-as-being and dead-story-as-non-being.
Sartre:	I think it is towards the second conception that Heidegger's theory of nothingness goes beyond that of Hegel. The importance of Heidegger's work to story is that it questions the beingness of story. There is a pre-ontological aspect of story that is involved in storying

---

16 Paraphrasing of Bakhtin (1990: 1–2).

17 See Holquist introduction to Bakhtin (1990: xxiii) *Art and Answerability*.

18 Stein's comment on 'wild and while' are from her 1931 *How to Write* book.

'human reality.' Stories also pick up a comprehension of nothingness: hate, regret, anguish, and foreboding.

Boje: Managerialist storytelling organizations are a synthetic complex of instrumentally storied realities where the counter-stories don't annihilate the official stories. More accurately managerial control stories and counter-stories annihilate each other in more multilineal or polyphonic settings. The intertextuality of Dorothy stories and counter-stories occurs in ever widening spheres that are becoming dialogic, but without resolution or synthesis. The organization's story control is all the narratives' order being imposed on the family storytelling as some king of totality, exercising control over family member's social constructions. The living stories are suspended in nothingness of organization narratives, and what employees are prohibited from telling.

Sartre: Story arises as an emergence of being in non-being and on the other hand is suspended in nothingness of perpetual nihilation.[19]

Boje: Every story is touched by death. The dead stories of the three wives threaten to live again. Vernon's wife, *Gentle Creature*'s wife, and my own are dead, yet live on. The living stories of the three husbands are surrounded by a ghostly present. I was interested in relating Dorothy's 'alleged' suicide to *The Gentle Creature*...

Dostoevsky: Boje is a vile man! Actually, I was lying now, and just before when I said you were spiteful.

Boje: Actually, I felt spiteful, and suddenly, in a flash, I changed, and felt some kind of empathy for my Uncle Vernon. I don't have the forensics to decide one way or the other, suicide or murder.

Dostoevsky: You seem to indulge yourself in a mystery of many opposite narrative fragments of these organizations. I think your uncle had become some kind of interrogator for you. And you submitted to his inquisition. You certainly submitted him to one.

Boje: That may because I was reading *A Gentle Creature* and started to run parallels in my head with Dorothy. Then as I assembled the narrative fragments held by various organizations and family members, I realized, I was reflecting upon the death of my dad and my ex-wife. The intercourse among the transorganization of narrators began to feel like a prison. Dorothy's story, my dad's, my

---

19 Sartre (1943/1956 p. 18) is a paraphrase of the concept of perpetual nihilation, that I am applying.

	ex-wife's and my own juvenile delinquency narratives were locked away in organization archives. The stories began to take being. The narratives seemed threatening.
Heidegger:	Stories are non-beings. Narratives do not threaten anything. Yours is a very transcendental conception of story. Is story complexity more material?
Boje:	Maybe we can talk more about forensic method. There are some material traces of the manner of deliberation, and the ways of story control. We can look at the stylistics of the oral, visual, and textual remains.
Bakhtin:	There are separate yet connected styles. You have a poem shaped like a diamond, a file you cannot access at the Coroner's Office, a memorial, your inner speech, official written records, an obituary and news story, emails, phone call, diary, and family gossip. It's a multifarious variety of stylistic genres. Was your point to be stylistically dialogic?
Boje:	Actually I wanted to try out a living story method that would allow for the possibility of story emergence among all kinds of dead texts. I did write it much like a diary, and wanted to cross the boundary between personal life and organization life. I also wanted to be forensic, and follow traces.
Stein:	Narrative is what is the matter with history. Newspapers are one kind of history. What newspaper does not do is say anything meaningful. It tells what it tells by narrating a beginning and ending. It tells in its ways of telling. Boje, you seem to be experimenting a forensic method, in trying to do something in a way that the organizations are not willingly telling. The organizations are not listening to your ways of telling. There were a few moments when you were in the Present. Mostly you were narrating some other way that something happened, or in saying you will call your uncle, will it happen.
Dostoevsky:	Boje, you seemed seized by revenge. The uncle had offended you. You charged about like a mad bull. You lowered your horns and went after every organization with any record of Dorothy. I'll bet you barely knew her. It's an excuse for going on a conquest. A very mystic one, with references to the Catholic Church.[20]
Stein:	I think you are renarrating Boje in your own image. Are you listening.[21] The fact that everybody is always telling and not really listening to everything being told is very

---

20 Paraphrase from Dostoevsky (1876/1955b) section III of *Notes from the Underground* (p. 114–15).
21 Note, Stein does not use commas or question marks.

interesting. Even as I am telling I am telling something different inside. Boje as you listen you also move away from what I am saying and are telling some other story to yourself. This telling inside you and listening to other ways of telling is going on all at the same time. I do not believe that any linear narrative way of telling is at all interesting. What is more interesting is what narrative is not telling. In organizations narrative is not telling what is really happening. It is not even all that retrospective about what has been happening. I think the lust for developmental narrative is to blame. There are so many ways of telling that are without beginning or ending.[22]

Bakhtin: Refractions are difficult to study. Organizations are a flood of generative ideologies, a quagmire of stylistics, and chronotopes. The stylistic flesh of Dorothy is refracted in socioeconomic elements by a network of organizations. The abyss is endless.

Stein: It's the differences in the narrative fragments that is very telling. Forensics is a way of following up.

Bakhtin: I agree. Differences in fragments follow from differences in narrative templates organizations have for making sense. What does not fit the organization's narrative template is a sense that is tossed aside. It seems only a superficial forensics method would look only at one or two styles of telling. That would make it quite the 'closed system.'[23] Yet, dialogically, utterances of one context become part of another context. Forensic tracing must follow the currents of thought and emotion. Fragments of those organization and family narratives do get woven into what you call emergent story!

Dostoevsky: It's getting late. I feel the need to return to my grave. Why don't you wrap this up?

Boje: I do apologize for disturbing your slumber.

Sartre: Hey, I'm ready to come out of the abyss anytime.

Ricoeur: Yes, thanks for inviting us to your Storytelling Symposium. Next time invite Socrates. Always wanted to meet him.

Stein: Boje your forensic model of story tracing does not make things too easy. Or should I say our model. I like that. Forensics is not easy. I think you get at the interplay of telling and listening talking and hearing by following

---

22 Stein's (1935, 1998) discourse is a paraphrasing and extension of her Narration lectures given to University of Chicago in 1935.

23 Volsinov (1929/1973: 3) refers to 'closed system.' On p. 5 there is about utterance removed from original context migrating to some other utterance, as in this *Symposium*.

clues. Your emergent story disappears as narrators start telling you they do not mean to control your story.

Heidegger: I gave you a difficult time. These questions about story and narrative being are quite difficult. Maybe you better have the last word. Then we must depart. But, we already are!

Boje: There is an ontological collision between the eight, maybe more, modes of story sensemaking. The sensemaking is part of the complexity of systemicity, how systems are unfinalized and ever rearranging and changing. Instead of one collective memory there are many. Forensic story methods need to address this nexus. One or more sensemaking modes and intergroup collective memories are always background or foreground to the others. An antenarrative thread can come into being and engage some more fully petrified coherent narrative. Or, several antenarrative threads can combine. They get interwoven with one another to emerge as some different emergent story fabric. Only for an instant! Narrative expectations imprison it. The Storytelling Organization recomposes and decomposes narrative fragments and pretentious whole narratives in collective memories. Emergent threads I have in mind are mere thoughts, emotions, and impressions. They can become transformative idea forces that emerge into ontological Being. Narrative fragments interpenetrate the body. Some bodies are being interpenetrating by some mode of story emergence. Storytelling organizations do a complexity-organizing act. Sensemaking, systemicity, collective memory, and a good deal of forensics to chase the inter-dialogic polypi are necessary. We can use story forensics to investigate strategy story ways of deliberation. We can use it to assess story consulting. Ultimately we never get to the beginning or end of story forensics. The heart of complexity of the Storytelling Organization is always in the middle, just becoming, restorying, never leaving anything settled.

GLOSSARY

After each definition, the chapter or chapters in which they are developed are listed in square brackets.

Aesthetic–Sensory Memory is defined as the collective body of individuals' memories, organizational archives of documents, films, videos, and websites record aesthetic–sensory memory (smell, taste, touch, visual, and acoustic) [Chapter 3; see also Cognitive– Rational and Emotive–Ethical Memory types].

Answerability has two types. First is content answerability, which suits narrative, for its obsession with verification. Second is moral answerability, being answerable as the only person in once-occurent being who can act, who is obligated to intervene. Mikhail Bakhtin in notebooks develops the philosophy of answerability as a young man, summarized in two books, *Art and Answerability* (1990) and *Toward a Philosophy of the Act* (1993: Chapter 7, *Answerability*, (defined as how one domain of discourse answers another) [Introduction, Chapter 7].

Antenarrative is defined as 'nonlinear, incoherent, collective, unplotted, and pre-narrative speculation, a bet, a proper narrative can be constituted' (Boje, 2001a: 1) Antenarratives morph as they travel, picking up and depositing context as they move [Introduction].

Architectonic Dialogism is defined as the interanimation of three societal discourses: cognitive, aesthetic, and ethic. Cognitive architectonic was invented by Immanuel Kant (1781/1900: 466): 'By the term Architectonic I mean the art of constructing a system...' and expanded by Bakhtin (1990, 1991) to the three discourses interanimating. Chapter 2 is an introduction to varied dialogism, while Chapter 7 looks at Bakhtin's 'mutual answerability' aspects of architectonic dialogism [Chapters 2 and 7; see also Architectonic Strategy Story].

Architectonic Strategy is defined as 'aesthetic visions' cognition of actions to transform 'aesthetic environment' (Bakhtin, 1990: 279–80) and ethical discursive environment [Chapter 7].

Architectonic Strategy Story is defined as orchestration of ethics in relation to aesthetic and cognitive aspects of storytelling. For it to be dialogic, the three discourses become more fully answerable to one another, not just image management [Chapter 7, see also Architectonic Dialogism, Architectonic Theatric Inquiry Method].

Architectonic Theatric Inquiry Method   Bakhtin (1990: 84–97) develops a dramaturgical architectonic method defined as the interplay of *Authors*, *Beholders* (spectators), *Characters* (i.e. heroes, villains), and *Directors* [Chapter 7].

BME is defined as the Beginning, Middle and End progressive sequencing of retrospective narrative, the five-senses wholeness with imposed coherency that is in vogue since Aristotle [Introduction].

Branding is defined as sensemaking control by centralizing and unifying coherence [Chapter 5; see also stylistic Strategy Story Orchestration, or McStyle].

Chronotope is defined by Bakhtin (1981) as relativity of space and time in narrative. Chronotope becomes a dialogized manner of narrating when multiple chronotopes interact [Chapters 4 and 6; see also Chronotopic Dialogism].

Chronotopic Dialogism   There are ten ways Bakhtin (1973, 1981) conceptualized 'chronotope' defined as the relativity of time/space in the novel. The theory is the chronotopes are embodied in ways of writing, visualizing, and telling stories and narratives. I have sorted the types into my own categories (adventure, folkloric, and castle room) [Chapter 2 and 6].

Chronotopic Strategy Story is defined as the juxtaposition, or possible dialogism among several ways in which space and time are being narrated [Chapter 6].

Cognitive–Rational Memory of whom, what, when, where, and why, set in retrospective memory. Includes cognitive, more transactive memory processes [Chapter 3; see also aesthetic–sensory and emotive–ethical types].

Collective Memory is defined to be like a tapestry of group's and some errant individuals' collective memories, interpenetrated by strands or threads of thoughts interwoven across the groups. The point is there are a multiplicity of them and several types [Chapter 3]:

- Managerial (Horizontal and vertical lines to retrospective center point)
- Punctual (Didactic silos, horizontal and diagonal, some feigning of multiplicity)
- Multilineal (Transhistorical, break with horizontal or vertical points)
- Polyphonic (Acts of anti-memory, mutations make points indiscernible)

Collective memory may be defined as the variegated, fragmented, discontinuous organizational processes for transforming and appropriating emergent story types into control narratives through modes of deliberation.

Collective Memory Dynamics are defined as a multiplicity of valuative standpoints on past, present, and future, and are permeated with three kinds of memory: cognitive, aesthetic, and emotive-volitional [Chapter 3].

Collusion is defined as a defense technique of image management that seduces tacit agreement be maintained between audience and performers not to think too critically, and spoil the illusion [Chapter 5].

Complexity Properties are defined as Boulding's frameworks, mechanistic, control, open, organic, image, symbol, network roles and transcendental [Chapter 1, Figure 1.2].

Critical Antenarratology is defined as a method to trace and pre-deconstruct an ongoing interweaving living story narrating and antenarrating that is always composing and self-deconstructing. Some deconstructed living stories die a quick death. There has been increasing interest in antenarrative theory and research (Barge 2002; Boje, 2001, 2002, 2007a; Boje et al., 2004; Collins and Rainwater, 2005; Vickers, 2005) [Chapter 11].

Critical Discourse Analysis is defined as opening up the 'infinite space where doubles reverberate' (Foucault, 1977b: 59) [Chapter 5].

Critical Spirituality is defined as the study of how people at work engage the transcendental. It assumes that various religions and spiritualities define transcendental quite differently. The word 'critical' refers to critical theory and critical postmodern theory. Critical Theory of the Frankfurt School (i.e., Benjamin, Horkheimer, Adorno, Marcuse, and Fromm) rejects organizational religious or spiritual metaphysics and classifies these as ideology used to exploit the consumer culture industry [Chapter 8].

Dialectics is defined as diversity of transcendental a priori conceptions of spatiality and temporality (see chronotope) to retrospective sensory (see BME), and/or I-we, even Hegelian dialectics (thesis, antithesis, synthesis); can be debate among fragment tellers, but is always about tracing transformations across the social field of Being [Introduction].

Dialogism is a word Bakhtin never used. *Dialogism* is defined as different voices, styles, and ideas expressing a plurality of logics in different ways, but not always in the same place and time. Dialogism is different from dialogue, debate, and various dialectics (Hegel, Marx, and Mead). Dialogic story is in 'heteroglossia,' 'dialogized' with fully embodied voices, logics, or viewpoints (Bakhtin, 1981: 273). Five types of dialogism: polyphonic, stylistic, chronotopic, architectonic, and polypi (dialogism of these dialogisms, at more complex order of systemic complexity than each is individually) [Chapter 2].

Dialogue can be broadly defined as, one person addressing themselves orally, in writing, or in (theatric) gesture to another person, to a third person. The emphasis in dialogue coaching is on the pursuit of order, often defined as overcoming resistance to change through active listening, and attaining consensus [Chapter 9].

Discourse is defined as 'the infinite play of differences in meanings mediated through socially constructed hegemonic practices, especially in stories (Boje, 1991:

107; Clegg, 1989: 178; Cooper and Burrell, 1988; Laclau, 1983, 1988)' (from Boje, 1995). Story is a domain of discourse [Chapter 5, see Critical Discourse Analysis].

Dramaturgy is defined as a theatrics of stylistic assemblage. It can range for texts, photos and décor to behavioral gestures. At issue here is the ways in which stylistic sensemaking modes interplay as either a control narrative (centripetal) or the counterforce of story divergence (centrifugal).

Ecriture is defined by Foucault (1977b: 117) as acts of writing and authoring that make a work of writing as well as authors a metaphysical event of the interplay of presence and absence. The écriture of frameworks is the interplay of presence and absence of authors and works, to erect and classify schools, to slight with silence and lack of invitation [Chapter 7].

Emergence is defined as an absolute novelty, spontaneity, and improvisation, without past/future [Chapter 2]. Ralph Stacey (1996: 287) defines it this way [Chapter 1]:

> Emergence is the production of global patterns of behavior by agents in a complex system interacting according to their own local rules of behavior, without intending the global patterns of behavior that come about. In emergence, global patterns cannot be predicted from the local rules of behavior that produce them. To put it another way, global patterns cannot be reduced to individual behavior.

Emergent Story can be defined as absolute novelty, spontaneity, and improvisation, without past/future. Emergent stories are conceived in the here-and-now co-presence of social communicative intercourse of narrative-memory prisons ready to capture and translate emergence [Chapter 2].

Emotive–Ethical sensemaking is defined as embodied memory that provokes present ethical inquiry, and answerability [Introduction].

Emotive–Ethical Memory In the Introduction and again in Chapter 1, I spoke of a new type of sensemaking called 'emotive–ethical memory.' Emotive-ethical has its own special registry. Its individual and collective body memory is etched in emotions of bogey rumors (fear), pipedreams (hopes), wedgedrivers (distrust), and projection (stereotypes) [Chapter 3, see also Aesthetic–Sensory, and Cognitive–Rational Memory types].

Ethics, here, is defined, as being about how, and for whom, systemicity is consummated [Chapter 7].

Fad or E3 is defined as a type of emergent story, part of fashion and what stylistic image is in vogue. The ephemeral fad quickly fades away [Chapter 3].

Folktale is defined as a narrative, which dissociates heroic, or spiritual value link to leadership, and is retold for entertainment value. It's more about the esteem of the performer than veracity or exactitude of content [Chapter 3].

Founding Story is defined as a sentence or paragraph (or longer) that answers the question, where did we come from? [Chapter 4].

Fragmentation defined as narrative fragments that are terse, interrupted, non-linear and moving, rearranging [Introduction].

Genealogy is defined as traces of the emergences, accidents, deviations, and reversals and false appraisals (Foucault, 1977b: 146; Bauer, 1999; Nietzsche, 1956) [Chapter 3].

GLR Framework is defined here as an associative typology, putting narratives into sameness or difference bins, and then supplementing it with a linear GLR (General Linear Reality) plot line (Abbott, 1988).[Chapter 3].

Gossip or E1 is defined as a type of emergent story, divulging personal information by 'those in the know' about others. Secrets are usually confined within a social group, or organization [Chapter 3].

Greek Romantic Adventure is defined as an abstract, formal system of space and time in adventure. Andrews' SWOT is an example of Greek Romantic adventure chronotope [Chapter 6].

Growth Culture is defined by Normann (1977) as an institution with strategic ideas embodied in signification actions of powerful actors in a learning process of socialization and 'knowledge-development' (p. 35) [Chapter 4].

Hailing   Althusser (1969: 41; 1998: 302) defines hailing as a process by which the person being hailed recognizes themself as the subject of the hail, and knows to respond (it's me). Althusser uses the example of the police officer yelling, 'Hey you!' [Chapter 5].

Heteroglossia is defined as opposing language forces of centripetal (centralizing deviation-counteraction) and centrifugal (decentering variety-amplification). 'Polyphonic manner of the story' is only one of the dialogisms implicated in story's relation to narrative control (Bakhtin, 1981: 60) [Chapter 2].

Holographic Inquiry is defined as interrelationships of storytelling-sensemaking and complexity-properties in any order, with from 1 to 13 or more dimensions (facets) reflecting 1 another [Chapter 1, see also Complexity Properties, Sensemaking].

Horsesense defined by Grace Ann Rosile as embodied telling and listening in the social moment of answering [Introduction].

Improv or E7 is defined as a type of emergent story. Spontaneous theatrics works best (Boal, 1979, 1992, 1995; Stacey, 2006) [Chapter 3].

Innovation or E6 is defined in managerial circles as a type of emergent story. It is what Schumpeter calls *creative destruction* [Chapter 3].

Legend is defined as a type of retro control narrative where an historic event testifies to the greatness of people and/or organization lineage [Chapter 3].

Living Story Theory is defined here as the emergence, trajectory, and morphing of living story from antenarrative-conception to the death of decomposition and forgetting to tell anymore (Boje, 2007b). Living story is neither being nor non-being; it is a form of haunting. The living story is in-between dead and alive, between forgotten fragments and revitalizing those into one's own life [Chapter 11].

Logo is defined as the symbol of the corporation, often not a sentence, but can be a letter or image (e.g. Nike's 'Checkmark' or 'SWOOSH' sound) [Chapter 4].

Managerialism is defined as the manager's view, that comes to dominate the polyphony of voices, as the only legitimate voice, as the agent's voice who controls on behalf of the owners or shareholders. Yin and Yang of Tao, idea that managerial control does not exist without the uncontrollable [Introduction].

Master Narrative Metaphorizations are defined as frame, machine, thermostat, cell, and plant [Chapter 1, Figure 1.2].

McStyle is defined as an orchestrated juxtaposition of architectural and décor styles for McDonald's restaurants in France [Chapter 5 see also Stylistic Strategy Story Orchestration, or Branding].

Metascript is defined as the multiplicity of scripts (mostly unwritten ones) that define the field of actions, where strategies are plotted, characters get trained in their lines, and many feel con-scripted (imprisoned) in their character roles [Chapter 10].

Mission is defined as a sentence that answers the questions, who are our customers, why do we exist? (e.g. Nike's 2006 Annual Report: New CEO Mark Parker asks, 'what part of the Nike story should I focus on?' then mentions brand 8 times, Nike 2006 10-K 26 'NIKE designs, develops and markets high quality footwear, apparel, equipment and accessory products worldwide' [Chapter 4].

Monogon is defined as monologic, monovocality, and mono-languagedness of one-dimensional system theory. See personality (Bakhtin, 1973: 65) [Chapter 1].

Monovocal Strategy Story is defined as what is told or written by an expert, or a dominant coalition of voices that are rather exclusionary of any wider stakeholder set of voices [Chapter 4].

Monumental History is defined by Foucault (1977b: 161) as 'a history given to the recovery of works, actions, and creations through the monogram of their personal essence' [Chapter 6].

Motto is defined as a sentence (sometimes a word or skaz-phrase) stating the moral sentiment that binds logo to the sentences that follow (e.g. Nike: 'Just Do It!') [Chapter 4].

Myth is defined as a type of retrospective control narrative about heroic beings, arranged in coherent, also most offing in linear BME (beginning, middle, and end) or cyclic sequence [Chapter 3].

Narrative is defined by Aristotle as requiring 'imitation of an action that is complete in itself, as a whole of some magnitude... Now a whole is that which has beginning, middle, and end': the definition of coherent narrative (Aristotle, 350 BCE: 1450b: 25, p. 233) [Intro, Chapter 11].

Plot is defined as a sentence stating sequence of events that will get enterprise from mission to vision (e.g. Nike: 'In 1962 Phil Knight wrote a term paper with the plot, low-priced shoe exports from Japan could replace Germany's domination over US running shoe industry' [Chapter 4].

Polyphonic Dialogism is defined as fully embodied plurality of multi-voicedness and unmerged consciousnesses, viewpoints or ideologies where none takes primary importance, not able to impose monovocal or monologic synthesis or consensus integration [Chapter 2].

Polyphonic Strategy Story is defined as one written, visualized or orally told by all the stakeholders to an organization. Very rare [Chapter 4].

Polyphony is defined as 'the plurality of independent and unmerged voices and consciousnesses' (Bakhtin, 1973: 4). Polyphony is 'destruction of the organic unity of the ... narrative fabric'; it is the multi-story 'whirlwind movement of events' (p. 11) [Chapter 9].

Polypi defined as dialogism of four types of dialogisms [Introduction]:

- Polyphonic dialogism of multiple voices in interactive moment of the event horizon
- Stylistic dialogism of types of telling (orality, textuality and visuality) that juxtapose
- Chronotopic dialogism of varied ways of narrating temporality and spatiality that interplay
- Architectonic dialogism, the interanimation vibrations of cognitive, aesthetic, and ethical social or societal discourses

Polypi dialogism is defined as the dialogism of dialogisms of systemicity complexity (Boje, 2005, 2007b, forthcoming b) [Chapter 2].

Polypi Strategy Storying is defined as multi-dialogized complexity whereupon polyphonic, stylistic, chronotopic, and architectonic dialogism collide. It is unlikely to be a something that is orchestratable [Chapter 8].

Propaganda or E4 is defined as a type of emergent story, one that is premeditated, and planted to spread, and transform hero into fool, villain into victim, rogue into idol, victim into martyr, or any combinations of idol, clown, rogue, fool, hero, villain, or victim [Chapter 3].

Quasi object or E8 is defined as a type of collective emergent story. It's the focus of collective action [Chapter 3].

Rebellion or E5 is defined as a type of emergent story characterization. Deviants from collective status quo stir up controversy, sometimes rebellion [Chapter 3].

Restorying is defined as deconstructing any dominant story, in order to develop a story out of fragments, that can be liberatory from oppression (White and Epston, 1990) [Chapter 9].

Rhizome is defined as stem roots that penetrate a lawn or envelope a tree trunk, rupturing in discontinuity and multiplicity [Chapter 3].

Role was defined by Mintzberg (1973: 36) as 'a set of certain behavioral rules associated with a concrete organization or post' [Chapter 6].

Rumor or E2 is defined as a type of emergent story that jumps the official or agreed channels of communication [Chapter 3].

Sensemaking Story/Narrative Types In alphabetical order (and any order is feasible) [see Introduction]:

1 *Antenarrative clusters* can be variety making or be control narrative fragments that morph as they traverse local contexts picking up and dispensing fragments.
2 *BME-Retrospective* is the most ancient of control narrative, positing progressive sequence and wholeness everywhere while ignoring fragmentation.
3 *Emotive–ethical* is what is most ignored in system thinking, yet so obviously is a part of everyday sensemaking.
4 *Fragments-Retrospective* can be control narrative when one fragment is an answer to others that might disagree.
5 *Horsesense* is embodiment, a way people make sense with their bodies, can become control narrative when other ways of sensemaking are ignored.
6 *I-we* (Mead), *transcendental* (Kant), *psychodynamic* (Carr and Lapp), and *historicity dialectics* (Hegel or Marx) are quite diverse, yet can become a control narrative when one kind of dialectic is hegemonic to other ways.
7 *Polypi of dialogisms* can become a control narrative when the order of them is seen as hierarchic, rather than allowing any one to relate to any other one, and to any other way of sensemaking.
8 *Tamara* is the dispersion of storytelling in space–time context where local rules of behavior do not overcome the constraint that people are not everywhere at once: that people arriving in same room from different sequence of rooms will make sense differently regardless of local rules of behavior. It can become a control narrative when one way of thinking dominates all the rooms.

Story is defined as 'an oral or written performance involving two or more people interpreting past or anticipated experience' (Boje, 1991: 111) [Introduction]. I would now add an architectural expression interpreting or expressing experience. By 'story' I mean a highly 'dialogized story' (Bakhtin, 1981: 25), not only the polyphonic (many-voiced) story, but one dialogized with multi-stylistic expression, diverse chronotopicities, and the architectonics of interanimating societal discourses.

Story fabric is defined by four qualities along landscape and temporal dimensions: simultaneity, fragmentation, trajectory, and morphing [Chapter 11].

Storying is defined as the more or less continuous behavior of getting story realized, getting others to take roles, to be part of either a managed and directed story, or one that is more emergent and even collectively enacted [Chapter 8].

Story Turn is defined as a priori, transcendental logic and transcendental aesthetics. I have distinguished between 'narrative', defined in Aristotelian ways, versus more 'storyist' coap which I define in terms of Kantian transcendental metaphysics, the Bakhtinian 'dialogic manner of story' (as in the polypi of dialogisms), and Stein's aversion to developmental narrative [Chapter 9].

Story Rights are defined differently in oral tradition than property rights, since each story is assumed to be owned by a memory of a community, and can only be retold by another with explicit permission. Once in written form, and published on paper or on line, it can be cited [Chapter 3].

Storytelling Organization is defined as, 'collective storytelling system[icity] in which the performance of stories is a key part of members' sense-making and a means to allow them to supplement individual memories with institutional memory' (Boje, 1991: 106, bracketed amendment, mine) [Chapter 1].

Strategy Narrative Forensics is defined as detection of clues to solve a storytelling mystery. Forensics traces the history written by an elite and the genealogy of those left out of history. Strategy forensics is defined as search for clue traces of elaborated argument, high or low involvement of stakeholders, in notes left by strategy scribes (espoused), as compared to those left in strategy enacted [Chapter 4].

Strategy Narrative is defined as a paragraph which has – one sentence each for motto, plot, mission, vision and founding story (which can be a paragraph, or longer) [Chapter 4; see Motto, Plot, Mission, Vision, and Founding Story].

Stylistic Dialogicality is defined as a plurality of multi-stylistic story and narrative modes of expression (orality, textuality and visuality of architectural and gesture expressivity) [Chapter 2].

Stylistic Strategy Story is defined as orchestration of image, or more of a dialogism, among oral, print and video media, websites, gesture-theatrics, décor and architecture modes of image expression [Chapter 5].

Stylistic Strategy Story Orchestration is defined as the juxtaposition of varied styles for image management. It is the manner of influencing and orchestrating image in diverse stylistic modes of narrative control over emergent story [Chapter 5].

Stylistic Strategy Story Dialogism is defined as the interactivity of various modes of expressing organization image within narrative control [Chapter 5].

Systemicity is defined as the dynamic unfinished, unfinalized, and unmerged, and the interactivity of complexity properties with storytelling and narrative processes. Storytelling shapes systemicity, and systemicity shapes storytelling with ways of sensemaking [Chapter 1].

Tamara is defined as landscape of space-time distribution of rooms or hallways in which storytelling and narrating is moving. Narrative meaning depends upon what rooms you have been to, or not, and what was enacted therein, and where your experience is in the present [Introduction].

Third Cybernetics Revolution is defined as the substitution of Polypi Dialogism Theory for the Shannon and Weaver (1949) Information Processing Theory (sender-receiver-feedback loop) model that has been in vogue since von Bertalanffy's (1956) 'General System Theory.' The first cybernetic revolution was mechanistic, cybernetics of deviation-counteraction; in Bakhtin's term it is centripetal forces of language, including retro-narrative. The second cybernetic revolution was the open system (cell) narrative of deviation-amplification, known as Law of Requisite Variety, including variety making [Chapter 1].

Transcendental Kant (1781/1900: 15) defines 'Transcendental' as 'all knowledge which is not so much occupied with objects as with the mode of our cognition of these objects, so far as this mode of cognition is *a priori*' [Chapter 8].

Transcendental Logic or 'Pure Reason' is defined by Kant (1781/1900: 15) as 'the faculty which contains the principles of cognizing anything absolutely *a priori*' [Chapter 8].

Transcendental Strategy is defined as an all reflexive strategy that is not derived from retrospective sensemaking of experience. Polypi and transcendental strategies interplay [Chapter 8].

Transorganizational Development (TD) is defined as a planned change in the collective relationships of a variety of stakeholders to accomplish something beyond the capability of any single organization or individual (Culbert et al., 1972) [Chapter 10].

Triple Narrative is defined as when two or more orchestrated narratives (such as narrative rhetoric and surface stylistic narrative) give rise to a third, more emergently dialogized story of thick empirics [Chapter 5].

Vision is defined as a sentence that answers the question, where are we going? (e. g. Nike: for every sport brand, a team or sports legend to sell it; McDonald's 2005 Annual Report: 4: 'Our mission. Becoming our customers' favorite place and way to eat' (note their vision and mission are same); IBM's 2005 Annual Report, 10: 'vision … "Innovation that matters"') [Chapter 4].

REFERENCES

Abbott, A. 1988. Transcending general linear reality. *Sociological Theory*, 6 (Fall): 169–86.

Ackoff, R. 1974. *Redesigning the Future*. New York: Wiley.

Ackoff, R. L. and Emery, F. E. 1972. *On Purposeful Systems*. London: Tavistock Publications.

Adorno, T. W. 1951/1974 *Minima Moralia. Reflections from Damaged Life*. First published in German in 1951 (Frankfurt Suhrkamp). English version trans. F. N. Jephcott. London: Verso New Left Books.

Alderson, W. 1980 *The Wayne Alderson Story: Stronger than Steel*. San Francisco: Harper & Row.

Alderson, W. T. and McDonell, N. 1994 *Theory R Management*. Nashville, TN: Thomas Nelson.

Alfino, M., Caputo, J. S. and Wynyard, R. 1998 *McDonaldization Revisited: Critical Essays on Consumer Culture*. Westport, CT: Praeger.

Aldrich, H. E. 1979. *Organizations and Environments*. Englewood Cliffs, NJ: Prentice-Hall.

Alinsky, S. 1946. *Reveille for Radicals*. New York: Vintage Books.

Alinsky, S. 1971. *Rules for Radicals, A Pragmatic Primer for Realistic Radicals*. New York: Vintage Books. (1989 revised edition.)

Allison, G. T. 1971. *Essence of Decision: Explaining the Cuban Missile Crisis*. Boston: Little Brown.

Althusser, L. 1998. Ideology and ideological state apparatuses, pp. 294–304 in J. Rivkin and M. Ryan (eds) *Literary Theory: An Anthology*. Malden: Blackwell Publishers.

Alvesson, M. and Johansson, A. W. (2002) Professionalism and politics in management consultancy work, in T. Clark and R. Fincham (eds) *Critical Consulting: New Perspectives on the Management Advice Industry*. pp. 228–46.

Andersen, H. C. 1974 *Hans Christian Andersen: The Complete Fairy Tales and Stories*. Translated from the Danish by Erik Christian Haugaard with the Foreword by Virginia Haviland. Garden City, NY: Doubleday & Company, Inc.

Andrews, K. R. 1965/1969. In E. P. Learned, C. R. Christensen, K. R. Andrews and W. D. Guth 1965. *Business Policy: Text and Cases*. Homewood, IL: Irwin. (1965 1st edition; 1969 revised edition.) *Note*: Andrews is not sole author of any chapter, nor editor of the book, he is a co-author; I include this strange reference since it is how Mintzberg et al. 1998, 1999, 2003 mistakenly cite Andrews.

Ansoff, H. I. 1957. Strategies for diversification. *Harvard Business Review*, 35 (15): 113–24.

Ansoff, H. I. 1965. *Corporate Strategy*. New York: McGraw-Hill.

Argyris, C. and Schön, D. 1974. *Theory in Practice. Increasing Professional Effectiveness*. San Francisco: Jossey-Bass.

Argyris, C. and Schön, D. A. 1978. *Organizational Learning: A Theory of Action Perspective*. Reading, MA: Addison-Wesley.

Argyris, C. and Schön, D. 1996. *Organizational Learning II: Theory, Method and Practice.* Reading, MA: Addison-Wesley.

Aristotle (written 350 BCE) (1954) translation *Aristotle: Rhetoric and Poetics.* Intro by Friedrich Solmsen; *Rhetoric* translated by W. Rhys Roberts; *Poetics* translated by Ingram Bywater. New York: The Modern Library (Random House).

Astley, W. G. 1984. Toward an appreciation of collective strategy. *Academy of Management Review,* 9 (3): 526–35.

Bakhtin, M. M. 1940/1968. *Rabelais and His World.* Translated by Hélène Iswolsky. Cambridge/London: The M.I.T. Press. (1940 date dissertation first submitted; 1968 English publication.)

Bakhtin, M. 1973. *Problems of Dostoevsky's Poetics* (trans R. W. Rostel) Ann Arbor, MI: Ardis.

Bakhtin, M. M. 1981. *The Dialogic Imagination: Four Essays by M. M. Bakhtin* (ed. M. Holquist). Austin, TX: University of Texas Press.

Bakhtin, M. 1984 *Problems of Dostoevsky's Poetics* (translated and edited by C. Emerson). Manchester: Manchester University Press.

Bakhtin, M. M. 1986. *Speech Genres and Other Late Essays* (C. Emerson, trans.). Minneapolis, MN: University of Minnesota Press.

Bakhtin, M. M. 1990. *Art and Answerability* (Michael Holquist and Vadim Liapunov, eds; translation and notes by Vadim Liapunov; supplement translated by Kenneth Brostrom). Austin, TX: University of Texas Press. (From Bakhtin's first published article and his early 1920s notebooks.)

Bakhtin, M. M. 1993. *Toward a Philosophy of the Act* (translation and notes by Vadim Liapunov; Michael Holquist and Vadim Liapunov, eds). Austin, TX: University of Texas Press. (From Bakhtin's early 1920s notebooks; 1993 is first English printing.)

Bal, M., Crewe, J. and Spitzer, L. 1999 *Acts of Memory: Cultural Recall in the Present.* London and Hanover: University Press of New England.

Barge, Kevin J. 2002. Antenarrative and managerial practice. Working paper, University of Georgia. Accepted for publication in revised form at *Communication Studies.*

Barney, J. B. 1991. Firm resources and sustained competitive advantage. *Journal of Management,* 17: 99–120.

Barney, J. B. 1995. Looking inside for competitive advantage. *Academy of Management Executive,* 9 (4): 49–61.

Barrera, Hop H, Hasen, Beny, Biberman, Mathews, Bakke, 2005 - p. 307

Barry, D. 1997 Telling changes: From narrative family therapy to organizational change and development. *Journal of Organizational Change Management* 10 (1): 30–46.

Barry, D. and Elmes, M. 1997. Strategy retold: Toward a narrative view of strategic discourse. *Academy of Management Review,* 22 (2): 429–52.

Bartlett, C. A. 1979 Mutinational structural evolution: The changing decision environment in international divisions. Doctoral dissertation, Harvard Business School.

Bate, S. P. 1997. Whatever happened to organizational anthropology? A review of the field of organizational ethnography and anthropological studies. *Human Relations,* 50: 1147–75.

Bate, S. P. 2000. Changing the culture of a hospital: from hierarchy to networked community. *Public Administration,* 78 (3): 485–512.

Bauer, K. 1999. *Adorno's Nietzchean Narratives: Critiques of Ideology, Readings of Wagner.* New York: State University of New York Press.

Bauman, Z. 1993. *Postmodern Ethics.* Oxford: Blackwell Publishers.

Benjamin, Walter. 1936/1955/1968. The Storyteller: Reflections on the works of Nikolai Leskov, pp. 883–110 in *Illuminations* (Edited with introduction by Hannah Arendt; Translated by Harry Zohn). New York: Harcourt, Brace & World, Inc. (1955 in

German, 1968 in English. 1936 was original publication of 'The Storyteller': Orient und Oksident, 1936)

Boal, A. 1979. *Theatre of the Oppressed* (translation by A. Charles and Maria-Odillia Leal McBride. Originally published in Spanish as *Teatro de Oprimido* in 1974). New York: Theatre Communications Group.

Boal, A. 1992. *Games for Actors and Non-Actors.* (translated by Adrian Jackson. A conflation of two books, *Stop C'est Magique* (Paris: Hachette, 1980) and *Jeuz pour acteurs et non-acteurs* (Paris: La Découverte, 1989) with additions by Boal). London/New York: Routledge.

Boal, A. 1995. *Rainbow of Desire, The Boal Method of Theatre and Therapy.* New York: Routledge.

Boas, A. M. and Chain, S. 1976 *Big Mac: The Unauthorized Story of McDonald's.* New York: E. P. Dutton.

Boisot, M. 1995. *Information Space: A Framework for Learning in Organizations, Institutions and Cultures.* London: Routledge.

Boisot, M. 1998. *Knowledge Assets: Securing Competitive Advantage in the Information Economy.* Oxford: Oxford University Press.

Boje, David M. 1979. 'The Change Agent as Revolutionary: Activist Interventions into Inter organizational Networks,' Transorganizational Development Session of the Academy of Management Meetings, Atlanta, Georgia, August.

Boje, D. M. 1981. Organization Lore in Transorganizational Praxis. Invited paper for the Academy of Folklore Meetings, in San Antonio, Texas, October 22–4.

Boje, D. M. 1991. The storytelling organization: A study of storytelling performance in an office supply firm. *Administrative Science Quarterly,* 36: 106–26.

Boje, D. M. 1994. 'Organizational storytelling: The struggles of pre-modern, modern & postmodern organizational learning discourses. *Management Learning Journal,* 25 (3): 433–61.

Boje, D. M. 1995. Stories of the storytelling organization: A postmodern analysis of Disney as 'Tamara-land'. *Academy of Management Journal,* 38 (4): 997–1035.

Boje, D. M. 1999a. Nike, Greek goddess of victory or cruelty? Women's stories of Asian factory life. *Journal of Organizational Change Management,* 11 (8): 461–80.

Boje, D. M. 1999b. Is Nike roadrunner or Wile E. Coyote? A postmodern organization analysis of double logic. *Journal of Business and Entrepreneurship,* March, II: 77–109.

Boje, D. M. 2000a. Phenomenal complexity theory and change at Disney: Response to Letiche. *Journal of Organizational Change Management,* 13 (6): 558–66.

Boje, D. M. 2000b. Nike corporate writing of academic, business, and cultural Practices. *Management Communication Quarterly,* issue on Essays for the Popular Management Forum, 4 (3): 507–16.

Boje, D. M. 2001a. *Narrative Methods for Organizational and Communication Research.* London: Sage.

Boje, D. M. 2001b. Carnivalesque resistance to global spectacle: A critical postmodern theory of public administration. *Administrative Theory & Praxis,* 23 (3): 431–58.

Boje, D. M. 2002. Critical dramaturgical analysis of Enron antenarratives and metatheatre. Plenary keynote presentation to 5th International Conference on Organizational Discourse: From Micro-Utterances to Macro-Inferences, 24–26 July (London).

Boje, D. M. 2004b. Beyond Open Systems: Commentary on 'Complexity, Stories, and Knowing'. *Emergence: Complexity and Organization Journal,* 6 (4): 88–9.

Boje, D. M. 2005. Wilda. *Journal of Management Sprituality & Religion,* 2 (3): 342–64, 399–405 (with accompanying commentaries by Eduardo Barrera, Heather Höpfl, Hans Hansen, David Barry, Gerald Biberman, Robin Matthews and John W. Bakke).

Boje, D. M. 2006a. Pitfalls in Storytelling Advice and Praxis. *Academy of Management Review,* 31 (1): 218–24.

Boje, D. M. 2006b. The Dark Side of Knowledge Reengineering Meets Narrative/Story. *Organization Journal, The Critical Journal of Organizations, Theory and Society,*

268

13 (5): 739–45. Book Review of *Knowledge Management and Narratives: Organizational Effectiveness Through Storytelling*, edited by Georg Schreyögg and Jochen Koch. Berlin: Erich Schmidt Verlag GmbH & Co.

Boje, D. M. 2007a. The antenarrative cultural turn in narrative studies. In Mark Zachry and Charlotte Thralls (eds),*The Cultural Turn Communicative Practices in Workplaces and the Professions*. Amityville, NY: Baywood Publishing.

Boje, D. M. 2007b. From Wilda to Disney: Living Stories in Family and Organization Research. In Jean Clandinin (ed.) *Handbook of Narrative Inquiry.* London: Sage.

Boje, D. M. 2007c. Wal-Mart founding story in relation to theory and research on shifts in strategy, identity, and reputation. Paper presented at 'Emergent Story and Control Narratives'. Critical Management Studies Conference, Manchester, UK.

Boje, D. M. forthcoming a. Antenarrative in management research. In Richard Thorpe, Luiz Mountinho and Graeme Hutchinson (eds), *Sage Dictionary of Management Research.*

Boje, D. M. forthcoming b. Dialogism in management research. In Richard Thorpe, Luiz Mountinho and Graeme Hutchinson (Eds), *Sage Dictionary of Management Research.*

Boje, D. M. and Dennehy, R. 1993 *Managing in a Postmodern World: America's Revolution against Exploitation*. Dubuque, IA: Kendall Hunt Publishing.

Boje, D. M. and Al Arkoubi, K. 2005. Third Cybernetic Revolution: beyond open to dialogic system theories. *Tamara Journal,* 4 (4): 139–51.

Boje, D. M. and Baskin, K. 2005. Emergence of Third Cybernetics. E:CO Emergence: Complexity & Organization Journal, Vol. 7 (3–4): v–viii.

Boje, D. M. and Cai, Y. 2004. McDonald's: Grotesque method and the metamorphosis of the three spheres: McDonald's, McDonaldland, and McDonaldization. *Metamorphosis Journal*, 3 (1): 15–33.

Boje, D. M. and Cai, Y. 2005. A Laclau and mouffe discursive critique of McJob. In Nico Carpentier (ed.), *Discourse Theory and Cultural Analysis.* London: Sage.

Boje, D. M. and Rosile, G.A. 2008 Specters of Wal-Mart: A critical discourse analysis of stories of Sam Walton's Ghost, *Critical Discourse Studies Journals* (forthcoming).

Boje, D. M. and Haley, U.C.V 2008 *Strategy and Critical Theory Ethics for Business and Public Administration.* Charlotte, NC: Information Age Press.

Boje, D. M and Hillon, M. 2008 Transorganizational development, in T. Cummings (ed) *Handbook of Organization Development.* Thousand Oaks, CA: Sage. pp. 651–54.

Boje, D. M. and Khadija, A. A. 2005 Third cybernetic revolution: Beyond open dialogic system theories, *Tamara Journal* 4 (2): 138–150.

Boje, D. M. and Khadija, A. A. 2005a Toward a dialogic system theory. Proceedings of standing conference for management and organizational inquiry (sc'MOI) edited by Carolyn Gardner. http://www.peaceaware.com.scmoi/abstracts_2005/Boje_ Khidija_Dialogic_System_Theory.doc.

Boje, D. M. and Rhodes, C. 2005a. The leadership of Ronald McDonald: double narration and stylistic lines of transformation. *Leadership Quarterly Journal,* 17 (1): 94–103.

Boje, D. M. and Rhodes, C. 2005b. The virtual leader construct: the mass mediatization and simulation of transformational leadership. *Leadership Journal,* 4 (1): 407–28.

Boje, D. M. and Rosile, G. A. 2002. Enron whodunit? *Ephemera*, 2 (4); 315–27.

Boje, D. M. and Rosile, G. A. 2003a. Life imitates art: Enron's epic and tragic narration. *Management Communication Quarterly*, 17 (1): 85–125.

Boje, D. M. and Rosile, G. A. 2003b. Comparison of socio-economic and other transorganizational development methods. *Journal of Organizational Change Management*, 16 (1): 10–20.

Boje, D. M., Rosile, G., Dennehy, B. and Summers. D. 1997 'Restorying reengineering: Some deconstructions and postmodern alternatives'. Special issue on Throwaway Employees, *Journal of Communication Research* 24(6): 631–68.

Boje, D. M. and Whetten, D. A. 1981. Effects of organizational strategies and constraints on centrality and attributions of influence in interorganizational networks. *Administrative Science Quarterly*, 26: 378–97.

Boje, D. M. and Wolfe, T. 1989 Transorganizational development: Contributions to theory and practice, in H. Leavitt, L. R. Pondy and D. M. Boje, *Readings in Managerial Psychology*, 3rd edn. Chicago: University of Chicago Press. pp. 733–53.

Boje, D. M., White, J. and Wolfe, T. 1994. The consultant's dilemma: a multiple frame analysis of a public housing community. In R. W. Woodman and B. Passmore (eds), *Research in Organizational Change & Development*, 8: 181–242.

Boje, D. M., Luhman, J. and Baack, D. 1999. Hegemonic tales of the field: a telling research encounter between storytelling organizations. *Journal of Management Inquiry*, 8 (4): 340–60.

Boje, D. M., Rosile, G. A., Durant, R. A. and Luhman, J. T. 2004. Enron spectacles: a critical dramaturgical analysis. Special Issue on Theatre and Organizations edited by Georg Schreyögg and Heather Höpfl, *Organization Studies*, 25 (5): 751–74.

Boje, D. M., Driver, M. and Cai, Y. 2005a. Fiction and Humor in Transforming McDonald's Narrative Strategies. *Culture and Organization*, 11 (3): 195–208.

Boje, D. M., Enríquez, E. González, M. T. and Macías, E. 2005b. Architectonics of McDonald's cohabitation with Wal-Mart: an exploratory study of ethnocentricity. *Critical Perspectives on International Business Journal*, 1(4): 241–62.

Boje, D. M., Gardner, C. and Smith, W. L. 2006. (Mis)using numbers in the Enron story. *Organizational Research Methodologies Journal*, 9 (4): 456–74.

Boje, D. M. Cai, Y. and Thomas, E. 2007. Regenerating McDonaldland: a play of grotesque humor. In Robert Westwood and Carl Rhodes (eds) *Humour, Work and Organisation*. Abingdon: Routledge.

Bonnet, M. and Cristallini, V. 2003 Enhancing the efficiency of networks in an urban area through socio-economic intervention. *Journal of Organizational Change Management* 16 (1): 78–82.

Booth, C. 1998 Critical approaches to strategy: An introduction to the special issue. *Electronic Journal of Radical Organization Theory* 4(1).

Boulding, K. E. 1956. General Systems Theory – The skeleton of science. In *General Systems; Toward a General Theory of Growth, Volume I*: pp. 11–17 and 66–75.

Boyce, M. E. 1995. Collective centering and collective sensemaking. *Organizational Studies*, 16: 107–30.

Braybrooke, D. and Lindboim, C. E. 1963. *A Strategy of Decision*. New York: Free Press.

Brown, Steven D. 1999. Caught up in the rapture: Serres translates Mandelbrot. Presentation at the CSTT/ESRC Poststructuralism and Complexity workshop at Keele University, 15 Jan. Accessed on the web 29 Dec 2001 at http://www.keele.ac.uk/depts./stt/cstt2/comp/rapture.htm

Bruner, Jerome 1986. *Actual Minds, Possible Worlds*. Cambridge, MA: Harvard University Press.

Bryant, M. and Cox, J. W. 2004. Conversion stories as shifting narratives of organizational change. *Journal of Organizational Change Management*, 17 (6): 578–92.

Burke, K. 1937. *Attitudes Toward History*. Las Altos, CA: Hermes Publications.

Burke, K. 1945. *A Grammar of Motives*. Berkeley: University of California Press.

Burke, K. 1972. *Dramatism and Development*. Barre, MA: Clark University Press with Barre Publishers.

Burns, T, and Stalker, G.M. 1961 *The Management of Innovation*. London: Tavistock.

Burrell, G. and Morgan, G. 1979 *Sociological Paradigms and Organisational Analysis*. London: Heinemann.

Butts, D. 1997. Joblessness, pain, power, pathology and promise. *Journal of Organizational Change Management*, 10 (2): 111–29.

Cai, Yue. 2006. Story strategy dialogisms at Motorola Corporation. Unpublished Doctoral dissertation, Management Department, New Mexico State University.

Calas, B. M. and Smircich, L. 1996. From the woman's' point of view: feminist approaches to organisation studies. In S. Clegg, C. Hardy and W. Nord (eds) *Handbook of Organization Studies*. London: Sage Publications.

Chan, A. 2000 *Critically Constituting Organization*. Amsterdam and Philadelphia: John Betjemans Publishing Company.

Chandler, A. D. Jr. 1962. *Strategy and Structure: Chapters in the History of the American Industrial Enterprise*. Cambridge/London: The MIT Press.

Chappell, T. 1994. The soul of a business. *Science of Mind*, 67 (9): 24– 30.

Child, J. 1972. Organization structure, environment and performance – the role of strategic choice. *Sociology*, 6: 1–22.

Chisholm, R. F. 1998. *Developing Network Organizations: Learning for Practice and Theory*. Reading, MA: Addison-Wesley OD Series.

Clegg, S. R. 1989. *Frameworks of Power*. London: Sage.

Cole, A. H. 1959. *Business Enterprise in its Social Setting*. Cambridge, MA: Harvard University Press.

Collingwood, R. G. 1946/1993. *The Idea of History* (first edition 1946; revised edition 1993). New York/Oxford: Oxford University Press.

Collins, D. 1998. *Organizational Change: Sociological Perspectives*. New York/London: Routledge.

Collins, D. and Rainwater, K. 2005. Managing change at Sears: a sideways look at a tale of corporate transformation. *Journal of Organizational Change Management*, 18 (1): 16–30.

Cooper, R. 1989. Modernism, postmodernism and organizational analysis: the contribution of Jacques Derrida. *Organization Studies*, 10 (4): 479–502.

Cooper, R. and Burrell, G. 1988 Modernism, postmodernism and organizational analysis: An introduction. *Organization Studies* 9: 91–112.

Cooperrider, D. L., and Srivastra, S. 1987. Appreciative inquiry in organizational life. *Research in Organizational Change and Development*, 1: 129–69.

Coupland, D. 1991. *Generation X: Tales for an Accelerated Culture*. New York: St Martin's Press.

Culbert, Samuel A., Elden, J. M., McWhinney, W., Schmidt, W. and Tannenbaum, R. 1972. Trans-organizational praxis: A search beyond organizational development. *International Associations*, XXIV (issue 10, October).

Cummings, T. 1984 Transorganizational development, in B. Staw and T. Cummings (eds) *Research in Organizational Behavior* 6: 367–422.

Cyert, R. R., and March, J. G. 1963. *A Behavioral Theory of the Firm*. Englewood Cliffs, NJ: Prentice-Hall.

Czarniawska, B. 1997. *Narrating the Organization: Dramas of Institutional Identity*. Chicago: University of Chicago Press.

Czarniawska, B. 1998. *A Narrative Approach to Organization Studies*. Qualitative research methods Series Vol. 43. Thousand Oaks, CA; Sage Publications, Inc.

Czarniawska, B. 2004. *Narratives in Social Science Research*. London: Sage.

Debord, G. 1967 Society of the Spectacle. La Societe du Spectacle first published in 1967 by Editions Buchet-Chastel (Paris); reprinted in 1971 by Champ Libre (Paris). The full text is available in English at: http://www.nothingness. org/SI/debord/index. html. It is customary to refer to parapgraph numbers in citing this work.

De Cock, C. 1999. Organizational change and discourse: hegemony, resistance and reconstitution. Article published in *M@nagement Journal,* http://www.dmsp.dauphine.fr/Management/PapersMgmt/11DeCock.html

Deetz, S. 2000 Putting the community into organizational science: Exploring the construction of knowledge claims. *Organization Science* 11: 732–38.

Deleuze, G. and Guattari, F. 1987 A *Thousand Plateaus: Capitalism and Schizophrenia*, (Translation B. Massumi). Minneapolis: University of Minneapolis Press.

Delgado, G. 1986. *Organizing the Movement: The Roots and Growth of ACORN*. Philadelphia: Temple University Press.

Denning, S. 2005. Stories that tame the grapevine, pp. 73–100 in Georg Schreyogg and Jochen Koch (eds), *Knowledge Management and Narratives; Organizational Effectiveness Through Storytelling*. Berlin: Erich Schmidt Verlag GmbH & Co.

Denzin, N. 1997. *Interpretive Ethnography*. Thousand Oaks, CA: Sage.

Derrida, J. 1978. *Writing and Difference*. London: Routledge and Kegan Paul.

Denzin, N. 1989 *Interpretive Biography*. Newbury Park, CA: Sage.

Derrida, J. 1991. *The Derrida Reader: Between the Blinds*. (Trans by Peggy Kamuf (editor)) New York: Columbia University Press.

Dewar, R., Whetten, D. and Boje, D. M. 1980. An examination of the reliability and validity of the Aiken and Hage scales of centralization, formulation and task routineness. *Administrative Science Quarterly*, 25: 120–8.

Dostoevsky, F. 1876/1955a. A Gentle Creature: A Fantastic Story. pp. 241–96 in David Magarshack (ed.), *The Best Short Stories of Dostoevsky*. New York: The Modern Library. (1876 Russian edition; 1955 English edition by Magarshack)

Dostoevsky, F. 1876/1955b. Notes from the underground, pp. 107–240 in David Magarshack (ed.) *The Best Short Stories of Dostoevsky*. New York: The Modern Library. (1876 Russian edition; 1955 English edition by Magarshack)

Doz, Y. 1976 National policies and multinational management, unpublished PhD dissertation, Harvard Business School.

Emery, F. E. 1977. *Futures We are In*. Leiden, Australia: Martinus Nijhoff Social Sciences Division.

Emery, F. E. and Trist, E. L. 1965. The causal texture of organizational environments. *Human Relations*, 18: 21–32.

Emery, M. 1993. *Participative Design for Participative Democracy*. Center for Continuing Education, Canberra, Australia.

Emery, M. 1994. The search conference: state of the art. Unpublished paper, Center for Continuing Education. Canberra, Australia.

Emery, M. 1997. Open systems is alive and well. Paper presented at the Academy of Management National Conference, Boston, MA, August.

Feldman, S. P. 1986 Management in context: An essay on the relevance of culture to understanding of organizational change. *Journal of Management Studies* 23 (6): 587–607.

Ferguson, A. 1991. *Sexual Democracy*. Boulder, CO: Westview Press.

Fisher, W. 1984. Narration as a human communication paradigm: The case of public moral argument. *Communication Monographs*, 51: 1–22.

Fisher, Walter R. 1985a. The narrative paradigm: an elaboration. *Communication Monographs*, 52 (December): 347–67.

Fisher, W. 1985b. The narrative paradigm: in the beginning. *Journal of Communication*, 35: 75–89.

Fisher, Walter R. 1989. Clarifying the Narrative Paradigm. *Communication Monographs:* 56: 55–8.

Foucault, M. 1977a. *Discipline and Punish*. (Trans. by Alan Sheridan; 1975 in French.) New York: Pantheon Books.

Foucault, M. 1977b. *Language, Counter-Memory, Practice: Selected Essays and Interviews by Michel Foucault*, D. F. Bouchard (ed.), trans. and intro. Ithaca, NY: Cornell University Press.

Gabriel, Y. A. 2000. *Storytelling in Organizations: Facts, Fictions, and Fantasies*. London: Oxford University Press.

Gardiner, M. 1992. *The Dialogics of Critique*. London: Routledge.

Garfinkel, H. 1967. *Ethnomethodology*. New York: Prentice-Hall.

Gephart, R. P. 1991. Succession, sensemaking, and organizational change: a story of a deviant college president. *Journal of Organizational Change Management*, 4 (3): 35–44.

Gergen, K. J. 1994. *Realities and Relationships: Soundings in Social Construction*. Cambridge: Harvard University Press.

Ghoshal, S. 1986 The innovative multinational: A differentiated network of organizational roles and management processes. Unpublished doctoral dissertation, Harvard Business School.

Goffman, E. 1974. *Frame Analysis*. New York: Harper Colophon Books.

Goffman, E. 1959. *The Presentation of Self in Everyday Life*. Harmondsworth: Penguin Books.

Goldstein, J. 1999 Emergence as a construct: History and issues. *Emergence* 1(1): 49–72.

Green, Joshua D., Sommerville, R. Brian, Nystrom, Leigh E., Darley, John M., and Cohen, Jonathan D. 2001. An fMRI investigation of emotional engagement in moral judgment. *Science,* 293 (14 Sept): 2105–8 .

Halbwachs, M. 1950/1980. *Collective Memory*. New York: Harper & Row. (Translated from the French by Francis J. Ditter, Jr. and Vida Yazdi Ditter, from a 1950 text, *La Memoire Collective,* (Presses Universitaires de France.)

Hamel, G. and Prahalad, C. K. 1993. Strategy as stretch and leverage. *Harvard Business Review*, Mar–Apr: 75–84.

Hammer, M. and Champy, J. 1993 *Reengineering the Corporation*. New York: HarperCollins.

Hannan, M. T., and Freeman, J. 1977. The population ecology of organizations. *American Journal of Sociology,* 82: 929–64.

Harfield, T. (1998) Strategic management and Michael Porter: A postmodern reading. *Electronic Journal of Radical Organization Theory* 4(1).

Hatten K. J., and Schendel, D. E. 1977. Heterogeneity within an industry: firm conduct in the US brewing industry: 1952–1971. *Journal of Industrial Economics*, 26: 97–113.

Hazen, M. A. 1993. Toward polyphonic organization. *Journal of Organizational Change Management*, 6 (5): 15–24.

Hazen, M. A. 1994. Multiplicity and change in persons and organizations. *Journal of Organizational Change Management*, 7 (5): 72–81.

Heidegger, M. 1927/1962. *Being and Time*, translated by John Macquarrie and Edward Robinson. London: SCM Press. (1st English edition, 1962; first published in German, 1927)

Heidegger, M. 1962 *Being and Time*. Translated by John Macquarie and Edward Robinson. New York: Harper & Row.

Heisenberg, W. 1927 Uber den anschaulichen inhalt der quantentheoretischen kinematik und mechanic, Zeitschrift fur Physik 43: 172–198. English translation by J. A. Wheeler and H. Zurek, (1983) *Quantum Theory and Measurement*. Princeton, NJ: Princeton University Press. pp. 62–84.

Hill, N. 1960 *Think and Grow Rich*. New York: Fawcette Crest.

Hirsch, M. 1999 Projected memory: Holocaust photographs in personal and public fantasy, in M. Bal, J. Crewe and L. Spitzer (eds) (1999) *Acts of Memory: Cultural Recall in the Present*. London and Hanover: University Press of New England. pp. 3–23.

Hobbes, T. 1958. *Leviathan Parts One and Two,* with introduction by Herbert W. Schneider. Original published 1651. Indianapolis, IN/New York: The Liberal Arts Press, Inc. (Bobbs-Merrill Company, Inc.).

Holland, J. H. 1998 *Emergence: From Chaos to Order*. Reading, MA: Helix.

Holquist, M. 1990. *Dialogism: Bakhtin and his World*. New York/London: Routledge.

Horkheimer, M. and Adorno, T. 1972 *Dialectic of Enlightenment*. Translated by John Cumming. New York: Herder and Herder Publishers. Original edition (1944) *Dielektik der Aufklarung,* New York: Social Studies Association, Inc.

Illich, I. 1993. *In the Vineyard of the Text: A Commentary to Hugh's Didascalicon*. Chicago/London: University of Chicago Press.

Kant, I. 1781/1900. *Critique of Pure Reason*. Introduction by translator, J. M. D. Meiklejohn and special introduction by Brandt V. B. Dixon. New York: The Colonial Press. (First edition 1781; revised edition, 1900)

Kant, I. 1785/1993. *Grounding for the Metaphysics of Morals: On A Supposed Right to Lie because of Philanthropic Concerns*. Translated by James W. Ellington. Indianapolis, IN: Hackett Publishing Company. (1785 in German; 1993, third edition, English)

Katz, D. 1951 Social psychology and group processes, in C.P Stone and D.W.Taylor (eds) *Annual Review of Psychology*, Vol. II (Stanford, CA: Annual Reviews, Inc.) p.144.

Kauffman, S. 1996 *At Home in the Universe: The Search for Laws of Complexity*. Harmondsworth: Penguin.

Kaye, M. 1996. *Myth-makers and Story-tellers*. Sydney, NSW, Australia: Business & Professional Publishing Pty Ltd.

Kincheloe, J.L. 2002 *The Sign of the Burger: McDonald's and the Culture of Power*. Philadelphia, PN: Temple University Press.

Kroc, R. and Anderson, R. 1977 *Grinding it Out: The Making of McDonalds*. Chicago: Henry Regnery Company.

Laclau, E. 1983 Socialism, the people, democracy: The transformation of hegemonic logic. Social Text. 7: 115–19.

Laclau, E. 1988 Politics and the limits of modernity, in A. Ross (ed) *Universal Abandon: The Politics of Postmodernism*. pp. 63–82. Minneapolis University of Minnesota Press.

Landrum, N. E. and Gardner, C. L. 2005. Using integral theory to effect strategic change. *Journal of Organizational Change Management*, 18 (3): 247–58.

Lang, K. and Lang, G. E. 1961. *Collective Dynamics*. New York: Thomas Y. Crowell Company.

Langton, C.G. 1990 Computation at the Edge of Chaos: Phase Transitions and Emergent Computation. Physica D Archive 42 (1–3) June: 12–37.

Latour, B. 1987. *Science In Action. How to Follow Scientists and Engineers Through Society*. Cambridge, MA: Harvard University Press.

Latour, B. 1988a. *The Pasteurization of France*. Cambridge, MA: Harvard University Press.

Latour, B. 1988b. A Relativist Account of Einstein's Relativity. *Social Studies of Science*, 18: 3–44.

Latour, B. 1996. Do scientific objects have a history? Pasteur and Whitehead in a bath of lactic acid. *Common Knowledge*, 5 (1): 76–91.

Leidner, R. 1993 *Fast Food, Fast Talk: Service Work and the Routinization of Everyday Life*. Berkeley, CA: University of California Press.

Letiche, H. 2000. Phenomenal complexity theory as informed by Bergson. *Journal of Organizational Change Management*, 13 (6): 545–58.

Levy, D. L., Alvesson, M. and Willmott, H. 2003. Critical approaches to strategic management, pp. 92–110. In M. Alvesson and H. Willmott (eds), *Studying Management Critically*. Newbury Park, CA: Sage.

Lewin, R. 1993 *Complexity: Life on the Edge of Chaos*. London: Phoenix.

Lévy, P. 1995. *L'Intelligence Collective: Pour une Anthropologie du cyberspace*. Paris: Éditions La Découverte.

Lévy, P. 1995 *Qu'est-ce que le Virtuel?* Paris: Éditions las Découverte.

Lévy, P. 1997. *Collective Intelligence: Mankind's Emerging World in Cyberspace*. New York: Plenum Press.

Levy, P. 1998 *Becoming Virtual: Reality in the Digital Age*. New York: Plenum Press.

Lindblom, C. 1959. The science of muddling through. *Public Administration*, 19: 59–79.

Love, J.F. 1995 *McDonald's: Behind The Arches*. New York: Bantam Books.

Luhman, J.T. and Boje, D.M. 2001 What is complexity science? A possible answer from narrative research. *Emergence* 3 (1): 1158–68.

Lyotard, J. F. 1979/1984. *The Postmodern Condition*, translated by G. Bennington and B. Massumi. Minneapolis, MN: University of Minnesota Press. (1979 French edition; 1984 English edition)

Maier, T. 2002 3 Initials Spelled Disaster. *Newsday,* 26 January.

Malinowski, B. 1954. *Magic, Science and Religion and Other Essays*. Garden City, NY: Doubleday Anchor Books.

March, J. G. and Simon, H. A. 1958. *Organizations*. New York: Wiley.

Marcuse, H. 1964. *One-Dimensinal Man: Studies in the Ideology of Advanced Industrial Society*. Boston, MA: Beacon Press.

Maruyama, M. 2003. Causal loops, interaction and creativity. *International Review of Sociology*, 13 (3): 607–8.

Mead, G. H. 1934. *Mind, Self and Society from the Standpoint of a Social Behaviorist*. Chicago, IL: University of Chicago Press.

Medvedov, P.N. 1928/1978. *The Formal Method in Literary Scholarship: A Critical Introduction to Sociological Poetics*. Baltimore/London: The John Hopkins University Press. (1928 in Russian edition)

Metcalfe, J.L. 1974 Systems models, economic models and the casual texture of organizational environments. *Human Relations* 27(7): 639–663.

Michael, D.N. 1973 *On Learning to Plan – and Planning to Learn*. San Francisco: Jossey-Bass.

Mihata, K. 1997 The Persistence of 'Emergence', in A.E. Raymond, S. Horsfall and M.E. Lee (eds) *Chaos, Complexity and Sociology: Myths, Models and Theories*. Thousand Oaks, CA: Sage. pp.30–38.

Miles, R. E. and Snow, C. C. 1978. *Organizational Strategy, Structure, and Process*. New York: McGraw-Hill.

Miller, D. and Friesen, P. 1977 Strategy making in context: Ten empirical archetypes. *Journal of Management Studies*, Vol. 14: 259–80.

Miller, D., and Friesen, P. H. 1984. *Organizations: A Quantum View*. Englewood Cliffs, NJ: Prentice-Hall.

Mills, J. A. and Tancred, P. 1992. *Gendering Organizational Analysis*. Thousand Oaks, CA: Sage Publications.

Mintzberg, H. 1973. *The Nature of Managerial Work*. New York: Harper & Row.

Mintzberg, H. 1978 Patterns in strategy formation. *Management Science* 24 (9): 934–48, May.

Mintzberg, H. 1979. *The Structuring of Organizations*. Englewood Cliffs, NJ: Prentice-Hall.

Mintzberg, H. and Lampel, J. 1999. Reflecting on the strategy process. *Sloan Management Review*, 40 (3): 21–30.

Mintzberg, H., Ahlstrand, B. and Lampel, J. 1998 *Strategy Safari: A Guided Tour Through the Wilds of Strategic Management*. New York: The Free Press.

Mintzberg, H. and Lampel, J. 1999 Reflecting on the strategy process. *Sloan Management Review* 40 (3): 21–30.

Mintzberg, H., Lampel, J., Quinn, J. B. and Ghoshal, S. 2003 *The Strategy Process: Concepts, Contexts, Cases*, 4th edn. Upper Saddle River, NJ: Prentice-Hall.

Mintzberg, H., Lampel, J., Quinn, J. B. and Ghoshal, S. 2003. *The Strategy Process: Concepts, Contexts, Cases,* 4th edn. Upper Saddle River, NJ: Prentice-Hall.

Mitroff, I. I. and Denton, E. A. 1999 *A Spiritual Audit of Corporate America*. San Francisco: Jossey-Bass.

Morin, E. 1977. *La Methode. I. La Nature de la Nature*. Paris: Seuil.

Morin, E. 1992. From the concept of system to the paradigm of complexity, translated by Sean Kelly. *Journal of Social and Evolutionary Systems,* 15 (4): 371–85.

Morin, E. 1996. A new way of thinking. *UNESCO Courier*, February; 10–14.

Mumby, D. 1994. Review of *Cultures in Organizations* (by J. Martin). *Academy of Management Review*, 19 (1): 156–9.

Motamedi. K. 1978. The evolution from interorganizational design to trans-organizational development. Paper presented at the Academy of Management Meetings in San Francisco.

Nevaskar, B. 1971. *Capitalists Without Capitalism: The Jains of Indian and the Quakers of the West*. Westport, CN: Greenwood Publishing Corporation.

Newman, W. H. 1951. *Administrative Action: The Techniques of Organization and Management*. Englewood Cliffs, NJ: Prentice-Hall.

Newton, A. Z. 1995. *Narrative Ethics*. Cambridge: Harvard University Press.

Ng, W. and de Cock, C. 2002. Battle in the boardroom: a discursive perspective. *Journal of Management Studies*, 39 (1): 23–49.

Nietzsche, F. 1990 *Beyond Good and Evil*. Translated by R.J. Hollingdale. Introduction byt Michael Tanner. London and New York: Penguin Books.

Nietzsche, F. 1956. *The Birth of Tragedy* (1872) and *The Genealogy of Morals* (1887), trans. F. Golffing, New York: Anchor Books.

Nietzsche, F. 1967. *The Will to Power*, Translated by Walter Kaufmann and R. J. Hollingdale, W. Kaufmann (ed). New York: Vintage Books.

Normann, R. 1977. *Management for Growth*. New York: Wiley.

O'Conner, E. 2002. Storied business: typology, intertextuality, and traffic in entrepreneurial narrative. *The Journal of Business Communication,* 39 (1): 36–54.

Ong, W. J. 1982. *Orality and Literacy: The Technologizing of the World*. London/ New York: Routledge.

Oswick, C., Anthony, P., Keenoy, T., Mangham, I. L. and Grant, D. 2000. A dialogic analysis of organizational learning. *Journal of Management Studies*, 37 (6): 887–901.

Owens, H. (ed.) 1995. *Tales From Open Space*. Cabin John, MD: Abbott Publishing (out of print) pdf version available on line at http://openspaceworld.com/Tales.pdf

Palmer, I. and Dunford, R. 1996. Conflicting uses of metaphors: reconceptualizing their use in the field of organizational change. *Academy of Management Review*, 21 (3): 691–717.

Parsons, T. 1964 *Social Structure and Personality*. New York: New York Free Press.

Pate, L. E. and Boje, D. M 1989 Retrospective sensemaking on a mentor and his magic: An introduction to the contributions of Louis R. Pondy, 1938–1987, *Journal of Organizational Change Management*, 2 (2): 5–14.

Payne, S. L. and Calton, J. M. 2002. Towards a managerial practice of stakeholder engagement: developing multi-stakeholder learning dialogues. *Journal of Corporate Citizenship*, 6: 37–52.

Peale, N. V. 1952 *Power of Positive Thinking*. New York: Prentice-Hall, Inc.

Penrose, E. T. 1959. *The Theory of the Growth of the Firm*. New York: Wiley.

Pepper, S.C. 1942 *World Hypotheses: A Study in Evidence*. Berkeley, CA: University of California Press.

Perrow, C. 1986 *Complex Organizations: A Critical Essay*. New York: Random House.

Pfeffer, J., and Salancik, G. R. 1978. *The External Control of Organizations: A Resource Dependence Perspective*. New York: Harper & Row.

Phillips, N. 1995 Telling organizational tales: On the role of narrative fiction in the study of organizations. *Organization Studies* 16 (4): 625–49.

Pirsig, R. M. 1974 *Zen and the Art of Motorcycle Maintenance: An Inquiry into Values*. New York: Morrow.

Plato 1957 *Plato's Theory of Knowledge: The* Theaetetus *and the* Sophist *of Plato*. Translated by Francis M. Cornford. New York: The Bobbs-Merrill Company Inc.

Polanyi, M. 1966 *The Tacit Dimension*. New York: Doubleday.

Polkinghorne, D. E. 1988. *Narrative Knowing and the Human Sciences*. Albany, NY: State of New York University Press.

Pondy L. R. 1978. Leadership as a language game, pp. 87–99 in M.W. McCall, and M.W. Lombardo, (eds), *Leadership: Where Else Can We Go*? Durham, NC: Duke University Press.

Pondy, L. R. 1976. Beyond open system models of organization, in B. Straw (ed.) (1979) *Research in Organizational Behavior*. Greenwich, CT: JAI, pp. 3–39.

Pondy, L. and Mitroff, I. 1979 Beyond open system models of organization, in B. Straw (ed.) *Research in Organizational Behavior*, Vol. 1, pp. 3–39. Greenwich, CT: JAI.

Pondy, L. and Boje, D. M. 1980. Bringing mind back in: paradigm development as a frontier problem in organizational theory, pp. 83–101, in Evan Williams (ed.) *Frontiers in Organization & Management*. New York: Praeger Publishers.

Porter, M. 1980. *Competitive Strategy: Techniques for Analyzing Industries and Competitors*. New York: Free Press.

Porter, M. E. 1985. *Competitive Advantage Creating and Sustaining Superior Performance*. New York: Free Press.

Prahalad, C.K. 1975 The strategic process in a multinational corporation. Unpublished doctoral dissertation, Graduate School of Business Administration, Harvard University.

Prahalad, C. K. and Hamel, G. 1990. The core competence of the corporation. *Harvard Business Review*, May-June: 79–91.

Pugh, D. S., Hickson, D. J., Hinings, C. R., and Turner, C. (1968). Dimensions of organizational structure. *Administrative Science Quarterly*, 13: 65–105.

Quinn, J. B. 1980. *Strategies for Change Logical Incrementalism*. Homewood, IL: Irwin.

Reiter, E. 1991 *Making Fast Food: From the Frying Pan into the Fryer*. New York: McGill-Queens University Press.

Rhenman, E. 1973. *Organization Theory for Long-Range Planning*. London: Wiley.

Ricoeur, P. 1983/1984. *Time and Narrative*, Volume 1, translated by Kathleen McLaughlin and David Pellauer. Chicago/London: The University of Chicago Press. (1983, first French printing (Pemps et Recit, Deidtions du Seuil, France); 1983 first English printing.)

Ricoeur, P. 1992. *Oneself as Another*, translated by Kathleen Blamey. Chicago/London: The University of Chicago Press.

Ritzer, G. 1993/2002. *The McDonaldization of Society*. Newbury Park, CA: Pine Forge. (First edition 1993; second edition 2002)

Rosile, G. A. 1998 Restorying for Strategic Organizational Planning and Development. The Case of the Sci Fi Organization. IABD Presentation (now independent conference and renamed Standing Conference for Management and Organizational Inquiry) Orlando, Florida. See sc'MOI at http://scmoi.org and http://web.nmsu.edu/~garosile/iabdscifi98.html

Rosile, G. A. 1999. Horsesense at work. Invited paper to an invitational scholar's conference on Narrative Studies, Ohio State University, May 14–16, hosted by Jeffrey Ford. For more on horsesense, see http:horsesenseatwork.com

Rosile, G. A. and Boje, D. M. 2002 Restorying and postmodern organization theatre: consultation in the storytelling organization, pp. 271–90 in Ronald R. Sims (ed.), *Changing the Way We Manage Change*. Wesport, CT/London: Quorum Books.

Roth, G. L. and Kleiner, A. 1998 Developing organizational memory through learning histories. *Organizational Dynamics* 27 (2): 43–60.

Roy, A. 1997 *The God of Small Things*. New York: Random House.

Rumelt, R. P. 1974 *Strategy, Structure and Economic Performance*. Boston: Harvard University Press.

Ryan, B. A. 1984. *Gertrude Stein's Theatre of the Absolute*. Ann Arbor, MI: UMI Research Press.

Sartre, J-P. 1943/1956. *Being and Nothingness: An Essay on Phenomenological Ontology*, translated with introduction by Hazel E. Barnes. New York: Philosophical Library. (1956 first English edition; 1943 French publication of *L'Être et le Néant*)

Savall, H., Zardet, V. and Bonnet, M. 2000. Releasing the untapped potential of enterprises through Socio-Economic Management. International Labor Organization publication. Contact Socio-Economic Institute of Firms and Organiztions (Research Center), 15, chemin du Petit Bois, 69130 Ecully, France. ISBN 92-2-112089-9.

Schein, E. 1969 *Process Consultation: Its Role in Organization Development*. Reading, MA: Addison-Wesley.

Schein, Edgar H. 1984. Coming to a new awareness of organizational culture. *Sloan Management Review,* 25(2): p. 3–16.

Schein, E. 1985 *Organizational Culture and Leadership*. San Francisco, CA: Jossey-Bass.

Schein, E. H. 1993. On dialogue, culture, and organizational learning. *Organizational Dynamics*, 22 (2): 40–51.

Schein, E. H. 1996. Three cultures of management: the key to organizational learning. *Sloan Management Review*, Fall: 9–20.

Schein, E. 1999 *Corporatel Culture Survival Guide*. San Francisco, CA: Jossey-Bass.

Schlosser, E. 2001. *Fast Food Nation: The Dark Side of the All-American Meal*. Boston: Houghton Mifflin.

Schon, D. 1971 *Beyond the Stable State*. London: Temple Smith.

Schumpeter, J. A. 1942 *Capitalism, Socialism, and Democracy*. New York: Harper.

Schumpeter, J. A. 1934. *The Theory of Economic Development*. Cambridge, MA: Harvard University Press.

Schumpeter, J. A. 1950. *Capitalism, Socialism, and Democracy*. New York: Harper & Row.

Selznick, P. 1957. *Leadership in Administration: A Sociological Interpretation*. Evanston, IL: Row, Peterson.

Semler, R. 1993. *Maverick: The Success Story Behind the World's Most Unusual Workplace*. London: Century.

Senge, P. 1990. *The Fifth Discipline: The Art and Practice of the Learning Organization*. New York: Doubleday.

Senge, P. M. 1992 *The Fifth Discipline: The Art and Practice of the Learning Organization*. Random House.

Senge, P. 1994. *The Fifth Discipline Fieldbook: Strategies and Tools for Building a Learning Organization*. New York: Currency Doubleday.

Serres, M. 1983. *Hermes: Literature, Science, Philosophy*. Baltimore, MD: The John Hopkins University Press,

Serres, M. 1987. *Statues*. Paris: Franois Bourin.

Serres, M with Latour, B. 1995. *Conversations on Science, Culture and Time*, translated by R. Lapidus. Ann Arbor, MI: University of Michigan Press.

Shannon, Claude E. and Weaver, W. 1949. *The Mathematical Theory of Communication*. Urbana: The University of Illinois Press.

Shotter, John 1993. *Conversational Realities*. London: Sage.

Simon, H. A. 1947. *Administrative Behavior*. New York: Macmillan.

Sinclair, U. 1906 *The Jungle*. New York: Doubleday, Page and Company.

Smircich, L., Calas, M., and Morgan, G. 1992a. New intellectual currents in organization and management theory. *Academy of Management Review*, 17: 404–6.

Smircich, L., Calas, M., and Morgan, G. 1992b. Afterward/after words: open(ing) spaces. *Academy of Management Review*, 17: 607–11.

Spender, J. C. 1996. Making knowledge the basis of a dynamic theory of the firm. *Strategic Management Journal,* 17: 45–62.

Stacey, R. 1992 *Managing the Unknowable: Strategic Boundaries between Order and Chaos in Organizations*. San Francisco: Jossey-Bass.

Stacey, R. 1996 *Complexity and Creativity in Organizations*. San Francisco: Berrett-Koehler.

Stacey, R. 2006. Complex responsive processes as a theory of organizational improvisation, pp. 128–41 in Patricia Shaw and Ralph Stacey (eds), *Experiencing Risk, Spontaneity and Improvisation in Organizational Change: Working Live*. London/New York: Routledge.

Stanislavski, C. 1936/1986 *An Actor Prepares*. Trans. Elizabeth Reynolds Hapgood. London: Methuen. First published 1936.

Stein, G. 1931. *How to Write*. Westgrove, VT: Something Else Press, Inc.

Stein, G. 1935. *Narration: Four Lectures*, introduction by Thornton Wilder. Chicago, IL: University of Chicago Press.

Stein, G. 1998. *Gertrude Stein: Writings 1932–1946*. New York: Literary Classics of the United States, Inc.

Steingard, D. S. and Fitzgibbons, D. E. 1995. Challenging the juggernaut of globalization: a manifesto for academic praxis. *Journal of Organizational Change Management* 8 (4): 30–54.

Stoney, C. 1998 Lifting the lid on strategic management: A sociological narrative. *Electronic Journal of Radical Organization Theory* 4(1).

Sun Tzu 1971 *The Art of War*. Translation and commentary by Samuel B. Griffith. New York: Oxford University Press.

Talwar, J. P. 2002 *Fast Food, Fast Track Immigrants, Big Business and the American Dream*. Cambridge, MA: Westview Press (Perseus Books).

Tawney, R. H. 1926 *Religion and the Rise of Capitalism*. London: John Murray.

Thomas, P. 1998 Ideology and the discourse of strategic management. A critical research framework. *Electronic Journal of Radical Organization Theory* 4(1).

TwoTrees, K. 1997 *Stories with mind*. Session presented at the April 1997 International Academy of Business Disciplines conference, postmodern organization theory track (now independent and renamed Standing Conference for Management and Organizational Inquiry) Orlando, Florida meeting. See sc'MOI at http://scmoi.org.

Vattimo, G. 1988 *The End of Modernity: Nihilism and Hermeneutics in Postmodern Culture*. English translation with introduction by Jon R. Snyder. Baltimore, MD: The Johns Hopkins University Press. Italian translation 1985.

Vickers, G. 1965 *The Art of Judgement*. New York: Basic Books.

Vickers, M. H. 2005. Illness, work and organization: postmodernism and antenarratives for the reinstatement of voice. *Tamara: Journal of Critical Postmodern Organizational Science*, 3 (2): 1–15.

Volosinov, V. 1929/1973. *Marxism and the Philosophy of Language*. Seminar Press. Russian original, 1929; English version 1973.

von Bertalanffy, L. 1956. General Systems Theory, General Systems. *Yearbook of the Society for the Advancement of General System Theory*, 1: 1—10.

Walck, C. L. 1995. Global ideals, local realities: the development project and missionary management in Russia. *Journal of Organizational Change Management*, 8 (4): 69–84.

Waldrop, M. M. 1993 *Complexity: The Emerging Science at the Edge of Order and Chaos*. London: Viking.

Weber, M. 1904/1930. *The Protestant Ethic and the Spirit of Capitalism*, translated by Talcott Parson. New York: Charles Scribner's Sons.

Weick, K. E. 1969. *The Social Psychology of Organizing*. Reading, MA: Addison-Wesley.

Weick, K. E. 1995. *Sensemaking in Organizations*. Thousand Oaks, CA: Sage.

Weick, K. E., Sutcliffe, K., and Obstfeld, D. 2005. Organizing and the process of sensemaking. *Organization Science*, 16 (4): 409–21.

Weisbord, M. R. (ed.). 1992. *Discovering Common Ground*. San Francisco, CA: Berrett-Koehler Publishers, Inc.

Westman, P. 1980 *Ray Kroc: Mayor of McDonalds*. Minneapolis: Dillon Press Inc.

White, M. and Epston, D. 1990. *Narrative Means to Therapeutic Ends*. New York/London: W. W. Norton & Company.

Wilber, K. 1996. *A Brief History of Everything*. Boston: Shambhala.

Witzel, K. M. 1994/1997 American Drive-in. Osceola, WI: Motorbooks International Publishers and Wholesalers. First edition published 1993.

Woodward, J. 1965. *Industrial Organization: Theory and Practice*. London: Oxford University Press.

Woodward, J. 1958 Management and Technology. London: Problems of Progress in Industry, Series No. 3. HMSO.

INDEX

NOTE: Page numbers in **bold type** refer to glossary.

13615922R00160

Printed in Great Britain
by Amazon.co.uk, Ltd.,
Marston Gate.